Hippocrene USA Guide to

AMERICA'S
HEARTLAND

Other Books by Tom Weil
A Clearing in the Jungle
A Balance of Power
Last at the Fair

Hippocrene USA Guide to

AMERICA'S HEARTLAND

A Travel Guide to the Back Roads of Illinois, Indiana, Iowa and Missouri

TOM WEIL

HIPPOCRENE BOOKS
New York

For information, address: Hippocrene Books, Inc.,
171 Madison Avenue, New York, NY 10016.

Library of Congress Cataloging-in-Publication Data

Weil, Tom.
  America's heartland : a travel guide to the back roads of Illinois,
Indiana, Iowa and Missouri / Tom Weil. (Hippocrene USA guide)
  Bibliography
  Includes index.
  ISBN 0-87052-748-7
  1. Middle West—Description and travel—1981— —Guide-books.
2. Automobiles—Road guides—Middle West. I. Title. II. Series.
F355.W36 1989   88-38241
915.6'045—dc19   **CIP**

Printed in the United States of America

This book is for Edith,
who roamed the back roads of the Heartland with me

CONTENTS

A Welcome to the Reader   xi

I An Introduction to the American Heartland
1. Voices from the Heartland   1
2. Practical Advice   13

II Indiana
1. Indiana: Middle America   21
2. Covered Bridges and Maple Sugar Country   26
3. Old Indiana   32
4. Abe Lincoln Meets Santa Claus   41
5. College, Country and Columbus   46
6. The Ohio River Country   54
7. Overland Waterway, Cross-Country
      Railroad, Underground Railway   61
8. Verses and Villages of the Nineteenth
      Century   65

9. North of the Old National Road 69

III Illinois
1. Illinois: Land of Linking 77
2. The Cradle of Illinois 83
3. Illinois's Egypt 96
4. England in Illinois 110
5. Land of Lincoln 123
6. Spoon River Country and Beyond 139
7. Riverlands 154
8. Skirting Chicago 173
9. The River Road Back to the Beginning 184

IV Iowa
1. Iowa: Land of the Land 195
2. Valley Villages, Pleasant Places 201
3. May Festival and Maytags, "Go West" and Wild West 214
4. "Amana That Was and Amana That Is" 226
5. A College Town, A President's Hamlet 234
6. New World Symphony, Old World Settlers 246
7. Northern Iowa 252
8. Covered Wagons and Covered Bridges 259
9. The Great River Road 269

V Missouri
1. Missouri: The United State of America 281
2. Missouri's Missouri River Valley 287
3. Mark Twain Country 304
4. From Mickey Mouse to Pony Express 314
5. Missouri's Wild West 324
6. Mid-Missouri 336
7. Kicks on 66 and Float Trips on Pristine Streams 345
8. The Hills 'n' Hollows of Missouri's Ozarks 352
9. The River Road South 364

Sources and Resources   377
Index   415

Maps

The American Heartland   2
Indiana   22
Illinois   78
Iowa   196
Missouri   282

A Welcome to the Reader

This book is a travel guide to the four Middle Western states that form the core of the American heartland: Indiana, Illinois, Iowa and Missouri. But, hopefully, the book is also a bit more than that. Time quickly overtakes most travel guides, making them soon out of date. "Every age makes its own guidebooks, and the old ones are used for waste paper," Herman Melville wrote in *Redburn*. I've tried to make this book something less disposable—and thus less likely to end its days as wastepaper—by including in it information more timeless than that which appears in most guides. Instead of simply tediously listing places, hotels and restaurants, with capsule descriptions of each, the book offers a narrative that will not only guide the reader to the region's attractions but which I hope will also give him or her the flavor of the Middle West. It is my further hope that even armchair travelers will enjoy this book, for the text abounds with anecdotes, stories of colorful characters both famous and obscure, and descriptions of lesser known interesting or unusual places, all of which both travelers and readers who don't visit the areas covered may find entertaining. For readers who travel through the heartland, the book presents a series of itineraries. The table of contents can serve as a sort of general guide. Information on places not listed in the headings in each section of the text can usually be found by consulting the narrative preceding or following discussion of the nearest important sight. So if you want to read about an out-of-the-way place near Springfield, Illinois, you can probably find the appropriate passage in the text near the material on Springfield. Since this book emphasizes those out-of-the-way, back road, lesser known corners of the Middle West, big cities have been omitted. Also omitted—under the theory that the reader is resourceful enough to locate the necessary hotels, motels and restaurants, amenities which the heartland offers in a wide variety of types and price ranges— are long lists of places to stay and to eat. But mention is made of such establishments if they offer a special ambiance or an interesting historical connection. To keep the narrative uncluttered, addresses, phone numbers and other such practical information have been grouped together by state at the back of the book, listed in the order in which the relevant places appear in the text. Also listed in chronological order are some of the more interesting or useful books I have consulted on each state. Frequent references in the text to sights listed on the National Register of Historic Places arise because Register listing, although not infallible, seems to me to indicate the probable merit of an attraction. (In the text this is referred to as the National Register.)

The reader will also find in the text a number of cross references from one chapter—that is, one state—to another. These cross-references indicate a similar or related sight in another state. Such references imply a certain cohesion be-

tween the four states covered. The history of those states—
Indiana, Illinois, Iowa and Missouri—is in a certain way less
fragmented than the boundaries between them and the
quartet of separate chapters might suggest. Neither people
nor events were necessarily restricted to just one state. To cite
a few examples: George Rogers Clark captured Kaskaskia
and Cahokia in Illinois before marching on to take Vincennes
in Indiana; Lincoln lived in both Indiana and Illinois and
Mark Twain lived in Iowa for a time after leaving his boyhood home in Hannibal, Missouri; the Mormons moved
from Missouri to Illinois, while the Lewis and Clark Expedition traveled from Illinois through Missouri and along the
western border of Iowa. So the histories of the four states
have to a certain extent become entwined over the years, and
that is one reason it seems appropriate to cover Indiana,
Illinois, Iowa and Missouri as a cohesive area. Another reason
is that those states form the American heartland, a reasonably
distinctive region with its own definable culture. As many
definitions of the Middle West exist as there are attempts to
delineate the area. Many writers include in the region Michigan, Wisconsin and Minnesota but those are better described
as the Upper Midwest, an area that in certain subtle ways
differs from the heartland, while Ohio, also sometimes included, seems to me somewhat too industrialized to fit. So I
have restricted this book to the core of the country, the true
heartland—what might be called "the inner Midwest," a
phrase used in *The North American Midwest: A Regional Geography* by John H. Garland.

I hope the reader will not find my view of the Middle West
parochial. My travels have not been restricted to the American heartland. In visiting well over a hundred countries I
have journeyed to the far corners of the earth—Timbuktu,
Samarkand, the Khyber Pass, the Sahara Desert, the Amazon
jungle, Angel Falls and Devil's Island, all through Asia, Africa and the Americas, to remote corners of the Orient, little

known areas of Latin America, isolated villages in Africa, virtually all of Europe, the fifty United States and much else, all of which I mention not as an exercise in braggadocio (there is a Braggadocio in Missouri but I am not from that hamlet) but to suggest that I am able to approach the Middle West with a certain seasoned perspective gained from years of roaming the globe. So I do not bring to the heartland—my own land—a provincial eye, for it is with an awareness of the greater world that I put forth the claim that the American Middle West boasts a history, folklore, culture and traditions well worth consideration, and attractions and scenery well worth visiting. I am quite aware that many people regard the Middle West, if they regard it at all, as "Dullsville," but I submit that any fair-minded person—and perhaps even a few unfair-minded souls—will agree with me after they've visited "the inner Midwest" or even after simply reading this book that the heartland offers much of interest.

As for my own familiarity with the Middle West, I have lived in the heartland all my life and for many years have roamed the region's roads, for the last decade gathering material for my column "Roaming with Weil" which appears regularly in the *St Louis Post-Dispatch*. I have also contributed many articles on the Middle West and its attractions to newspapers coast to coast, from the *New York Times* to the *Los Angeles Times* and to such other papers as the *Chicago Tribune, Kansas City Star, Des Moines Register, Milwaukee Journal* and *Atlanta Journal*. So for many years I have experienced the Middle West as a resident, as a tourist and as a writer: the Midwest is a part of me as I, for a time, am part of it.

It was almost exactly a hundred years ago when my grandfather—my grandfather-to-be—immigrated to Missouri from the Rhineland in Germany, so the roots of my family in the heartland are by now fully a century deep. My father was born in Missouri, as was I, and both my grandfather and father repose in Missouri soil where someday, most likely, I, too—my travels at an end—shall lie. It is a privilege for someone with such a long and familiar connection with an area to have the opportunity to write about it. With heartfelt sincerity I welcome you, reader, to the heartland and to the book, and hope that you enjoy your time in the Middle West—my past, my land, my home.

ACKNOWLEDGMENTS

My thanks to *St. Louis Post-Dispatch* travel editor Joan Dames, who for the last ten years has run my column "Roaming With Weil" in that paper. Many of the places described in this book I visited during my roamings to gather material for the column. My thanks also to the National Endowment for the Arts, whose writing fellowship grant encouraged me to complete this book on the American Heartland.

. . . the laws of nature and the initial conditions are such as to make the universe as interesting as possible.
—Freeman J. Dyson, *Infinity In All Directions*

I

An Introduction to the American Heartland

1. Voices from the Heartland:

Impressions of the Middle West

Perhaps the most striking feature of the Middle West is the cycle of the seasons. That elemental process typifies the heartland, an earthy landlocked and land-dominated region whose fortunes and very appearance so depend on natural forces. The changing seasons color the character of the Middle West and season its people. As the year begins to wane, the weather—so extreme and so influential in the American heartland—suddenly turns from the relentless heat of the

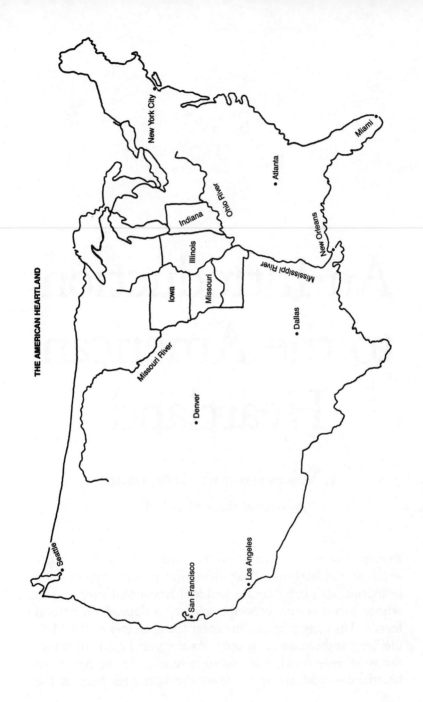

THE AMERICAN HEARTLAND

Seattle

San Francisco

Los Angeles

Denver

Missouri River

Iowa

Missouri

Illinois

Indiana

Ohio River

Mississippi River

Dallas

New Orleans

Atlanta

Miami

New York City

long summer to a more temperate presence. The days grow short and the leaves turn to flame. "The foliage slowly takes on those remarkable shades and colors," noted Graham Hutton in *Midwest at Noon*. "The skies become more brightly blue than at any other time of the year. The air is mildly imbued with the thin and acrid smell of wood smoke. . . . Over all, a different suffused light from the sloping sun strikes street and building, forest and field, in a strange way, throwing shadows into unexpected places and illuminating what for most of the year lay in shadow. The sunsets, always imposing in the Midwest, now reach their majestic climax."

And then arrives Indian summer, when the chill of fall momentarily retreats and a certain mellow warmth again pervades the land. John Parsons, a Virginian who traveled through Indiana in 1840, described in his diary "the beauty of the Indian summer in this state, of the colors of the trees and the opalescent haze that hangs o'er woods and prairie." The harvest moon hangs high and farmers gather in the crop, fruits of a rich topsoil good enough to eat without putting vegetables through it, so claimed Robert Frost. And then comes the frost, and the summer—that of Indian and paleface alike—ends, and before long that winter which "cracks your skull," as Iowa poet Paul Engle described it, sweeps across the land. Then, finally, spring, when the Middle West again comes into its own—rich with the new cycle of crops, "fat as a hog and so fertile you felt that if you stuck a fork in the earth the juice would spurt—one thousand miles of fat, flat, green, hog-fat fertility—barns, houses, silos, towns," wrote Thomas Wolfe after a visit to Indiana in 1938.

Those towns Wolfe mentioned dot the Midwestern landscape: "The American Middle West is still a region of small towns, towns permanently small," noted Richard Rhodes in *The Inland Ground*. Some of the towns are renowned—Twain's Hannibal or the seven villages that comprise Iowa's Amana Colony—and others obscure. But in all of them may be seen or, on a passing visit, at least visualized, the old-fashioned ways of life that seem to endure in a more pronounced way in the heartland than elsewhere. "One is aware of the continuing stream of life," noted Earnest Elmo Calkins (in *They Broke the Prairie*) about one such town—Galesburg, Illinois, in the late nineteenth century. "Mankind is seen as a whole, in all of its relations, instead of such detached segments as impinge on one's consciousness among the milling crowds of a great city. You may behold the span of five generations, births, marriages, deaths, the vagaries of heredity, the changing fortunes in human lives." Back then, around the turn of the century, was the golden age of small towns, when "under an overarching blue dome of sky one could well believe that one's town and one's country were good places, that life itself was good, that the same slow rhythmic heartbeat of the days would continue down through the years," observed Richard Lingeman in *Small Town America*. And in the heartland that heartbeat has continued up to the present time, for in the Middle West there still remains a lingering afterglow of the good old days and ways.

From the beginning life was good in the Middle West. The land was bountiful: Englishman William Blane, who visited Illinois in 1822, saw terrain of such fertility that the corn's stature called to his mind Jack's legendary giant beanstalk. And, too, the land was free. Many an early settler commented on the lack of constraints in the great American heartland. William Fischer, a mid-nineteenth-century immigrant from Germany, wrote to a friend from his new home in Iowa: "I am no longer a shackled subject of Prussia, but a free citizen of the United States of North America. Here it is not necessary to show a pass to every petty official or gendarme. . . . Here people are not divided into classes as in Germany. One person is as good as another." Midwestern writer Eugene Field took up the theme in his poem "Plaint of the Missouri 'Coon in the Berlin Zoological Gardens": A caged raccoon, noticing Americans visiting the zoo, recalls his life in Cole County, Missouri, and complains about the food in Germany—onion tarts and beer-soaked sausages. The homesick animal longs for his tasty native cuisine of "worms and things," and says he'd willingly give up his pampered existence as a zoo pet in Berlin for his previous life in America, where he was free.

The freedom, the openness—both political and geographic—in the Middle West attracted to the area a generation of optimistic and forward-looking settlers and even a scattering of utopians who founded communal settlements. Some took hold, for a time at least, and such places as New Harmony, Indiana, Bishop Hill, Illinois, the Amana Colony in Iowa and Missouri's Bethal still survive today as delightful historic remnants of those nineteenth-century utopian experiments. That freedom also nurtured an informal and unpretentious sort of society. Ferdinand Ernst, a wealthy settler from Germany, remarked in 1819 after taking tea with the Illinois governor, on "the banishment from higher and lower society of all so-called etiquette and unnecessary compliments. The American never greets one by taking off the hat, but by a cordial grasp of the hand." That "hail-fellow-well-met" sort of temperament still survives in the Middle West, where the people tend to be rather blunt, direct and—like the land—open. "The people of the [mid-] west, and of Illinois, have much plain, blunt, but sincere hospitality," noted J. M. Peck in his 1834 *A Gazetteer of Illinois*. J. H. Buckingham, son of a Boston newspaper publisher, described a certain Illinois politician he encountered on a carriage ride through that state in 1847:

[The candidate] knew, or appeared to know, everybody we met, the name of the tenant of every farmhouse, and the owner of every plat of ground. Such a shaking of hands—such a how-d'ye do—such a greeting of different kinds, as we saw, was never seen before; it seemed as if he knew everything, and he had a kind word, a smile and a bow for everybody on the road, even to the horses, and the cattle and the swine.

This down-to-earth campaigner was a young fellow by the name of Abe Lincoln who, even as a mature and successful politician, retained his earthy manner. Sent a gift of soap by an admirer during the 1860 presidential campaign, the candidate responded: "Some specimens of your soap have been used at our house and Mrs. L declares it is a superb article. She at the same time protests that I have never given sufficient attention to the 'soap question' to be a competent judge."

That Midwestern openness and directness typified by Lincoln's whimsical comment is a trait the early settlers favored and one that still survives today in the heartland. Such directness developed in part no doubt because the pioneers had to deal with the vicissitudes of the natural forces that constantly confronted those early settlers. If the people were to survive, then the earth, the seasons, the weather had to be dealt with. Practical problems involving "the labor of bringing from raw materials anything at all presentable for family use" (as Christiana Holmes Tillson put it in *A Woman's Story of Pioneer Illinois*) challenged the early Midwesterners from the day of their arrival, and those challenges demanded practical solutions. De Tocqueville remarked on how the American mind fixed "upon purely practical objects. His passions, his wants, his education, and everything about him, seem to unite in drawing the native of the United States earthward." In the Middle West, where the land is intrinsic to the culture, the people were literally drawn earthward, and forced to eschew the theoretical or the frivolous. Cultivation of the land left little time for cultivating sensibilities. "A well-ploughed lot is more satisfactory to their eye than the most exquisite painting of a Raphael," observed an 1840 traveler in the Middle West. In *The Disney Version,* a biography of Missourian Walt Disney, whose down-home, wholesome and quaintly old-fashioned stories seem a sort of metaphor for his native land, Richard Schickel writes: "The American Midwest is a highly practical place. Its habit is to ask how much, how big, how far, and, sometimes, simply how. It rarely asks why. The bluff and hearty manner it affects is not a conscious pose: it believes in its own friendliness and good spirits."

The Midwesterner, then, has his feet on the ground and his head not in the clouds but perhaps scanning the sky, observing the clouds to gauge the chances of rain, for rain is a practical thing; it waters the crops, cools the air, feeds the streams, fills the ponds—and affects the futures market. The *Indiana Gazetteer,* published in 1826, notes the eminently practical reply a preacher gave "when receiving furs and skins for his salary, [he] was asked 'whether it was not poor pay?' 'Yes,' he said, but he 'gave poor preaching in return.'" Faced with a dawdling pair of cattle, James Hearst, an Iowa farm boy (and later poet), devised a direct, practical solution for

the slowest team on the farm—I can still see their broad fat rumps ambling down the corn rows. [My brother] Bob, impatient and eager to show progress, tried yelling and line slapping to move the team along. A cob had been left in the toolbox to clean off the shovels, and at my suggestion Bob jammed it in Topsy's rear end. The effect was electric. Up the corn row we went at a gallop, Topsy alternately trying to push the cob out, and then because it hurt, clamping her tail down tight on it and driving it in.

A more genteel but no less practical attitude extended to the realm of romance in the Middle West. In 1885 a would-be bride in Salem, Illinois, decided just before the ceremony not to tie the knot, whereupon her younger sister stepped forward to offer herself to the jilted groom. Having already paid

for a wedding license, he accepted the proposal, changed the
name of the bride on the certificate and proceeded with the
ceremony. The May 3, 1848, *Iowa City Standard* reported a
similar substitution:

> Quite a mistake took place in a [local] love affair. A couple of
> young fools agreed to elope together, and by some mistake in
> the preliminary arrangements, the male lover put his ladder up
> to the window next to that in which her mamma, a handsome
> widow, reposed. She turned the mistake to her own advantage,
> got into his arms, returned his embraces, was borne by him to
> the carriage, and by preserving a becoming silence until
> daylight, kept him in error, and then by the potent power of her
> blandishments, actually charmed him into matrimony with her-
> self.

An element of practicality underlies even less romantic
encounters in the Middle West. When people in the region's
small towns and countryside gather to gossip the chatter
often involves more than simply idle chit-chat. As Douglas
Bauer, in *Prairie City, Iowa,* puts it: "These men do not come
together to compete with their finest stories. Escape, diver-
sion, the drawing in of others are inherent in the art of the
Southern lie. But these Midwestern farmers seem to have
exactly the opposite motive. They practice an inquiring journalism, compared with the Southerners' flowing fiction,
gathering facts about the methods of labor, the movement of
land, not looking to escape their working lives but, rather,
getting even nearer to them." One early Midwestern newspaper took such a direct, no-nonsense approach to its handling of the published news. When Jonathan Baldwin Turner,
who edited the *Illinois Statesman* in 1843–4, renounced frivolous reports in order to save space for more practical items, he
printed under a heading "Crimes and Casualties" the following notice: "Our paper is small, and if our readers will for the

present just have the goodness to imagine a certain due proportion of fires, tornadoes, murders, thefts, robberies and bully fights, from week to week, it will do just as well, for we can assure them they actually take place."

Part of the desire—necessity, even—to exchange hard news and useful information in rural Midwestern get-togethers stems no doubt from the isolation of farmers and of country towns. The sense of distance, of openness and space, in the heartland is one of the area's most distinctive characteristics. Even today in the information-saturated television and computer age, many towns in the region remain seemingly remote from the outside world and retain a pronounced atmosphere of yesteryear. Villages, hamlets, really, such as Arrow Rock in Missouri, Illinois's Elsah and Bentonsport in Iowa are beguiling pockets of the past with an endearing simplicity that seems far from the here and now. And even larger settlements—delightful nineteenth-century river towns like Madison, Indiana on the Ohio, Galena in Illinois just by the Mississippi, Missouri's Weston on the Missouri and Keosauqua on Iowa's Des Moines River—still seem of another era. Those Midwestern river towns and many another waterside settlement thrived during the steamboat era. The age of the riverboat reached high tide about mid-century and then receded, leaving many towns high and dry and like the places mentioned above, frozen in time.

But even if the paddle-wheelers are long gone the waterways they plied remain as pervasive presences in the heartland. Rivers, streams, brooks and creeks vein the Midwestern landscape and the rhythms of the waters pulse in the very veins of the heartland's natives. "One of the most impressive features of this magnificent land is the magnitude of its streams," wrote early Illinois settler Eliza W. Farnham in her 1846 book *Life in Prairie Land*. "One can form no adequate conception of the effect which these watercourses have on the mind: the smallest of them that is ever entered by steamboats, larger than the most vaunted rivers of the east; the largest, half spanning a continent." Beginning with the original residents of the region, the Indians, the rivers have somehow seeped into the essential being of the locals. In his last speech, made at a July 4, 1838, celebration at Fort Madison, Iowa, three months before he died, Indian leader Black Hawk reminisced: "I am now old; I have looked upon the Mississippi River; I have been a child; I love the great river; I have dwelt on its banks from the time I was an infant; I look upon it now." And still today the waterways of the Middle West exert on the area's residents a certain incantatory effect, such as described by William E. Wilson in *The Wabash:* "A man who lives near a river cannot go for long without a visit to the riverbank. Anyone who has lived near flowing water—and most Americans have—knows that. The river draws him to it like a magnet, and on its banks he will stand for hours, simply watching the water glide past."

The rivers, along with such other natural features as the woods, the fields, the hills (the heartland is definitely not all flat) contribute to the area's essential beauty. Englishman Graham Hutton noted in *Midwest at Noon* that a traveler "through the Midwest countryside cannot fail to be struck by majestic beauty on all sides." Such beauty resides not only in the natural landscape but in the cultivated areas as well. As one-time Iowa farmboy Herbert Quick wrote in his 1925 autobiography *One Man's Life:* "There is nothing more beautiful in its way than a well-cultivated Iowa cornfield, with its deep green rows of maize slanting in the breeze; or a field of oats of a still morning, with its nodding heads jeweled with dew; or a green pasture, with its grazing herd." Some Midwestern landscapes equal those anywhere for beauty. You would have to travel far to find areas more attractive than the Ohio River country east of Madison, Indiana, the Mississippi River and bluffs just north of Alton, Illinois, highway 94 near the Missouri River in eastern Missouri, or Iowa's rolling hills and picture-perfect farms in the northeastern part of the state. And there is not only the land but also the sky. Hutton, quoted above, commented that "I have not seen in over twenty countries starlit heavens to compare with those of the Midwest," an echo, or a reflection, of Walt Whitman's verse: "Give me nights perfectly quiet as on high plateaus west of the Mississippi, and I looking up at the stars." Along with the stars that dot the Midwestern nights glow other bits of brightness: "Few at first, they seemed like stars here and there; but they increased in number, till every tree seemed alive with wandering stars. Flitting in brilliant sparkles from leaf to leaf, they made the whole dark wood alive with light. As I called my companion's attention to them, some men at the station informed us, 'Them's the lightning bugs!'" So William Ferguson, a Scottish scientist, described the fireflies he spotted during his visit to southern Illinois in 1855.

But the Midwest is essentially a land of the earth, not the heavens, and of a soil that has nurtured an extraordinary variety of cultures and people as well as crops. Anyone who believes America has become bland and homogeneous need only travel through the heartland, there to see more a mosaic than a melting pot. To the region migrated all manner of men and women, and some of the early colonies they established still survive, their ethnic flavor intact. Pella, Iowa, is a Dutch town, and that state's Spillville quite Czech; Missouri's Hermann remains German and its Ste. Genevieve, French; while Highland, Illinois, still seems Swiss. And as for the people of the Midwest, the region has produced, or attracted to it, a rich crop of varied types. Any number of characters, colorful and shady, populated the heartland and are recalled in the pages that follow. You can take your pick of presidential personalities and styles—Lincoln, Grant and Reagan of Illinois, the Harrisons from Indiana, Iowa's Hoover and Missouri's Truman—or of lawmen and adventurers such as Wyatt

Earp, Bat Masterson, Buffalo Bill and Wild Bill Hickok. You'll meet the Cherry sisters of Cedar Rapids, Iowa; Indiana's sex researcher Alfred Kinsey; "Mother" Jones, the labor organizer from Illinois, and Illinois's Allen Pinkerton, America's first private eye; Walt Disney, J. C. Penney, General John J. Pershing and Jesse James from Missouri; Robert G. Ingersoll ("the great agnostic") and William Jennings Bryan ("the great commoner") from Illinois; writers Mark Twain, Edgar Lee Masters, Carl Sandburg, James Whitcomb Riley, Ernie Pyle and Ernie Hemingway.

Now to return, full cycle, back to the changing seasons, where this impressionistic glimpse of the Middle West began, the epitaph of Hemingway, that son of the Middle West, well encapsulates the elemental components—the seasons, the landscape—that shape the heartland's essential being:

> Best of all he loved the fall
> The leaves yellow on the cottonwoods
> Leaves floating on the trout streams
> And above the hills the high blue windless skies
> Now he will be a part of them forever.

Forever. There is, indeed, something eternal and timeless about the Middle West. Perhaps it stems from the pervasive influence, there in the heartland, of those eternal elements: the seasons, the trees, the streams, the hills, the skies, the land. An elemental, organic earthiness underlies the Middle West's nature, and a certain enduring quality pervades the place. There seems to be a permanence there, a continuity, as if, somehow, the people, the animals, the crops, the villages with their frozen-in-time settings, the small towns with their trim frame houses—along with the broad fields, the great rivers, the overarching starlit sky and the changing seasons—have been and will be there forever.

2. Practical Advice:

Being a Few Suggestions to Coast Dwellers,
Yankees, Southerners, Foreigners, Europeans,
Peddlers, Hobos, Confidence Men, Outsiders,
Transients, Tourists, Visitors
and Other Strangers Who Venture by Chance
or by Choice into the Midwestern Territory

Do not shrink, dear traveler, from venturing to visit the great American heartland. Help is at hand. This brief discussion will introduce you to a few of the many quirks, peculiarities and unusual (some might say strange) characteristics that typify the Midwest, that curious land so remote from the civilized coastal regions, and its natives. These comments, designed to help people unfamiliar with the Territory travel through the area, are necessarily brief because, as everyone knows, when you come right down to it there's really not all that much to say about the Midwest. In fact, the very first thing to realize about the place is that things out there in the Territory won't interest you like the more refined and developed parts of the world. Truth to tell, farms occupy much of the Midwest, and there isn't too much to say about hayseeds or cornstalks or hogs. Tractors or cows, say, may momentarily fascinate city folks. But how many Deeres or steers can you look at without getting bored? Let's face it: Once you've seen one green farm machine or one udder, you've seen them all. No two ways about it. And as far as the towns, if they were truly interesting places they obviously wouldn't be content to remain in the Midwest: Cedar Rapids would lie in the Loire Valley (and perhaps be called Loire Rapids), Peoria would embellish the Rhineland, and Dubuque would be neatly nestled in Italy's hill country. "Dubuque" even sounds sort of Italian if you pronounce the "e"; it's possible the place emigrated from Italy to Iowa, in which case it's a wonder the city, on first seeing the Midwest, didn't turn right around and return immediately to Italian soil. Located elsewhere, those cities would be truly fascinating. But stuck out there in the Midwest—no way there can be much of interest in that part of the world. The very name "Midwest" strikes fear in the heart of the true world traveler.

But suppose that one day you happen to find yourself in, of all places, the U.S. Midwest. What on earth do you do? How do you cope with this rather remote and obscure part of the country. All is not lost, even if you are. For one thing, you'll find that the natives are real friendly. They may be slow—half-witted perhaps, possibly even quarter-witted—and a bit dull to boot, and so laid back they seem to be way behind the times, but by and large the locals cotton to outsiders. Of course Midwesterners, contrary to what outsiders may suppose, are only human, and they may get a little peeved at you if you criticize their (a) accent, (b) old-fashioned attitudes, (c) down-home clothes, (d) basketball team (especially dangerous in Indiana), (e) horse team, (f) livestock, (g) corn crop, (h) quilt patterns or (i) grub (except for something called country fried steak, which even Midwesterners find a mess of a dish). But feel free to joke about their lack of culture or make fun of their provincial ways, because most of the locals will be too dense to understand what you're talking about. In fact, one of the great pleasures of traveling in the Midwest is to make witty comments about how backward the way of life is out there. A German poet named Heine (expired 1856) once said that he wanted to go to England to die because everything happened twenty years behind the times there. That fellow would've done better to move to the Midwest, for in that slow-paced region he'd still be alive.

When you travel through the Territory you may occasionally meet a few of the locals. It's advisable to carry with you candy to hand to the children and perhaps some cheap pens as well. By the way, when you offer someone a pen make sure you explain it's for writing: in the Midwest the natives usually think of pens as enclosures for hogs and cattle. And be sure the prospective recipient knows how to write. Most educated Midwesterners usually move away to New York or California or anywhere outside the Territory. Why get educated only to stay in the Midwest? Locals will also appreciate receiving postcards of your hometown, photos of places like the Pentagon or the Empire State Building or the Brooklyn or Golden Gate Bridges. But a word of caution is in order here: don't try to sell those places to the natives. Many Midwesterners have already bought the Brooklyn Bridge, and the like, from your predecessors, and the new owners of the structures don't need another one: one Brooklyn Bridge per family is quite enough. Don't fail to take lots of film with you, because you'll encounter many colorful characters. You may see an Indian or two but, truth to tell, a lot more redskins inhabit the Florida beaches than the Midwest. As for cowboys, they do exist in the heartland but they tend to spend their time with cows rather than with tourists. Your best bet is to look for farmers. The Midwest is full of them. In big cities it's hard to know what people do for a living just by looking at them, but out in the Territory it's easy to tell who's a farmer: they're the ones clad in dungarees and with dung clinging to their shoes, dirt on their hands, hayseeds in their hair, a government subsidy in their pocket. When talking to city slickers farmers often play dumb. Of course—let's face it—some of them aren't just playing dumb. After all, if they had any smarts they wouldn't be plain old farm folk in the Midwest, would they? But remember, when the farmer thinks about your side of the conversation he may conclude that you're playing dumb, too. Can you tell the difference between a combine and a harvester, between wheat and sorghum, between Holstein and Guernsey cows, between a tornado and a cyclone, between a horse and a nag, between fertile and exhausted soil? In fact, there's not much worn-out soil out there in the Midwest. Most of the land is rich and so are its farmers, although they don't dress the part.

But even if the heartland is an agricultural utopia, the region remains a cultural desert. That is a well-known fact. Since culture is so scarce in the Territory, you should definitely bring along whatever you need to nourish your intellectual requirements while traveling in the mindless Midwest. Otherwise you'll face mental starvation. Stash in your luggage cassettes of classical music, coffee table volumes of art (no need to bring a table, for there's furniture a-plenty in the Midwest, but coffee is somewhat scarce as cows give only milk) and plenty of other books. Of course, printed matter does exist in the Territory, but mainly such uninspiring items as Bibles, paperback romances, comic books, cookbooks, World Book encyclopedias (in untouched, mint condition) and the like. You'll also find a lot of Sears Roebuck catalogs, but they're usually missing a bunch of pages. Museums out there are few and far between but they do exist and you may want to visit one or two just to say that you've seen a great collection of butter churns, cookie jars or barbed wire, or a memorable exhibit of harnesses or cow bells. The folks back home will surely envy you. A few museums in the Midwest contain paintings, mainly of horses or barns or fields. But why look at pictures when you can see the real thing all around you? In fact, why even look at the real thing? But if you find yourself stuck out there in the heartland, here's a word to the wise: bring your culture with you—you won't find very much of that stuff in the Midwest.

What you will find out there, however, is easy traveling. First and by far most important: you can drink the water everywhere. In that respect, even if in no other, the Midwest can be considered more civilized than Third World countries.

For another thing, very nearly everybody in the Territory speaks English—of a sort. Oh, you'll come across the occasional twang, or the stray strange word or two or three, or some hard-to-understand pronunciation, or a provincial dialect beyond human comprehension. Or maybe the locals will from time to time be at a loss for words: some of the natives suffer from a limited vocabulary. But by and large you'll experience no communication problems in the Midwest. Just remember to speak slowly, ever so slowly, and very clearly so the natives will understand. If they don't grasp what you're getting at, try repeating the sentence even more slowly, S-L-O-W down. Remember, you're not in New York City or on the Santa Monica freeway now, you're out there in the wilds of the heartland. If your listener keeps scratching his head and grinning like an idiot, a not untypical reaction, you might try writing down what you want to express. You may have to show your words around a while until you can find somebody who can read. After all, this is not a hotbed of culture and learning like Cambridge or the Upper West Side or Georgetown or Beverly Hills—it's only the Midwest. But don't give up; usually each Territory town, no matter how small, boasts a few people who can read. However, when trying to communicate with the locals by speech or by writing it is highly recommended that you avoid such words or expressions as "Soho," "Bloomies," "Valley Girl," "Perrier," "spritzer," "Safire," "Rodeo Drive," "Skull and Bones," "Dunster House," "the Beltway," "the Main Line" and the like. Such references will go completely unrecognized in the Midwest.

Another reason you'll find travel in the Territory so easy is that your money will go farther there—and not only because the distances are so great in the Midwest. For what an evening out in New York City would cost, you can spend a month or more in the Midwest. This may not be desirable—but it's true. You'll be amazed at the prices. Hotels charge what in New York or California would be only the room tax, while meals run less than what you'd leave as a tip in a restaurant at home. In the Midwest you can actually buy a house for what a bar mitzvah in New York City or a movie studio party in Beverly Hills or a retainer with a D.C. lawyer would cost. Try not to bring plastic money with you out to the Territory. They've all heard of the Pony Express out there in the Midwest and some folks are familiar with Federal Express, but only a few know of American Express. You'll be able to change cash money—fives, tens and twenties—in most stores and banks in the Territory but try not to bring any fifty dollar (or larger) bills to the area because most of the natives have never seen anything larger than a twenty, if that. And by the way, make sure you count your change. It's not that Midwesterners are dishonest (quite the contrary) but, truth to tell, some of them don't know how to reckon very well. And be forewarned that in a few remote areas, such as the Ozark Hills, you won't be able to change money at all, for all transactions take place by barter only. So come prepared to swap some sort of trinket for a meal or lodging. The hillbillies like shiny objects—tinfoil, say, or bright new paper clips—and are also known to fancy such hard-to-get (in the back country) treasures as soap and pipe tobacco (especially appreciated by the women).

A further advantage to traveling in the Midwest is that the states there are so easy to understand. You'll find none of the complexities that vex visitors in the rest of the world, no confusion over whether you're in North or South (as in the Carolinas or the Dakotas) or in New or old (as in York, Hampshire, England and the like). In the Midwest the states are quite simple, just like the people, and easily defined. Indiana, for example, that's the place where the Hoosiers live. Not much of a life out there, not much going on—but that's where the Hoosiers live, and that's about all you need to know about Indiana. Illinois? That's the place where Lincoln, a politician who had a car and a life insurance company named after him, came from. Not much more to say about Illinois. Iowa: corn. That says it all about Iowa. That's Iowa in a nutshell, or a corncob. Missouri is a bit more confusing. It's hard to remember if it's a state or a river. The answer: it's both. Then what about Mississippi? That's a state (not in the Midwest), but it's also a river—one that borders Missouri, the state. Maybe this will help: Missouri is in the center of the country but not in the center of things. After all, Missouri didn't get where it is, stuck out there in the Midwest, by being a significant place. In fact, the state's main function is to be unimportant so places like New York, Washington and California can, by comparison, be very important. Missouri—excellent mediocrity: that's Missouri's claim to fame.

Of course, once you're actually out there in the territory you might become a mite confused, as all those cows and farmers and fields look about the same. So please, good traveler, reread the previous paragraph so that you won't get the Midwestern states all mixed up. That's only too easy to do, for places out there can be really confusing. For one thing, believe it or not there's no "East Side" or "West Side" in the Midwest. You do have inside and outside there, but that doesn't really help you keep things straight. One helpful hint: with a slight nick to "Missouri," the names of all the states begin with "I." So if you can't remember where you're headed, just ask how to get to that "I" state. Of course, you may end up in Idaho rather than in Indiana, Illinois, Iowa or Issouri, but no matter: even that's better than being stuck in the Midwest. To take another example of how confusing things can be in the heartland, try to remember that Kansas City lies mainly in Missouri and only partly in Kansas (that's the state next to Missouri). After all, Midwesterners don't think Los Angeles is in the neighboring state of Hawaii. In fact, most people in the Territory don't think of Los Angeles at all and have no idea where (or what) Hawaii is. If you can't use a Hawaii on the farm, the Midwestern has no interest in it. And if you're, say, a New Yorker who happens to find yourself in Grundy County, Iowa, try to avoid the temptation to observe that you've never heard of the place. After all, most of the people in Grundy County have never heard of New York. In fact, the Midwest's reputation for being isolationist is definitely deserved. Midwesterners seldom travel abroad because they find too many foreigners over there. This is admittedly a bit baffling, for the Midwest was itself once a foreign country—three foreign countries, in fact: French, Spanish and English flags flew over the land where Six Flags banners now wave. But the experience didn't take, as Midwesterners view Europeans with a mixture of indifference and difference—all foreigners and outsiders are seen to be different. But do not let that deter you from venturing into the Territory. You'll find out there quaint customs, old-fashioned (some would say out of date) ways, simple people, tall corn, fat hogs, thin culture, cow-clotted landscapes and a pace so slow you'll feel you've stepped back into the '50s— the 1850s. As that quintessential Midwesterner Mark Twain never said: "I thought the Midwest, where I was born at a very young age, was a great and a wonderful place. Then I grew up." So come out to the Territory for a visit; you'll never forget it—much as you may want to!

II

Indiana

1. Indiana:

Middle America

Indiana, truly a state of middle America, is a Middle Western state located in the middle of the country. In 1937 the state adopted the motto "The Crossroads of America," an appropriate designation, as more highways intersect in Indiana than in any other state. As George Ade, an Indiana wit and writer, observed, "Indiana is not Out West or Way Down East or Up North or South in Dixie." It is, rather, smack in the middle. Early explorers and immigrants converged on the crossroads state from different directions. The French floated down from the north on the St. Joseph and then the Wabash rivers to the south; the English and, later, the Americans traveled from the east on the Ohio River. In time, Indiana became the demographic middle of the nation: America's population center was located there, beginning in 1890, and remained in Indiana for sixty years, longer than any other state.

INDIANA

South Bend • • Elkhart

• N. Webster

Fort Wayne •

• Peru

• Kokomo

• Crawfordsville

Richmond •

• Rockville   • Indianapolis

• Terre Haute   Metamora •

Nashville
Bloomington •   • Columbus

• Bedford

Madison •

Wabash River

• Vincennes

New Albany •

• New Harmony

Ohio   River

Indianians seem proud to claim that they are middle Americans, moderate in temperament and average in ability. Indianian Thomas R. Marshall, vice-president under Woodrow Wilson, wrote: "Yes, the old state, as the days have come and gone, has struck a right good average. It has perhaps had no towering mountain peaks, but it has surely furnished as many first-grade second-class men in every department of life as any state in the Union." Marshall, who gave the nation the above-average witticism "What this country needs is a good five-cent cigar," was one of four vice-presidents from Indiana, a phenomenon that prompted humorist Irvin S. Cobb to observe that "the average Indianian makes suitable vice-presidential material because he is absolutely just that—average." And more recently Vice-President Dan Quayle of Indiana has maintained the state's reputation for political averageness. Dick and Jane, those average child characters in reading primers, were created by an Indiana native, and Robert S. and Helen Merrell Lynd chose Muncie, Indiana, as the nation's most typical town, which they described in their 1924 classic *Middletown,* an appropriate title for that middle American city in the Middle Western state of Indiana.

Being Middle Western, a kind of down-home, old-fashioned, rural atmosphere pervades Indiana. Until 1830 the entire population of the state was classified as rural by the federal census. Only in 1920 did urban inhabitants outnumber rural ones. Back in 1840 William Henry Harrison, who'd previously served as governor of the Indiana Territory, ran for president as the "log cabin and hard cider" candidate against Martin Van Buren, portrayed as an aristocratic dandy who fancied silk stockings, doused himself with scent and drank only the finest French wines. Harrison won the race, although he was hardly a "log cabin" type, as you'll see when you visit Grouseland, his elegant mansion in Vincennes.

But the Hoosier Harrison's pose of simplicity wasn't entirely a sham, for Indianians do tend to favor a laid-back, basic sort of existence. As Irving Leibowitz wrote in *My Indiana,* "Generally speaking, Hoosiers have learned the value of the simple things in life. They are in no great rush and are not overawed by wealth, position or prestige. Hoosiers may live in the present and plan for the future, but they jealously guard the past." That past is preserved around the state in such nineteenth-century settlements as Madison, a beautifully conserved Ohio River town; New Harmony, the site, a century and a half ago, of two utopian experiments and still today a delightful old-time village; and many others, such as Zionsville, Metamora, Conner Prairie Settlement—described in the pages that follow.

Those small towns in a way typify Indiana. James Whitcomb Riley, whose poetry captured the state's heart and soul and very essence, preceded his poem "My Ruthers" ("druthers") with the parenthetical comment: "(Writ durin' State Fair at Indianapolis, whilse visitin' a soninlaw then residin' thare, who has sence got back to the country whare he says a man that's raised thare ort to a-stayed in the first place)." Indianians seem to idealize the small town or country way of life. In fact, they do more than idealize it; Hoosiers live such a life. In his 1947 reminiscence *Home Country,* Hoosier Ernie Pyle, the famous journalist and war correspondent whose boyhood home is described in the next section of this chapter, wrote of the outpouring of "good neighbor" help after his mother's stroke. "For forty years my mother was the one who went to all these people when they needed help. They hadn't forgotten, and now they were coming to her in droves. Indiana farmers know what a 'good neighbor' policy is. It's born in them."

With some imagination, perhaps you'll be able to visualize as you travel through Indiana's old towns and country attractions life as it was (and to a certain extent still is) there is the

American heartland, for the past somehow seems to linger in the Hoosier state. Maybe you'll manage to imagine the panorama of the past at old Vincennes, Indiana's earliest surviving settlement, as did John Parsons who wrote in his diary when visiting the town in 1840: "When I close my eyes I can see, against the background of forest, the picturesque figures, the painted Indians, the Jesuit father, the French coureur-dubois, the English soldier, the titled visitors, the backwoodsman with his rifle." And maybe, catching a glimpse of an Amish carriage in Elkhart County or one of the nineteenth-century round barns in Fulton County or a serene scene at one of Indiana's eighty-eight thousand farms, you'll conjure up in your mind visions of country life a century ago, such as described by J. A. Lemcke, who recalled in *Reminiscences of an Indianian* "log rollings, house and barn raisings and corn shuckings. I greatly delighted in gatherings of this sort, especially when there was a quilting bee. . . . After supper we boys and girls danced to the tune of 'Old Dan Tucker,' scraped out on a hoarse fiddle; or played kissing games, in which hands were held in a circling march."

Such is the sort of basic, old-time, small town atmosphere you'll find as you roam the byways and back roads of Indiana. In a reminiscence of his Indianapolis school days, Indiana native Kurt Vonnegut, Jr. recalled a poem in his 1940 Shortridge High School yearbook that addressed the question "Where go the years?" The novelist quoted with approval the poem's answer—that the years "ride forgotten moonbeams to the sky." But in the Hoosier state not all the past has vanished on those forgotten moonbeams in the sky, as you'll see when you visit the old-fashioned corners and historic towns of old Indiana described in the following pages.

2. Covered Bridges and Maple Sugar Country:

Parke County
Ernie Pyle House
Terre Haute

Like much of the Middle West, Parke County is a land for all seasons. It's pleasant to tour the rustic area in the spring and summer, while fall is the time when the silvery harvest moon hangs high in the sky, the leaves turn gold and "When the frost is on the pumpkin and the fodder's in the shock," as James Whitcomb Riley, Indiana's poet laureate, wrote. The second week in October, Parke hosts a covered-bridge festival with a farmer's market and bazaar crammed with handicrafts and harvest delights such as pumpkins, popcorn, persimmons, squaw corn and much else. In the winter—the last weekend of February and the first weekend of March—the Parke County maple sugar festival includes tours of the maple camps, sheep shearing, hog butchering and a "Home Folk's" market with locally made crafts and such maple treats as syrup, candy, sugar and pralines.

Parke County, located in far western Indiana twenty-five miles north of Terre Haute, boasts more covered bridges than any other county in the country. The nation's stock of old covered bridges is gradually dwindling: in the last twenty years, half have disappeared, leaving in the land fewer than a thousand. Parke County, whose picturesque bridges were listed on the National Register in 1978, is a good place to see some fine examples of the surviving specimens. Parke originally boasted fifty two and a half covered bridges, the "half" being a span across the Wabash River leading to an adjoining county. Thirty-five survive, all but ten still in daily use.

It's one of the Midwest's true travel delights to wander Parke's back roads, passing by some of the county's seven hundred or so farms, now and again crossing by covered bridge over Sugar or Raccoon Creek or one of the other pristine streams. The floorboards of the old wooden spans rhythmically rattle as you inch your way over them. "Cross this bridge at a walk" caution signs on many of the bridges, a remnant of the horse and carriage days when it was feared that vibrations from the animals' hooves might damage the structure.

It's hard to pick and choose among the rustic roads that criss-cross the fertile farm area, leading you to the region's nearly three dozen covered bridges. The county has divided itineraries into Yellow, Blue, Brown and Red Routes. At the tourist office in Rockville you can pick up a map that shows each itinerary outlined in the color which designates it. On the Red Route you'll visit Crooks Bridge, the county's oldest (1856), as well as a spot from which you can see three covered bridges at once—the only place in the country affording such a view. By Bridgeton Bridge rises an 1868 mill thought to be the oldest continually operating grist mill west of the Allegheny Mountains. The mill still produces cornmeal and whole wheat, rye and buckwheat flours on sale in the area.

The Blue Route takes you past the Catlin Bridge, originally built (in 1907) to serve the village of Catlin but later moved to its present place on the Rockville golf course. Farther north, in the village of Marshall, you'll pass the Federated Church. One of the few such sanctuaries in the country, the church serves various denominations—including Friends, Methodists and Presbyterians—who worship together in a "federated" congregation.

On the Brown and the Yellow Routes, which follow the same roads for about seven and a half miles out of Rockville, you'll see Mecca's old iron jail, near the bridge that spans Big Raccoon Creek, as well as the county's shortest and longest covered bridges. The shortest, at forty-three feet, is the 1909 Phillips Bridge, while the longest is the West Union Bridge, a three-hundred-and-fifteen-foot double-span affair constructed in 1876. The West Union Bridge is no longer used by vehicles, so the nearby two hundred and seven foot long Jackson Bridge takes the prize for being the world's longest single-span covered wooden bridge still used for automobile traffic.

Because the October covered-bridge festival offers not only Mother Nature's autumn leaf spectacular but also quilt and antique sales, square dancing, a pig roast, a scarecrow contest and other treats of the season and region, the county fairly bursts with tourists then. An estimated five hundred thousand people visit Parke County for the fall festivities, so if you prefer to enjoy the villages, rustic roads and picturesque bridges without bumper-to-bumper traffic it's best to see the area at other times.

The winter Maple Fair, for example, is considerably less busy than the covered-bridge festival but its crafts booths, farm demonstrations and other country activities, still give you the flavor of Parke County's old-time rural atmosphere. Indiana has a long maple sugar tradition. In 1815 Caleb Lownes, who settled in Vincennes that year, referred to the state's stands of maple trees with the alluring phrase "sugar orchards." Even before that, Indians, who would gash the hard trees with a stone axe and collect the drippings in a birchbark pail, would gather sugar water from Indiana's maples. These days the people of Parke County use similar, though less primitive, methods. During the first warm days of late winter, when the weather is freezing at night and thawing by day, the locals tap the trees with a spile (a three-inch-long, tapered metal cylinder) and then process the liquid in evaporators that boil off the water to leave a residue of syrup. It takes about fifty to seventy gallons of sugar water to produce a gallon of maple syrup.

During Maple Fair time you'll see these operations at Parke County's four functioning sugar maple camps. Four miles northwest of Rockville, the county seat, is the Williams and Teague Camp, founded by owner John Teague's grandfather. Even older is the Smiley family camp, about twelve miles east of Rockville, which four generations of Smileys have operated for some hundred and fifty years. One of the most rustic camps is Foxworthy's Sugar Bush, just north of Turkey Run State Park, which lies ten miles north of Rockville. At Foxworthy's a wood-fired furnace and a century-old one-room school house—where such goodies as maple syrup cookies, sassafras candy, cider and homemade jam, jelly and apple butter are offered—provide a warm, old-fashioned atmosphere. About five miles southwest of Foxworthy you'll reach Heath Camp, located in a natural wooded area near Sugar Creek, named by the Indians "Pungosiconi," or "waters of many sugar trees." Some of the oldest trees bear hatchet scars left from the days when Indians tapped the maples.

One of the most attractive places in the area to stay is the Turkey Run Inn at Turkey Run State Park. Especially delightful are the individual cabins, which give you a backwoods feeling of privacy. The unusual name originated from the great flocks of wild turkeys that once inhabited the terrain, sheltering themselves beneath the area's overhanging cliffs. Within the park is the Narrows covered bridge, an 1882 span that crosses Sugar Creek and that bears on the north portal the legend "$5.00 Fine for Driving or Riding Over This Bridge Faster Than a Walk." On a hill north of the bridge rises the brick house built in 1841 by Salmon Rusk, who in 1826 settled there on a land grant given him for his military service.

Before leaving the Parke County area it's worth visiting the Ernie Pyle house in Dana, fourteen miles west of Rockville and just by the Illinois state line. Built in the 1850s, the white wood residence where the famous World War II newspaper correspondent first saw the light of day (in 1900) is a typical nineteenth-century Midwest farmhouse. Much of the "Country Victorian"-style furniture which fills the four first-floor rooms, dining room, kitchen, parlor and bedroom, belonged originally to the Pyle family.

Pyle began his illustrious journalism career in the northern Indiana town of Laporte where he joined the *Herald* in 1922 after leaving Indiana University just six months before he was scheduled to graduate. By 1935 he'd become a roving columnist, writing features from all around the country. When war broke out, Pyle covered the conflict in Europe from 1940 to 1945, by which time his column appeared in seven hundred papers. Pyle was assigned to the Pacific theater, where a Japanese sniper's bullet killed him on April 18, 1945. The famous journalist was buried, far from the Indiana farm area of his origins, in the National Memorial Cemetery of the Pacific in Honolulu under a simple flat stone, Number D 109, with the inscription "Ernest Taylor Pyle, Indiana" and the dates of his birth and death.

At the Pyle house in Dana, displays trace the life and career of the Pulitzer Prize-winning writer. Photos, scrapbooks and memorabilia recall his early days as an Indiana farm boy and his later years as a reporter, columnist and correspondent from the front. One of the items on display seems to encapsulate the small town Hoosier's successful career out in the big wide world beyond the Midwest—a canvas satchel bag stencilled with the simple legend "Ernie Pyle, War Correspondent."

Terre Haute, about twenty miles south of Dana, was the boyhood home of another famous American writer—Theodore Dreiser. Born in 1871, the Indianian became famous for his biting novels such as *The Financier, The Titan* and, best known of all, *An American Tragedy,* attacking high finance and low jinks among the upper classes. Dreiser's book of essays about his Indiana boyhood, *A Hoosier Holiday* (1916), captures in a delightful way the experience of growing up in the Middle West in the late nineteenth century. Although Dreiser's birthplace hasn't been memorialized, that of his elder brother, Paul Dresser, is open to visitors. The residence, listed on the National Register of Historic Places, is a typical workingman's house of the period. Dresser was an accomplished writer in his own right: One year, 1898, nine of his songs appeared on the hit list of best-selling sheet music. Dresser also wrote what in 1913 became Indiana's state song, "On the Banks of the Wabash—Far Away." The Terre Haute house (moved to its present site in 1963) is but a stone's throw from the Wabash River Dresser memorialized in his song, one of the most bittersweet and nostalgic state songs imaginable and one that gives an evocative glimpse of the Middle West:

Oh, the moonlight's fair tonight along the Wabash
From the fields there comes the breath of new mown hay.
Thro' the sycamores the candle lights are gleaming,
On the banks of the Wabash, far away.

A few blocks east of the Dresser birthplace stands the more imposing mansion, also listed on the National Register, of famous labor leader Eugene V. Debs. Debs was a Terre Hautean born, bred, and settled. Born there in 1855, Debs grew up in Terre Haute and for nearly fifty years occupied the two and a half story frame house he built (for $4,500) in 1880. Eight rooms of the spacious house, a typical example of Midwestern late-Victorian-style architecture, are crammed with exhibits, period furniture, family photos, memorabilia and other items recalling Debs's tumultuous career as a labor leader and social activist. Debs organized the American Railway Union (1893), participated in the famous 1894 Pullman strike in Chicago and organized the Social Democratic Party.

Debs ran as the party's nominee for president five times, the last in 1920 as convict number 2273 in the Atlanta federal penitentiary, where he was confined for anti-war activities. Campaigning from behind bars, Debs received nearly one million votes. The third-floor walls of the house are covered with colorful murals, painted by John Joseph Laska, professor of art at nearby Indiana State University. The scenes depict the history of the American labor movement and Debs's role in the growth of the unions.

If you're a bibliophile, one little-known corner of Terre Haute worth visiting is the Cunningham Memorial Library at Indiana State University, just a few blocks from the Debs house. The Cordell Collection there contains a large number of rare books dating from 1475 up to the twentieth century. The library also owns one of the world's largest collections of Dr. Samuel Johnson's famous dictionary, starting with the first edition in 1755 up to a 1963 version. If the charms of Parke County's covered bridges, Ernie Pyle's house and the attractions of Terre Haute leave you at a loss for words, you can find all you need in the more than two hundred editions of Johnson dictionaries at the Cunningham Library.

3. Old Indiana:

Vincennes and New Harmony

Unlike many states, Indiana was first settled in the west. In 1717 French officers and traders established a small fort on the Wabash River below present-day Lafayette. That settlement, the first European outpost in what became Indiana, predated such historic eastern cities as Savannah, Georgia; Buffalo, New York; and Richmond, Virginia. Some ten or fifteen years later another fort, called Vincennes, was established farther south along the Wabash and there Indiana began, for Vincennes is the state's oldest surviving settlement. This pleasant river town of nineteen thousand people is rather a rarity in the Midwest, for it boasts a large number of remnants from the eighteenth and early nineteenth centuries—truly early days in the middle part of the country. In fact, you can trace much of the area's rich and colorful history by visiting Vincennes' various attractions.

A good place to start is the Old Cathedral, founded in 1732, which recalls the days when French missionaries arrived to bring religion to Indians and fur trappers. Although the present building dates only from 1826, it occupies the spot where the original log cabin church stood. By the cathedral stretches the Old French Cemetery, filled with graves of Vincennes' founding fathers and mothers. You'll find there the oldest marked grave in the state, that of Jeanne Bonneau, second wife of a French nobleman who accompanied Lafayette to America. She died November 15, 1800, at the age of twenty-eight. In the courtyard to the left of the church stands the Cathedral Library, the state's oldest library (1840). It contains more than eleven thousand books and rare documents, most printed between the fifteenth and eighteenth centuries, with the oldest—a papal document—dating from 1319.

A short walk from the Old Cathedral over to the George Rogers Clark Memorial will take you forward a half century in time. Between the days when the French founded Vincennes and American troops, led by Clark, captured the fort from the British in 1779, the town saw many changes. During the middle of the eighteenth century the French and the English vied to control the Indian tribes and the fur trade in what was then the far west. Typical of the rivalry was the 1765 mission of George Croghan, an Indian agent for the English sent west to parley with the redskins and convert them to the English cause. Near the mouth of the Wabash, eighty Kickapoos attacked Croghan's party. Of the hatchet blow on the head he received, Croghan later wrote: "my Scull being pretty thick the hatchett wou'd not enter, so you may see a thick Scull is of Service on some Occasions." The English eventually won out—perhaps their skulls were more durable than the French ones—and in the 1763 Treaty of Paris the French ceded Vincennes and the surrounding area to Great Britain, and by the 1770s the fort had become one of the principal British outposts in the west.

George Rogers Clark saw the need for American forces to capture Vincennes from the British, so in a now-famous exploit Clark and his men marched on the enemy stronghold and captured it from the British commander, Colonel Henry Hamilton, known as "hair buyer" for his practice of purchasing Yankee scalps from the Indians. The Clark Memorial, a rotunda, dedicated by President Franklin Roosevelt in 1936, commemorates the famous victory, which assured American control of the continent's interior and led to the westward expansion of the United States. A series of seven large murals vividly portray episodes in Clark's career on the western frontier. One scene shows him leading his men across the flood waters of the Wabash on the way to capture Vincennes, while another pictures the attack on the fort.

After the Americans took over Vincennes, civilization gradually began to mature the frontier town. A short drive, ten blocks east from the Clark Memorial, will take you another quarter of a century ahead in the history of old Vincennes. In a small park stand two white frame buildings that recall the early days of the Indiana Territory, a huge domain including all or a substantial part of five states carved out of the old Northwest Territory in 1800. One building is a replica of the printing office of Elihu Stout, who published the Territory's first newspaper. Stout came to Vincennes from Lexington, Kentucky, where he'd worked on the *Kentucky Gazette*. Using a second-hand printing press and type he'd brought with him, the twenty-two-year-old founded the *Indiana Gazette* in the summer of 1804. "The Editor pledges himself that the columns of the *Gazette* shall never be tarnished with matter that can offend the eye of decency, or raise a blush upon the cheek of modesty and virtue," Stout avowed in one of the early issues. The paper appeared weekly until April 1806 when a fire destroyed the printing shop. On July 4, 1807, the young editor started up a new paper called *The Western Sun,* whose descendant, the *Sun-Commercial,* still publishes in Vincennes. In March 1830 Abe Lincoln, then twenty-one, paid a visit to the *Sun's* offices where he saw for the first time the process of printing.

Next to the *Sun* rises the first capital of the Indiana Territory, a small two-story building with the governor's office on the lower floor and the legislative assembly hall upstairs. William Henry Harrison served as the Territory's first governor. Harrison (who became ninth President of the United States, although only for a month—he died of pneumonia) was the son of Benjamin Harrison, a prominent politician who served three terms as governor of Virginia and signed the Declaration of Independence, and was the grandfather of another Benjamin Harrison, twenty-third president of the U.S. Soon after his arrival at Vincennes, William Henry Harrison wrote to a friend in Cincinnati on October 15, 1801: "I am much pleased with this country. Nothing can exceed its beauty and fertility." In those early days, however, Vincennes lacked certain amenities so Harrison, now in a more practical vein, went on: "How comes on the distillery? I wish you to send me some whisky as soon as possible." Harrison was essentially the man who subdued the redskins and acquired for the United States vast tracts of Indiana lands. In 1803 President Jefferson commissioned Harrison to enter into treaties with the Indians, "touching a quill," as the Indians called signing an agreement. Losing no time, Harrison concluded a number of land treaties with various tribes. But in

the spring of 1808 the famous chief Tecumseh arrived at
Vincennes to complain about the loss of land. Harrison replied, "The long knives [Americans] are not less brave [than
the Indians] and you know their numbers be as the blades of
grass on the plains, as the sands on the river shore." Over the
next three years Harrison and the great chief parleyed and
skirmished until, finally, on November 7, 1811, at the Battle
of Tippecanoe—near present-day Lafayette—the Americans
defeated Tecumseh's braves once and for all. After that, the
Indian pressure and threat in Indiana began to recede. Harrison had consolidated American control of the Territory.

Just by the old state capital and only a hundred yards or so
from the Wabash stands Grouseland, Harrison's home for
eight years. An impressive twenty-six-room, red brick mansion built (1803–4) in the style of an old Virginia plantation
house, the residence, listed on the National Register in 1961,
is a remarkably civilized place for such early days on the
western frontier. Elegant period furnishings, many belonging to the Harrison family, fill the attractively restored house.
The dining room table is set for a formal dinner, as if Governor Harrison and his party were expected at any moment.
But all is not refinement and civilization within: a dining
room shutter bears a bullet hole left there from an attempt by
Indians on Harrison's life.

As the nineteenth century wore on, Vincennes developed
into a tidy little town with a certain grace and sense of the
past. Writing in his diary on July 24, 1840, John Parsons, a
Virginian traveling in Indiana, noted, in regard to Vincennes,
"my amazement over the beauty, the antiquity, the interest of
this town," with a site "of great loveliness" and inhabited by
"extraordinarily interesting, high-bred people." Still today a
lingering atmosphere of the past pervades the old Wabash
River town, where you can get the flavor of what the western
frontier was like two centuries and more ago.

Tucked in by the banks of the Wabash some fifty miles

south of Vincennes, in the far southwest corner of the state, nestles an entire village that is a picture out of the past—the nineteenth-century settlement of New Harmony. New Harmony is a living museum of past attempts to create a utopian society there in the far reaches of the Middle West. A charismatic maverick German Lutheran minister named George Rapp and eight hundred followers founded the settlement in 1814. Over the next eleven years the Harmonists, as they called themselves, cultivated two thousand acres, planting vineyards and orchards; built dormitories and more than a hundred brick, frame or log houses; and established two distilleries, a brewery, a shoe factory, and woolen, cotton, hemp and saw mills. The rather severe, serious sect managed to create at New Harmony a prosperous colony that Rapp decided to move back east to Pennsylvania, nearer to the main textile markets; so in 1825 he advertised the town for sale. Robert Owen, a Scottish industrialist and idealist, purchased the place for $190,000 and proceeded to establish a second utopian community in New Harmony, a kind of intellectual colony devoted to the life of the mind. Many of the scientists and teachers Owen imported into the settlement arrived in January 1826 on a flatboat dubbed the "boatload of knowledge."

In a certain way New Harmony was brilliantly successful, although Owen's experiment failed. In that remote early nineteenth century outpost in a corner of Indiana was founded America's first infant school, first trade school, first free public school system, first free library, first civic drama club and first office of the U.S. Geological Survey. But disharmony thrived at New Harmony. Paul Brown, a New Yorker who in 1826 enthusiastically joined Robert Owen's experiment, soon became disillusioned by what he described in his book *Twelve Months in New-Harmony* as "all the lingering turmoils of this place, all the agitations, all the embarrassments" that divided the residents. Almost immediately after arriving, he encountered friction with Owen, whom Brown accused of "selling and buying, doing and undoing, taking and retaking, turning and overturning and re-overturning, bargaining, bantering, scheming, and manoeuvring." Such was the atmosphere at New Harmony under Owen, according to at least one disappointed utopian. In the end the great experiment failed. Owen dissolved the operation in 1827 and returned to England. But during the so-called afterglow period, the colony became a delightful village, eminently livable and very visitable. A description of New Harmony written for the Indianapolis *Sentinal* by John H. Holliday after his visit there in July 1869 still well describes the town today:

> The village is slow going and conservative in comparison with most of our towns. Comparatively isolated as it has always been by not being on any direct line of travel, it has retained many old-fashioned notions and customs, and there is a freedom and restfulness about its existence that is fascinating when contrasted with the hurry and bustle of city life. For years it was miles away from the railroad and the telegraph, but at last these arms of modern life have grasped it, and, while their coming has wrought some change and in time may create greater ones, they cannot efface the marks of the past, for it is still in many things as anomalous as in the Community days and deserving par excellence the title of "*The* Indiana Village."

To visit "*the* Indiana village," it's well to begin at the striking Atheneum, a combination museum, visitor's center and modern-day landmark. It's impossible to miss the Atheneum. A glossy white porcelain building, it rises near the Wabash River like an oversized White Castle, one of those famous "greasy spoon" hamburger establishments that dot the Middlewestern landscape like displaced igloos. (No true Middlewesterner can survive for long without a fix of "belly bombers," as connoisseurs of the delicacy sometimes call the

White Castle burgers.) At the Atheneum you can view a brief movie that recounts the history of New Harmony. Books, maps, pamphlets and information on the colony are also available, as well as tickets for the two and a half hour "Historic New Harmony Tour," which leaves regularly from the Atheneum. The advantage of the tour is that it takes you inside some of the buildings that are not otherwise open.

On the tour you'll visit the West Street Quarter, with a 1775 double log house and Harmonist-built houses that show you the colonist's way of life; in the Tavern Street Quarter you visit the mid-nineteenth-century Lichtenberger Building that houses a collection of paintings of the American west (now Midwest) by Karl Bodmer, a Swiss artist who traveled through the country in 1833; the Brewery Street Quarter includes stops at a cooper shop (1819) and the 1823 Solomon Wolf house where a scale model of New Harmony in 1824 is displayed; finally, on Main Street you stop in at the Museum and the Restoration Shops, each installed in a late nineteenth-century building.

After the tour it's pleasant to stroll at your own pace to explore some of the side streets and off-the-beaten-track corners of town you don't visit with the guide. At the Harmonist Burial Ground, near the Atheneum, repose two hundred and thirty members of the Harmonie (as Rapp spelled the name) Society. They lie in the same ground as prehistoric Woodland Indians interred there a millenium earlier. The nearby strikingly stark Roofless Church, designed by architect Phillip Johnson and built in 1959, is an interdenominational sanctuary (if you can call a building without a roof a sanctuary) decorated with a bronze sculpture by Jacques Lipchitz. Steps away is Tillich Park, where theologian Paul Tillich lies buried in a lovely verdant enclave embellished with quotations from his works incised on boulders. Eight blocks south of town coil the hedges of the Labyrinth, a maze (you can walk through) planted by the Harmonists as a metaphor for life to symbolize the virtue of making correct choices.

Apart from the fact that there's enough to see in New Harmony to delay you for a full day or even a weekend, it's worth remaining in the village overnight just to stay in the delightful New Harmony Inn. In keeping with the simplicity of the early Harmonists, the Inn is a beautifully understated place, its forty-five rooms outfitted with pleasingly plain furniture rather than fancy new-fangled sorts of fixtures. An alcove off the lobby serves as a small chapel, while by the fireplace appears a quotation that sets forth the Inn's philosophy of hospitality: "The man who comes away from his work is like one who has been wounded. He needs to be cared for in a calm atmosphere: do not treat him with violence! Help him to relax. Give him some encouragement! Show some interest in the things he does."

For meals the Red Geranium, a block from the Inn, is the place to go. This rustic restaurant, with its polished brick floor and turn-of-the-century display cases, features tasty meals in a pleasant atmosphere. One specialty is old-fashioned Shaker lemon pie.

Any time of year is a good time to visit New Harmony, but June is an especially delightful month. In the last half of June burst into bloom the golden rain trees, Chinese by origin, and planted in New Harmony by Thomas Say, a famous naturalist who lived in the colony. The magnificent trees gild the village with splashes of bright yellow blossoms—a kind of annual revival of golden days in New Harmony recalling the time when a brave utopian experiment thrived and then vanished in a secluded corner of America's Midwest a long time ago.

4. Abe Lincoln Meets Santa Claus:

Santa Claus, Indiana
Lincoln Boyhood National Memorial
St. Meinrad's Abbey
The Spa Towns of French Lick and West Baden
The Bedford Limestone Quarries

If you thought Santa Claus lived at the North Pole, a visit to the town of Santa Claus, Indiana, might change your mind. Santa Claus is a hamlet of three hundred people in southern Indiana about sixty miles due east of New Harmony. Although only a tiny one-street town, Santa Claus boasts a large first-class-category post office, installed in a castle-like stone building, which processes some one million pieces of mail yearly, mostly during the holiday season. Stamped envelopes (mailed in bulk) pour in from all over the country to receive the unique "Santa Claus" cancellation from the post office, which was established in 1856. In Santa Claus Park, atop the highest hill in the village, stands a granite statue of a smiling, jolly Saint Nick dedicated to the "children of the world."

Founded in 1846, the village took its unusual name when the first suggestion, Santa Fe, was rejected because a town by that name already existed in Indiana. Since Christmas season was at hand, someone jokingly suggested an alternative, and the name "Santa Claus" stuck. In the 1930s a Santa Claus College operated in the village. A man named Charles W. Howard wanted to perk up the normally unconvincing department store Santas, so he opened a school to train aspiring Saint Nicks. Graduates of the course received a "B.S.C." degree—Bachelor of Santa Clausing.

These days Santa's Indiana outpost includes Holiday

World, a one-hundred-and-eighty-acre amusement park with rides, a petting zoo, a wax museum, a spin ride called "The Arctic Circle," stage shows, a mini-train you can ride, Mrs. Claus's kitchen and, of course, Santa Claus himself, who poses for photos the year round. (Another Midwestern Christmassy village—Noel—lies in southwestern Missouri: see Chapter V, section 8.)

A few miles west of Santa Claus, once lived one of Indiana's most famous residents, young Abe Lincoln. Who knows?—perhaps the two renowned whiskered folk heroes once met there in the southern Indiana farm country. Lincoln came to Indiana at the age of seven when his family moved there from Kentucky in 1816. Years later Lincoln recounted for a presidential biographer a description of pioneer life in the state: "Indiana was a wild region with many bears and wild animals in the woods. My father settled in an unbroken forest; and the clearing away of surplus wood was the great task ahead. Abraham, very large for his age, had an axe put into his hand at once; and from that moment till well into his twenty-third year, he was almost constantly handling that most useful instrument." Life was hard on the frontier back then. Potatoes were the only food the family could count on. At one meal, Thomas Lincoln asked his son for a blessing over a dish of roasted potatoes, to which young Abe responded "that they were mighty poor blessings."

At the Lincoln Boyhood National Memorial you'll see a number of attractions recalling young Abe's days on the hundred and sixty acre farm. A twenty-five minute film called "Here I Grew Up," shown at the Visitor Center, offers a good introduction to the history of the site. Also at the center is a museum as well as books, postcards and information on the Memorial. Although the Lincoln cabin there is a reconstruction, both it and the working pioneer farmstead—with the split-rail fences, outbuildings, animals, costumed attendants, gardens—give a vivid example of life as it was for the Lincolns there in the early nineteenth century. Beyond the grave of Nancy Hanks, Lincoln's mother, who died in October 1818 of "milk sickness," runs a trail past fields of corn and wheat and patches of cotton, flax and tobacco. A bronze marker indicates the site of the original Lincoln home. Beyond stands a log cabin, smokehouse, carpenter shop, barn, corn crib and chicken house. This "Living Historical Farm," as it's called, includes animals and cultivated fields which locals plow, plant and harvest, so the land the Lincoln family cleared and worked more than a century and a half ago is still being farmed.

From the Lincoln Memorial it's only a short drive to St. Meinrad, nine miles northeast of Santa Claus, where a huge old Benedictine abbey towers over the peaceful little village. This is a picture out of a European landscape, perhaps Switzerland, the country where the original Saint Meinrad lived in the ninth century. A thousand years later his latter-day disciples came to the New World and established in rural Indiana a religious community that now includes a church, monastery, seminary, library and an active publishing operation called the Abbey Press. The church, a huge stone pile of pure romanesque design, is open daily for self-guided tours. An especially enchanting time to visit the abbey is when the Gregorian choir sings. The medieval chants sound and resound through St. Meinrad's hallowed halls, seemingly transporting one to a time and world far removed from the twentieth century and Indiana farm country in America's heartland.

A somewhat more worldly, bodily experience awaits you in the spa towns of West Baden and French Lick, some thirty-five miles north of St. Meinrad. Back in 1840 an entrepreneur named Dr. William A. Bowles promoted the local spring water as beneficial to the health. Bowles built the first French Lick Springs Hotel and dubbed the product of the spring "Pluto Water." Meanwhile, Dr. John Lane erected a resort hotel a mile or so away at West Baden, named after the German spa town of Wiesbaden. He called the water there "Sprudel Water," and before long locals hotly debated the merits of Sprudel versus Pluto. The area soon became fashionable. The Monon Railroad brought wealthy visitors in private cars to the area to "take the water" during the "watering season." After the stock market crash (the one in 1929, not that of 1987), the Depression brought hard times to the spa towns. In 1934 the Jesuits bought the huge, rotund West Baden Hotel and established a seminary there. Twelve years later they moved away and eventually the hotel closed, but plans have been made to restore the old dowager to its original use. As for the vast French Lick Springs Hotel, it's still functioning much as in the old days, and there you'll find all the amenities of a leading resort hotel—tennis courts, a golf course, skeet and trap shooting, horseback riding, bowling, surrey rides and, of course, a health spa where you can take the waters. Also available are boating on nearby Patoka Lake and, in the winter, skiing at Paoli Peaks.

While whiling away a pleasant day or two at the spa you may want some diversions. Two possibilities in French Lick are the House of Clocks and the Railway Museum. The collection at the clock museum, installed in a frame house near the hotel, includes more than a thousand timepieces, some dating back to the early 1800s when Eli Terry established America's first clock factory. The Railway Museum houses six locomotives and twenty-one old-time railroad cars. A 1930s-vintage trolley car, labeled "Springs Valley Electric Railway," carries visitors from the train station, where the museum is located, to the West Baden Springs Hotel. For a more extensive trip, a 1925 Baldwin steam locomotive pulls old cars on a twenty-mile ride through the Hoosier National Forest, the twenty-two-hundred-foot Burton Tunnel and limestone rock cuts.

Indiana is famous for its limestone. Bedford, about thirty

miles north of French Lick-West Baden, is the heart of the state's limestone industry. The towns of Oolitic and East Oolitic near Bedford furnish reminders of the rock's profusion in the area, oolite being a kind of limestone. Recognizing the possibilities of the local limestone as a building material, Dr. William Foote, who in 1818 settled in Indiana from Connecticut, in 1832 persuaded a Louisville stonecutter to come to Bedford and start his trade there. Soon the limestone, prized for its unusual combination of being easy to quarry and carve but also durable and fire resistant, was being shipped out on the New Albany & Salem Railroad. Later, workers devised machinery for use in quarrying the stone, and in 1877 Davis Harrison formalized the industry when he organized the Dark Hollow Quarry Company.

Holes that pock the ground around Bedford evidence the great chunks of limestone carted away to build such well-known structures as the Empire State Building, Chicago's Tribune Towers and the Art Institute, the Mellon Institute in Pittsburgh, New York City's St. John the Divine Cathedral (still-building) and many of the buildings in Washington's Federal Triangle area. More recently, Indiana limestone was used to replace crumbling sandstone along the cornice and seven hundred feet of entablature on the U.S. Capitol's west front. A good part of the state of Indiana has thus migrated and ended up scattered around the country.

At the quarries, giant saws slice out ten- to twenty-ton stone blocks. Some are left as is and transported to construction projects all over the nation. Other blocks are carved and embellished with designs or scenes. The craftsmen who work the limestone were popularized in the 1979 movie *Breaking Away,* set in nearby Bloomington, seat of the University of Indiana, twenty-three miles north of Bedford.

5. College, Country and Columbus:

Indiana University at Bloomington
Rustic Brown County
The Modern Architecture of Columbus

Indiana highway 46 needs only thirty-five miles to go from Bloomington to Columbus by way of Brown County. But that short stretch of road takes you on a widely varied itinerary that includes what is perhaps the state's most scenic countryside as well as two of Indiana's most culturally rich towns.

Completely dominated by Indiana University, Bloomington seems the quintessential Midwestern college town, with its cozy cafes and pubs, bookstores and swarms of young people thronging the tree-filled campus. In one Bloomington pub (called the Book Nook) of the sort that abound on Kirkwood Avenue, Indiana University graduate Hoagy Carmichael first picked out the notes of "Stardust."

With more than thirty-two thousand students these days, it's hard to imagine the school a century and a half ago when it was chartered as a university. That was back in 1829, when the endowment amounted to $80,000 and when "The fees in the College proper are $24 a year; in the Preparatory Department, $17; in the Law Department, $20. Students can board and lodge with private families at from $1.25 to $1.50 per week. Bloomington is beautifully situated; the neighborhood is favorable to the health, and to the promotion of good morals." So advised the *Indiana Gazetteer,* a fact book on the state published in the mid-nineteenth century.

Bloomington doesn't seem to have changed much in the subsequent century. In a reminiscence entitled *The Indiana Years 1903–1941* Walter B. Hendrickson, a history and government professor, recalls the town in the mid-thirties: "In the 1936–1937 academic year there were only about three thousand students on the Bloomington campus, which extended over a very small area compared with the great post-World War II expansions. Most of the buildings faced on a beautiful wooded area, which was especially lovely in the spring when it reminded me of an Indiana farm wood lot."

After the war the university grew—the campus now occupies eighteen hundred and fifty acres, with many of the buildings made of limestone from the Bedford area—and became more worldly. In the late forties and early fifties Dr. Alfred Kinsey, the famous sex researcher, brought national attention to the university town in the supposedly conservative Middle West. Indiana parents complained about Kinsey's sex studies and threatened to withdraw their children from Indiana University. Stripteaser Rose La Rose, appearing in Indianapolis's Fox Burlesque, criticized Kinsey as "a literary peeping Tom." *Time* magazine had Kinsey's wife saying, "I hardly ever see him at night anymore since he took up sex." Kinsey's Institute for Sex Research at the University assembled what is probably the world's largest collection of pornographic material, right there in little ol' Bloomington in the Hoosier state of Indiana.

Unless you have a provable professional interest in sex—a healthy amateur interest won't suffice—the Institute collection isn't open to view. But there are a few other places at the University well worth visiting, even if somewhat less stimulating. One is the Lilly Library, named for the Lilly pharmeceutical family of Indianapolis. Among the library's more than four hundred thousand books and four million manuscripts are the only Gutenberg Bible to be seen between America's coasts and a Coverdale Bible (1535), the first Bible printed in English. Also at the library are a desk from Lincoln's Springfield, Illinois, law office; a portrait gallery of famous writers painted by such artists as Sir Thomas Lawrence and Joshua Reynolds; and a collection of more than eight hundred film scripts, including those for such classics as *Citizen Kane, Jaws, The Godfather* and *Gone With the Wind*. Across from Lilly Library stands the ultra-modern University Art Museum, designed by well-known architect I. M. Pei. Dedicated in October 1982, the museum contains works by Durer, Ribera, Goya, Manet, Monet and Picasso as well as art from Asia, Africa, the Middle East and a pre-Columbian Latin American collection. A one-hundred-and-ten-foot-high atrium topped by a skylight highlights the interior of the striking reinforced concrete building. More art can be seen in the nearby Indiana University Auditorium, where a series of murals by Missouri artist Thomas Hart Benton (Chapter V, section 8) depict Indiana's history. If you remain overnight in Bloomington, an attractive place to stay is the two-hundred-room University Memorial Union. This puts you right in the heart of the campus, where you can best experience the flavor of the University.

From Bloomington it's only seventeen miles on highway 41 to Nashville, the center of scenic, colorful Brown County, whose hamlets bear such names as Beanblossom and Gnaw Bone. Wooded hills, a scattering of log cabins, barns decorated with old-fashioned painted "Chew Mail Pouch Tobacco" ads set the mood for this rustic area. Back in the summer of 1940 Hoosier native Ernie Pyle, the famous writer and journalist, spent two weeks visiting Brown County. "I have fallen head over heels for the place, and the people, and the hills, and the whole general air of peacefulness," he proclaimed, succumbing to the spell Brown County has exerted on any number of visitors.

At Belmont, about halfway between Bloomington and Nashville, it's worth leaving highway 41 for a one-and-a-half-mile detour south to the Theodore Steele State Memorial. Steele, who moved to a remote corner of Brown County in 1907, became famous for his paintings of the beguiling landscapes in the area. At a secluded two-hundred-and-eleven-acre site Steele and his wife Selma built an eleven-room residence, two studios and a guest house. In her memoir *The House of the Singing Wings: Life and Work of T. C. Steele,* Selma Steele recalled her first visit, in April 1907, to the area where they settled. "I was overwhelmed by the beauty of the countryside. I had no idea the Indiana landscape could be so fine," she wrote. After reaching Belmont—still little bigger than the "general store, blacksmith shop, and a few houses" Mrs. Steele found—they proceeded down "the worst road imaginable" and finally "reached the brow of the hill and faced the panorama of hills and skies," a perfect place for Steele to use "for the continuance of his work. There was everything to meet his requirements. There was an incomparable quality of beauty to the hills."

At the Steele State Memorial, listed on the National Register, you'll see that "incomparable" scenery as well as the house and other buildings the Steeles built. The two studios house the painter's personal effects and some hundred of his canvases. Their titles typify his subject matter: "Village in the Valley," "The Ravine in Autumn," "House Nestled in the Trees." Inscribed over the fireplace of the main house appears the artist's credo: "Every morning I take off my hat to the beauty of the world."

From the Steele Memorial you can proceed slowly on to Nashville, whose seven hundred or so inhabitants make it the metropolis of Brown County. "Slowly" because you'll want to savor the delicious sights and scenes of Brown County. If you're there in the spring, redbuds and dogwoods will color the countryside, while in the fall maples will blaze with their autumn foliage. Log cabins tucked into the hillsides add rustic, old-fashioned touches. It wasn't so long ago that the area, still isolated and remote from the greater world beyond, offered scenes such as described by Meredith Nicholson in *The Hoosiers,* published in 1915: "In the hills of Brown County the traveler passes here and there a rude wagon drawn by oxen. A dusty native walks beside the team, and seated on the floor of the wagon is an old grandmother, smoking a clay pipe with great contentment." Truth to tell, that sense of rural innocence and contentment no longer pervades Brown County. But the area still represents "to visitors a world that was lost and a chance to idealize a rural past of genial community and individual contentment," as James H. Madison put it in *The Indiana Way, A State History* (1986). So you'll find in Brown County these days a sort of relic of a place, an echo of the past where you can get the feel for how things used to be but, for the most part, are no more.

Nashville, perhaps inevitably, is a bit commercial now but the profusion of art galleries, antique stores, craft shops and other such establishments don't detract from the town's intrinsic charm. Old wooden houses and stately trees line the streets and a certain slow-paced way of life keeps things low key. On Van Buren, the main street (although there's also a Main Street), stands the Brown County Playhouse which offers stage shows and, nearby, the atmospheric old Nashville House, a restaurant built on the site of a Civil War-era hotel. Even if you don't eat there, it's well worth looking around inside, where you'll find an old country store with turn-of-the-century utensils and posters on display and items such as sorghum, apple butter, sassafras tea and "galluses" (firemen's red suspenders) on offer.

Somewhat less in keeping with the town's rustic tone is the John Dillinger Historical Museum. Displays there include the famous bank robber's death mask, a toy wooden gun he used to escape from jail and the trousers he wore when F.B.I. agents killed him outside the Biograph Theater in Chicago on July 22, 1934. More typical of Brown County's old-time air is the historic Hook Drug Store on highway 46 a mile or so from town. After being moved in 1975 from Indianapolis, where it had been established in 1900, the store was reassembled in Nashville complete with its early advertising signs, an old-fashioned soda fountain and antique apothecary containers holding such old-time nostrums as Carter's pills "for blood and nerves."

Back in the village you might want to idle away part of the day at the courthouse, where the "Liar's Bench" still occasionally attracts a tall-tale-teller or two. There you may hear stories such as those told by Charles Porter (of Odon, Indiana; he's the only Hoosier to win the World Champion Liar title in the annual competition held in Wisconsin), who recounts how one summer was so dry the trees would follow dogs around, and that another summer was so hot you could toss a frozen hamburger patty in the air and when it descended the meat was cooked—and well done, at that!

Perhaps the best known spinner of Brown County tales and witticisms was a local character named Abe Martin, created by Hoosier Kin Hubbard who for years published in the Indianapolis *News* sketches and sayings of the scarecrow-like, cracker barrel country sage. Abe and his Brown County cohorts—such as Miss Tawney Apple, ticket seller at the local picture show, mule-breeder Tipton Bud, millinary trimmer Miss Germ Williams and Tilford Moots, a hoop-pole magnate—became famous for observations such as:

> Nothin' upsets a woman like sombuddy gitti' married
> she didn't even know had a beau

> A restaurant waiter allus lays your check on the table
> upside down so you won't choke t' death

> Th' husband that has t' git his breakfast downtown is
> liable t' be late fer supper

> Nothin'll dispel enthusiasm like a small admission fee

> A grocer often goes t' th' th-ater just t' see if th'
> folks that owe him are still in town

Stew Nugent has decided to go t' work till he kin find
somethin' better

Some fellers get credit fer bein' conservative when
ther only stupid

One character once locked his whiskers up in the cash register drawer. Another, acquitted of murdering his wife, allowed after the trial, "I never would have shot her if I'd knowed I'd have t' go thru so much red tape." Another fellow, asked why he hadn't spoken to his wife in three years, replied, "I didn't want t' interrupt her." James Whitcomb Riley, Indiana's best loved poet, once wrote of the sage of Brown County: "ABE MARTIN!—Dad-burn his old picture!/P'tends he's a Brown County fixture—/A kind of comical mixture/Of hoss-sense and no sense at all!"

As a tribute to the local boy who made good, the lodge at Brown County State Park, a few miles east of Nashville, is named for Abe Martin. One road that leads into the park (at 15,543 acres, Indiana's largest) crosses the state's oldest covered bridge. Brown County Park, a beautiful wooded area with hiking and riding trails, lakes and wildlife, is the area's most delightful place to stay. Both the Abe Martin Lodge and clusters of cabins—named after Martin's fellow characters—offer rustic, pleasant accommodations.

From the back country's precincts of Brown County to the ultra-modern architecture of Columbus, Indiana, is only a few miles in distance but light years away in atmosphere. In sharp contrast to the old-time rural mood of Brown County, Columbus presents an urban setting for nearly fifty modern buildings designed by the most famous names in contemporary architecture. Columbus once discovered America and now America, so it seems, is discovering Columbus: the renowned architecture of the city attracts more visitors—

some fifty thousand a year—than the number of inhabitants, thirty-two thousand.

This unusual collection of distinguished modern structures began in 1942 when famous Finnish architect Eliel Saarinen designed the First Christian Church, a glassy, boxy building with a detached tall, elegant clock tower. Later, J. Irwin Miller, then head of Cummins Engine Company, headquartered in Columbus, decided that attractive, stylish buildings would improve the city's quality of life, so in 1957 the company foundation offered to pay architect's fees for innovative designs. Since then, strikingly modern structures have risen to embellish the otherwise rather nondescript Indiana town.

At the Visitor's Center, installed in a restored nineteenth-century house downtown, you can get maps for walking and driving itineraries as well as information about guided tours by bus. The downtown walking itinerary takes you to eighteen buildings, among them the library, designed by I. M. Pei; the first privately designed post office in the U.S., by Kevin Roche; and Saarinen's First Christian Church, near which stands a 1971 Henry Moore sculpture. Perhaps downtown's most striking structure is Skidmore, Owings and Merrill's creation for *The Republic*. The newspaper is housed in a long, low, boxy building with huge plate glass windows through which the offices and a row of bright yellow presses are all open to view. The various shapes, lines and colors form what seems to be a giant abstract painting.

The well-marked driving tour—signs guide you all along the route—takes you to some thirty modern schools, churches and office buildings around Columbus. The most famous is Eero Saarinen's (the son of Eliel) 1964 North Christian Church, a low-slung hexagon topped by a soaring one-hundred-ninety-two-foot, needle-thin spire: eight feet higher and the spire would have to carry a red light to warn low-flying aircraft. Other sites include such usually prosaic places

as a fire station, a bank, suburban office buildings, a retirement center and a golf club house, all in the sleek modern
style which has made the architecture of Columbus, Indiana,
famous. Once you've had your fill of the new style in architecture, then you might want to head south forty-five miles
to an Ohio River town where you'll find a completely different sort of place—old Madison, virtually unchanged from
a century ago, with dozens of delightful nineteenth-century
structures.

6. The Ohio River Country:

Madison
Vevey and Indiana's Switzerland
The Howard Steamboat Museum and
The "Louisville Slugger" Bat
Factory in Jeffersonville

Madison is a gem of a town, its setting a small enclave
between the Ohio River and steep wooded bluffs that rise not
far from the water. Irving Leibowitz, in *My Indiana,* calls
Madison "the loveliest town in Indiana"—no exaggeration,
for the settlement is one of the most attractive and best
preserved in the entire Midwest. Dozens of nineteenth-century buildings at Madison remain untouched by time. In
1978 virtually the entire town, one hundred and thirty-three
blocks comprising the heart of the century-and-a-half-old
Ohio River settlement, was listed on the National Register of
Historic Places. Madison so well represents small town, old-
time America that in World War II the Office of War Information chose the picturesque place as a "typical American
town," filming there a movie, issued in thirty-two languages

and distributed the world over to inspire overseas GIs and to show citizens of other lands the sort of life the Americans were fighting to preserve. (Later, in the late fifties, *Some Came Running,* with Frank Sinatra, was filmed in the photogenic old town.)

Founded in 1809, Madison had by 1850 become the largest town in the state, with five thousand inhabitants (these days thirteen thousand people live there). Steamboat traffic brought prosperity to the river town. The first steamboat appeared on the Ohio in 1811; in 1816 the *Indiana Republican* at Madison remarked on the steamboat *Harriet* which passed by the town "at the rate of twelve miles an hour." As early as 1826 the *Indiana Gazetteer,* a fact book on the state, noted that "There are more brick houses, and the dwelling houses in Madison are better in quality, in proportion to their number, than in any other town in the state."

Madison soon became a center of culture. On April 11, 1851, circus and theater impresario P.T. Barnum produced an appearance there by singer Jenny Lind, the "Swedish Nightingale." Caroline C. Barnum, P.T.'s daughter, commented in her diary about Madison: "It is the most beautifully situated town I have seen in a long while. It is almost surrounded by hills, all of them covered with the richest verdure and foliage. The town is small and nestled in among these hills, it presents a most pleasing appearance."

The star performed to a packed house in a packing house: "Miss Lind sang in a pork house at this place, it being the largest room in the town, [and] we have had great fun about it . . . I asked Belletti [Giovanni Belletti, a baritone who accompanied Miss Lind on tour] how he liked to sing in a Pork House, [and] he said, 'I do not like to sing for so much pigs.'" Perhaps his response was prompted by the collection problems Barnum encountered. As Caroline recounted: "The concert had been sold for $5,000 but when Father demanded the money the man refused to pay him, but Father succeeded in getting 3,000 of it being swindled out of the remainder, it was a shameful proceeding altogether."

For your visit to Madison, it's best to stop first at the Chamber of Commerce where you can pick up a pair of pamphlets with detailed walking tours. The "East" tour takes you to the Old Jail; the historic "Fair Play" Fire House Company Number 1 building; the English Gothic-style Christ Episcopal Church (1848); the 1835 Auditorium, a Greek Revival-style structure believed to be the town's oldest public building; the cozy-looking two-story brick Hutchings Memorial, restored as a nineteenth-century doctor's office; and the 1830s-vintage buildings on Mulberry Street, the center of old Madison, where you'll see rows of shop fronts virtually unchanged since they were built a century and a half ago.

On the "West" tour you'll visit many of Madison's most important old houses. Among them are Sullivan House, an 1818 Federal-style building considered the town's first mansion; Schofield House, Madison's first two-story brick residence (1817); and the Regency-style Shrewsbury, with a well-known free-standing three-story spiral staircase. The walk also takes you to Madison's most imposing building, the 1844 James Lanier mansion, a classic-style residence overlooking the Ohio River. Lanier—a lawyer, politician and banker—lived in the house only a few years before moving to New York where he became a prosperous railroad financier. Period furnishings fill the stately house, giving one a feel for the antebellum days when Lanier hosted elegant social gatherings there. A pleasant place to stay in Madison is the Victorian Inn, a cozy chalet-type house nestled below one of the bluffs at the edge of town.

Along the Ohio River east of Madison, highway 56 winds through unspoiled, little-visited country. The road takes you to Vevey, seat of Switzerland County. In 1802 a group of immigrants from Vevey, Switzerland, settled in the area where they began the cultivation of grapes. Before long, their wine became a favorite of visitors to the area. In a journal entry for September 3, 1811, Mrs. Lydia Bacon, wife of Lieutenant Josiah Bacon, sent out from Boston to Vincennes in his capacity as a U.S. Infantry quartermaster, tells of the Swiss families who settled there along the Ohio and "planted Vineyards, the produce of which, enables them to realize what they had fondly anticipated in an exchange of Countries. Their Wine made from the Maderia & Clarret Grapes is excellent. We purchased some. This place is called Veva, it is in New Swiss." (Mrs. Bacon had a whimsical sense of humor. On October 18, a few days after leaving Vincennes, she noted: "We live very well as to quality of our victuals & have enough, plenty of elegant Bacon (nothing better).") Although tobacco is now the main local crop, Vevey's Swiss heritage is recalled every year the first week in August when the town provides a Swiss Alpine Festival.

Vevey these days is a sleepy town of two thousand where a certain sense of isolation prevails, but for that very reason it's worth visiting for you can find there a leisurely way of life common a century and more ago. The town's most noteworthy attraction is the two-story brick boyhood home of Edward Eggleston. Born there in 1837, Eggleston became famous as author of *The Hoosier Schoolmaster* (1871), which some consider the first classic American novel to come out of the Midwest. The book was based on the experiences of Eggleston and his younger brother, George, in the rather primitive local schools. Edward's work is somewhat overdrawn but in 1903 George published a more balanced reminiscence of those early Indiana school days, recalling in *The First of the Hoosiers* the erudite master who "knew the whole arithmetic" at the local log cabin "loud school," so called because the pupils were required to study out loud so the master could be sure they were really working. "On his way to school every morning," Eggleston recalled, "the master cut and trimmed eight or ten stout beechen 'switches' . . . for instant use when needed." Other schoolmasters tended "to reduce the use of the rod somewhat, by the substitution of such devices as the fools' caps, dunces' stools and the like."

Downtown Vevey, with more than three hundred mid-nineteenth-century structures, is a virtually intact historic area with examples of Victorian, Greek Revival, Gothic and other styles, including vernacular folk architecture. The Switzerland County Historical Museum, housed in the old Presbyterian church, contains Eggleston memorabilia and other displays relating to the area's past.

If you continue east along the river you'll follow the Ohio River as it curves and heads north to Rising Sun, named for the sunrise over the Kentucky hills above the town of Rabbit Hash across the river. You'll find there a delightful old (1845) courthouse which, with its quartet of tall white columns, recalls a southern plantation mansion. An open stairway leads to the second-floor courtroom. Farther north, also on the Ohio, is the town of Aurora where stately old homes high on the hillside overlook the river. The most imposing of the mansions is Hillforest, the restored mid-nineteenth-century residence—listed on the National Register—of steamboat fleet owner Thomas Gaff. With its rounded central colonnade and pilot-house-like cupola, the mansion, in fact, looks like a steamboat.

For even more steamboat lore the highway west and then south of Madison will lead you forty-four miles to Jefferson-ville, just across from Louisville, where the Howard Steam-boat Museum contains a large collection of navigational equipment, paddle wheels and riverboat replicas. The museum occupies the huge red brick Victorian-era Howard mansion, furnished with the family's original possessions. The family operated the Howard Shipyards at Front Street between Fulton and Watts, virtually without interruption from 1834 until 1931. Here many of the early Mississippi River packets and some of the first steamers used on the

Yukon River in Alaska were built. A latter-day firm, the Jeffboat Company, continues the shipbuilding tradition at Jeffersonville, which boasts the nation's largest inland shipyard. Located across from the Steamboat Museum, the company, founded in 1938, has built more than six thousand vessels.

It's only a short drive from the steamboat era and area in Jeffersonville to another part of town with one of Indiana's most typical attractions of Americana, the "Louisville Slugger" baseball bat factory at Hillerich and Bradsby Company's Slugger Park plant. The very name "Louisville Slugger" brings back to most red-blooded Americans memories of long hot summers and thwacks of ball against bat. Tours at Slugger Park take you through the factory where the famous bats are produced.

Tours start in a museum room where one item on display is a century-old bat used by one Pete "the Old Gladiator" Browning. It seems that one summer day back in 1884 the "Old Gladiator" was at the plate for the Louisville Eclipse baseball team. Browning waited patiently for the pitch. Then came the delivery. Taking a hefty swing, Browning cracked his bat beyond repair. In the stands that day sat a seventeen-year-old fan named J. A. "Bud" Hillerich, son of a local woodworker who made such products as wooden bowling balls and butter churns. After the game, Hillerich took "Old Gladiator" Browning to the woodworking shop where they carved out a custom-made baseball bat. Thus was born the world's first "Louisville Slugger," which Browning used the next day to crack out three hits.

The fabled wood piece should now be renamed the "Indiana Slugger," for in 1974 the bat production line moved from Louisville, just across the Ohio River, to Jeffersonville. The display room contains exhibits pertaining to the lore, legends and history of the renowned sports implement. You'll find there bats used by such stars as Hank Aaron, Ty

Cobb, Lou Gehrig, Babe Ruth and Stan Musial. The handle of Musial's bat—at ³⁄₃₂ of an inch—is the thinnest on record, while "the Babe's" bat bears tiny notches he carved after each of the twenty-one home runs the "Sultan of Swat" hit with it. On one wall hangs the front page of the New York *Journal American* for August 19, 1948, which reports news of Ruth's funeral.

From the exhibit room, visitors proceed to the factory to see how forty-inch boards of northern white ash, from trees at least seventy-five years old, are turned into "Louisville Sluggers." Cut from the two hundred thousand trees a year chopped down in Pennsylvania and New York forests for the bats, the boards season for six to eight months. The wood is then sorted for quality, with 10 percent set aside for professional bats (each major leaguer uses about six dozen a year) and the balance used to make bats destined for the consumer market. The boards are shaped, sanded, stamped with the famous oval Hillerich and Bradsby trademark, then dipped in lacquer to preserve the wood. Slugger Park produces some one million bats a year. Those for the pros are hand turned, a process that takes fifteen minutes. Sluggers for retail sale are shaped on semiautomatic lathes that churn out a piece every eight seconds.

As for "Old Gladiator" Browning, the player who started the whole thing, he lies buried in a Louisville cemetery. A few years ago Hillerich and Bradsby Company paid part of the cost of a new gravestone for Browning. The marker is embellished with a crossed pair of bats, carved stone replicas of the "Louisville Slugger" the "Old Gladiator" helped to invent more than a century ago.

7. Overland Waterway, Cross-Country Railroad, Underground Railway:

The Old Whitewater Canal at Metamora
Oldenburg, "the Village of Spires"
The Whitewater Valley Steam Train
The Levi P. Coffin House
The Rose City of Richmond
Wilbur Wright State Memorial

America has always been a land on the move. As a crossroads state—"The Crossroads State," so its motto has it—Indiana has seen more than its fair share of transportation history. Across the center of the state ran the National Road, the nation's first major highway constructed with federal funds and the main artery connecting the Atlantic coast with the Midwest in the early nineteenth century. Steamboats plied the Ohio (the first appeared in 1811) and the Wabash, eventually (in 1821) managing to churn their way as far north as Terre Haute. Along the Buffalo Trace, which ran from Louisville to Vincennes, Indiana's first stagecoach line began operations in the spring of 1820. Indiana was even the scene of the world's first train robbery when the Reno Gang of Jackson County leaped onto an Ohio & Mississippi train at Seymour, south of Columbus, the night of October 6, 1866, and made off with $15,000 from the Adams Express Agency man.

The east central part of the state abounds in examples of Indiana's early efforts at improving transportation links. One especially unusual place is the old Whitewater Canal at Metamora. Now an Indiana State Historic Site, the seventy-six-mile-long canal was completed in 1847. Intended to connect the Ohio River with the National Road in central Indiana, the canal soon became obsolete with the advent of the railroad. But at Metamora you can see, still preserved as it was, part of the original canal as well as an 1845 grist mill and the unique Aqueduct, believed to be the only such structure in the U.S., which carries the canal waters over Duck Creek just above its mouth on the Whitewater River. The original covered bridge-type structure was built in 1843, then replaced five years later when flood waters washed it away. You can experience how it felt in the old days to float down the canal by taking the forty-four-foot horse-drawn *Ben Franklin,* bright white with red trim, on a half-hour cruise across the Duck Creek Aqueduct then east to Gordon's Lock Number 24 at Millville and back again to Metamora. A good hundred shops, galleries, cafes and other commercial establishments line the canal-side streets of Metamora. One unusual touch: a bright yellow flag hangs from each building where a shop is open for business.

While in the area you might want to stop at the village of Oldenburg, an Old World-type religious settlement ten miles south of Metamora. This German Catholic community is called the "village of spires" for the many steeples which rise from the 1862 Church of the Holy Family and other religious buildings, including a convent and a Franciscan monastery. Nestled in the hills, with tree-lined sidewalks and German street signs, Oldenburg recalls a Bavarian village tucked away in a remote Alpine valley.

At Connersville, north of Metamora, another relic of old-time Indiana transportation history recalls bygone days—the Whitewater Valley Railroad. Early twentieth-century Baldwin steam locomotives pull an excursion train that travels the sixteen miles and forty-three curves between Connersville and Metamora and then returns. During the trip you'll see along the way some of the original canal locks. The Whitewater Valley Railroad—the "Canal Route," as it's called—was incorporated in 1865 and the roadbed built on the towpath of the old canal. In December 1972 local residents revived the railroad and in 1984 finally acquired the track from a successor of the defunct Penn Central corporation.

At Fountain City, northeast of Connersville, you'll find another sort of railway—the "Underground Railroad" of Civil War days. In the town stands the painted red brick tin-roofed Levi Coffin House, home of the Midwest organizer of the secret system of escape routes that slaves used to flee their masters in the south. Although a southerner by birth (he was born in North Carolina), Coffin became an abolitionist and after moving to Indiana helped set up fugitive slave routes from Cincinnati, the Indiana towns of Madison and Jeffersonville, and other Ohio River settlements. Many of the escape "tracks" converged on Coffin's house, the "grand central station" of the Underground Railroad. An estimated two thousand slaves passed through the house, now a museum listed on the National Register, on their way to freedom. Among them, so legend has it, was the prototype for Eliza Harris, the heroine of *Uncle Tom's Cabin* by Harriet Beecher Stowe, whom Coffin knew in Cincinnati. Coffin supposedly cared for the real-life Eliza after she crossed the Ohio on the ice, her child in her arms and bloodhounds from her outraged master baying at her heels. In his memoirs Coffin recalled the famous Underground Railroad he helped run: "The roads were always in running order, the connections were good, the conductors active and zealous, and there was no lack of passengers. Seldom a week passed without our receiving passengers by this mysterious road." Once the slaves reached Wayne County they were safe, thanks to the area's many abolitionist-minded Quakers, a group Hoosier-born writer Jessamyn West told about in her novel *The Friendly Persuasion*.

A number of Quakers live in Richmond, the county's principal city, which straddles the old National Road—now highway 40 but still designated "National Road" in Richmond—that cuts across the center of the state. Some forty acres of hothouses for the cultivation of roses have given Richmond the name "the city of roses." A mayor with the appropriately botanical name of Lester E. Meadows used to embellish his stationary with the slogan "Richmond the beautiful." The town's main attraction is Earlham College, where the world's only Quaker seminary, established in 1960, turns out some twenty graduates a year. The college's Moore Museum, dating from 1853, was Indiana's first natural history museum. At another Richmond museum, Wayne County Historical Museum, is installed an old-time nineteenth-century general store. Perhaps the most delightful activity in town, and certainly the most fragrant, is to tour the Hill Floral Products greenhouses, forty acres crammed with roses, chrysanthemums and other flowers. The third week in June Richmond celebrates its annual rose festival.

At Millville, about twenty miles west of Richmond, stands another monument to the history of transportation. A two-story white frame house (reconstructed in 1972 on the foundation of the original residence which burned in 1884) is where early aviation pioneer Wilbur Wright was born in 1867. Victorian country-style items typical of the 1860s when Wilbur lived there furnish the farmhouse. His brother Orville was born after the family moved elsewhere. It's curious that the three other Wright children all graduated from college, while Wilbur and Orville, the great inventors, never even finished high school. Parked at the Wright House, an Indiana State Memorial, is an F-84 jet placed there to symbolize the modern-day advances in air transportation, an era which began back on December 17, 1903, with the simple flying machine the Wright brothers flew at Kitty Hawk, North Carolina. Stage coaches, steamboats, horse-drawn canal boats, steam-driven locomotives—those relics of the old days in early Indiana—now belonged to history. With the Wright invention a new era of transportation had dawned, and the nineteenth-century way of life was gone forever.

8. Verses and Villages of the Nineteenth Century:

The James Whitcomb Riley House at Greenfield
Conner Prairie Pioneer Settlement at Noblesville
The Nineteenth-Century Village of Zionsville

At the center of the state are a few attractions near Indianapolis, the capital and metropolis of Indiana, that stand apart from the big city and still retain their small town ambiance.

At Greenfield, ten miles east of Marion County, which encompasses greater Indianapolis, stands the birthplace of James Whitcomb Riley, the poet who best captured the flavor of nineteenth-century Indiana. As William E. Wilson, in *Indiana, A History*, wrote of Riley's poetry: "It carried the scent of Indiana's woods and fields, echoed the voices of its country people, stirred memories of years never to be relived, painted rich and mellow Hoosier scenery, and captured the tempo of easy, comfortable Hoosier manners." The ten-room frame house is crammed with period furniture and with Riley memorabilia. Riley was born in 1849 in a log cabin that now forms the kitchen of the present house, built around the cabin the following year. Visiting the homestead, it's not hard to imagine the settings and sources of Riley's poems. Nearby runs the old National Road (now highway 40), the early nineteenth-century highway which Riley called a thoroughfare that "blossoms with romance," so colorful and varied were the early travelers on it. At the house is the porch which Little Orphan Annie shooed chickens away from, she of the famous warning—

> An' the Gobble-uns 'at gits you
> Ef you

Don't
Watch
Out!

(Annie Gray, a Riley family employee who inspired "Little Orphan Annie," lived in a white cottage at Philadelphia, a few miles west of Greenfield.) In the eastern part of town lies the "Old Swimmin' Hole," which gave its name to the title poem of Riley's first book (1883). Writing of swimming holes, of back roads on which sunshine spreads "as thick as butter on country bread," of *Home Folks* (the title of his 1900 book), Riley is indeed the poet laureate of the heartland—of the vanished Middle West of bygone days. "O the days gone by! O the days gone by!" he writes, "When life was like a story holding neither sob nor sigh,/In the golden olden glory of the days gone by."

Those olden and—who knows?—perhaps golden days have been frozen in time at two nineteenth-century villages north of Indianapolis that recall daily life of yesteryear in Indiana. Just south of Noblesville is the Conner Prairie Pioneer Settlement, a recreated 1836 village run by Earlham College, the Quaker school in Richmond, Indiana. In 1818 William Conner, Indian trader and Hamilton County's first settler, established a trading post in a log cabin. Conner knew how to trade with the redskins: Indians had captured him when a boy and raised him as a member of the tribe, and Conner later married an Indian. In January 1820 a commission appointed by Governor Jennings, meeting at Conner's trading post, selected what became Indianapolis for the site of the new state capital. On the terrain where the log cabin once stood rises the two-story federal-style brick house (now open for tours) that Conner built in 1823. Listed on the National Register, the house recalls the pioneer days when William Conner was carving a new settlement out of the previously unbroken prairie land.

In a reminiscence entitled *Sweet Memories of "Old Indianie" in 1870* Sarah Brown DeBra wrote of her rural life and the endless cycle of seasons on an Indiana farm a century and more ago, a life much as those at Conner Prairie might have experienced. "How days fly into weeks—weeks into months and months into years!" She tells of idyllic roamings in the countryside, one day coming upon "a bunch of beautiful silver birch trees, with bark that was silvery white. They were very pretty with a delicate foliage. And then we came to the field of buck-wheat, in full bloom. The bees, and bees, and bees were all over it getting the sweet honey. And next to the buck-wheat was the field of clover, to make hay for the cows and horses." And then came autumn: "The spring and summer months now seemed like a pleasant dream." Now, at harvest time—"gathering in" season—appeared wild geese and ducks on the lake. Finally, winter: "And now winter has come and snow is every where."

At the Conner Prairie Pioneer Settlement some of the sights, sounds and smells of "old Indianie" will greet you. Village "residents" dressed in period costumes add authenticity to the setting. You'll meet the carpenter, blacksmith, doctor, schoolmarm and other locals. At the Pioneer Adventure Center you can participate "hands on" in activities common in the old days—weaving, splitting and carving wood, making candles or lye soap, basketry, dulcimer playing. Many of the pioneer-style crafts made by Conner Prairie artisans are on sale in the Settlement's museum shop.

Unlike the Conner Prairie Settlement, the village of Zionsville, southwest of Noblesville, isn't a re-created town but an authentic well-preserved carryover of a nineteenth-century settlement. The tree-lined cobblestone streets of Zionsville, named for surveyor William Zion in 1852, bear such woodsy names as Oak, Cedar, Maple, Poplar, Elm, Pine and Walnut—a veritable forest of thoroughfares. The town's Lincoln Park recalls the day, February 11, 1861, when the president-elect spoke at Zionsville from the rear platform of the train taking him to Washington for his inauguration. "I would like to spend more time here," Lincoln allowed, "but there is an event to take place in Washington which cannot start until I get there."

It's pleasant to wander the shady streets of old Zionsville, looking in every now and then at a crafts shop or antique store or stopping at the Green Apple or the Friendly Tavern for a snack. One unusual place in town is the Patrick Henry Sullivan Museum, established in memory of Boone County's first permanent settler. Specializing in genealogy, the museum has marriage records from 1830 and birth and death documents dating back to 1882.

Zionsville is a good example of those villages found all over Indiana which still today are so typical of the state and of the entire Midwest as well. In *The Indiana Way, A State History,* published in 1986, James H. Madison writes: "Small towns dotted the landscape and shaped much of the state's character. Neither urban or rural, they provided a small agricultural hinterland with essential economic, social, and political services: a few retail stores and a grain elevator, a high school and two or three churches, lawyers, doctors, fraternal lodges and women's clubs, and perhaps the county courthouse and weekly newspaper. They were the proverbial neighborly places where nearly everyone was known by name to nearly everyone else, where all important communication was face to face, where life could be secure and comfortable."

Such is the way of life typified by both Conner Prairie Settlement, a throwback to those "golden olden" days James Whitcomb Riley so nostalgically wrote about, and Zionsville, an old-fashioned but contemporary village similar to dozens of small towns, obscure and timeless, that still exist in Indiana and throughout the great American heartland.

9. North of the Old National Road:

Huntington
Wabash
Peru and Kokomo
South Bend
Elkhart
Amish Acres at Nappanee
The Camelot Town of North Webster
Tippecanoe Battlefield
Crawfordsville

Scattered across the state's northern landscape is a sprinkling of attractions that recall old Indiana of a century and more ago. Huntington, twenty-five miles southwest of Fort Wayne, boasts an attractive district of century-old homes and the unusual Jefferson Street Bridge, a block of shops and businesses spanning the Little Wabash River. Reminiscent of the famous stall-lined Ponte Vecchio in Florence, Italy, the bridge is said to be the only such structure in the U.S.

Twenty-one miles to the west at Wabash, a pleasant tree-shaded town tucked into the side of a hill overlooking the Wabash River, you'll see displayed at the courthouse one of the original "Brush lamps" used to light the building's dome, starting on March 31, 1880. That antique carbon lamp commemorates Wabash's claim that it was the world's first town to be wholly illuminated by electric light.

At Peru, another fourteen miles west, it's fun to visit the Circus City Museum with its exhibits of miniature circuses, costumes, a flying trapeze, items from the Wallace Circus and photos of circus days of long ago. Back in 1883 Ben Wallace started Peru on the road to becoming a circus center when he bought a defunct traveling show that included a bandwagon and a few animals, including an elephant named Diamond, which the new owner trained in a railroad roundhouse. The show opened in Peru and later became the well-known Hagenbeck-Wallace Circus, which toured the country. Later, the American Circus Corporation was established in Peru to provide winter quarters for many of America's leading circuses. The third week of July every year Peru holds its annual Circus Festival.

Another famous show business phenomenon originated in Peru. Composer Cole Porter was born there in 1892 in a large frame house, now a duplex apartment, at the northeast corner of Huntington and East 3d Streets. Porter grew up in a three-story, white-columned red brick Georgian-style mansion out on the old Slocum Indian Trail. Porter, that most sophisticated of song writers, shows in his work no evidence of his Hoosier origins: Indiana innocence was somehow bred out of him, even though he studied under a French composer with a name reminiscent of his home state—Vincent D'Indy. But in the end Indiana reclaimed him, for Porter now lies buried in Peru's Mt. Hope Cemetery, back in the Middle West of his origins.

Twenty-one miles south of Peru lies Kokomo, that melodiously named town called such after the even more euphonically named Indian chief Kokomoko. The Elwood Haynes Museum at Kokomo commemorates the inventor of the nation's first successful commercial automobile. Installed in Haynes's residence, the museum contains exhibits, including 1905 and 1924 models of Haynes cars, recalling the career of the auto pioneer, who also invented stainless steel and stellite (a metal used in space craft). In his book *The Complete Motorist,* published in Kokomo in 1914, Haynes recalled how he realized, while traveling by horse through the countryside one day in 1890, that transportation would be more certain "if I didn't have to depend on the horse for locomotion. From then on my mind dwelt a great deal upon the subject of a self-propelled vehicle." After experimenting at Apperson Brothers machine shop with various energy sources—steam, battery and finally gasoline—on July 4, 1894, Haynes was ready to test drive his contraption out on Pumpkin Vine Pike. "It moved off at once at a speed of about seven miles per hour, and was driven about one and a half miles farther into the country. It was then turned about, and ran all the way into the city without making a single stop." A memorial at U.S. 31 Bypass and Pumpkin Vine Pike marks the great event.

Indiana played an important role in the development of the auto industry. At Auburn, in the northeast corner of the state, an Auburn-Cord-Duesenberg Museum contains more than one hundred and forty of those and other makes of old cars displayed in the Art Deco-style original showroom of the Auburn Automobile Company. At South Bend, in the far northern part of the state, two museums recall the early days of Indiana's car industry. The Discovery Hall Museum houses a large collection of old Studebakers, as well as exhibits on South Bend's industrial history, while at the Studebaker National Museum you can see more old autos, the Studebaker Company's archives, and such other vehicles as the carriage Lincoln rode to his fateful evening at Ford's Theatre in Washington. The Studebaker brothers, Clement and Henry, opened a blacksmith and wagon shop in South Bend in 1852. There they built wagons that carried pioneers to the West. The contract between the two boys was a model of simplicity. "I, Henry Studebaker, agree to sell all the wagons my brother Clem can make. [Signed] Henry Studebaker." The second and final clause read: "I agree to make all he can sell. [Signed] Clem Studebaker." Their vehicles were used at the Battle of Gettysburg and also by presidents in Washington. Wagon production continued as late as 1920 but in the meantime, starting in 1902, the Studebaker brothers began making autos, the firm eventually becoming the nation's fifth largest car company.

Founded in 1820 as a fur-trading post along the south-ernmost bend of the St. Joseph River, South Bend has pre-served some of its early history in six sections of town now designated historic districts. Two are listed on the National Register: the West Washington District, which includes some of the city's oldest buildings, one a 1906 Frank Lloyd Wright-designed residence; and the Chopin Park District, a neigh-borhood of old houses lining brick streets where old-time lamplights add a turn-of-the-century touch. South Bend's most famous institution is Notre Dame, founded in 1842. It's worth visiting on the university's campus the Snite Art Mu-seum, with works by Chagall, Picasso, Rodin and other leading artists, and the Church of the Sacred Heart (1871), with French stained-glass windows and North America's oldest carillon.

West of South Bend lies Indiana's heavy-industry region, centered in Gary, the largest city in the U.S. founded in the twentieth century (1906). Near Gary, along Lake Michigan, stretch the pristine sands of the Indiana Dunes National Lakeshore. Fourteen miles east of South Bend lies Elkhart, which clusters around the confluence of the St. Joseph and Elkhart Rivers. The town took its name from an island there whose shape an early Indian thought resembled an elk's heart. The town is the home of Alka-Seltzer and the Conn Com-pany, the first of the fifteen firms that now manufacture some 50 percent of the nation's band instruments. At the Miles Laboratories Visitors' Center you can see an archive and museum devoted to the history and lore of Alka-Seltzer, developed by Dr. Franklin Miles as a tonic for nervous females, while the 1847 Colonel C. G. Conn home recalls the founder of the Conn Band Instrument Company, whose traveling salesmen—truly drummers—supposedly suggested the character Harold Hill, hero of the musical *The Music Man*. (For Mason City, Iowa, home of Meredith Willson, the musi-cal's composer, see Chapter IV, section 7.) Also worth visiting in Elkhart is the Midwest Museum of American Art, installed in the former St. Joseph Valley Bank Building, a Greek Revival-style structure built in 1922. The collection includes a large number of Norman Rockwell lithographs as well as works by Iowa artist Grant Wood, Frederick Remington, Grandma Moses and other artists of Americana.

As you head back south toward the heart of Indiana, away from the northern areas near the Michigan border, you'll come to more of the rustic small town and country attractions the state offers. At Nappanee, sixteen miles south of Elkhart, the center of the mint and onion growing country, is Amish Acres, a restored Amish farm, with a bakery, a cheese and meat shop and an old-fashioned soda fountain. Decorated in early American style, the restaurant at Amish Acres features Amish homestyle food. As you drive along the area's country roads, or in Nappanee itself, you're likely to see Amish horse-drawn covered buggies.

A bit to the southeast lies the curious village of North Webster. If you're looking for an old-fashioned sort of place, *really* old-fashioned, North Webster is the place to go. Much of the town is modeled after King Arthur's Camelot in the "Old England" of medieval times. In the early 1970s local banker Homer Shoop decided the northern Indiana town of five hundred people needed some new attractions—or, rather, some very old ones—so he suggested that North Webster adopt a Camelot style. Shops took names like Ye Olde Tobacco Box, Ye Olde Double Dip & Dunk It, King's Keg liquor store, Camelot Beauty Salon, Read's Castle of Values (a motorcycle dealership); and Shoop changed the name of his Farmer's State Bank to the Counting House Bank. He also built a block-long grey castle-like structure—complete with watchtowers, arches and a crenellated roof—that houses the International Palace of Sports, a princely name for what is simply a wax museum filled with likenesses of famous athletes. In the "palace's" lobby stands a replica of

Excalibur, King Arthur's legendary sword, stuck in a block of stone. Many of the stores along Main Street were remodeled in "Camelot Modern" style, adding battlements, archways, portcullises, towers, turrets and signs in Gothic script. In North Webster time hasn't stood still; it's regressed. (A more genuine English Midwestern village is at Le Mars, Iowa; see Chapter IV, section 8.)

You'll find a more authentic holdover from the old days in Fulton County, just to the southwest of the Indiana Camelot. Scattered around the Fulton County landscape are nearly a dozen round barns, turn-of-the-century touches that lend the countryside an old-fashioned air. At Rochester, the county seat, you can pick up a map giving locations of these unusual old barns.

As you continue on toward the southwest, across the flat fertile farmland of central Indiana, you may want to stop off at one of the state's most historic sites, the Tippecanoe Battlefield, just north of Lafayette. Here, as recounted in section 3, on Vincennes, William Henry Harrison and his troops defeated Tecumseh's band of Indian warriors in November 1811, an engagement that tamed much of the redskin threat in the Indiana Territory. An eighty-five-foot-high pillar marks the site of Harrison's encampment, while at the museum, listed on the National Register, exhibits recall the historic battle from the points of view of both sides.

Twenty-seven miles south of Lafayette lies Crawfordsville, where you'll find the unusual Old Jail Museum. The 1882 jailhouse is a lazy sheriff's delight: a hand-operated crank turns the two-story cylindrical cell block, enabling him to check on the prisoners without ever taking a step. The Old Jail is believed to be the country's only operating rotary cell block. (A similar such jail is located at Council Bluffs, Iowa; see Chapter IV, section 8.) Because of the various writers who lived in Crawfordsville, the town is known as the "Athens of the Hoosier State." The most famous author was

Lew Wallace, best known for his 1880 novel *Ben-Hur*. Wallace settled in Crawfordsville in 1853 and died there in 1905 after an active career as an army officer, politician and diplomat. Still preserved in town is the Lew Wallace Study, the author's writing quarters where he penned *Ben-Hur*. Oil paintings, turn-of-the-century wooden furniture, shelves of books, photos, manuscripts, mementos of Wallace's careers and other memorabilia fill the cozy old room.

Maurice Thompson, author of the historical romance *Alice of Old Vincennes,* also lived in Crawfordsville, where he spent most of his life. Vincennes is where Indiana began two and a half centuries ago, while just west of Crawfordsville lies Parke County, with its covered bridges and maple sugar camps, where we began our tour of the Hoosier state. So now that we've traveled full circle in time and in place, we can end our excursions into the past and on the byways and back roads of Indiana, that typical Midwestern state so rich in the afterglow of what James Whitcomb Riley called "time's all-golden yesterdays."

III

Illinois

1. Illinois:

Land of Linking

Although Illinois is often called the "Land of Lincoln," as the state's license plates proclaim, it is just as much a land of linking. The state seems to tie together between its watery borders urban Chicago, and all that metropolis represents, and the more simple rural and small town areas typical of the Midwest, found down-, up-, and out-state. Chicago dwarfs the rest: its population tops three million. Rockford, Peoria and Springfield, the capital, the three next largest cities, each has less than a hundred and fifty thousand inhabitants; and no other town claims more than a hundred thousand. The world's busiest stretch of road, the Dan Ryan Expressway at 59th Street in Chicago (some quarter of a million vehicles a day rush past) contrasts with such remote down-state areas as Calhoun County, isolated between the Mississippi and Illinois Rivers just north of St. Louis, where you can drive the back roads for hours and scarcely find another moving car.

ILLINOIS

Galena

Rockford

Mount Carroll

St. Charles

Dixon

Chicago

River

Rock Island

Princeton

Mississippi

Galesburg

Peoria

Bloomington

Champaign Urbana

Quincy

Springfield

Alton

Vandalia

Albion

Mount Vernon

Kaskaskia

Shawneetown

River

Grand Tower

Ohio

Metropolis

Cairo

Chicago wasn't always so dominant. Back in 1818, when Illinois entered the Union, only the southern part of the state was settled. At Fort Dearborn (now Chicago) resided only a handful of soldiers—commanded by Captain John Whistler, grandfather of artist James McNeill Whistler—and a few civilians, while the down-state river cities, Kaskaskia, Illinois's first capital, on the Mississippi, and Shawneetown, on the Ohio, thrived. Kaskaskia boasted the state's first newspaper, the *Illinois Herald,* founded in 1814, and Shawneetown the second, the *Illinois Immigrant* (1818). Back in the 1830s a delegation of citizens traveled the three hundred miles from newly established Chicago to Shawneetown to borrow money for the tiny Lake Michigan settlement. Adjudging Chicago to be too distant from Shawneetown to succeed, the bankers refused the loan. Between 1850 and 1870, however, Chicago's population increased tenfold, from thirty thousand to nearly three hundred thousand, perhaps the fastest growing urban area in history. Kaskaskia now lies under water, a victim of the Mississippi's whims, while Shawneetown is now but a backwater, a relic with some four hundred inhabitants.

The contrast between the big city's fortune, and fortuncs, and those of the rest of Illinois seems to symbolize the difference between the two areas—Chicagoland, its face toward the lake and its back turned toward the state, and the rest. The town of Metropolis, with some seven thousand residents, definitely the metropolis of Massac County (on the Ohio down river from Shawneetown) is only a dot on the map compared to the metropolis of the north. Galesburg-born and bred Carl Sandburg's famous description of Chicago, "Hog Butcher for the World," appeared in his 1915 volume *Chicago Poems,* but in 1918 he also published a less renowned collection of verses on the rural part of Illinois, entitled *Cornhuskers.* It's that part of the state—the villages, the back roads, the historic old towns—you'll read about in this chapter, places where the hogs are grown, not butchered, like the farmstead of the early settler who observed that it took a powerful long time for his pigs to fatten but concluded it didn't really matter, for "What is time to a hog?"

It's there in those old-time, slow-time, out-state areas where the essence of Illinois resides. Naturalist and author Donald Culross Peattie, an Illinois native, referred in his 1959 article "The Best State of the Fifty" to those places—"the old-timeiness of Illinois towns, with their streets deep-shaded in vaulted elms and their yards never fenced against neighbors so that the children run in and out of each other's frame houses or play those favorite dusk games all over the block, while the June bugs bang against the screens."

Illinois links together not only urban and rural but also, to a certain extent, the northern and the southern temperament. The distance from the Wisconsin border to Cairo, at the state's southern tip, is greater than that between New York and North Carolina, and that wide stretch of territory in Illinois encompasses differences typical of those found above and below the Mason-Dixon Line. As if to accentuate the two areas, even the first rail lines bore geographical names: the Northern Cross (1838), the Southern Cross and later (1856), as if to mediate between the two, the Illinois Central. The 1848 state constitution compromised between the township system brought from the north and the county type of plan from the south by providing for both kinds of local organizations. To this day, of Illinois's one hundred and two units seventeen are officially counties while eighty-four are townships. (In case you're counting, the total of the two omits one—namely Cook, the Chicago area, a combination of county and township.) Reflecting the urban-rural, north-south dichotomy, the 1848 constitution, designed for what was then primarily a farm state, was superseded in 1870 by a new document, with special provisions for the boom area of

Cook County and Chicago, to bring Illinois into the industrial age.

North clashed with south in Illinois in the temperance movement, the sober missionaries from New England conflicting with the more freely imbibing southern Baptists. When William Kinney, a Baptist preacher, compaigned for governor in 1830 he took the precaution of carrying a Bible in one pocket and a bottle of liquor in the other. The two views divided a Baptist church near New Salem—where young Abe Lincoln lived before he moved to Springfield and his destiny—when the congregation expelled one member for favoring temperance and another for drunkenness, leading a parishioner to brandish a flask of booze and ask, "Now, brethren, how much of this critter have I got to drink to have good standing among you?" Lincoln and his great rival Stephen A. Douglas personify some of the differences in Illinois, many of which boiled to the surface during the Civil War period when Egypt, as the southern part of the state is called, actually threatened to secede and form a new state. Lincoln, the southerner (from Kentucky) was the great abolitionist while Douglas, a Yankee (from Vermont) at least tolerated slavery. Their very appearances set them apart: a correspondent for the New York *Evening Post,* reporting from Ottawa August 21, 1858, on the first of their famous series of seven debates, wrote of "Douglas, a heavy, thick-set, burly man, with large round head, heavy hair, dark complexion, and fierce bull-dog bark" and of Lincoln, "in physique he is the opposite of Douglas. Built on the Kentucky type, he is very tall, slender and angular, awkward even, in gait and attire. His face is sharp, large-featured and unprepossessing. His eyes are deep set, under heavy brows; his forehead is high and retreating and his hair is dark and heavy." The two men typify the sort of mix that came to form Illinois, not so much a melting pot as a kind of "burgoo"—a pioneer-era stew with a variety of meats and a veritable garden of vegetables simmered in a large kettle and, nowadays, served up at the annual October Burgoo Festival at Utica on the Illinois River near Ottawa.

Perhaps Illinois's various strands when linked together serve to strengthen the state, which enjoys a certain balanced way of life that encompasses a metropolis as well as a Metropolis, dairy country—Gail Borden and J. L. Kraft started their companies in northern Illinois—and the south's cotton land, Lincoln and Douglas, downstate Deere (farm machinery) and Chicago-based Sears. The great Chicago mail-order houses, a Midwestern institution, are a kind of amalgam of urban and rural cultures, for they were partly formed (Montgomery Ward in 1872, Sears Roebuck in 1886) in response to the Grange movement's complaints about the high profits supposedly enjoyed by retail middlemen. As Clyde C. Walton noted in *An Illinois Reader:* "Of the various circumstances which have given the state a peculiar heritage, the chief is unquestionably its combination of remarkable diversities within a general unity." The farms, the towns and Chicago—the strands which form one pattern of that diverse texture—are not only geographical entities but also temporal ones, for they represent ways of life typical of different times: areas echo eras. Many of the rural regions you'll pass through as you tour Illinois seem nineteenth-century places, the sleepy villages often recall the early twentieth century, while in some of the cities the past has almost disappeared. As for Chicago it's by and large tomorrow-new, the last word in everything the end of the twentieth century has to offer—high-tech futures trading, state-of-the-art slums, the latest fashions and much else. Albert Britt alluded to this sort of geographical time warp that exists between country and city in *An America That Was* when he described his move as a young man from farm to town: "The shift from the simplicities of farm living to the urban civilization of Galesburg, population about fifteen thousand, seemed bewildering to me. In reality it was merely a change from one aspect of early midwestern America to another. College, town, and farm were different phases of the same time and place, characteristic products of identical forces."

So, as you wander the back roads of the diverse state of Illinois, you'll pass from town to country, from now to then, through the thriving north and into Egypt, "south of prosperity," as Baker Brownell described the lower part of the state in *The Other Illinois*. It's all enclosed by the rivers that form all but three hundred and five of the state's eleven hundred and sixty mile borders—as if, somehow, those watery boundaries and the dozens of rivers that criss-cross the state hold together in a permanent but ever-changing network the diversities that comprise the "land of linking."

2. The Cradle of Illinois:

French Cahokia
Early Indians at Cahokia Mounds, A World Heritage Site
Waterloo and Mayestown
The French at Fort de Chartres and Prairie du Rocher
The Octagonal Schoolhouse
The Pierre Menard Home
Chester: Home of Popeye
Kaskaskia: Illinois's First Capital

Like Indiana, but unlike most states, Illinois was first settled in the west. In the late nineteenth century the French established in the wilderness along the Mississippi River outposts whose traces still today remain. The French explorers Marquette and Joliet (sometimes spelled Jolliet) were the first

Europeans to visit what later became the state of Illinois. They left from the northern part of Lake Michigan in May 1673 and made their way by water south. Indians along the way, noted Marquette in his journal, warned the explorers that on their proposed route dwelled fierce tribes "who never show mercy to Strangers." Marquette thanked the redskins for their cautionary advice, then the expedition pressed on. Led by local braves, the Europeans carried their canoes across "a portage of 2,700 paces" and then the guides "returned home, leaving us alone in this Unknown country, in the hands of providence. Thus we left the Waters flowing to Quebeq, 4 or 500 Leagues from here, to float on those that would thence forward Take us through strange lands." And so began the European exploration of Illinois.

There is something both poignant and exhilarating about Marquette's comments. Looking back, with a perspective of three hundred and more years, it's hard for us to imagine how the now settled and developed Mississippi River valley appeared to the early explorers. All was new, all was unknown. Marquette's observations evoke that sense of anticipation, mingled with a certain anxiety, felt by all explorers and adventurers, for his words well express the expedition's fateful transition from the familiar waters connected with Quebec and the past to new, unexplored rivers carrying the French forward to strange places and a problematic future. That future soon arrived when French Jesuits traveled south from Quebec to establish missions in the Illinois country. In 1696 a Mission of the Guardian Angel started up on the site of the future city of Chicago but the settlement soon disbanded. Two years later the head of Foreign Missions in Quebec sent three priests to start a religious outpost among Indian tribes south of the mouth of the Illinois River, and in the spring of 1699 a mission took hold at Cahokia, just across the river from what is now St. Louis, founded much later—in 1764. In 1703 another mission sprang up about fifty miles south near where the Kaskaskia River entered the Mississippi, and soon French settlers began to trickle into the area. After a few decades all of twelve Europeans lived in Cahokia and nearly two hundred in Kaskaskia. To protect those early French settlers along the Mississippi, the French built Fort de Chartres, ten miles northwest of Kaskaskia. Such were the beginnings of the French presence in the middle Mississippi River valley, ruled back then from Paris—in effect, the first capital of Illinois.

Still today, nearly three centuries later, travelers can find at Cahokia, Fort de Chartres and Kaskaskia buildings and other relics from those very early days on the western frontier, an area which in time became the Midwest. In Cahokia ("wild geese" in Indian language), the oldest town in Illinois, stands a vivid reminder of the missionary era—Holy Family Church, a log sanctuary built in 1799, exactly a century after the original missionary chapel was constructed. Listed on the National Register, the church is constructed in the French palisade style which uses vertical rather than horizontal log alignments. Behind the sanctuary, still occasionally used for services, lies a small cemetery—thought to be the oldest European burial ground west of the Alleghenies—with graves of early town settlers, including Vital Jarrot who lived in the nearby Jarrot Mansion, the oldest brick residence (completed in 1806) in Illinois. In 1809 Cahokia's first school occupied the second floor of the house owned by Jarrot, an Indian trader who was the second largest landowner (twenty-five thousand acres) in what became the state of Illinois. Because the mansion stood on floodland, water occasionally flowed into the residence, a phenomenon that enabled the Jarrot children, so it's said, to learn to swim in their hallway.

A few blocks away (just off highway 3) stands the Saucier House, which predates the Jarrot Mansion by nearly three-quarters of a century. Constructed about 1737 by Captain Jean Baptiste Saucier, builder of Fort de Chartres down river, the log house, listed on the National Register, is thought to be the oldest private dwelling in the Midwest. In 1793, three years after the founding of St. Clair County—which extended north to Canada and included Peoria, Chicago and Green Bay, Wisconsin—the government acquired the house from Saucier's son François, and it was there where the first U.S. court sessions and the first election in Illinois took place. Historical displays and the restored courtroom recall the days when Illinois's eighty northern counties were governed from Cahokia. Now a state memorial, the building, believed the oldest courthouse west of the Alleghenies, bears extended eaves around its entire structure, a feature common in early dwellings in the area and brought there by French settlers from the West Indies where the practice of adding overhanging roofs developed as protection against tropical rains and sun. In 1904 the Cahokia Courthouse was dismantled for removal to the St. Louis World's Fair as a display, after which the well-traveled building moved to Chicago where the antique stood in Jackson Park until its return to the original site in 1939.

Long before the French arrived in Illinois, even before France existed, Indians dwelled in the Mississippi River valley. Around A.D. 700 prehistoric Indians of the Late Woodland culture settled in an area near present-day Collinsville, a few miles north of Cahokia. A century or two later another culture, called Mississippian, emerged in the area and established there the center of an advanced civilization which enjoyed an efficient agricultural system and a sophisticated political, social and religious structure. The Indian city of Cahokia, not to be confused with the present-day Cahokia, of French pedigree, occupied more than six and a half square miles and contained some forty thousand inhabitants, twice as many as today's Cahokia. Around A.D. 1300 the population began to decline—possibly because of food or materials shortages, a change in climate, war, disease or social unrest; no one knows for sure—and by 1500 the site had been abandoned. When the Europeans arrived two hundred years later latter-day Indians referred to those early native Americans as "the ancient ones." Although they disappeared from old Cahokia, "the ancient ones" hardly vanished without a trace, for they left behind what is now one of the world's great archeological sites and sights: the Cahokia Mounds. It is no exaggeration to claim that the ancient formations comprise one of the world's leading attractions of antiquity, for in 1982 Cahokia Mounds was designated a World Heritage Site, one of little more than a hundred such cultural treasures around the globe chosen by UNESCO (the Paris-based United Nations Educational, Scientific and Cultural Organization) as a place of universal significance.

The millenium-old mounds (about sixty-five of the original hundred lie within the historic site's boundaries) are the New World's equivalent of the great constructs civilizations through the ages raised to mark their existence, and perhaps to defy time. Like the Parthenon or the Pyramids and the towers and monuments of the ancient Middle East, the Middle West's mounds form links in the great chain of being that unites generations and cultures around the world and through the ages. Writing in what he described as a Dadaist vein, Henry Miller, in *Tropic of Capricorn,* described a New World that "turned out to be a far older world than any we have known. I saw beneath the superficial physiognomy of skin and bone the indestructible world which man has always carried within him; it was neither old nor new, really, but the eternally true world. . . . When my companions left me of an evening I would often sit down and write to my friends . . . the Mound Builders of the Mississippi Valley. . . . Any primitive man would have understood me, any man of archaic epochs would have understood me." For a present-day visitor to understand primitive man of the sort who built the mounds, it's well to begin at the brand new thirty-three thousand-square-foot museum and interpretive center where displays based on the theme "Cahokia, An Urban Center" trace the history of the mound builders and their constructions. The mounds are comprised entirely of earth, dug with primitive tools and carried in baskets on workers' backs to the construction sites. Although a few of the mounds served for burial purposes—Mound 72 yielded nearly three hundred bodies, along with grave offerings such as copper and mica objects, some eight hundred arrowheads and a blanket made of twenty thousand marine shell beads—the Indians built most of the hillocks for ceremonial activities. The crown jewel of the collection is the famous Monks Mound, so named for the group of Trappist brothers who in 1809 built a monastery nearby. With a base covering more than fourteen acres and four terraces rising to a height of a hundred feet, Monks is the largest Indian mound in the U.S. and the biggest prehistoric earthen construction in the New World. Flights of (modern-day) wooden stairs lead to the top from where you can enjoy a view over the mound-dotted landscape across which, long ago, rose the once-great city, believed to be the largest prehistoric settlement north of Mexico. To the south, where the highway cuts through the green terrain, stretched the spacious plazas, while to the east now stands a reproduction of part of the two-mile-long stockade wall that once surrounded the ancient city's center. Up there atop Monks Mound, with the perspective of the height and the years, it's perhaps impossible to avoid meditating on the ebb and flow of civilizations and the vicissitudes of time. In Lanford Wilson's 1975 play *The Mound Builders,* about a group of archaeologists hurriedly excavating ancient mounds in southern Illinois before a nearby lake floods the site, the phrase "vanished without a trace" echoes through the text. The huge earthen construction beneath one's feet testifies that such wasn't the fate of the mound builders at old Cahokia, the city that time remembered.

To continue on the trail of the old French settlements along the Mississippi, head south from the Cahokia-Cahokia Mounds area on route 3, which will take you to Waterloo. On the west side of the highway at the north edge of town stands Peterstown House, a two-story, white frame, green-shuttered building which is the only remaining stagecoach stop on the Cahokia-Kaskaskia Trail. Listed on the National Register, the house was built in the mid-eighteenth century by Emory Peter Rogers, a settler from Massachusetts who became a leading businessman in Peterstown, as Waterloo was once called. Period furnishings and an old wooden trough, along with a sign proclaiming "Stage Coach Stop," lend the building a touch of yesteryear. Two nineteenth-century log cabins stand in the yard behind the house. Waterloo's central section, also listed on the National Register, offers a scattering of late nineteenth-century brick houses and other century-old structures.

You'll find another National Register group of buildings at Maeystown, an isolated hamlet of a hundred or so people eight miles south of Waterloo on route 7. Sleepy Maeystown is an unspoiled corner that provides a scene out of the last century. Virtually the entire village, which nestles in a small valley watered by a bucolic stream, is listed on the Register. Atop a hill overlooking the town towers the attractive stone St. John's Church, founded more than a century and a quarter ago. Over the door stained glass inscribed with the phrase "Evangelische St. Johannes Kirche" recalls the German families who settled in the lovely little hollow in the mid-eighteen hundreds. Down in town all roads lead to Hoefft's Village Inn, Maeystown's only commercial establishment apart from a feed mill. Hoefft's occupies a historic tavern little changed from a century or so ago when the pub's predecessor first opened. Antique display cases, turn-of-the-century photos and a well-worn wooden bar recall the old days which, in laid-back Maeystown, probably greatly resembled more recent times.

From Maeystown the road that takes you south toward Fort de Chartres passes near Renault, a village whose name recalls the French presence in the area. The town was named for Phillipe François Renault, director-general of mining operations for John Law's so-called "Mississippi Bubble," a speculative promotion organized in Europe to exploit North America's mineral resources. Renault imported some five hundred slaves from the French West Indies to work the mines near the Mississippi River. The "Bubble" burst in 1720, but for two centuries afterward descendants of those slaves in Renault continued to speak a French patois and to cling to French customs. (For the French-exploited lead mines across the river in Missouri, see Chapter V, section 9.)

A few miles south of Maeystown lies Fort de Chartres, for more than half a century the stronghold of French power in the Mississippi valley. After two early forts built in 1720 and in 1727 fell into disrepair the French government decided in 1751 to build a more substantial structure. Under the direction of engineer François Saucier, the early settler whose house still stands in Cahokia, construction began in 1753. The limestone fort the visitor sees today is a rebuilt version of that third fortress, completed in 1756. The ramparts of the reconstructed gatehouse, which towers over the site, afford a view of the complex: foundations of two barracks buildings; the original squat, solid 1756 powder magazine, one of Illinois's oldest structures; and two other stone structures, one containing a guardhouse and a tiny gothic chapel, the other housing the Peithmann Museum. Displays there include exhibits pertaining to the French presence in the area—military objects, French playing cards, fur trade implements and pelts, a Latin missal and breviary printed in France in the mid-eighteenth century, and brandy bottles with high kicks in the bottom designed to limit the contents and so cheat the Indians who purchased the "fire water."

The French never had occasion to war from Fort de Chartres. "Never a volley from France's folly," one wag joked, and by the 1763 Treaty of Paris, which ended the French and Indian War, France ceded to England all claimed lands east of the Mississippi, except New Orleans. London thus became the Illinois territory's second capital. Dr. Samuel Johnson, the famous London literary figure, didn't think much of England's new acquisition in the New World wilderness. "Sir," he opined, "large tracts of America have been added by the last war to the British dominions. . . . [The] barren parts of the continent, the refuse of the earlier adventures, which the French, who came last, had taken as better than nothing." The British military in America apparently found the territory only slightly better than nothing, for in 1772 they abandoned the fort, which soon deteriorated. An American general who visited the area in August 1787 on an inspection tour of the Northwest Territory reported to the Secretary of War: "I passed by the ruins of Fort Chartres. . . . It was built of stone and must have been a considerable fortification formerly, but the part next to the river had been carried away by the floods . . . [and it was] all a thicket within." Over the years local settlers gradually dismantled the great fortress, removing stones and timbers to build houses. Finally, in 1913, the state of Illinois acquired the ruin and partially restored the fort to its former glory. The first weekend in June every year that glory revives when Fort de Chartres comes alive with period music, militia maneuvers, tomahawk throwing, birchbark canoe races and demonstrations of old-time crafts.

Four miles east of the fort lies Prairie du Rocher ("Rock Prairie"), a sleepy village of seven hundred people, well garnished with large trees that shade the quiet streets. On Market Street a French sign or two recall the old days when

France controlled the area, while Conner's store, established in 1839, offers another carryover from the past. As you head south on highway 3 toward Fort Kaskaskia State Park you may want to detour a few miles west at Evansville to Schuline where you'll find an unusual eight-sided school house, one of the very few remaining octagonal schools in the country (another is Diamond Rock School in Valley Forge, Pennsylvania, and near Watkins Woolen Mill not far from Kansas City, Missouri, stands the 1856 octagonal Franklin School; see Chapter V, section 5). Built in the early 1870s and used as a school until 1953, the brick building, topped by an octagonal wooden cupola, replaced a classroom structure destroyed by a tornado in 1870. The eight-sided design was thought to be better able to resist strong winds and, with windows on each face, would afford more light than a conventional building. It was certainly no idle threat to the forty or so pupils—increased to perhaps fifty or more when the older boys had gathered the fall crops and then arrived for book learning—that they might be disciplined by being sent to a corner: the octagonal structure encompassed all too many corners available to punish the mischievous.

Farther south, on the hills overlooking the Mississippi at Fort Kaskaskia State Park, stand the earthworks and foundations of the old palisade fort, built by the French in 1733. In 1766 the people of Kaskaskia, one of the early French villages (1703), destroyed the fort rather than have it occupied by the British, who took control of the area the previous year. Near the fort's remains lies Garrison Hill Cemetery, filled with graves of the early settlers in Kaskaskia. A monument recalls those adventurous souls who braved the hazards of the frontier: "Those who sleep here were . . . the early pioneers of the great Mississippi valley. They planted free institutions in a wilderness and were the founders of a great commonwealth." The park's overlook affords an extensive view across the Mississippi to Kaskaskia Island, site of the original town of

Kaskaskia which in 1818 became the first capital of the new state of Illinois. The island forms a curious appendage to Illinois, for it lies west of the Mississippi, which changed courses in 1881 and sliced the area away from the mainland.

Before proceeding to that isolated corner of Illinois west of the great river, it's worth descending from the high road to the Mississippi to visit the lovely old Pierre Menard house. Born in Quebec, Menard established a trading business in Cahokia in the early 1790s. Menard's second wife was Angelique Saucier, granddaughter of François Saucier, Cahokia resident and the engineer who built Fort de Chartres, not far up river. In 1802 Menard, who in 1818 became Illinois's first lieutenant governor, began construction of his home, known as "The Mt. Vernon of the West." The impeccably restored French colonial-style house and its furnishings, some of them original, recall the French-American upper-class way of life in the early nineteenth century. Installed on the ground floor is a one-room museum displaying such items as Indian artifacts (a tomahawk, trading beads, moccasins), Menard's surveying compass, his personal tax ledgers—taxes hardly intimidated him, for he was the tax assessor—and the silk slippers worn by his daughter at a ball given for the Marquis de Lafayette in 1824 when the famous French general visited Kaskaskia.

From the Menard house you can proceed south to Chester where Shadrach Bond (died 1832), Illinois's first governor, lies buried in Evergreen Cemetery. In a park near Chester stands St. Mary's covered bridge, remnant of the 1853 Randolph County Plank Road Company's toll road that connected Chester and Sparta. The ninety-foot-long slightly swayback span served traffic from 1854 to 1930. Back in the mid-nineteenth century Chester and Sparta became great competitors in the castor oil trade. Randolph County was then the nation's largest producer of the oil, made from castor beans and used not for the digestive system but as a lubricant, an application petroleum subsequently replaced. Years later a local figure popularized, or at least publicized, another agricultural product when spinach-munching Popeye appeared on the scene. The famous cartoon character first saw the light of day in 1929 when Chester-born (in 1894) Elzie Crisler Segar created Popeye from his recollection of Frank "Rocky" Fiegel, a local tough. The spinach-loving sailorman first appeared as a character in "Thimble Theatre," the forerunner of "Popeye," on January 17, 1929. William "Windy Bill" Schuchert, Chester movie house owner and Segar's benefactor, inspired the part of Wimpy, the hamburger addict, while Olive Oyl was based on Dora Paskell, who ran a general store in Chester. By the Mississippi River bridge in Chester stands a six-foot-tall bronze statue of the famous sailorman, complete with his characteristic knobby knees and puffy cheeks and puffing on his pipe, tilted—as always—at a jaunty angle.

To reach Kaskaskia Island, cross the bridge and continue on through Missouri for about ten miles to the town of St. Mary's, gateway to that small Illinois enclave west of the Mississippi. The isolated island seems forlorn and forgotten. Electricity reached the remote and desolate lowland, a fourteen-thousand-acre spread inhabited by a handful of farmers, only in 1948. On the island stands the Church of the Immaculate Conception, a latter-day structure built on the spot where the original sanctuary, established in 1675 by explorer Jacques Marquette, was located. Nearby is a memorial building that houses the so-called "Liberty Bell of the West." Eleven years older than *the* Liberty Bell in Philadelphia, this bell was cast in France in 1741 for the church at Kaskaskia. The bell received its name after being rung the night of July 4, 1778, when George Rogers Clark captured the town from the British on his way to Vincennes, Indiana (see Chapter II, section 3). A French inscription on the bell, ornamented with the fleur-de-lys emblem of France, reads "For the church of

Illinois—by the gift of the King." Thus a present from King Louis XV of far-off France remains to recall the French colonial days in the Illinois region of the Mississippi River valley.

Little else, however, survives to memorialize the time when Kaskaskia was Illinois's largest city and first capital. Back in the early years of the nineteenth century Kaskaskia glittered with society and pulsated with activity. Prominent citizens included Daniel Cook—lawyer, judge, newspaper owner, U.S. Congressman for eight years and the man for whom Cook County (which includes Chicago) was named; William Morrison (buried in Garrison Hill Cemetery in Kaskaskia State Park, across the Mississippi), a successful trader who entertained Lafayette during the Frenchman's 1825 visit and who in 1804 stocked a trading expedition which was the first commercial venture to travel over what later became the Sante Fe Trail (for the origins of the Trail in Missouri, see Chapter V, section 5); and Shadrach Bond and Pierre Menard, Illinois's first governor and lieutenant governor. Kaskaskia began to decline in 1820 when the state capital was moved to Vandalia. In 1844 a flood nearly destroyed the town, and in 1881 the Mississippi changed course and washed away much of the historic old settlement. Each recurring spring flood ate away more land until finally the last vestiges of old Kaskaskia slipped into the Mississippi, and now diesel-powered tugboats push long barge trains over the site of Illinois's first important city and one-time state capital.

3. Illinois's Egypt:

The River Road to Grand Tower and Thebes
The Inland Route to Carbondale, Marion, Pomona, Cobden
and Jonesboro
Cairo, Capital of Little Egypt
Metropolis: Home of Superman
Vintage Ohio River Towns: Golconda, Elizabethtown, Cave-
in-Rock and Its Bandit Lair
Old Shawneetown

For more than a century and a half southern Illinois, that part of the state wedged between the Wabash, Ohio and Mississippi Rivers, has been known as Egypt. No Nile washes through the area, but one of Egypt's main cities is Cairo, pronounced in these parts "Kay-row." That curious designation for the region supposedly originated after the winter of 1830–31, the most severe and one of the longest in the state's history. The extended cold spell so shortened the growing season in central Illinois that farmers there were forced to travel south, like the sons of Jacob "going down to Egypt for corn," to procure corn for their animals. Illinois's Egypt doesn't glitter with Pharaonic splendor but, at its lower regions along the Ohio, it does exude a certain southern charm. That part of the state in fact extends farther south than most of Virginia and Kentucky, and many of the early settlers who arrived by flatboat on the Ohio River came from the south. During the Civil War citizens of the area agitated to set up Egypt as a separate state aligned with the south. Still today the region's slow pace and rural atmosphere stand in contrast to the quicker tempo in more industrialized central and northern Illinois.

One way to reach Cairo, which lies at the very southern tip

of Egypt, is highway 3, the River Road that parallels, but which for the most part is not within view of, the Mississippi. Between Gorham and Grand Tower, villages on highway 3, lies the Boone family cemetery where many relatives of the famous frontiersman Daniel Boone lie buried. (In his later years Boone lived in Missouri. See Chapter V, section 2.) A tall triangular stone marker commemorates Benningsen Boon (he spelled the name without an "e"), first non-Indian child born in Jackson County. The father of Boon, who fought in the 1832 Black Hawk War that led to the removal of the last Indians from Illinois, was Captain William Boon, an officer of the Illinois Riflemen in the Battle of New Orleans and the county's first permanent settler. More early history haunts Devil's Backbone Park, an enclave by the Mississippi just north of Grand Tower. The park marks the 1803 camp site of a U.S. cavalry unit, led by Colonel Zebulon Davis, uncle of Confederate President Jefferson Davis, sent to the area to break up a stronghold of pirates who had menaced river travelers. Two now-vanished iron furnaces utilizing iron ore from Missouri and coal from Murphysboro, Illinois, operated at the site until after the Civil War. Andrew Carnegie supposedly once considered turning Grand Tower into a Pittsburgh of the west. The town was named for Tower Rock, a sixty-foot-high limestone hulk that rises from the Mississippi near the Missouri side. This part of "Old Man River" was especially hazardous: An 1867 survey recorded one hundred and thirty-three sunken hulks between Cairo and St. Louis, a stretch of river ominously known as "The Graveyard." In 1871, when the river was being cleared of navigation hazards, President U.S. Grant (from Galena, Illinois: see section 7) ordered federal engineers to preserve Tower Rock as a pillar for a bridge. The order still stands but not the bridge, which was never built. Now listed on the National Register, one-quarter-square-mile Tower Rock is no doubt America's smallest natural national monument. Various Indian legends are attached to the Rock—or perhaps detached is the word—for one tale tells of a leap off the pinnacle by an Indian maiden thwarted in love.

Tower Rock is now a rather scruffy river town little changed from a century or so ago when Mark Twain wrote that the place "seemed to need some repairs here and there, and a new coat of whitewash all over." But the village is worth visiting if for no other reason than to eat at Ma Hale's Boarding House Restaurant, a cozy establishment with an old-time atmosphere reminiscent of the era when steamboats plied the Mississippi. About a half century ago a veteran river captain who boarded with the Hale family found the food so good he asked Mrs. Hale to cook for his entire crew. In 1940 Melissa Hale opened the Boarding House restaurant that she ran until her death thirty-one years later at age seventy-one. Her son then operated the establishment until 1979 when a Mississippi and Ohio River ship pilot bought the restaurant. Ouside stands a statue of Melissa "Mom" Hale, the plaque noting that for more than thirty years she served some million and a half home-cooked meals to all comers. The inscription concludes: "Those of us who enjoyed her cooking affectionately dedicate this plaque to her." Old photos and Hale family mementos decorate the polished wood walls of the restaurant. Friendly waitresses and a folksy ambiance create an informal boarding house-type atmosphere, but no "boarding house reach" is necessary at Hale's, where maximum helpings of minimum-priced all-you-can-eat food (fifteen or so different items) crowd your table.

If you can still squeeze behind your car's steering wheel after your Hale and hearty feast, continue south from Grand Tower on highway 3 to Thebes, a hamlet of four hundred and fifty people just below the city of Cape Girardeau on the Missouri side of the Mississippi (Chapter V, section 9). On a hill overlooking the river and the tiny town, part of which perches atop a rise by the Mississippi, stands the 1848 sand-

stone and hewn timber courthouse, seat of Alexander
County until 1864 when Cairo succeeded Thebes as the center of county government. Old books, an antique iron stove,
venerable wooden chairs and a high-backed old judge's chair
furnish the interior in the manner of a nineteenth-century
courtroom. For a time Dred Scott, the slave whose famous
trial took place at St. Louis a decade before the Civil War, was
confined in the dungeon beneath the Thebes courthouse.
Originally called Sparhawk's Landing, Thebes was at one
time a thriving river port. It was there where Captain Andy
Hawks of the *Cotton Blossom* in Edna Ferber's *Show Boat*
lived. Or, rather, his house was there but his home and
perhaps his heart were elsewhere, for "Despite the prim little
house in Thebes," Ferber wrote, "home, to Andy, was a
boat." His daughter Magnolia, however, stayed at home in
the "little white house at Thebes" where she would gaze out
her window at the river and the passing showboats, "their
lights shining golden yellow through the boat's many windows." It's pleasant to linger in Thebes and for a moment or
two imagine Magnolia watching the old river boats chugging
by in the darkness. The night-shrouded waters would now
and again brighten with the lights of a passing steamer, its
paddle wheel churning and splashing as the golden rectangles
glide along. Then the lights would disappear, leaving the
river once again in darkness as it flowed silently through the
night on down to the sea.

The inland route from south-central Illinois down to Cairo
also offers a few off-the-beaten-track places of interest. Instead of taking highway 3 via Grand Tower and Thebes you
can head south along highway 127. You'll pass near Carbondale, seat of Southern Illinois University—Egypt's cultural
and educational oasis. In keeping with the area's name, the
University's mascot is the Saluki, the royal Egyptian hunting
dog. A bronze marker at the entrance of Woodlawn Cemetery in Carbondale proclaims that the site saw the first organ-

ized observance of Decoration Day, held there April 29, 1866, when a group of Civil War veterans organized a memorial service at the graveyard. The following year, when May 30 was designated as the day of mourning, the event became formalized. Farther east, at the edge of Crab Orchard National Wildlife Refuge, lies Marion, headquarters of an old-time short-line train company with the delightful name Crab Apple and Egyptian Railroad. Although thirty-five hundred steam locomotives and some eight passenger-carrying steam trains still operate in the U.S., the Crab Orchard and Egyptian is believed to be the nation's only common carrier that runs a steam engine to haul freight. Engine Number 17, a one-hundred-and-fifteen-ton four-thousand-horsepower behemoth, serves the line's twenty or so customers along an eight-and-a-half-mile stretch of track that connects with a Union Pacific through line. The schedule of Crab Orchard and Egyptian, which ended passenger service and began hauling freight in 1977, is based on shippers' needs, so if you want to see Number 17 in action it's advisable to call ahead. But even if the train isn't operating, you can see the engine in all its gleaming splendor at the line's depot in Marion.

Back on highway 127 toward the west you'll reach Pomona, a village in Shawnee National Forest. At Pomona is an old-time general store, while north of town (and three miles west of 127) stands a well-known local landmark—a ninety-foot-long natural bridge across which it's said a peg-legged local fellow named Frank Hawk once drove a horse and buggy. Covering more than a quarter of a million acres across much of southern Illinois, Shawnee Forest offers an extensive range of trails, camp sites, wildlife, water sports and other outdoor activities. A few miles south of Pomona you'll pass through Alto Pass—near which rises a one-hundred-and-eleven-foot-tall cross, supposedly the tallest Christian monument in North America—on the way to Cobden, named for English economist and politician Richard Cobden who visited the area in 1859 to inspect the new railroad lines he'd promoted in Britain. From Cobden, center of a fruit-growing area, departed in 1858 the nation's first refrigerated car shipment, a load of strawberries. A few miles south at Anna—whose modernistic limestone library was designed by Walter Burley Griffin, one of Frank Lloyd Wright's students—you can drive west one mile to reach Jonesboro, where a stone marker at what was the town fairgrounds indicates the site at which Lincoln debated Douglas in the third of the series of seven famous confrontations between the two Senatorial candidates in 1858. As might be expected in the Egypt area of Illinois, the crowd of some hundred people—the smallest any of the debates drew—was strongly Democratic and pro-slavery. The night before the debate, held September 15, Lincoln stayed at the appropriately named (for him) Union Hotel, from the porch of which he watched Donati's comet flash through the sky and then disappear into the night. Near town stands the Austrian-style Kornthal Church, an 1860 sanctuary listed on the National Register, with handmade pews and a pulpit modeled after the one in George Washington's church in Alexandria, Virginia. The canopied pulpit, attached to the front wall above the altar, is reached by a dozen steps representing the twelve apostles; legend has it that if a step ever breaks that was the one symbolizing Judas Iscariot.

Whether you've chosen the River Road, via Grand Tower and Thebes, or the inland route through Carbondale, Marion, Cobden and Jonesboro, you can continue south on the highway you've selected to reach Cairo, a city once destined to be the metropolis of Egypt. But destiny had other plans and Cairo never became a metropolis, although a city so named lies a few miles east on the Ohio River. At one time Cairo was a city of promise but it turned out to be only a place of promises. William Ferguson, a Scottish scientist who visited the town in June 1855, observed that Cairo, thanks to its strategic location at the confluence of the Ohio and Mississippi Rivers, was "likely to become a great shipping-place" for goods and passengers. But by the time Edward Dicey, a journalist for the London *Daily Telegraph,* visited the city in 1862, he found a less alluring scene: "There are some places in the world which, when you get to, your first thought is—how shall I get away again; and of these Cairo is one."

Twenty years earlier a more famous English writer—Charles Dickens—found Cairo a similarly unpleasant place, but his perceptions were no doubt colored by his worthless investment in a local development company. In 1837 promoters incorporated the Cairo City and Canal Company, a firm organized to develop the area where the Ohio met the Mississippi. The promoters arranged with the London banking house of John Wright and Company to sell Cairo bonds in England. In August 1839 the promoters, with the help of a fat fee, persuaded Daniel Webster, a lawyer and U.S. Senator then visiting London, to render a favorable legal opinion on the land titles and a few other matters in regard to the offering. The house of Wright then sold one million two hundred fifty thousand dollars of bonds, one unsuspecting investor being Charles Dickens. In 1842 Dickens traveled to America to inspect the property which backed his by then worthless bonds. The renowned novelist was, to say the least, unimpressed. Describing his trip down the Ohio River into the area, Dickens gave Cairo the dickens:

> At length, upon the morning of the third day, we arrived at a spot so much more desolate than any we had yet beheld, that the forlornest places we had passed were, in comparison with it, full of interest. At the junction of the two rivers, on ground so flat and low and marshy, that at certain seasons of the year it is inundated to the house-tops, lies a breeding-place of fever, ague, and death; vaunted in England as a mine of Golden Hope, and speculated in, on the faith of monstrous representations, to many people's ruins.

Nor did even the great "Father of Waters" impress Dickens, who wrote of "the hateful Mississippi circling and eddying before [Cairo], and turning off upon its southern course a slimy monster hideous to behold." Then he concluded by dismissing Cairo as "a hotbed of disease, an ugly sepulchre, a grave uncheered by any gleam of promise; a place without one single quality, in earth or air or water, to commend it; such is this dismal Cairo."*

Today Cairo, now protected from the river's whims by levees, is a quiet town of six thousand people with a definite southern feel to it. The southern atmosphere echoes in the redolently named Magnolia Manor, a four-story, fourteen-room, red brick Victorian mansion listed on the National Register, built in 1872 by Charles Galigher, a local milling magnate. To help the structure withstand the damp river air the house boasts double brick walls with a ten-inch insulation space between them. In 1880 former President and Mrs. Ulysses S. Grant attended a gala reception at the house after their return from a world tour. The Galighers had befriended Grant when the Union army general installed his headquarters at Cairo's Fort Defiance while planning and launching his siege of the South. Civil War reminders abound in the area. At Ft. Defiance State Park you can enjoy a view onto the confluence of the Ohio and Mississippi Rivers, while at Mound City National Cemetery, six miles north of Cairo, lie nearly five thousand Union and Confederate soldiers. A series of bronze markers bear stanzas of the poem "The Bivouac of the Dead"—"The muffled drum has beat the soldier's last tattoo"—while a short distance south of the large granite memorial near the center of the cemetery is the grave of

---

*So incensed did Dickens's comments make former Illinois lieutenant governor William Kinney that in the fall of 1842 he contributed to the Belleville *Advocate* a series of articles responding to the Englishman, arguing that Cairo would soon "appear in the attitude of a fat turkey" such that "hungry hunters for prosperity [will then] desire a slice from Cairo's breast."

Union Brigadier General John B. Turchin, who once served
as an officer in the Russian Czar's army. Mound City was the
site of a U.S. Naval Hospital where casualties from the Battle
of Shiloh and other encounters were treated, and also in the
town is the Marine Ways, a riverside works where gunboats
and steamships were made and repaired.

Mound City is the first of the old settlements by the Ohio
on the Illinois side worth a stop. All along that river lie towns
and villages of interest. Randall Parrish, in *Historic Illinois*,
published in 1906, vividly summarizes Illinois's Ohio River
country:

> All of this Illinois shore is historic, and has witnessed many a
> strange flotilla sweep by, both in peace and in war. Along every
> nook and bend have been the camping spots of wearied emi-
> grants, of war-worn soldiers, of adventurous hunters and prey-
> ing outlaws. Here the great family arks have drifted down the
> current . . . here have been seen the uniforms of French gre-
> nadiers, British Highlanders, and the buff and blue of the Conti-
> nental troops. . . . The towns one sees nestling along the bank
> are old, their names associated with early State history, their
> houses telling of that interesting past in which they bore part
> bravely and well—Elizabethtown, Golconda, Metropolis,
> America, Post Wilkins—all a part of the great story of coloniza-
> tion and development, of early privation and achievement.

Just beyond Mound City lies tiny America (you can see all of
America in just a minute or two) and farther on is Metropolis—with seventy-two-hundred inhabitants, definitely the
metropolis of Massac County. But Metropolis boasts a
greater claim to fame—it's the hometown of Superman,
whose colorful portrait decorates the otherwise rather plain
place. It's fun to drive around Metropolis looking for portraits of Superman, clad in his familiar bright red and blue
outfit. A seventy-foot-wide billboard on the outskirts wel-
comes visitors with a portrayal of the comic book hero

flying, left arm outstretched and right fist clenched. In town the water tower bears a representation of mild-mannered Clark Kent pulling off his white shirt to reveal the Superman workclothes beneath. On the courthouse lawn stands a presumably larger-than-life seven-and-a-half-foot statue showing the famous strong man with his hands poised on his hips. The masthead of the town newspaper—which is, of course, called the *Planet*—sports a drawing of the cartoon character, and affixed to the window of the paper's office at Ferry and West Seventh Streets is a large "S" insignia. At the Chamber of Commerce, which bears on its facade a mural of an airborne Superman, is a small museum with photos and displays of items connected with the famous hero, as well as a red and blue phone booth where you can contact Superman—maybe even hire him for an assignment or two. If you fancy a Superman memento, a few places in town sell souvenirs (T-shirts, towels, ashtrays, knick-knacks) bearing his likeness. In early June, Metropolis holds its annual Superman Celebration, featuring a mock bank robbery foiled by the city's favorite law enforcer.

One other famous resident of Metropolis was the well-known agnostic Robert G. Ingersoll, who in 1852 taught in a log cabin school there. Ingersoll, "the Great Agnostic," as he came to be called, once commented during a confab in Metropolis that the best way to conduct a baptism was to "soap up" the candidate so that he or she could at least be bathed during the ceremony. The flippant remark led to Ingersoll's dismissal from his teaching position and he moved from Metropolis to Shawneetown, an Illinois Ohio River settlement to the east where he studied law.

Just east of Metropolis lies Illinois's first state park, established in 1908, where you'll find a reconstruction of historic old Fort Massac. With its palisade fences and quartet of two-story block houses at each corner, the fort vividly evokes the frontier days. For Superman, Fort Massac would be a pushover but in the eighteenth and nineteenth centuries the fortress helped the occupying power—first the French, then the English, finally the Americans—control the surrounding territory. Soon after French soldiers constructed the first fort in 1757 Indians captured the stronghold without firing an arrow. One day a band of redskins appeared just outside the installation covered with bearskins and walking on all fours. When the French soldiers left their posts to pursue the "bears" a group of Indians rushed in to take possession of the fort and massacred many of the Europeans. In 1765 British troops occupied the outpost, which they lost in 1778 to Colonel George Rogers Clark and his band of "long knives," who then proceeded from Fort Massac to Kaskaskia (see section 2), a hundred miles northwest, after which they marched on Vincennes, Indiana (Chapter II, section 3). In the early nineteenth century Fort Massac helped protect U.S. military and commercial interests in the area, while during the Civil War Yankee troops occupied the outpost.

Famous personalities connected with the historic fort include Zebulon Pike of Pike's Peak fame, stationed there in the mid-1790s; Meriwether Lewis and William Clark, who stopped at Fort Massac in 1803 before proceeding on their expedition up the Missouri River to the Pacific Northwest (see section 9); General Andrew Jackson; and Aaron Burr. It was at Fort Massac where Burr, former U.S. vice-president, met with General James Wilkinson in 1805 to discuss their plan to take over the southwestern territory, a scheme later known in history as the "Burr Conspiracy." The Burr-Wilkinson plotting at Fort Massac forms the basis of the plot for Edward Everett Hale's famous historical novel *The Man Without a Country*. A small museum at the fort contains well-mounted exhibits tracing those and other historic events connected with the outpost, whose past presents a kind of microcosm of America's frontier history.

From the Metropolis-Fort Massac area you can make your

way northeast, keeping your eye peeled for a blue blur flying
"faster than a speeding bullet," over to Golconda, an old-time
river town, a National Register historic district, with a nineteenth-century atmosphere. A block from the courthouse
stands the nearly century-old Victorian-style Riverview
Mansion, once the home of steamboat owner John Gilbert
and now a delightful bed-and-breakfast inn whose fourteen
rooms are outfitted with original furnishings and other
period pieces. Up river a few miles at Rosiclare, named for
both of the founder's daughters so neither of them would
sulk, are two attractions that recall the area's early mineral
activity—the Hardin County Fluorspar Museum (fluorspar is
used in the manufacture of plastics) and, on Hog Thief
Creek, just north of town, the Illinois Iron Furnace, the
state's first charcoal-fired iron furnace, a restored fifty-two-
foot-high structure, listed on the National Register, in which
iron was produced during the Civil War. A few miles east lies
Elizabethtown, locally known as E'town, named for the wife
of James McFarland who in 1812 built a tavern-hotel which,
until it finally closed in the late 1970s, was the oldest continuously operated hostelry in Illinois and perhaps in the Midwest. Back in the early years meals there cost twenty-five
cents, a bed half as much and a quart of beer or half pint of
whiskey the same as a bed and perhaps more conducive to
sleep.

For years the place was known as the Rose Hotel after
Sarah Rose, a widow who in 1884 took over the establishment and ran it until 1939 when her daughter started to
manage it. Although the hotel no longer receives guests, the
venerable white brick building, a handsome structure with a
spacious second-floor verandah affording views of the Ohio
River, still stands.

A few miles east of E'town lies Cave-in-Rock, a fabled
limestone cavern on the Ohio River where one Sam Mason,
said to be America's first brigand, installed himself and a

band of robbers in 1797. Mason, once an officer in George Washington's army, converted the cave into a tavern which he named "Cave-Inn-Rock" and set up on the banks of the Ohio a billboard advertising his "Liquor Vault and House of Entertainment." Few red-blooded boatmen could pass that sign without stopping in to check out the attractions at the "Inn" where they found no hard liquor or soft women, no bourbon or belles, but a den of cutthroat thieves who relieved the rivermen of their possessions and sometimes their lives. After Mason's day many other brigands, outlaws, pirates and n'er-do-wells occupied the cave, from which they terrorized the Ohio River boat traffic until finally, around 1834, the authorities chased away the last of the desperados. The legendary cave, where scenes from such adventure movies as *How the West Was Won* and the Disney TV series *Davy Crockett and the River Pirates* were filmed, now forms part of an Illinois state park.

Before proceeding on to Old Shawneetown, now a mere remnant of what was one of Illinois's leading cities back in the early nineteenth century, you might want to stop in at Ridgway, self-proclaimed "Popcorn Center of the World," which holds an annual Popcorn Day on a Saturday in early September. One early-day local promoter of the product once observed that "popcorn isn't peanuts." At Junction, a few miles away, stands the 1834 Old Slave House—a handsome red structure with a large two-tier white porch—where, local legend has it, slaves who worked the nearby Equality Salt Wells lived. Although the Northwest Ordinance prohibited slavery and Illinois was a free state, special provisions permitted exceptions at the salines area, which thus was the only part of Illinois where slavery legally existed. On view at the mansion, outfitted with its original furnishings, are the cramped quarters that housed the slaves.

Nearby Old Shawneetown was laid out in 1810 by the federal government, which for years retained an interest in the salt deposits in the area. For more than a century Shawneetown could boast that it and Washington, D.C., were the only two cities in the country platted by the national government. At the time Illinois joined the Union in 1818 it was the second largest state in size but the smallest in population. Only thirty-five thousand people lived there, many of them scattered about the state in small communities. The only two settlements that enjoyed any semblance of being true towns were Kaskaskia (see section 2) and Shawneetown, the latter a rather rough and raucous river port with stores, hotels and even a bank, the first—founded in 1816—in the Illinois Territory. Little of that early thriving community remains, but John Marshall's two-story brick home, which housed the first bank, survives. Nearby rises the more substantial and imposing building of the first bank's successor, a beautifully proportioned Greek Revival-style structure constructed in 1839 at a cost of eighty thousand dollars, then a break-the-bank-size fortune. A narrow flight of steps leads up to five fluted Doric columns that stand before the sandstone portico. This classic and classy building is one of the state's most elegant structures, a historic treasure and treasury, that recalls the days when Shawneetown served as an important commercial and financial center. John Woods, an English farmer who in 1819 passed through Shawneetown on his way to the English Prairie near Albion, a settlement of British some fifty miles north (see section 4), described the Ohio River town in its heyday: "There is a bank called the 'Bank of Illinois,' in good repute, many stores, and several taverns [inns], the principal one the Steam-Boat Hotel. . . . There are about 80 houses, mostly of wood, and a wooden jail." Now, with a shade under four hundred inhabitants, Old Shawneetown is a mere shadow of its former self—just another of those sleepy river towns, residues of history, that line the Mississippi and Ohio in the Illinois southland known as Egypt.

4. England in Illinois:

The English at Albion

History and Natural History in Fairfield, West Salem, Olney
and Salem
North to Teutopolis, The Old State Capital at Vandalia,
Greenville, The Swiss Town of Highland, and the Grave of
"Mother Jones" at Mt. Olive
The Southern Route to Carmi, McLeansboro, Mt. Vernon,
The Spa Town of Okawville, and Charles Dickens's Lebanon

When two men propose marriage to the same woman at the same time, something has to give. In 1817 both Morris Birkbeck and George Flower asked for Eliza Andrews's hand in marriage. She had two hands but accepted only one offer—that of Flower—and the men then fell out over the matter. The rivals had previously traveled together from England to America to establish a colony for their fellow countrymen. At the U.S. land office in Shawneetown (see previous section) the two Englishmen acquired fourteen hundred and forty acres of Illinois prairieland for two dollars an acre. When the two men broke, their followers also divided, Flower's group settling in Albion and Birkbeck's in Wanborough, named for his property in County Surrey near London. The English Settlement, as the colony was called, became a success but in 1825 Birkbeck drowned while returning from the communal village at nearby New Harmony, Indiana (Chapter II, section 3), and without his leadership Wanborough eventually faded from existence. Today, few traces of the English Settlement remain. (For another early English prairie settlement—Le Mars, in Iowa—see Chapter IV, section 8.) At Albion, a town of twenty-three hundred people in south-central Illinois near the Indiana border, a marker in the town square recalls Birkbeck and Flower, while a pleasant old residence with gingerbread trim houses the local museum and library, the latter a descendant of the original English Settlement's book collection and thus seemingly Illinois's oldest public library.

But Birkbeck and his fellow Englishmen left to Illinois one important legacy that had a lasting effect on the state. Birkbeck was the first person to realize that the virgin prairie—the nearly treeless grassland which covered much of Illinois—could be cultivated. Settlers in the state from the south doubted that soil which produced virtually no trees was fertile enough to grow crops. After Birkbeck proved the doubters wrong, pioneers in "the Prairie State," as Illinois is often called, rapidly began to cultivate the prairies. In the early days the prairie exerted a strong impression on people. In *Illinois As It Is,* published in 1857, Fred Gerhard noted that "The most remarkable and striking feature, distinguishing the State of Illinois from the other States of the Union, consists in her extensive prairies." The book takes seven and a half pages to list and briefly describe the state's various prairies. From the wooded areas there gradually extended out into the prairie new farms, spacious stretches of cultivated earth that epitomize the bountiful Midwest, an area where, seemingly, the land—like the region's rivers—rolls on to the far reaches of the earth. Gerhard wrote: "The sight of such a farm on a rolling prairie, partly in grass, partly in corn, partly in grain and garden vegetables, as the sun chases over it the cloudy shadows, and the light breeze waves the distant grove, to a lover of the beautful is perfectly enchanting." And then there was the rhythm of the changing seasons on the prairie, a delight poetically evoked by Eliza W. Farnham in her 1846 book *Life in Prairie Land:*

> Summer had worn away, with its wealth of golden grains and flowers. The luxuriant harvest had disappeared from the farms in

the adjacent country, the tall corn was in its sere and yellow leaf, the late fruits began to ripen, the prairies faded from their rich green, save where here and there a "late burn" showed the tender grass, like an emerald island in the vast brown ocean. Autumn in the prairie land is scarcely excelled for the richness of its charms by any other season.

Alas, such delights no longer enrapture the traveler through Illinois, for virtually the entire prairie has, in the hundred and seventy or so years since Birkbeck first cultivated the virgin soil, been plowed under and planted over with crops. The state's only surviving prairie of any size is eighteen hundred acres preserved at Goose Lake Prairie State Park, southwest of Joliet in northern Illinois (section 8). But it's nice to recall that the great agricultural areas you'll see as you criss-cross "the Prairie State" were once, many moons and harvests ago, that "perfectly enchanting" prairieland broken and farmed for the first time around Albion.

From Albion you can find places of interest in all directions. The northern route out of Albion begins in the next paragraph; the southern itinerary follows. As for the west, seventeen miles away in that direction lies the town of Fairfield. On the way there you'll pass close to the hamlet of Golden Gate near which, it's believed, western lawman and Indian fighter William "Bat" Masterson was born in 1853. Also born near Fairfield (in 1865) on a farm six miles northeast of town was William E. Borah who became a famous U.S. Senator, serving six terms from Idaho. Perhaps growing up in a boisterous family of ten noisy children persuaded Borah to become "the Great Isolationist," the name given to him for his anti-foreign attitude, as outlined in his most famous Senate speech, delivered November 19, 1919, opposing the League of Nations. Fairfield also claims another political connection. A marker on the courthouse lawn recalls that the town was the site of Lincoln's very first formal endorsement for president when, on March 3, 1860, the Wayne County Republican convention "Resolved—that the Hon. Abe Lincoln is the Unanimous choice of the Republicans of Wayne County for the presidential nomination of the National Convention at Chicago." The road north out of Albion takes you via Bone Gap, so named for a cache of animal bones left by Indians in a gap in the forest, to the town of West Salem, which boasts the only Moravian church in Illinois. The first Moravians arrived in the area in 1821. When the early settlers sent back glowing reports to the Moravian community in Salem, North Carolina, additional Moravians trekked out to Illinois and by 1848 more than forty families of the sect lived in the town. The following year, forty-six Moravians arrived from Germany and that complicated matters. Unable to speak or understand each other's language, the American and German groups alternated services in the local church until 1858 when the English-speaking members departed and built a house of worship at the south side of the square. In 1902 the Germans also constructed a sanctuary, an attractive brick structure with slim Gothic-style windows and a large belfry that houses two bells, one brought over from the 1858 church. Off to the east, near St. Francisville, a town by the Indiana border, stands the bridge once used by the famous "Wabash Cannonball," the New York Central train between Chicago and Florida. (The legendary train's praises have been widely sung; for a verse from the renowned song about the "Cannonball," see Chapter IV, section 7.) North of St. Francisville and just inside the Illinois state line, across from Vincennes, Indiana, the Lincoln Trail State Memorial marks the place where the now famous family entered "The Land of Lincoln" in 1830 when emigrating from their Indiana farmstead (see Chapter II, section 4). Heading west from the Memorial on highway 50 you'll arrive at Olney, passing on the way Red Hills State Park where the western-most edge of the first land in Illinois ceded by the Indians (in 1795) to the U.S. government lies. In 1950 the center of the nation's population (now in eastern Missouri: see Chapter V, section 9) was located along highway 130 nine miles north of Olney. Back on November 1, 1858, the Olney *Times* published a front-page banner headline: "For President in 1860, Abraham Lincoln of Illinois," believed to be the first newspaper endorsement in the U.S. of Lincoln's candidacy. These days Olney is known—at least in Illinois; well, perhaps just in Richland County; well, maybe just in Olney itself—for its white squirrels. It seems that sometime in the first decade of the century someone let a pair of albino squirrels loose in town. At one time thousands of the white creatures frolicked in the city, but as they mated with grey squirrels the pure whites grew rather rare. In fact, you'll probably see around town more white squirrels as signs and emblems, such as those that decorate the local police uniforms, than the animals themselves. But such is Olney's somewhat squirrelly claim to fame.

From Olney you may want to swing north to Effingham where the period-piece 1871 County Courthouse remains one of the few in Illinois that hasn't undergone any extensive changes. At Teutopolis, a mile or so east, you can visit an unusual museum that occupies the quarters of a Franciscan monastery established in 1858. After the monks left the grounds in 1968 the monastery was converted into a museum, with many of the thirty-two rooms preserved as they appeared when the brothers occupied them. Books, pictures, furniture, tools and other objects used by the Franciscans in the 1800s recall the retreat's early days. Heading southwest toward Salem you'll pass Kinmundy where Ingram's Log Cabin Village boasts a collection of nineteen original log buildings—twelve authentically furnished—dating from 1818 to 1860. Brought to the site from all over the Midwest, the log buildings form a pieced-together pioneer village that gives the flavor of old Illinois.

In Salem stands the two-story white frame house where three-time presidential candidate William Jennings Bryan was born in 1860. At the house, listed on the National Register, you can see memorabilia from the legal and political careers of "the Great Commoner," as Bryan was called. Items on display include a well-worn leather chair the politician used as Secretary of State in the Wilson administration, a photo of him taken during the famous Scopes's "Monkey Trial" evolution case in Tennessee in which Bryan acted as prosecutor, a life mask, and Bryan's 1893 Illinois law license. The precocious young man began his political involvement at an early age. When his parents were away from Salem attending the 1876 Centennial Exposition at Philadelphia, the sixteen-year-old Bryan made his way to St. Louis where he snuck through a window of the hall housing the Democratic National Convention then in progress. A mere twenty years later Bryan attended a similar gathering, the 1896 Democratic Convention in Chicago, where he delivered his famous "Cross of Gold" speech and was nominated for president, the youngest candidate of a major party in the nation's history. Ten miles east of Salem on the north side of highway 50— which follows the original "trace" that ran between Vincennes and St. Louis—stands the restored Halfway Tavern, located at the midway point between the two cities. The stagecoach stop, built in 1818, the year Illinois became a state, offered meals for man or beast at a cost of twenty-five cents per feed, while lodging or half a pint of whiskey set a traveler back twelve and a half cents; the same quantity of rum sold for twice that price.

At Vandalia, northwest of Salem, stands the handsome 1836 Federal-style capitol building, the third built there. The state capital was moved from Kaskaskia (section 2) to Vandalia in 1819 where it remained until 1839 when Springfield became the center of government. The century-and-a-half old building has seen much history: In 1832 the city of

Chicago received its first village charter there; in March 1837 a twenty-eight-year-old lawyer named Abraham Lincoln entered the roll of attorneys at the Supreme Court, located in the capitol; Lincoln's rival Stephen Douglas supposedly rode a donkey up the stairway to celebrate a Democratic victory; and in 1837, so the story goes, Lincoln, leader of a coterie of tall legislators known as the "Long Nine," jumped from a second-story window to break not his leg but a quorum that would've kept the state capital in Vandalia rather than removing it to Springfield, Abe's town. Next to the old capitol building stands the Madonna of the Trail Monument, one of twelve such markers erected by the Daughters of the American Revolution in each state through which early roads ran (another Trail Madonna is at Lexington, Missouri; Chapter V, section 5). A Kansas City politician named Harry S Truman was scheduled to speak at the 1928 ceremony to dedicate the monument but he couldn't attend. The statue, showing a pioneer mother, babe in arms, striding forward to the west, marks the end of the historic National (or Cumberland) Road that stretched across the country in the early part of the nineteenth century. At the monument linger ghostly memories of the hundreds of Conestoga wagons, the so-called prairie schooners, and canvas-covered carts and just plain walkers that rolled or strode along the long National Road on their way west as the continent opened up. After the capital moved to Springfield, Vandalia settled into the ordinary workaday existence of a small mid-American town, a place Joseph P. Lyford described as a typical heart-of-the-country community in his 1965 study, *The Talk of Vandalia*. Lyford encapsulates much about Midwestern small-town life in his comments on reasons why people choose to stay in Vandalia: "Underlying them all seems to be a desire to be able to know the whole of one's town, to be 'some kind of a somebody' in it, and to be part of a social arrangement where there are certain justified assumptions about how people will deal with each other." If a transient population and new cities typify such far-out (from the heartland) coastal areas as California and Florida and Texas, one of the Midwest's defining characteristics is a sense of community—the desire to be part of a familiar place. Thus is the Midwest justifiably viewed as conservative: the people of the center favor conserving ties to place, people and past.

Continuing west on highway 40 from Vandalia you'll arrive at Greenville, a pleasant tree-shaded college town and county seat. A gallery in the 1855 Almira House at Greenville College contains sculpture and archives of Richard W. Bock, a "Prairie School"-style artist associated with Frank Lloyd Wright, some of whose works are also on display. Farther west you'll reach Highland, a trim little town settled in the 1830s by emigrants from Switzerland, who named the village Helvetia. Highland is believed to be the nation's oldest and largest Swiss community. Reminders of the town's heritage abound: colorful Swiss canton shields on the buildings, many in the Swiss chalet style; a memorial and chapel to members of the John Suppiger family, drowned off the coast of England when returning to Switzerland for a visit in 1875; a granite memorial erected in 1909 by the Swiss Society of America to poet Heinrich Bosshard, who lived in Highland from 1851 to 1877 and whose poem *Sempacher Lied* was in part incorporated into the Swiss national anthem. The homestead of local resident Louis Latzer, founder of the Pet Milk Company, is now a museum, while another commercial connection in Highland is the Wicks Organ Company, founded in 1906, where you can see custom-built pipe organs being crafted.

From Highland you might want to swing north for twenty-nine miles to Mt. Olive, an old coal mining town. On the northwest side of the city lies the Union Miners Cemetery where Mary Harris, an Irish-born labor activist better known as "Mother" Jones, reposes. Until her husband

and four children died in 1867, Mrs. Jones was a homemaker and a dressmaker. After losing her family she became a labor leader, touring the country clad in her trademark black bonnet to organize strikes, protests and demonstrations by mine workers. "Mother" Jones expressed a desire to be buried at Mt. Olive's Miners Cemetery; so when she finally died in 1930 at age one hundred the old lady was laid to rest there. A granite monument near the grave memorializes "Mother" Jones and "the martyrs of the Virden [a mining town north of Mt. Olive] riot of 1898."

Such is the tour out of Albion (where this section began) off to the northwest of that town. Let's return now back across the state from Mt. Olive to the starting point of Albion to consider another possible itinerary, this one starting off to the southwest. The first stop on that route is Carmi, south and slightly to the west of Albion. At Carmi you'll find two historic structures, both housing museums and both listed on the National Register. The 1828 Ratcliff Inn—built by James Ratcliff, Carmi's first postmaster and probate judge—lodged many of the early travelers in the area, among them Abraham Lincoln who stayed at the inn in 1840 when he came to town to campaign for William Henry Harrison. Nearby stands the four-room Robinson-Stewart House Museum, installed in the residence of U.S. Senator John M. Robinson. After Robinson purchased the 1814 log structure in 1835 he applied clapboard siding and added the wings. Later his granddaughter, Mary Jane Stewart, lived in the house, which had served as the White County courthouse before Robinson acquired the property and which now is the county historical museum. Due west of Carmi lies McLeansboro, with the McCoy Memorial Library, an 1880 structure utilizing nine types of wood. Fireplaces with wooden mantels imported from around the world warm the interior, which houses on the upper level a collection of antiques from the McLeansboro area. Down the street stands the Peoples National Bank, an 1880-vintage building with an exterior preserved as it was a century ago. From McLeansboro highway 142 takes you northwest to Mt. Vernon, whose Times Square at the intersection of Broadway and Forty Second Street might make you feel at home, or homesick, if you're from New York City. Thanks to the generosity of local businessman John Mitchell and his wife Eleanor, Mt. Vernon boasts the Cedarhurst Cultural Center, an eight-acre estate with nature trails, an art center and an art museum with works by late nineteenth- and early twentieth-century American painters such as George Bellows, Mary Cassatt, John Singer Sargent and Andrew Wyeth. Unfortunately, however, that collection is often removed to accommodate traveling exhibits, so it's best to call ahead to see if the permanent items are on display. Over the winter Cedarhurst offers concerts and in mid-September the Cedarhurst Crafts Fair, featuring more than a hundred craftspeople from around the country, takes place on the grounds. In town stands the Appellate Courthouse where the southern division of the Illinois Supreme Court once convened. A graceful outdoor double stairway made of iron leads to the second floor of the attractive 1857 building, where in 1859 Lincoln won a famous tax case for the Illinois Central Railroad. In 1888 the courthouse served as a hospital under the direction of Clara Barton, founder of the American Red Cross, after a devastating tornado hit Mt. Vernon.

About halfway between Mt. Vernon and St. Louis lies the quiet little town of Okawville which boasts an attraction unique in Illinois, the state's only commercially operated mineral spring spa. The Original Mineral Springs Hotel and Bath House, built in 1892, still offers mineral water baths in a true nineteenth-century setting. With a wooden veranda bordering the two-story white frame hotel and, inside, old furniture and fixtures, the "Original" (listed on the National Register in 1978) seems little changed from the 1890s.

Okawville first became a spa town in 1867 after a St. Louis laboratory analyzed the water and found it contained enough minerals to give it medicinal qualities. You can stay at the venerable hotel—the rooms are rated as Good, Better, Best and Deluxe—even if you don't use the mineral water baths. A few blocks from the spa stands the 1904 Schlosser family house, also listed on the National Register. Now a museum, the house has been preserved as a turn-of-the-century period piece crammed with old furniture and memorabilia. Most interesting are the two former businesses on the property, a laundry and a harness shop, both left exactly as they appeared in the old days. In the laundry remain venerable celluloid collars, hand-cranked wooden washing machines (Mrs. Schlosser paid local lads ten cents a day to turn the cranks) and old receipt forms and stationary. The harness shop looks as if Frank Schlosser had just stepped away for a few minutes (he died in 1941); his chewing tobacco awaits him, and all the tools, materials and equipment remain in place. Old-time items on display there include tins of shoe grease, "makes work shoes manure proof," and a horse shawl with tassels that jiggle to keep flies away.

At Mascoutah, fourteen miles west of Okawville, a giant (forty by forty-six feet) mural on the old mill wall downtown depicts the history of the town and the Midwest, while in Shreve Park stands a restored L and N railroad station. Between 1970 and 1980 the population center of the U.S. was on highway 177 near Mascoutah (the center now lies near De Soto, Missouri: see Chapter V, section 9). Belleville, farther to the west, boasts a National Register district with more than seven hundred houses, many dating from the 1830s. Old-fashioned cast-iron street lamps embellish part of the district. The buildings in the historic area include the 1830 Emma Kunz house, considered the earliest brick Greek Revival-style residence in the state, and the 1866 Victorian-style mansion that houses the St. Clair County Historical Society Museum.

From Belleville it's only a short drive up to Lebanon, home of McKendree College, which occupies a compact leafy campus. Back when McKendree was founded in 1828 up to two-thirds of the tuition—eight dollars for five months—could be paid with pigs, a milk cow or foodstuffs. No longer are the fees chicken feed or payable by green beans rather than greenbacks, but back in the pioneer days that sort of arrangement wasn't unusual, for money then assumed all sorts of forms. The Indian leader Pontiac once issued birchbark vouchers bearing a painting of an otter and specifying an amount payable in pelts—perhaps the first checks used in North America. One Mt. Vernon, Illinois, pioneer paid his taxes with a wagonload of wolf skins, and on another occasion tendered a wolf skin to pay for a purchase at a store, whereupon the proprietor gave him an opossum skin for change. William Blane, an Englishman who visited Illinois in 1822, noted that raccoon skins were worth about twenty cents each, adding he was "much amused" by the tale that "some Yankees forged these notes, by sewing a raccoon's tail to a cat's skin, and thus destroyed the currency." Near downtown Lebanon stands an 1830 inn called the Mermaid House, which hosted various famous visitors back in the nineteenth century. One renowned guest at the Mermaid—so named by retired sea captain Lyman Adams, a relative of early patriots John and Samuel Adams, after the mermaids he'd claimed to have seen at sea—was Abraham Lincoln. What "Washington slept here" is to the east, "Lincoln slept . . . or supped . . . or spoke . . . or joked here" is to Illinois, for virtually no corner of the state lacks its Lincoln lore. The story is told that Lincoln was still eating breakfast at the Mermaid one morning when the stagecoach prepared to depart. Unperturbed, Lincoln remained at the table to finish his meal, commenting that the coach would soon return. After the vehicle left, the Mermaid's owner suddenly realized the inn's silver spoons had disappeared so he sent the law after the stage to recover the missing valuables. Officers forced the coach to return, whereupon Lincoln nonchalantly took the missing silver from beneath the table, then boarded the conveyance for his trip. Another famous visitor, Charles Dickens, spent the night of April 12, 1842, at Mermaid House. The famous English author had arrived in St. Louis on the steamboat *Fulton* the day before, after his visit to Cairo (see section 3). The morning of the twelfth the novelist traveled from St. Louis to the so-called Looking Glass Prairie, east of Lebanon, via Belleville, "a small collection of wooden houses, huddled together in the very heart of the bush and swamp," the writer recalled in his *American Notes*. "Returning to Lebanon that night," Dickens recounted, "we lay at the little inn at which we had halted in the afternoon." Dickens appreciated the Mermaid House: "In point of cleanliness and comfort," he wrote, "it would have suffered by no comparison with any village ale house, of a homely [homey] kind, in England."

Thus did Charles Dickens, the famous English writer, visit the prairie where his fellow countrymen Birkbeck and Flower a quarter of a century before had put down their roots at the English Settlement at Albion across the state. For the English pioneers, however, Albion was not just a homey place like Dickens found at the Mermaid but home itself. As Birkbeck wrote on Christmas day 1817 in a letter to England, published in his *Letters from Illinois:*

What *is* [a] country? the soil? Of this [in England] I was only an occupant. The government? I abhorred its deeds and its principles. The church? I did not believe in its doctrines, and had no reverence for the clergy. The army? No. The law? We have the same law here, with some omissions and some improvements. The people? Yes, but not the fund-holders, nor the soi-disant [so-called] House of Commons. [N]ot the consumers, nor the creators of taxes. My family and my friends [of which] I hope to have more, and then this will be my country.

So Birkbeck described the mentality underlying his trans-mutation from being an Old Worlder to that new kind of creature—an American. Of such transformations was a good part of the Middle West made.

5. Land of Lincoln:

Springfield
New Salem
Edgar Lee Masters's Petersburg
Clayville Rural Center at Pleasant Plains
Decatur
Bryant's Lincoln–Douglas Cottage at Bement
Mt. Pulaski Courthouse
Lincoln's Lincoln
Bloomington
Champaign
Urbana
Amish in Arcola and Arthur
Moore Home and Lincoln Log Cabin Park Near Charleston
Paris
Lincoln Lodged at Danville
Rossville
Lincoln's "Private Eye" Pinkerton at Onarga

One day in his home town of Springfield, Abe Lincoln mounted a platform to deliver an impromptu speech. When the stand began to give way, Lincoln exclaimed, "This must be a Democratic platform to threaten to go to pieces if a crowd tries to stand on it!" That platform is perhaps the only thing in Illinois Lincoln touched that has not been conserved—consecrated even—and labeled as having been used by the great man. All through central Illinois, where Lincoln lived for thirty-one years, are dozens of memorials, mementos, monuments and museums devoted to "the tall man [who] casts a long shadow," as A. J. Liebling wrote in a 1950 *New Yorker* article about Springfield. Arriving in Illinois from their Indiana farm (see Chapter II, section 4) in 1830, the Lincoln family settled on a site near Decatur. The following year young Abe moved to New Salem and in 1837 he settled in Springfield. Riding the Eighth Judicial Circuit, Lincoln practiced law at courthouses in Mt. Pulaski, Postville and other towns. Meanwhile, his father and stepmother settled on a farm near Charleston. All those places and more lie on the Illinois portion of the Lincoln Heritage Trail, a medallion-marked route established in 1963 to trace the great man's history (the Trail also includes sites in Kentucky and Indiana).

The best place to start a visit to the land of Lincoln—that area of central Illinois rich with Lincoln legends, lore and locations—is Springfield, where "Honest Abe" lived and lawyered from 1837 until February 11, 1861, when he left for Washington and the White House. Thanks both to Lincoln's long presence in the place and to its serving as Illinois's capital for, by now, a century and a half, Springfield, a town of a hundred thousand residents, offers more attractions than most cities of its size. Most of the sights cluster near the center of town within walking distance of one another. The centerpiece of the Lincoln presence in Springfield is the four-square-block Lincoln Home National Historic Site, visited by more than five hundred thousand people a year. A sign near the entrance to the area proclaims "Another World" and, indeed, you'll find in the enclave's tree-shaded streets lined with twelve old houses once occupied by Lincoln's neighbors, a corner of modern-day Springfield that seems like a time warp, so imbued with a nineteenth-century atmosphere is the site. Exhibits and information available at the Visitor Center will introduce you to the neighborhood where Lincoln purchased his house, the only residence he ever owned, in 1844 for fifteen hundred dollars. Abe and Mary Todd Lincoln's three younger sons were born there (Robert, the oldest, arrived earlier), and there the Lincolns lived for seventeen years. After the president's assassination in 1865 the family continued to own the house and rented it out until 1887 when Robert Todd Lincoln gave the residence to the state of Illinois. Lincoln's attachment to his hometown is evident in the moving farewell remarks the president-elect delivered upon his departure to Washington that rain-swept February morning in 1861 at the Great Western Depot a few blocks from the house. "My friends, no one not in my situation can appreciate my feeling of sadness at this parting. To this place, and the kindness of these people, I owe every thing. Here I have lived a quarter of a century and have passed from a young to an old man. Here my children have been born and one is buried. I now leave, not knowing when, or whether ever, I may return. . . . I hope in your prayers you will commend me, I bid you an affectionate farewell."

From the restored depot, which contains exhibits on Lincoln's departure from Springfield and his own house to Washington and the White House, you can make your way on foot toward the main square—perhaps via First Presbyterian Church, at Seventh and Capitol, where the Lincoln family pew is marked—to the Old State Capitol, an impeccably restored structure furnished with period pieces from the Lincoln era. On the ground floor is displayed one of the five surviving copies of the Gettysburg Address in the president's own handwriting, while upstairs on the second floor you can

see Representative Hall, which looks just as it did when
Lincoln delivered there in June 1858 his famous "A house
divided against itself cannot stand" speech and when, seven
years later, his body lay in state May 3–4, 1865, in the
chamber. Other Lincoln attractions adorn the square. At one
corner a sign with large black letters on white proclaims
"Lincoln-Herndon law offices." The three-story 1840 brick
building contains exhibits, old-time furniture and accoutre-
ments from the days when Lincoln practiced there (1843 to
1852), as well as the room which, between 1840 and 1855,
housed Illinois's only Federal court. Another attraction hides
within the hamburgery confines of the McDonald's eatery in
the middle of the block, where you'll find two over-sized
offerings—Big Macs and "the Long Nine" museum. Formerly located in nearby Athens, Ilinois, the museum features
seven dioramas portraying scenes from Lincoln's life, a life
mask of "Honest Abe" and pictures of the "Long Nine," nine
legislators (one of them Lincoln) with a combined height of
fifty-four feet who in 1837 successfully schemed to move the
state capital from Vandalia to Springfield. At another commercial establishment, the Marine Bank on the east side of
the square, you'll find displayed in the lobby the original
ledger book that records Abe Lincoln's account with the
institution. From March 1, 1853, when the lawyer deposited
three hundred and ten dollars to open an account, until the
day of his death, Lincoln banked at the Marine, Illinois's
oldest bank. The large ledger lies open to the pages recording
the famous customer's transactions from December 1860 to
August 1861, during which period plain old Mr. Abe Lincoln
became President Abraham Lincoln. Before leaving the
square it's worth descending to the quarters beneath the Old
State Capitol where the Illinois State Historical Library
houses one of the country's largest collections of Lincolnia—
some ten thousand manuscripts, books and documents. The
library's Lincoln Room contains family memorabilia, photos

and other remembrances of Springfield's most famous citizen.

From the square it's only a short walk south down Seventh Street to the Oliver P. Parks Telephone Museum, featuring one hundred and seventeen antique phones and other related items, and then over to Fifth to the antique-filled Governor's Mansion, a huge Georgian-style structure (open for tours). Just next door stands the 1846 house where poet Vachel Lindsay lived. In the yard of the two-and-a-half-story, blue-shuttered white frame house, listed on the National Register, stands a sign describing Lindsay as "Author of children's fantasies and animal poems. Designer of symbolic censers, flowers, trees and butterflies. Idealist stressing the importance of nature and beauty." Lindsay's *Art of the Moving Picture*, published in 1815, was one of the first serious commentaries on the then-new medium of movies. Born in the house in 1879, Lindsay grew up there and after long walking tours across the nation as a wandering minstrel, a vagabond versifier who paid his way by selling his poems, the writer in 1929 brought his own family to live in the home, where in 1931 he died of a self-administered overdose of Lysol. The house, crammed with original furnishings, artworks, writings and objects, is preserved as a memorial to Lindsay, who in his famous poem "Abraham Lincoln Walks at Midnight" tells of how "in our little town [Springfield]/A mourning figure walks, and will not rest. . . .It breaks his heart that kings must murder still,/That all his hours of travail here for men/Seem yet in vain." Another renowned Springfield residence, the Frank Lloyd Wright-designed Dana-Thomas House, occupies the corner of Fourth and Lawrence a few blocks away. Completed in 1905, the angular low-slung residence was one of the famous architect's first major "Prairie Style" homes. The interior contains dozens of Wright-designed features, including furniture, light fixtures, glass ornaments and windows. Susan Lawrence Dana, daughter of a

wealthy banker and silver-mine owner, built the sixteen-
room showplace only for herself, for by the time she moved
into the mansion Mrs. Dana's parents, two sons and two
husbands had died and a third spouse she'd divorced. Left
alone, Mrs. Dana dabbled in spiritualism, entertained and
traveled the world, collecting boxloads of objects, mementos
which for the most part gathered not praise but only dust, for
she left many of them untouched in their shipping cartons.
After Mrs. Dana was put into an institution in 1943 her
conservator opened safe deposit boxes belonging to the
dowager in five cities, finding in the containers a few stale
mining claims and jars of feathers from the old lady's favorite
parrot. Mrs. Dana died three years later at the age of eighty-
four.

A few blocks east of the Dana-Thomas House stands the
Grand Army of the Republic Memorial Museum featuring
displays relating to the Civil War; while to the west, near the
state capitol, is the Daughters of Union Veterans of the Civil
War National Headquarters and Museum, which also preserves books, documents and memorabilia from the war
between the states. Next to the capitol, whose rather thin, tall
superstructure and dome make the building seem top heavy,
is the Illinois State Museum with an eclectic range of exhibits
on natural history, anthropology, geology, art and other subjects. More art embellishes historic old Edwards Place, an
Italianate-style mansion listed on the National Register, built
in 1833 by a Springfield doctor. In 1843 Benjamin S. Edwards, the Yale-educated son of Ninian Edwards, third governor of Illinois and one of the state's first two U.S. Senators,
acquired the property where he and his wife lived for more
than sixty years. Among their friends were Abraham and
Mary Todd Lincoln, whom the Edwards often entertained at
the house, where today the Springfield Art Association maintains collections of paintings, ladies' fans, antique toys and
objects acquired around the world by Thomas Condell, the

Edwards's grandson. From Edwards Place it's only a short drive north to the Lincoln tomb in Oak Ridge Cemetery where the bodies of the president, his wife and three of their sons repose (the eldest, Robert Todd Lincoln, who served as Secretary of War and whose Chicago law firm—founded in 1872—survived until 1988, lies in Arlington National Cemetery just outside Washington). Every Tuesday at 7 p.m. in June, July and August a troupe of the Illinois Volunteer Infantry dressed in Civil War uniforms and armed with muskets performs a retreat ceremony at the tomb.

The Oak Ridge mausoleum represents Lincoln's end, his final resting place in the central Illinois land he called home. His beginnings in that region can be vividly visualized at the village of New Salem, a reconstruction of the hamlet where Lincoln settled in 1831. He lived in New Salem, twenty miles northwest of Springfield, until 1837, working there as a store clerk, postmaster and surveyor. After 1839, when the county seat moved from New Salem to Petersburg, two miles away, the settlement declined. Only in the 1930s was the village revived, and now twenty-two reproduced buildings—plus one original structure, the Onstot Cooper Shop—recall the Lincoln era. Among the old log buildings are houses, a "blab" schoolhouse (so-called because the students studied by blabbing their lessons out loud), general stores where young Abe worked, a blacksmith shop, a saw and grist mill and the tavern (inn) of James Rutledge, whose daughter Ann supposedly attracted Lincoln. From mid-June to mid-August three different plays performed on alternate evenings dramatize Lincoln's life, while an excursion on the steamer *Talisman*, a reproduction of the original craft Lincoln once piloted down the Sangamon River, recalls the old days of steamboat travel. "Travel in elegance and comfort without fear of Indian attack or abuse from frontier ruffians," boasts the ship's brochure, definitely truth-in-advertising, as Indian attacks are said to occur infrequently in the area these days.

At Oakland Cemetery in nearby Petersburg, so named in 1832 after New Salem resident Peter Lukins, who won that right in a card game, lies buried Ann Rutledge, whose epitaph comes from the poem about her in *Spoon River Anthology*, the famous book of verses by Edgar Lee Masters telling of lives the region's dead once lived. Masters himself reposes near the grave of Lincoln's first love. A block from courthouse square in Petersburg stands a white frame house where the Masters family lived in the 1870s before moving some forty miles north to Lewistown, center of the Spoon River country (described in the next section). Near the village of Pleasant Plains, south of New Salem and Petersburg and twelve miles west of Springfield, you'll find another early nineteenth-century settlement, the Clayville Rural Life Center, its centerpiece an 1820s-vintage two-story brick inn that served as a stagecoach hotel a century and a half ago. In addition to the inn, other buildings at the Center house exhibits and demonstrations of various old-time trades and crafts. Almost every weekend over the summer Clayville hosts special shows, sales or other events.

After visiting the Lincoln-land attractions west of Springfield you can head to points east of the capital where you'll find more Lincolnia. On the way to Decatur you'll pass Illiopolis, at the very center of the state, where the funky old (1854) six-room Illiopolis Hotel, now restored, offers overnight accommodations with an atmosphere that will take you back to the Lincoln era. The Lincolns first settled in this area at a site a few miles farther east marked by the Lincoln Trail Homestead State Memorial. There young Abe lived with his family when they arrived from Indiana in March 1830. The young man helped build their cabin (a replica stands at the Memorial) and he earned extra money by splitting fence rails for local farmers, a skill that later earned him the rustic nickname "the Railsplitter," first given to him in nearby Decatur at the May 1860 state Republican convention which nominated Lincoln for the presidency. In Decatur's Lincoln Square stands a statue of a pre-political, pre-presidential Lincoln, a barefoot and beardless young fellow. Fresh-faced young Lincoln lacked the craggy, haggard look which later typified him. In an 1860 speech Richard Yates, governor of Illinois during the Civil War, observed: "We know he does not look very handsome, and some of the papers say he is positively ugly. Well, if all the ugly men in the United States vote for him, he will surely be elected." And, indeed, the ugly man constituency triumphed. Once accused of being two-faced by his political rival Stephen Douglas, Lincoln replied, "I leave it to my audience. If I had another face to wear, do you think I would wear this one?" In Decatur, once home of the Staley Stars football team that in 1922 moved north to become the Chicago Bears, stand two nineteenth-century show houses, the 1876 red brick Victorian James Milliken Homestead and the Italian style Oglesby Mansion, residence of U.S. Senator and three-time Illinois governor Richard J. Oglesby. In addition, an architecturally rich eighty-acre tract in the city comprises the Decatur Historic District, with buildings from the Victorian era to Frank Lloyd Wright. Before heading north out of Decatur you might want to drive a few miles east over to Bement to see the Bryant Cottage, an 1856 house owned by town banker Francis E. Bryant, cousin of poet William Cullen Bryant. In July 1858 Senator and Mrs. Stephen Douglas lodged at the cottage prior to a speech Douglas was scheduled to deliver in nearby Monticello. On the way there the Douglases and Bryant encountered a covered wagon out of which suddenly jumped none other than Abe Lincoln, who asked Douglas where they could meet to arrange a series of debates. Bryant offered his cottage, and the evening of July 29, 1858, the two politicians met for two hours in the parlor there. You'll see at the historic house the marble-top table on which Douglas wrote a note accepting Lincoln's challenge to debate as well as the chair where Lincoln sat, still draped with crepe and a flag Bryant put there after the assassination. Just north of Bement lies Robert Allerton Park, with a sculpture garden and a thousand bird- and plant-crammed acres, designated a National Natural Landmark, while at nearby Monticello the Monticello and Sangamon Valley Railroad Museum features steam train excursions.

The town of Lincoln, thirty-four miles northwest of Decatur, was the first community in the nation to be named for the great man, who showed up there on August 27, 1853, to christen the new town with the juice of a watermelon. On the way to Lincoln you'll pass the lovely Greek Revival-style Mt. Pulaski courthouse, a National Historic Landmark, restored to its appearance as it was when Lincoln argued cases there. He tried a total of some three thousand during his career as he traveled the Eighth Judicial Circuit. In Lincoln stands the venue of another old Eighth Circuit stop the lawyer frequented—the Postville courthouse, replica of the original 1841 structure (now at Greenfield Village near Detroit) where the famous circuit-riding attorney received the nickname "Honest Abe" for his refusal to continue to defend a client he'd determined was guilty. Lincoln brims with Lincoln-related sights. On the campus of Lincoln College, whose University Hall is listed on the National Register, stands a statue of a youthful Lincoln portrayed as a student, while the college library houses a Lincoln Museum, with a large collection of memorabilia and books, as well as the Museum of Presidents, featuring a display of documents with the signatures of every U.S. chief executive. At the old Rustic Tavern in Lincoln a group of ne'er-do-wells hatched a plot to rob the late president's grave in Springfield and ransom the body, and not far away from the pub stands a plaque marking the spot where in 1848 Stephen Douglas addressed a rally assembled in a circus tent as Lincoln stood in the rear to monitor his opponent's speech.

If you're not by now Lincolned out you can stop at Clinton, on the way north to Bloomington, to see the Homestead, a restored Victorian mansion, also listed on the National Register, where Lincoln's law partner C. H. Moore once lived, and the Lincoln statue on courthouse square commemorating his comment addressed to Stephen Douglas in Clinton in 1848: "You can fool some of the people all of the time, and all of the people some of the time, but you can't fool all the people all of the time." In nearby Bloomington stands another Lincoln-associated house, Clover Lawn, owned by David Davis, whom Lincoln appointed to the U.S. Supreme Court and who later served as the assassinated president's executor. The 1843 Federal-style Miller-Davis Museum downtown houses the law offices used by Lincoln in Bloomington from 1845 to 1855. Lincoln won the presidency two times, while his fellow Illinoisian Adlai Stevenson II twice lost the great race, so the double loser—buried in Bloomington's Evergreen Cemetery along with his grandfather Adlai Stevenson I, a Lincoln contemporary and vicepresident under Cleveland—merits only a limited remembrance of his political career, the Stevenson Memorial Room at Illinois State University in Normal, adjacent to Bloomington. (Adlai I's house still stands at 901 North McLean in Bloomington.) The university also boasts what is said to be the world's largest college residence hall, twentyeight-story Watterson Towers, and four or five other museums or displays including those on agriculture, minerals, history and the Eyestone One Room School, preserved as it was in 1899, complete with old-fashioned desks, a woodburning stove and a dunce stool.

At Bloomington-Normal's hyphenated rival Champaign-Urbana, fifty miles southeast via Mahomet—where Lake of the Woods Park includes a covered bridge and a one-twentieth-scale replica of San Francisco's Golden Gate Bridge, while the nearby Early American Museum bursts with some three thousand items of old-time Americana—is the University of Illinois. This is one of those vast Big Ten or Big Seven state universities common in the middle part of the country, huge education factories that take small-town and farm-green youngsters and process them into—well, at least football fans, and Tri Delts and Phi Delts and, hopefully, Phi Beta Kappas. Although located in Champaign-Urbana, the school has a flavor less champagne than beer and a tone more downstate than urban or urbane. In his *Illinois, A Bicentennial History* Richard J. Jensen called the institution "a middle-class counterweight to the elite University of Chicago." But the campus does include a highbrow place or two, one of them the Krannert Art Museum, supposedly second among Illinois museums only to Chicago's Art Institute in size and value of the collection. The university also operates the World Heritage Museum, with displays ranging from prehistoric and ancient cultures to the present, while tucked away in a second-floor room of the Handing Band Building is a museum devoted to bandmaster John Phillip Sousa.

About thirty miles south of Champaign-Urbana you'll reach the Illinois Amish country. Scattered around the landscape between the towns of Arcola and Arthur are any number of Amish farms, maintained without the benefits of electricity or engine-powered vehicles. The farmhouses lack telephones and the only decorations allowed are the patterns on a family's china and dishes. The Amish, who arrived in the area from Pennsylvania after the Civil War, travel by old-fashioned carriages, evidenced by signs at village parking places advising "Horsedrawn Vehicles Only." Harness stores, blacksmith shops and retail establishments offering Amish crafts and food dot the countryside. At Arthur, where a sign proclaims "You're a stranger only once," you'll find an Amish cheese factory, the Arthur Country Inn, a farmers' market and black-garbed Amish families coming and going in their sleek black buggies. By prior reservation, parties of ten or more can eat in an Arthur Amish home, feasting on food prepared by the owner and other Amish women. At Sullivan, out of the Amish area but not far southwest of Arthur, the Little Theater on the Square, central Illinois's only professional stage, offers shows throughout the summer, while at Gays to the south stands a two-story outhouse mentioned in Ripley's "Believe It or Not." Back in the Amish country, Rockome Gardens, five miles west of Arcola, includes Old Bagdad Town, a re-created frontier village, a typical Amish home and dozens of rather curious fences, figures and other objects fashioned from rocks cemented together. The Family Style Restaurant there serves such Amish specialties as apple butter, noodles and shoo fly pie—this is called Illinois Dutch cooking—as does the Dutch Kitchen in nearby Arcola, where you'll also find the old-fashioned Rockome Store, as well as craft and antique shops.

Lest you imagine that you've now freed yourself from Lincoln land, your "emancipation proclamation" is not yet ready. Still more monuments to the famous Illinoisian exist near Charleston, southeast of Arcola. There's no getting away from Lincoln's long shadow, for memories of him haunt virtually all corners of central Illinois. After a miserably cold first winter on their small farm (now Lincoln Trail Homestead State Park) near Decatur, the Lincoln family started back to Indiana in the spring of 1831. On the way they stopped in Coles County and decided to give Illinois another chance. The family lived on three farms in the county before purchasing in 1840 the Goosenest Prairie Farm, now the Lincoln Log Cabin State Historic Site. This is the last place where Lincoln's father, Thomas, and his stepmother, Sarah Bush Lincoln, lived. Costumed guides relate the history of the eighty-six-acre site, which includes the reconstructed Lincoln cabin and an 1840s-era farmstead. At Shiloh Cemetery, a short distance west of the farm, lie Thomas and Sarah Lincoln. After her husband died in 1851, Sarah moved to a nearby residence, the Moore House, where she lived with her daughter until her own death in 1869. A few days before leaving Springfield for Washington in 1861 the president-elect visited his stepmother at the Moore house and, so dramatized Carl Sandburg in his Lincoln biography, they "put their arms around each other and listened to each other's heartbeats." Together they visited his father's and her husband's grave. Then Lincoln went off to Washington—and his destiny. Sarah was living in the Moore house when word came in 1865 of the president's assassination. In Charleston you'll find the venerable Coles County courthouse and a number of spacious old houses lining Sixth and Seventh Streets between the courthouse and Eastern Illinois University on the south side of town. During the fourth Lincoln-Douglas debate in September 1858 at the old county fairgrounds in the eastern part of Charleston, Douglas accused Lincoln of tailoring his views on slavery according to the locale. His opponent, Douglas charged, was "jet black in the North, a decent mulatto in the center, and almost white in the South."

Southeast of Charleston lies the little town of Marshall, setting for Indiana writer Booth Tarkington's *Penrod*. Another renowned writer—James Jones, author of *From Here to Eternity*—lived as a boy in Marshall, where Illinois's oldest band performs on the county courthouse lawn Friday evenings during the summer. On the way north to Danville you'll pass through Paris, an attractive little town with lovely old homes and a handsome courthouse listed on the National Register. Farther north, seven miles west of Danville, Kickapoo State Park occupies nearly seventeen hundred acres resurrected from a former strip mine on the site. Danville treasures its Lincoln lore and history: "We knew Abe *before* they called him Mr. President," boasts one local brochure. Indeed, Lincoln often visited the town, where one of his law partners, Ward Hill Lamon, lived. Lamon, whom Lincoln allegedly trusted "more than any other man," moved to

Washington and acted as the president's confidant and bodyguard during the Civil War. The 1850 Lamon house, built by a cousin of Lincoln's friend, stands in Lincoln Park and is said to be Danville's oldest frame residence. At the Reason Hooten house (207 Buchanan Street) occurred the only known instance of Lincoln consuming alcohol. While visiting there on one occasion Lincoln sampled a selection of homemade wines. He took a sip of each type, then facetiously proclaimed, "Fellers, I'm getting drunk" and there began and ended the Springfield attorney's imbibing of spirits. The Charles Addams-like Victorian-style residence that used to stand at 418 North Vermilion was home for half a century to Joseph G. Cannon, longtime U.S. Representative and from 1901 to 1911 Speaker of the House. First elected to Congress in 1873, Cannon served with a few interruptions until 1923. Although his career extends into modern times, Cannon started early enough to have met Lincoln, whom he first saw at the 1860 state Republican convention in Decatur. Cannon, then practicing law, encountered Lincoln at the post office. When someone in the crowd there expressed surprise at seeing Lincoln at the convention, the great man replied, "I'm too much of a candidate to be here, and not enough of one to stay away." The Vermilion County Museum includes an "Uncle Joe" Cannon room, with the Speaker's oversized desk, beaver hat, gavel and other personal effects on display. Also at the museum, installed in the 1855 house that belonged to William Fithian, is the bedroom used by Lincoln when he visited the house and the iron balcony from which he addressed a crowd assembled below on September 21, 1858. An herb garden at the house recalls the medications Dr. Fithian used to concoct for his patients from the plants.

Twenty miles north of Danville you'll come to Rossville, a small town crammed with antique and curio shops. More than thirty stores offer a wide variety of bric-a-brac, doodads, gizmos and other such miscellany. Aunt Jody's Christmas Bank, installed in the original First National Bank building, contains an extensive collection of Christmas ornaments from around the world. Three miles south of the town, formerly known as Henpeck, stands the simple but attractive red brick Mann's Chapel, one of central Illinois's oldest churches (1857). About forty miles northwest of Rossville lies Onarga, where the ruin of a one-time famous house known as The Larches recalls the colorful career of Allan Pinkerton, the "Private Eye" who became one of the most renowned detectives in American history. Born in Glasgow, Scotland, Pinkerton moved to West Dundee, Illinois, in 1843. After he discovered a gang of counterfeiters in the area, the authorities appointed Pinkerton deputy sheriff and later, in 1850, he became Chicago's first sheriff. Pinkerton subsequently formed the country's first private detective agency. After the Civil War he acquired a two-hundred-and-fifty-four-acre farm near Onarga, building there in 1873 The Larches, which he used not to live in but for entertaining, a function rather vividly evoked by the name the locals gave the place: "Whoopee house." Pinkerton meticulously maintained the lavish estate; visitors who drove their horses faster than a walk received five-dollar fines for stirring up dust that might fall on the flowers. After "The Eye," as Pinkerton became known, died in 1884 the estate fell into disrepair. There being no escape from the long shadow cast by Lincoln in Illinois, even Pinkerton had a connection with the great man. The president commissioned him to organize the U.S. Secret Service, while in 1861 Pinkerton, as Lincoln's personal bodyguard, arranged for the president secretly to change trains to thwart a feared assassination attempt against the chief executive in Baltimore. But, as the world knows, four years later an assassination attempt did succeed, and so Lincoln returned to his beloved Illinois not in triumph but in death and now in his tomb in his hometown of Springfield he belongs to the ages.

6. Spoon River Country and Beyond:

The Towns of Jacksonville, Beardstown, Rushville and
Macomb
Ancient Indians at Dickson Mounds
Edgar Lee Masters's Spoon River
Monmouth
Carl Sandburg and Lincoln-Douglas at Galesburg
The Swedish Settlement at Bishop Hill
Elmwood: Sculptor Lorado Taft's Town
Peoria and Pekin
Metamora Courthouse
Another Illinois President, at Eureka College

A few years after Jacksonville was founded in 1825 Elizabeth
Duncan arrived in the western Illinois town, thirty-four miles
west of Springfield, for the first time. Mrs. Duncan had met
her husband, Joseph, Illinois's sole Representative in Congress, at a dinner President John Quincy Adams hosted in
Washington. When the Duncans arrived in Jacksonville after
their wedding in the spring of 1828 Mrs. Duncan noted in the
diary she kept for many years how "as I was standing on the
doorsteps, an old man said to me: 'Sis, what brought you to
this rough country?' I replied: 'I followed my husband.'"
This surprised the old fellow, who supposed Mrs. Duncan,
fourteen years younger than her spouse, was his daughter.
"Men change their place of abode from ambition and interest,
women from affection," opined the old man. Such was Elizabeth Duncan's introduction to Jacksonville, where she settled
in the town's first frame home in a wooded area the Duncans
called Elm Grove. The "rough country" settlement of Jacksonville back then still belonged to the frontier: "the wild-

cats and the wolves prowled through the woods," she wrote. "Indians were frequent visitors. . . . The country was wild." But civilization gradually arrived. Joseph Duncan was elected governor of Illinois in 1834 and soon such political notables as Martin Van Buren, Abraham Lincoln and Stephen Douglas, who set up a law office in Jacksonville in 1834, came to call at Elm Grove. "In June 1837 we entertained Daniel Webster, his wife and niece," Elizabeth Duncan wrote in her diary. "Mr. Duncan gave him a barbecue down in the grove—northwest of the house; roasted a steer whole; Webster made a most eloquent speech, as was his wont." Over the years Jacksonville became an education and political center. In 1829 a group of Yale graduates founded there Illinois College, modeled after their alma mater. The school's first president was the Reverend Edward Beecher, brother of *Uncle Tom's Cabin* author Harriet Beecher Stowe. The college still operates, one of its graduates being three-time presidential candidate William Jennings Bryan (from Salem: see section 4) who started his law practice in Jacksonville in 1883, and so does MacMurray College, founded in 1846, the year famous social reformer Dorothea Dix visited Jacksonville. She persuaded the Illinois legislature to establish in the state a decent hospital for the mentally ill, a descendant of which institution exists in Jacksonville today. A drive around town will take you to those old institutions, including the two-story Georgian-style Duncan house, now occupied by the local DAR chapter, and Illinois College's 1829 Beecher Hall, which in the 1840s housed the state's first medical school. Also in Jacksonville are two unusual factories: ferris-wheel manufacturer Eli Bridge and Company, established in 1906; and the Capitol Records plant, where all the original Beatles recordings, among other discs, were pressed (tours available by reservation).

On the Illinois River northwest of Jacksonville lies the pleasant river town of Beardstown. Before the wall installed along the Illinois's banks tamed the flood-prone river, Beardstown suffered a more watery existence, the stream occasionally invading the city's streets. During the devastating flood of 1926 one resourceful local operated a water taxi, a small boat that ferried supplies and people around town. Beardstown's claim to fame involves the 1858 so-called almanac trial in which—yes, you guessed it!—Abraham Lincoln defended a man accused of murder by using the *Old Farmer's Almanac* to show that, contrary to the testimony of a supposed witness to the murder, no full moon shone the night of the killing. The chamber where the trial took place on the second floor of the 1844 city hall building remains unchanged from the day Lincoln pleaded his case there. Still used for Cass County trials, the courtroom is the only one yet functioning where Lincoln acted as a lawyer. The story goes that Lincoln, an officer in the 1832 Black Hawk War, was one day drilling a group of farm boys in a park at Beardstown. As the spread-out unit marched toward a narrow gate the neophyte captain, unsure of the proper command, improvised an order: "Company dismissed for two minutes. Fall in again on the other side of the gate." Before leaving courthouse square it's worth casting a glance at the cast-iron embellishments on the boxy house at the southeast corner. After Mississippi steamship skipper Charles Ebaugh bought the 1852 house in 1865 he added the elaborate two-story ornamental metal porch, a New Orleans French Quarter-type adornment, and he then supposedly ordered the molds destroyed so the cast iron grape cluster, leaf and branch design would remain unique.

Rushville, a few miles northwest of Beardstown, boasts an attractive town square anchored by a gazebo in the center. The Schuyler-Brown County Historical Society, just off the square, occupies unusual quarters—an old jailhouse—and one of the collections there is unusual as well: undertaker's sticks used to measure corpses for coffins. Scripps Park in

Rushville memorializes the famous newspaper family, whose founding father once lived in the town. John Scripps, born in London in 1785, left England in 1824 and emigrated to Illinois where he became a circuit-riding Methodist preacher. After settling in Rushville, Scripps ran a general store for fifteen years, then purchased the Rushville *Prairie Telegraph* in 1849. John Locke Scripps, the nephew of John Scripps, who died in Rushville in 1865, founded and edited the Chicago *Tribune;* a grand-nephew, James E. Scripps, started the Detroit *Evening News;* and Edward W. Scripps, another grand-nephew, established the Scripps-Howard chain. In 1923 Edward and his two sisters gave the park, site of John Scripps's house, to Rushville. Farther on at Macomb, Western Illinois University houses a cluster of museums, among them an art gallery, the Illinois Business Hall of Fame and a Western Museum featuring Indian costumes and Civil War artifacts. Other attractions in town include the Watson-Wiley School Museum, a restored 1890s-vintage schoolhouse, and the factory and store of Haeger Potteries, one of the country's leading manufacturers of flowerpots and art pottery.

In the Colchester area to the west of Macomb stand some unusual round barns, their shape chosen to provide larger feeding areas for livestock, while to the east of Macomb lies the Spoon River country. Before starting your drive through this delightful area, it's worth looking in at the Dickson Mounds Museum, which lies between the Illinois and the Spoon Rivers. Fulton County's more than three thousand known prehistoric sites, evidences of the early cultures that lived in the Illinois River valley as far back as ten thousand years ago, make it one of the nation's richest archeological areas. The museum, a National Historic Site, is most unusual for it encompasses a section of one of those ancient leavings— a large Indian burial mound where more than two hundred skeletons, partly excavated but otherwise exactly as they were when interred seven hundred years ago, lie in the ground. From an observation platform near the graves one can study the bones and the objects buried with the bodies. The museum also contains an extensive display of Indian artifacts retrieved from excavations conducted in the area. After the Dickson dig opened to the public in 1927 as a private museum (the state acquired the site in 1945), University of Chicago archeologists, digging in Fulton County in the 1930s, established many of the methods and field techniques used in modern archeology.

A mile or so from the museum begins the sixty-five-mile-long Spoon River Valley Scenic Drive, marked by red and white oval signs. At Waterford, the southern entry point, stands the 1850 wood cabin where tickets for the old plank road were sold. Farther on, at the sleepy hamlet of Lewistown, you'll find the two-story white frame house where *Spoon River Anthology* author Edgar Lee Masters lived from 1883 to 1891 after his family moved from Petersburg near New Salem (see section 5). The only trace of the family's presence at the house is a curbside stone block, used for descending from carriages, bearing the name "Masters." On the corner opposite the house stands the Rasmussen Blacksmith Shop, an establishment operated by the Rasmussen family from 1893 to 1969. Old equipment and tools and a collection of corrective horseshoes for animals with defective feet cram the shop's interior. The scene recalls Masters's Shack Dye, the Spoon River blacksmith who once entered his workplace to find "some horse-shoes crawling/Across the floor, as if alive." By way of a practical joke, one of Dye's friends "had put a magnet/Under the barrel of water" and drawn the shoes across the floor. A few blocks north of town lies Oak Hill Cemetery, thought to be the burial ground Masters refers to as "the hill" in the opening poem of the *Anthology*. Where, he asks, are the "weak of will, the strong of arm, the clown, the boozer, the fighter? All, all are sleeping on the hill." One of the graves belongs to William Cullen

Bryant, a relative of the poet of that name, who died in a hunting accident at age twenty-four in 1875. His father, H. C. Bryant, introduced Stephen Douglas when the politician spoke at Lewistown on August 16, 1858. The next day Lincoln also delivered a speech there, addressing the crowd from between a pair of stone pillars that then flanked the courthouse entrance and which now stand in the cemetery. From Lewistown you can wander the valley's quiet country roads to various corners of the Spoon River country. One possibility is Vermont, a little-visited hamlet to the south where you'll find a dozen or so pre-Civil War southern-style mansions. Another route leads to Bernadotte, a well-shaded settlement on Spoon River reached by a turn-of-the-century one-lane iron bridge. An early settler supposedly purchased the site from Indians in 1822 for fifty deerskins. Given three months to live, Isaiah Beethoven of the *Anthology* "crept to Bernadotte,/And sat by the mill for hours and hours/Where the gathered waters deeply moving/Seemed not to move." One of the Spoon's seven or so mills once turned at Bernadotte, but none now survive. A few miles up the road lies the hamlet of Ellisville where old storefronts line the main, and virtually the only, street. The Odd Fellows Hall houses a small nineteenth-century theater, complete with a painted curtain sporting a Venice scene and advertisements for such local practitioners as miller D. Sheckler, painter and paper hanger M. W. Griffith and Dr. Cluts, a physician. It's nine miles from Ellisville to London Mills, the northernmost point on the Spoon River Scenic Drive, where the old Ross Hotel now serves as a museum showing how an early 1900s rural Midwestern hostelry appeared. The tranquil riverside park at London Mills offers a pleasant place to linger and recall Masters's reflection on his beloved stream: "Spoon River still flows on, even as the years/Have also flown."

From the Spoon River country you can make your way northwest to Monmouth, named after Monmouth in New

Jersey where an early settler had originated, after locals rejected the designation Kosciusko (the famous Polish patriot) as being too hard to pronounce. Monmouth's most renowned native son was frontier lawman Wyatt Earp, born on a farm at the edge of town in 1848. The Earp family moved to Pella, Iowa (see Chapter IV, section 3) when Wyatt was a child and in 1864 on out to California, but he returned to Monmouth in 1868 to study law in his grandfather's office. Earp later again struck out for the west where he rode shotgun for Wells Fargo Express, hunted buffalo and ran a gambling establishment. The law business seems to have thrived in Monmouth. An early settler from Maine named Ebenezer Welch wrote his brother a letter from the Illinois town in September 1841 relating: "Rum drinking (or rather whiskey) is quite fashionable here, & it is not uncommon to see boys 8 or 9 years old *drunk*. But you can judge something of the society when I tell you that we employ 7 lawyers in this place & have a court nearly every day." This evidences the truth of the old Midwestern saying: a town that can't support one lawyer can always support two (or more). The old Warren County courthouse in Monmouth recalls those well-lawyered days, while the nearby Pioneer Cemetery contains graves of Wyatt Earp's relatives and other area settlers. Some attractive old houses along East Broadway and the tree-shaded campus of Monmouth College embellish the town, which also boasts Holt House, an elegant old Victorian structure where Pi Beta Phi, said to be the nation's first sorority, was founded. A few blocks away the Western Stoneware works (now called De Novo Ceramics), a long-established manufacturer of the wares, offers its products at a factory outlet called The Pottery Barn.

Galesburg, a town rich in history, lies fourteen miles east of Monmouth. Two blocks of restored old buildings on Seminary Street lend the center of town an atmosphere of yesteryear. A descendant of one of the pioneer families, Gale

Ferris, invented the Ferris wheel, first used at the 1893 Columbian Exposition in Chicago where the contraption amazed fair officials, both because the device actually functioned and because it "turned" a nice profit. Another prominent local resident was Mary "Mother" Bickerdyke, whose monument on the courthouse lawn bears William Tecumseh Sherman's compliment "she outranks me," a comment the Union general offered in praise of her organizing nursing services during the Civil War. Mrs. Bickerdyke, who traveled the country as a social activist after the war, died in 1901 and lies buried in Galesburg's Linwood Cemetery. From the early days of railroading in the mid-nineteenth century Galesburg has served as a rail center. The Railroad Museum, installed in an old Pullman parlor car, recalls some of the city's train activity, still going strong at the huge Burlington Northern complex, visible from the Fourth Street Bridge, which is among the largest rail-car classification yards in the world operated by one line. The annual Railroad Days festival the first weekend in June celebrates Galesburg's long-standing status as an important train town. Three blocks south of downtown lies Knox College, whose students have included Edgar Lee Masters, Broadway lyricist Otto Harback (*No No Nanette, Rose Marie* and other musicals) and Don Marquis, creator of the light verse characters "archy and mehitabel," who produced whimsical observations, such as this quatrain comment on the theory of relativity: "old doc einstein has/ abolished time but they/haven't got the news at/sing sing yet." Knox is best known as the site of the fifth Lincoln-Douglas debate, held October 7, 1858, in Old Main, the only venue of the seven debates still standing. Officials set up a speaking stand at the east end of Old Main away from the strong winds that spun through the city that day. After arriving by a four-horse carriage, the orators entered the front door of Old Main, walked to the east side and stepped out a window onto the platform, a maneuver that prompted Lincoln to observe that now he had gone through Knox College. During the debate, attended by some twenty thousand people, the largest crowd in the series, Stephen Douglas informed the listeners that Abe once worked at a grocery store where he sold sugar—innocent enough—to the ladies but that he also peddled liquor to the men, to which Lincoln, when his turn came, responded, "I did sell whiskey in those days, and Steve was my best customer." But the most lasting comment of the encounter was Lincoln's insistence on the moral aspects of slave-keeping, the first time "the Emancipator" so strongly articulated in public the philosophy underlying his opposition to the practice. "He is blowing out the moral lights around us, when he contends that whoever wants slaves has a right to hold them."

On October 7, 1893, the thirty-fifth anniversary of the great debate, college officials unveiled a commemorative tablet by the entrance to Old Main. A young Galesburgian of Swedish descent who scurried about town back then earning money by doing various odd jobs often stopped at Knox to read the plaque, which no doubt inspired the boy, for later in life the Galesburg native—Carl Sandburg by name—became known as one of Lincoln's greatest autobiographers. Sandburg was born in 1878 in a three-room white frame cottage not far from Knox and only a few steps away from tracks of the Chicago, Burlington and Quincy Railroad in whose blacksmith shop Sandburg's father, who never learned to write, worked for a dollar a day. The little house where baby Carl was born on a cornhusk mattress and diapered in flour sacks stood in an immigrant neighborhood filled with similar workingmen's cottages. The house today serves as a museum with displays that recall the career of Sandburg—poet, biographer, journalist and historian—who wrote more than forty books. One room honors Sandburg's monumental six-volume Lincoln biography, for part of which he won a Pulitzer Prize. Displays include a bust of Sandburg, an N.C. Wyeth portrait of Lincoln, the author's old-fashioned typewriter, an autographed collection of his books and other personal items. Behind the house stretches a small park where a large red granite boulder called Remembrance Rock, after the title of Sandburg's novel, marks the writer's final resting place. Beneath the rock repose the author's ashes, while on the marker appear his words: "For it could be a place to come and remember."

In the years before Carl Sandburg's birth Galesburg had become a very Swedish town. Although only six Swedes lived there in 1847, by 1859 some three thousand, a quarter of the town's entire population, had settled in Galesburg. The writer's father found so many people called Johnson, his original patronymic, that he changed his name to Sandburg, partly because he fell victim to frequent mix-ups in paychecks at the C.B. and Q. shop. Swedish names proved so confusing to the post office in Galesburg that Clark Carr, the postmaster, invented a "Swedish roll," a revolving rack that customers could turn from outside to see if they had any letters, which the patrons could then collect inside. Many of the Swedes who swelled Galesburg's population in the late '50s arrived from the Swedish settlement of Bishop Hill, about twenty-five miles northeast of town. Bishop Hill, one of those utopian communal colonies that dotted the Midwestern landscape in the nineteenth century, began to decline a few years after founder Eric Janson, who had led a group of immigrants from Sweden to the Illinois prairie in 1846, was murdered in open court in May 1850. Janson was shot by a colony member who'd forced his wife, Janson's cousin, to leave Bishop Hill when he'd abandoned the settlement, thus supposedly breaching an agreement that the woman would stay even if the man left. During the fifteen years the religious collective survived, more than a thousand immigrants arrived from Sweden. Bishop Hill may be unique in that the hamlet's present-day population of about two hundred includes many descendants (they comprise perhaps two thirds of today's residents) of the original settlers, so fifth- or sixth-generation Swedes are engaged in restoring the town their own ancestors founded. Self-styled "utopia on the prairie," Bishop Hill, National Historic Landmark, is a pleasant little enclave of the past and of rural Illinois. Fifteen of the original twenty main buildings have been restored, among them the old church, the colony's first permanent structure (the ground floor is devoted to apartments, while the sanctuary occupies the upper level), and the 1854 Steeple Building, a handsome three-story Greek-revival structure topped by a clock tower whose timepiece lacks a minute hand, an omission that helped keep the mechanism simple. The two buildings house more than one hundred delightful paintings of old Bishop Hill by Olof Krans, whose family settled there in 1850. The primitive-style pictures make the self-taught artist, who started painting at the age of fifty-eight, a kind of Grandpa Moses of the prairie. Other places on view include the 1857 blacksmith shop, the old colony school, the Bishop Hill store, which sells locally produced handicraft items, and the restored 1860 Bjorklund Hotel (no guests—it's now a museum) with a two-tiered tower used as a lookout to announce the arrival of the Peoria-Rock Island stagecoach.

Peoria lies about forty-five miles southeast of Bishop Hill on a wide stretch of the Illinois River called Peoria Lake. On the way there you might want to stop at Elmwood, an attractive little town between Galesburg and Peoria where the famous sculptor Lorado Taft was born in 1860. Memorials to the native son include a one-room museum devoted to Taft's life and works and his 1928 statue "The Pioneers" erected, the inscription notes, to the early settlers who "bridged the streams, subdued the soil, founded a state." With its portrayal of a pioneer couple and their child (and not to forget the family dog), the work seems an analogue to the "Madonna of the Trails" statue on the grounds of the Old Statehouse in

Vandalia (see section 4). Taft, who studied in Paris and then opened a studio in Chicago, also created the towering Black Hawk statue at Oregon, Illinois (see section 7). Taft's daughter married Paul Douglas, U.S. Senator from Illinois, and his sister married writer Hamlin Garland, while one of the artist's students was Gutzon Borglum, famous for the presidential faces he fashioned on Mount Rushmore in South Dakota.

From Elmwood it's only a short drive east to Peoria. Like Iowa's Dubuque (Chapter IV, section 9), Peoria is one of those Midwestern outposts that has come to symbolize provincialism. "How will it play in Peoria?" wonder the media magnates, politicians, anxious advertising moguls and Hollywood types huddled on the coasts far from the laid-back Midwest. If it "plays" in Peoria—that remote mid-American, middle-income, middle-class avatar of averageness—then, so it's supposed, plain folks everywhere will accept the concept. But when you visit Peoria you'll find that the city is only an average sort of average place. True, like cities everywhere, the town has its ups and downs, for Peoria is quite hilly, and the typical resident, statistics show, does have one dog, two children, three TV sets, a four-room house, five working days, a six-pack, 7-Up and V-8 juice in the refrigerator, 9 Lives cat food (cats are big in Peoria) and fully ten books (seven of them paperbacks, of which five are romances) in the house. Thus does Peoria number itself among the average of the nation. All that being said, if you fancy seeing where "it" might have played in Peoria, pay a visit to the Madison Theater (502 Main), a hall decorated in the sober classical style of the eighteenth-century Adam brothers of England. Built in 1920 at the beginning of the movie age, the theater saw the era's leading film and vaudeville performances, so the Madison is where "its" and hits played in Peoria. The Madison is listed on the National Register of Historic Places, as are the nearby Flemish Renaissance-style City Hall (Fulton and Madison Streets) and the

Beaux Arts-style Grand Army of the Republic Hall (416 Hamilton), built in 1909 as a meeting place for Civil War veterans. Adam style, Flemish Renaissance, Beaux Arts—can this be Peoria? Yes, those refined European styles have made their way even to Peoria. Outside the downtown area the John C. Flanagan House, built about 1837 and believed to be the city's oldest existing residence, and the 1868 Pettengill-Morron House, furnished with possessions acquired by a single family over a century and a half, are also listed on the National Register, as is the nearby Peoria Mineral Springs. From the spring bubble floods of pure water—said to have flowed there for fourteen thousand years—which attracted breweries and distilleries to Peoria, once the nation's leading distillery town. Although the Hiram Walker & Sons bourbon distillery, once the world's largest, no longer operates, another famous Peoria company—Caterpillar—offers a factory tour that takes you through the earth-moving equipment plant where the well-known yellow "Cats" are manufactured.

At the Mineral Springs in the 1840s Zealy Moss, father of Lydia Moss Bradley (a distiller's widow who in 1897 founded Peoria's Bradley University), established a bottling operation, forerunner of the bottled beverages (stronger than water) the town later produced. In the northern part of Peoria you'll find the Lakeview Museum, which offers a little of everything—fine arts, natural sciences, anthropological displays, decorative arts (much of that collection donated by Annette Smith Clemenceau, daughter-in-law of World War I French premier Georges Clemenceau)—while in Tower Park a glass-enclosed elevator whisks you up to an observation room affording a far panorama of the area. In the near distance below curves Grandview Drive, a scenic route bordering the Illinois River, which Teddy Roosevelt called "the world's most beautiful drive." On the way back toward town you'll pass near a statue of pot-bellied Robert G. Ingersoll (lower entrance of Glen Oak Park off Abington Street), the famous agnostic who lived in Peoria from 1857 to 1877. A southern Illinois boy, Ingersoll taught school in Mount Vernon and in Metropolis (see section 3), studied law in Marion and practiced in Shawneetown before moving to Peoria where, on September 14, 1869, he delivered his first major controversial speech, asserting that "all religions are inconsistent with mental freedom." Ingersoll, whom fellow Illinoisian Edgar Lee Masters described in a poem as "a general in the war of ideas for freedom," held that "A good deed is the best prayer. A loving life is the best religion." And that's how it plays in Peoria.

Nestled along the river to the south of Peoria is Pekin, where an exhibit at the Dirksen Congressional Center entitled "Congress: the Voice of the People" honors native son Everett McKinley Dirksen, longtime U.S. Senator from Illinois; while, to switch from politics to pumpkins, at nearby Morton you can tour the Libby, McNeil & Libby canning factory, which produces fully three-quarters of the world's canned pumpkin. At Metamora, north of Morton, stands the well-proportioned classic 1845 courthouse, preserved as it was during the dozen years Lincoln rode the Eighth Judicial Circuit. Apart from the courthouse at Mt. Pulaski (section 5), this is the only remaining court building in which Lincoln practiced law. Inside the attractive building, constructed of local timber and bricks baked in the village, is the restored courtroom along with displays of pioneer and other items, one a special table with a section sawed away so lanky Lincoln could bend his knees while working there. At one Metamora trial, Lincoln's client Melissa Goings lived up to her name when she found the evidence going against her. When Mrs. Goings failed to reappear after a recess Lincoln had requested, the judge accused the attorney of encouraging the defendant to flee. "Honest Abe" denied the charge, explaining that when his client had asked him where she could get a drink of water he merely observed that Tennessee offered darn good water. Another future president frequented the precincts of this area. A few miles southeast of Metamora stands Eureka College, Ronald Reagan's alma mater. At Eureka Reagan was first elected president, of the Student Senate, and he also started his acting life there, appearing in fourteen campus plays. A half century after Reagan graduated (class of '32), "Dutch," as he was called in college, returned to Eureka to announce for the first time, in a major foreign policy address, his goal for a Strategic Arms Reduction Treaty with the Soviet Union. The college's Melick Library houses a collection of more than eight hundred items relating to Reagan's acting career, his eight years as governor of California and his two presidential terms. Thus did Illinoisian Ronald Reagan follow in the footsteps of those other modestly born small-town Midwestern boys, like Lincoln, Hoover and Truman, whose improbable careers eventually led them to the White House.

7. Riverlands:

Old Buildings in Hennepin
Lovejoy House at Princeton
Utica: Canal Town
Lincoln–Douglas at Ottawa
Norway and "Wild Bill" Hickok Monuments
Sheffield's St. Peter's Danish Church and the Hennepin Canal
Quad Cities
Reagan Landmarks in Tampico and Dixon
Grand Detour, John Deere's Town
Lorado Taft at Oregon
Rockford
Via Freeport, Cedarville and Lena to Mount Carroll
Ulysses S. Grant's Galena

Three major rivers water upper western Illinois: the Illinois, the Rock and the Mississippi. Along and between those rivers lies a wide range of attractions—industrial towns, remote farm villages, historic cities—which reflect Illinois's variety. Clustered together on or near the Illinois River north of Peoria (see the previous section) is a series of cities that recall the state's early history. At Hennepin stands the 1839 Putnam County Courthouse (listed on the National Register), the oldest such building still in use in Illinois. Hennepin also boasts two especially venerable churches: United Methodist, believed to be the area's oldest church still in use, an 1859 Greek-revival structure with its unusual looking sanctuary located upstairs on the second floor; and its predecessor, the 1839 Methodist Meeting House, one of the oldest church buildings in Illinois still used for religious purposes. At Princeton, north of Hennepin, you'll find another historic old building, the spacious mid-nineteenth century two-story house where abolitionist Owen Lovejoy lived. Lovejoy was one of those Yankees who settled in the Midwest and brought their northern conscience with them. Born in Maine, he moved to Alton, Illinois in 1836 to join his brother Elijah, the crusading editor killed the following year by a mob angered by his abolitionist views (see section 9). Kneeling over the body of his slain brother, Owen Lovejoy vowed "never to forsake the cause that had been sprinkled with [Elijah's] blood." After studying for the ministry in Jacksonville, Owen settled in Princeton, making his homestead there an important station for runaway slaves on the Underground Railroad in Illinois. Ardent abolitionist Lovejoy, a five-term U.S. Representative, introduced the Emancipation Proclamation bill to Congress. His fifteen-room house, listed on the National Register, has been restored to the era when Lovejoy lived there. North of town on route 26 stands the 1863 Red Covered Bridge, also listed on the National Register, one of five remaining covered bridges in Illinois still in use. In town the Bureau County Historical Museum, installed in a three-tier white wedding cake-like mansion, contains a display of local items out of the past; while at the New Deal-style county courthouse stands a Civil War monument by Illinois sculptor Lorado Taft. Another Princeton abolitionist figure, John H. Bryant, brother of the renowned poet William Cullen Bryant, was a state legislator and a delegate to the 1860 Republican convention that nominated his friend Lincoln for the presidency. Like Lovejoy's house, Bryant's residence at 1518 South Main served as a stop on the Underground Railroad. The famous poet's four brothers all moved to central Illinois between 1830 and 1833, two of them, John and Cyrus Bryant (the latter lived in the house at 1110 South Main), arriving in the Princeton area in 1832 when they founded the town by building log cabins on the site. William Cullen Bryant's visit to his brothers in Illinois inspired him to write his poem "The Prairies": "The Prairies! I behold them for the first,/And my heart swells. . . Lo! they stretch/In airy undulations, far away,/as if the ocean in his gentlest swell,/stood still."

The tiny town of North Utica, called simply Utica by its thousand residents, nestles by and between the Illinois River and the Illinois-Michigan Canal about thirty miles east of Princeton. As might be expected, this well-watered village offers a sprinkling of river and canal-oriented attractions. A good place to begin your visit is the Illinois Waterway Visitors Center, with exhibits on the river and the canal, a National Heritage Corridor, and a view of the Starved Rock Lock and Dam. The one-hundred-and-twenty-mile canal opened in 1848 after twelve years of construction, to connect the Great Lakes and the Mississippi River. Next to the Visitors Center stands Half-Way House, an old stagecoach stop (Lincoln once lodged there) located on the Chicago-Peoria route. Across the Illinois River lies Starved Rock State Park, so named for an eighteenth-century Indian legend that recounts how a band of Illiniwek (the tribe that gave its name to the state) starved on the sandstone cliff there to avoid surrender to a fierce band of Potawatomi who surrounded the redoubt. If you overnight in the area, rustic Starved Rock State Lodge, a log structure built in the 1930s by the Civilian Conservation Corps, offers an attractive place to stay. On the canal back in Utica—which on the second weekend in October celebrates its annual "burgoo" craft fair and flea market festival, cooking up in large cauldrons gallons of that pioneer stew—stands the LaSalle County Historical Museum, which occupies a two-story 1848 stone warehouse building that once served as a general store supplying early settlers and travelers along the canal. Among the displays is the carriage that carried Lincoln from the Ottawa train station to the site of his debate with Douglas in that town.

On the way to Ottawa, which lies at the confluence of the Fox and Illinois Rivers a few miles east of Utica, you might want to drive by the rather odd earthwork effigies at Buffalo Rock State Park. After the land at an abandoned strip mine was reclaimed, an artist created in 1985 five large earthen figures—a snake, turtle, fish, frog and spider—which, extending more than a mile, is said to be the world's largest outdoor sculpture. At nearby Ottawa a boulder in Washington Park marks the first Lincoln-Douglas debate, held in the town August 21, 1858. Charles W. Marsh, who traveled down from De Kalb some forty miles north to attend the debate recalled the event in his *Recollections 1837–1910*. Owen Lovejoy, the abolitionist from Princeton (see above), sat on the dais, Marsh noted; suddenly one of Douglas's remarks "brought Lincoln to his feet, with a stern expression on his face, but before he had time to interrupt, as apparently he intended, Lovejoy, sitting behind, grabbed his coat, pulled him back and whispered something that induced him to resume his seat." Thus was Lincoln—"a man of much length. He was dressed in broadcloth and his long black coat gave him a ministerial look. . . . He was not handsome, neither was he ugly"—brought back to earth. But after the debate he rose even higher when his supporters ran to him "and despite his earnest protests, loaded him on their shoulders. I have never forgotten the expression on his face as they bore him along. It was seriocomic in the extreme." A year after the debate William Reddick built in Ottawa the twenty-two room, three-story, red brick Italianate mansion, listed on the National Register, which contains period furnishings and which served as a stop on the Underground Railroad. Back in those nineteenth-century days a man named John Edwin Scott ran a dry goods business in Ottawa before moving to Chicago where he joined with Samuel Carson and John T. Pirie to form Carson Pirie Scott department store. Out at the

Ottawa Avenue Cemetery you'll find a monument to another old-time local figure, W. D. Boyce, the man who started the Boy Scout movement in America.

At the hamlet of Norway, a few miles northeast of Ottawa, a monument recalls Cleng Peerson who in 1834 founded the community, the first permanent Norwegian settlement in America, while at Troy Grove, northwest of Ottawa, stands a memorial to James Butler ("Wild Bill") Hickok, born there in 1837. Like Illinois-born William "Bat" Masterson and Wyatt Earp, Hickok made his way west where he served as a lawman. "Wild Bill," who once used a bowie knife to dispose of a bear that attacked him, was also known to kill two-leggers. When Hickok was shot dead at Deadwood, South Dakota, in 1876 while playing poker—holding two aces and two eights, known ever since as the "dead man's hand"—his revolver bore seventy-two notches. After Charles W. Marsh (whose description of the Lincoln-Douglas debate in Ottawa is quoted above) met Hickok in 1872, Marsh cautiously noted, "I observed him closely, as any one would a man who had killed many men with his own hands." Four miles south of Mendota, to the north, is the huge Time Was Village Museum, with nine buildings crammed full of old toys, carriages, dolls, household objects and a miscellany of other items that seem straight out of granny's attic. In fact, one of the exhibits is a replica of an 1880s-era attic. In mid-August the town of Mendota hosts the annual Sweet Corn Festival.

Heading now back west, at Sheffield, twenty miles west of Princeton, stands St. Peter's Evangelical Lutheran Church, a late nineteenth-century sanctuary, reconsecrated in 1976 by the Queen of Denmark, that housed the first Danish Lutheran congregation in the U.S. Listed on the National Register, the attractively restored church also includes a museum. Near Sheffield is the visitor center for the Hennepin Canal Parkway, a ninety-six-mile swath that follows the waterway that extends from near Hennepin to the Mississippi

River. The canal, which served as a commercial waterway from 1907 to 1951 and is now no doubt the nation's most linear park, offers a combination of recreational and historic attractions with boat launches, fishing and camping sites and trails as well as the old locks, bridges and overseers' houses. Between Atkinson and Geneseo, self-styled "Hog Center of the World," to the west lies the Johnson 1910 Farm, a frozen-in-time farmstead with old machinery and equipment, a country schoolhouse and a ten-room pre-Civil War farmhouse.

It's a bit of a transition to travel from the old farmstead to the industrialized Quad Cities area along the Mississippi. At East Moline you can tour the International Harvester factory, the largest farm equipment production facility under one roof in the world, while in Moline stands the world headquarters of another farm implement manufacturer, John Deere & Company. Designed by the renowned architect Eero Saarinen, the glassy structure opened in 1964 and is one of the most stunning buildings in the Midwest. The ultramodern seven-story edifice, made of steel which has weathered and taken on a rich brown tone the color of freshly plowed Midwestern soil, rises from a wooded ravine near a lake that reflects the elegant structure. The interior of the headquarters, open for tours, is embellished by paintings, sculpture, an unusual historical collage-mural and equipment displays. Some of the founders of Moline—a word stemming from "moulin," French for "mill"—were Belgian, a heritage recalled at the Center for Belgian Culture where artisans fashion lace as it was woven in the old country. At Rock Island, one of the Quad Cities (the others, on the Iowa side of the Mississippi, are Davenport and Bettendorf; see Chapter IV, section 9), a railroad museum listed on the National Register occupies the 1901 train depot, while at the south edge of town by Rock River lies the historic Black Hawk State Park, with the Hauberg Museum that contains a large display relating to the area's Indian culture. About 1730 the Sauk and Mesquakie Indians settled at the riverside site, and over the next century Saukenuk—as the Sauk Nation capital was called—became one of the largest Indian centers in North America. In 1780 Saukenuk was the locale of the westernmost battle of the Revolutionary War when American forces destroyed the settlement because some of the Sauk had helped the British military effort. A statue of Black Hawk, a pro-British Sauk warrior, stands in the park which bears his name. In the late nineteenth and early twentieth centuries the area became a popular local amusement park, with balloon ascensions, outdoor movies projected on canvas screens and a "shoot the chute" tobaggan slide, a thrill ride invented in Rock Island.

In the middle of the Mississippi, between Rock Island city and Davenport, Iowa, stands the Rock Island itself, a sort of no-man's land or, as a federal enclave, everyman's land. The huge (three miles long, three-quarters of a mile wide) island boasts an eclectic mixture of sights, ranging from a historic house to a military base to a Mississippi River installation. The house belonged to Colonel George Davenport, who gave his name to the Iowa city just across the way. Built in 1833, the residence (listed on the National Register) hosted planning sessions for many early area endeavors, among them the founding in 1836 of Davenport, the establishment of the Rock Island Railroad in 1845 and construction of the first bridge across the Mississippi in 1856. Colonel Davenport never lived to see the historic day the railroad finally crossed the river. On July 4, 1846, seven bandits broke into the house and tortured Davenport to death in an effort to learn where he'd supposedly hidden twenty thousand dollars in gold. The bridge, too, suffered an unexpected assault. The span represented more than just a way across the Mississippi: it promised—and to the steamboaters threatened—an entirely new link between the east and the west, since trains could use the bridge to connect the two parts of the country. An official report related the high expectations for the bridge, to be built by "men of stout hearts and of iron nerve": "For many long years the Mississippi has been considered an insuperable obstacle to the continuity of all great thoroughfares, from the Atlantic to the Pacific. Happily for the best interests of the West, and indeed the whole world of commerce, a rare combination of natural facilities at this point, of the resources of modern science, of eastern capital and of western enterprise, has made the project practicable, and insured its completion within the present year. Its opening will mark a new era in the history of Commerce, and in the annals of the Great West." As might be expected, the river men became unhappy with the prospect of railroads extending their reach. In 1856 a boat named *Effie Afton* just happened to ram into a pier of the bridge, partly destroying it, whereupon boats all around the area sounded their whistles and bells in celebration. A court case ensued—things were no different back then than they are now—and a certain "distinguished lawyer," as a local paper described him, appeared in federal court representing the railroad interests in an action brought by the ship's owners charging obstruction of navigation. A hung jury resulted, so the railroad attorney—Abraham Lincoln by name—saved his clients from having to pay damages.

A drive around Rock Island will take you to the site of a Civil War prison for Confederate soldiers, a Confederate cemetery where the nearly two thousand southerners who died in the prison camp repose, a national cemetery, and the fifty-two room Quarters One dwelling, the second largest residential building—after the White House—owned by the U.S. Some of the buildings you'll pass form part of the still functioning Arsenal (listed on the National Register in 1969) where artillery parts, small arms and other weapon components are produced. The Arsenal Museum contains displays of more than thirteen hundred firearms, from French-made

Revolutionary War bronze cannons to modern-day weapons, including pieces captured from hostile Indians and from enemy forces in various wars. Opposite the 1865 Clock Tower building at the west end of the island stands the U.S. Army Corps of Engineers Mississippi River Visitor Center, which overlooks Lock and Dam 15. Displays relate a torrent of river information on such subjects as navigation, flood control, reservoirs, levees and the series of twenty-nine locks and dams on the Mississippi. The board inside the entrance of the center lists "Approaching Tows," so you can check there if a ship is expected during your visit. If so, through the picture window you'll be able to observe how the boat passes through the lock.

Northeast of the Quad Cities area lies the tiny town of Tampico, a hamlet of less than a thousand residents where Ronald Reagan first saw the light of day on February 6, 1911, in a six-room apartment above a bakery, later a bank. His father, Jack Reagan, then worked as a clerk at the H.C. Pitney general store in Tampico. The main floor of the simple two-story brick building houses a small museum, while the restored apartment now displays its turn-of-the-century appearance. Three months after the future president arrived, the family moved into a white frame house at 104 Glassburg Street. But Reagan's true home town is Dixon, northeast of Tampico, where he lived from age nine through high school. English novelist Anthony Trollope, who traveled in Illinois in February 1862, noted of Dixon: "Much of it has burned down, and more of it has never been built up." But, in fact, the place has been a busy river city almost from the time ferryboat proprietor John Dixon established the settlement in 1830. Until Reagan rose to fame, Dixon was better known as the birthplace of gossip columnist Louella Parsons, as the site of the nation's first Walgreen drug store, as "the Petunia Capital of the World" (a Petunia Festival blooms every year over Fourth of July weekend), and as the town where another president-to-be, Abe Lincoln, was stationed over the summer of 1832 during the Black Hawk War. On the north bank of the Rock River between the Lincoln and the Reagan bridges stands a statue of young Lincoln, an unusual portrayal showing him beardless, his face untouched by the ravages of time or the cares of office. But, for once in Illinois, Lincoln is overshadowed by another president, for Reagan memorials dominate the town. You can see there his boyhood home (one of five houses, all rented, the Reagans occupied in Dixon), South Side School (now called South Central) where he attended grade school, the First Christian Church he frequented (his father and older brother Neil were Catholic, Ronnie and his mother Protestant), and North Dixon High where he graduated in 1928, his class picture bearing the quote "life is just one grand sweet song, so start the music." Three miles north of town by the Rock River lies Lowell Park where young Ron, working as a lifeguard from 1926 to 1932, saved seventy-seven swimmers and once even retrieved a set of dentures from the river to earn himself a five-dollar reward. Lowell Park was named for poet James Russell Lowell's brother, who was so taken with the beauties of the Rock River Valley, visited on his honeymoon, that he bought a building plot which, never used, his daughter later gave to Dixon. Ghosts of presidents haunt the venerable Nachusa Hotel: not only did the three chief executives from Illinois— Lincoln, Ulysses S. Grant and Reagan—stay there, but also Theodore Roosevelt and William Howard Taft. Built in 1837, the hostelry was Illinois's oldest operating hotel and said to be the fifth oldest in the U.S. before it recently closed (it may have reopened by now). The Lincoln room at the Nachusa, which installed the first bathtub in Illinois, is decorated in mid-nineteenth-century style.

South of Dixon lies Amboy, site of the first Carson Pirie Scott Store, where a seventeen-room regional history museum occupies the century-old Illinois Central train depot, while to the west at Sterling—national award recipient for the finest park district in the nation in a city under twenty thousand—stands the Italian Renaissance-style 1857 Paul W. Dillon Home, occupied by the local businessman for ninety-six years from his birth (1883) to his death (1980). At Morrison, farther west, stands the 1858 Unionville grist mill, a four-story solid sandstone structure with a large six-spoke wheel. Near Malvern, nine miles northeast, you'll find another old mill, the Appel Mill, an angular white frame structure resembling an oversized barn. Neither building is open to the public but if you happen to be a mill aficionado it's worth trying to see the Appel Mill's interior, where the machinery and mechanisms remain especially well preserved. In a bend of the Rock River to the north of Dixon nestles the lovely hamlet of Grand Detour, well worth a detour to see. Early French traders named the area for the large horseshoe curve in the river there. The wide elm-shaded streets, large lawns, white picket fences and comfortable old clapboard houses recall a New England village. One New Englander who settled there was a young Vermonter named John Deere, who in 1837 came to Grand Detour where he set up a blacksmith shop. The following year Deere built the lovely white frame house which, along with the reconstructed blacksmith building, stands as a memorial to the man who invented the steel plow. After arriving in the west Deere discovered that the cast-iron plows then common were not only heavy and cumbersome but also required frequent sharpening and cleaning to remove the rich prairie soil that clung to the pitted surface. To assemble the first steel plow, in 1837, Deere used a broken discarded circular sawblade. When he tested the device on a field across the Rock River from Grand Detour, Deere found the new implement cut evenly and needed less animal power than iron plows. In 1838 Deere turned out three plows; the next year, ten; and by 1842 his shop produced an average of two a week. In 1847 Deere moved the operation to Moline, and by mid-century, production reached sixteen hundred plows a year. Incorporated in 1868, the Deere company is Illinois's oldest manufacturing business. One unusual feature at the Deere site, listed on the National Register, is an archeology display showing the excavated remains of the original blacksmith shop, with explanations of how it functioned.

A few miles up the Rock River lies Oregon where Illinois sculptor Lorado Taft (born in Elmwood: see section 6) spent his summers. A second-floor gallery at the public library houses a collection of Taft's works, while on the lawn of the late nineteenth-century Ogle County courthouse, listed on the National Register, stands the 1916 Soldiers Monument designed by the artist. Taft's most famous work embellishes Lowden State Park, a mile or two northeast of Oregon, where his nearly fifty-foot-tall concrete American Indian figure towers on a bluff three hundred feet above the Rock River. Although Taft designed the figure to represent Indiankind in general, the statue has come to be known as Black Hawk, the Sauk leader who roamed the area a century and a half ago. After the defeat of his people in the war named after him Black Hawk told the white victors: "Rock River was a beautiful country. I liked my towns, my corn fields, and the home of my people. I fought for it—it is now yours—keep it, as we did." In 1898 Lorado Taft and a group of colleagues established in the area an art colony (active until 1942) called "Eagles' Nest" after a starkly bare dead cedar tree on which eagles once nested. Beneath the tree's branches Margaret Fuller, a poet who belonged to the famous mid-nineteenth-century literary colony in Concord, Massachusetts, wrote her well-known poem "Ganymede to His Eagle" in 1843.

Highway 2, heading north along the Rock River to Rockford, affords one of Illinois's most scenic drives. Back in 1846, in *Life in Prairie Land,* Eliza W. Farnham described the area: "The country bordering on Rock River, in nearly its whole length, is one of the most beautiful that can be imagined. The stream itself is a clear and generally rapid current, running over ledges of lime rock or beds of fine gravel and sand. Its banks are beautifully diversified with grove and lawn, which sometimes form natural parks of many miles in extent." Rockford, by way of contrast, sprawls along both banks of the Rock, here no longer coddled by long stretches of greenery. Although its population numbers only about a hundred and fifty thousand, Rockford is Illinois's second largest city. Founded in 1834, the town took its name from the crossing point where the Frink, Walker and Company stagecoaches operating between Galena and Chicago forded the Rock River. Museums abound in Rockford: the Burpee Museum of Natural History and the nearby Burpee Museum of Art; the Rockford Museum Center, which encompasses a history and an industrial museum, as well as a turn-of-the-century village with an old-time bank, town hall, school house, church and replicas of a nineteenth-century hotel and hospital; the 1857 Graham-Ginestra house and the 1839 oak timber Stephen Mack home, both listed on the National Register; the Erlander Home Museum, with displays recalling the city's Swedish heritage; and even a museum devoted to scouting—the Zitelman Scout Museum.

If your time in Rockford is limited, two attractions there especially merit a visit. One is Tinker Swiss Cottage, a Swiss-style chalet perched on a limestone bluff by Kent Creek. Hawaii-born Robert Hall Tinker built the house in 1865 after a visit to Switzerland in 1862 introduced him to the style. After moving to Rockford in 1856 Tinker worked as a bookkeeper for Mary Manny, wealthy widow of inventor John H. Manny, whose reaper company, eventually merged into J. I. Case, enjoyed such great success (one machine could replace twenty scythe-wielding workers) that some locals wanted to rename the town Reaper City. Manny died in 1856, age thirty, just after winning a patent lawsuit brought by

Cyrus McCormick, a case in which a certain tall lean Springfield lawyer-politician acted as one of Manny's attorneys: by now no prize for guessing who that honest, rail-splitting—if not hair-splitting—lawyer was. Now the plot thickens, and so does Tinker's bank account: in 1870 he married Mrs. Manny, who lived in a spacious house (later razed) across Kent Creek. A suspension bridge connected Tinker's Swiss chalet and her residence, and the couple divided their time between the two places, staying in the cozy cottage during the winter and at the cool limestone mansion in the summer. After Mary Manny Tinker died in 1901 Robert kept the family connection by marrying her niece, Jessie Hurd, after whose demise in 1942 the Swiss cottage was opened to the public. Antiques, porcelain and art objects collected the world over by Robert and Mary Tinker cram the cottage, preserved as it was when the couple lived there. Unusual features that enhance the house include a small swinging door set into the larger sliding door in the parlor and a graceful walnut spiral stairway in the library, a room inspired by the library in Sir Walter Scott's house in Scotland. The other place in Rockford well worth a visit is the Time Museum, a collection of twenty-five hundred clocks, watches, sundials, astrolabes, chronometers, sand glasses and other keepers of time ranging from 3000 B.C. to present-day atomic clocks. Items in the fourteen chronologically arranged sections of the museum—located at the Clock Tower Inn, a hotel in east Rockford—include a 1664 clock with a candle inside to check the hour at night, an alarm clock which sets in motion at the appointed hour a lever that hits a flint to light a candle, and the huge late nineteenth-century Christian Gebhard console with dials everywhere and a Christ statue by which, every hour, one of the twelve disciples passes and pivots for a blessing—except for Judas who, carrying a box of silver, turns his head away.

From Rockford the road west leads to Freeport, twenty-nine miles away, a town supposedly so named when a farmer's wife found herself feeding so many people who stopped off on their way between Rockford and Galena she declared her kitchen a "free port." A Lincoln statue in City Park marks the site of the second Lincoln-Douglas debate, held in Freeport on August 27, 1858. The town's art museum contains a large collection of historical works and antiques, while displays at the Stephenson County Historical Society include a farm museum, a 1910 schoolhouse, an 1840s log cabin and exhibits pertaining to Jane Addams, the Nobel Prize-winning social worker who in 1889 founded in Chicago Hull House, an educational and social center for immigrants and the impoverished. Addams was born in 1860 in nearby Cedarville where her father, John, owned a grist mill. Her grave lies in the family burial plot at Cedarville where Addams's idyllic childhood, set in a "scene of rural beauty," she later recalled, contrasted with the urban inner-city world she subsequently inhabited in Chicago. At Lena, a few miles west of Cedarville, you can tour the Kolb-Lena cheese factory before continuing on to Galena.

The direct way from Lena to Galena takes one due west but a more roundabout route to the southwest offers some worthwhile attractions. That road passes through Lanark, where the century-old general store contains a museum of local history, on the way to Mount Carroll, a thoroughly delightful and unusually attractive town with an abundance of well-preserved old buildings. Much of the city's center section comprises a National Historic District, while the 1858 Carroll County Courthouse is itself listed on the National Register. Next to the courthouse stands a Civil War monument, topped by Lorado Taft's cavalryman statue, and nearby rises an annex to the monument, mentioned in Ripley's "Believe It or Not," bearing the names of the twelve hundred and eighty-four Carroll County men who fell in the conflict. A wide variety of styles—Federal, Greek Revival, Queen Anne,

Tudor, Italianate and others—enrich the town's historic district. Houses there include those which belonged to Nita Snook, Amelia Earhart's first flight instructor, and John Christian, an 1838 settler and patriarch of Mount Carroll's oldest continuous family, now in at least its eighth generation. The southernmost historic district attraction is the complex of 1905 Georgian buildings which once made up a local college, its predecessor headed by a woman with the endearing name Cinderella Gregory. The buildings now house the rather unusual Campbell Center for Historic Preservation Studies, an organization offering courses and workshops in many fields of restoration and preservation. Four miles from town stands the Oakville Country School Museum, with a restored one-room 1888 schoolhouse, blacksmith shop and two log cabins dating from the 1840s.

A few attractions of interest lie between Mount Carroll and Galena, another splendidly preserved old town forty-two miles north. About twelve miles northwest of Mount Carroll, Mississippi Palisades State Park offers a series of panoramic views onto the great river from atop steep limestone bluffs, reminiscent of those along New York's Hudson River, that border the Mississippi there. Farther north lies Hanover, which nestles by the Apple River that runs through Illinois's highest and hilliest region, an area the glaciers that covered much of the state thousands of years ago didn't level. (After Louisiana and Delaware, Illinois is the nation's flattest state.) Hanover locals claim that the nation's temperance movement originated there back in 1856 when Daniel Boone's granddaughter led a group of sixty women to a saloon which they dismantled. One of the women later moved to Guthrie, Oklahoma, where she supposedly influenced her neighbor Carry Nation (buried in Belton, Missouri: see Chapter V, section 5) to take up the temperance cause. Quacks abound in Hanover, not practitioners at some shady medical clinic but feathered fauna at the Whistling Wings Duck Hatchery, which breeds more than two hundred thousand mallards a year for eating, research and game preserve purposes. Five miles northwest of Hanover stands one of AT & T's seven U.S. earth stations (tours available), an installation with two hundred-foot-diameter, disk-shaped antennas which relay via satellite more than twenty-two thousand telephone circuits. At Stockton, off to the east of Jo Daviess (pronounced "Davis") County, is a Kraft cheese plant, descendant of the first such factory in the country, established there by J. L. Kraft who opened a creamery in the town. Seventeen miles north of Hanover lies Galena, a treasure trove of old architecture, history and atmosphere. In the mid-nineteenth century Galena became a mining boomtown, at one time supplying more than 80 percent of the nation's lead needs. Then—after the mines ran out—Galena, the name for lead ore, busted. By a certain perverse twist of fate the bad times which kept the town unchanged preserved it, frozen in time, so that now Galena can mine loads of silver from the pockets of the tourists who flock there rather than lodes of lead ore from the ground.

So many of Galena's buildings boast architecturally interesting features that fully 85 percent of the town's structures merit inclusion on the National Register of Historic Places. Galena is therefore one of those unusual American cities— like Natchez, Mississippi, or Charleston, South Carolina— which offers a coherent whole in style and tone, an integrated urban area with that pleasing sense of regularity and symmetry so common in Europe and so rare in this country. The largest house in town is twenty-two-room Belvedere built in 1857 by steamboat owner J. Russell Jones; the oldest is the 1826 Dowling House; among the most storied are the Washbourne House (its owner served as a Congressman, Secretary of State and minister to France) on whose lawn local resident Ulysses S. Grant drilled his volunteer troops, and the Melville House, occupied by the uncle of *Moby Dick* author

Herman Melville, who visited Galena in 1840; and the most historic is the residence Galena gave to Grant when he returned home in 1865 after leading Union forces to victory. Over the next fifteen years, during which Grant served two terms in the White House, the two-story brick residence at the edge of Galena was the president's home base. Now a State Historic Site, the house is furnished as in the days when Grant lived there. In town on Quality Hill stands the smaller house Grant occupied before the war when he worked in his father's leather shop on Main Street. On Main stand the General Store Museum, not named after General Grant but a re-creation of a nineteenth-century emporium, and the Galena *Gazette* Museum (the paper was founded in 1834). A few blocks away rises another venerable commercial building, the restored Old Market House where the City Council met from 1846 to 1938 in the upstairs hall while down below functioned farmers' and merchants' markets. Galena, a city of museums as well as a museum city, also offers the Vinegar Hill Lead Mine and Museum where you can tour one of the original local lead mines and see mining artifacts (an abandoned lead mine in Missouri is also open for tours: see Chapter V, section 9), and the Galena-Jo Daviess Historical Museum installed in the 1858 Barrows residence. The historical museum's most famous item is Thomas Nast's painting depicting General Robert E. Lee's surrender to Grant at Appomatox. The painting includes portraits of two of the nine Union Army generals from Galena—John A. Rawlings, who by the time he died at age thirty-seven had served not only as a major general but also as Grant's Secretary of War, and Ely S. Parker, a full-blooded Seneca Indian chief originally named Ha-sa-no-an-da who, refused admittance to the New York bar, which welcomed blue bloods but didn't accept redskins, became an engineer and later served as military secretary to Grant, who promoted Parker to brigadier general the day of the surrender. The many celebrities who visited Galena through the years lodged at the DeSoto House, but unfortunately the hotel closed for financial reasons in late 1988, two-and-a-half years after undergoing an $8 million renovation. In its heyday the DeSoto hosted such luminaries as Mark Twain, James Russell Lowell, Ralph Waldo Emerson, Susan B. Anthony, Horace Greeley and nine U.S. presidents. In 1856 Lincoln spoke from the balcony of the establishment, known as "the best hotel west of New York City," and in 1868 the DeSoto served as Grant's campaign headquarters. The hotel may eventually reopen, but in the meantime, Galena also offers a wide selection of bed and breakfast places in antique houses. So day or night, uptown or down, today or tomorrow you'll find yourself surrounded by the nineteenth century there in the hilly historic city—the town that time passed by—enabling us now, a century and a half later, to step back into the past there in old Galena.

8. Skirting Chicago:

Utopia at Zion
Through Waukegan, Glenview and the Antique Centers of
Long Grove and Richmond to Woodstock
Union's Museums, Barbed Wire at De Kalb
The Fox River Valley: Elgin, St. Charles, Geneva, Aurora
An Old Village at Naperville, Morton Arboretum at Lisle,
Oak Brook, Old Graue Mill and A Stage Coach Tavern at
Glen Ellyn
Publisher Robert R. McCormick, Preacher Billy Graham and
Pigskinner Red Grange at Wheaton
Oak Park: Home of Hemingway and Frank Lloyd Wright
Pullman Community
The Old Canal at Lockport and Old Homes at Joliet
Goose Lake Prairie Park and Kankakee

Traveling in northern Illinois it's hard to avoid the magnetic pull of Chicago, a "miracle of paradox and incongruity," as George W. Steevens, a journalist for *The Daily Mail* of London, described the metropolis after his visit there in 1896. "Chicago! Chicago, queen and guttersnipe of cities," he wrote, "cynosure and cesspool of the world! Not if I had a hundred tongues, every one shouting a different language in a different key, could I do justice to her splendid chaos. The most beautiful and the most squalid, girdled with a twofold zone of parks and slums; where the keen air from lake and prairies is ever in the nostrils, and the stench of foul smoke is never out of the throat." Let Steevens's capsule comment about the sprawling metropolis suffice, for our travels to Illinois's smaller cities and off-the-beaten-track attractions require us to shun Chicago. Chicago is an entire world unto itself, far removed from the state's more rustic spots, some of which lie near to but apart from the big city, keeping it at arm's length.

In the far northeastern corner of Illinois, near the Wisconsin border, lies the settlement of Zion, whose history is perhaps the most curious of any town in the state. On the last day of the nineteenth century a Scottish faith healer named John Alexander Dowie revealed himself as the man who'd purchased a large tract of land on the north shore along Lake Michigan. Soon the village of Zion sprang up there, and hundreds of Dowie's followers flocked to the area. A theocratic regime governed Zion: no liquor, tobacco or card games allowed, and even train stops on Sunday were banned. Apart from a lace factory owned by Chicago's Marshall Field and Company department store, the town controlled all local businesses. On Shiloh Boulevard—most of the settlement's streets bear biblical names—near Illinois Beach State Park stands Dowie's 1902 Shiloh House residence, which contains historical exhibits pertaining to Zion's utopian Christian era. As a carryover from the early days when Zionites performed a passion play every spring, the locals still present the Zion Passion Play on Saturday evenings in April and May. Illinois Beach State Park, which comprises a six-and-a-half-mile stretch of lakefront land, includes Illinois's only sand dunes, used during World War II by soldiers from nearby Fort Sheridan to practice tank maneuvers. In 1914 the first American western was filmed in the dunes; later, in the mid-'20s, the Essanay movie company shot a number of films at the sandy site, some starring Charlie Chaplin. In the southern part of the park runs—or most often does not run—the Dead River, a lagoon usually blocked from the lake by a sandbar that washes away during heavy rains when the pond then becomes a flowing stream. At Tempel Farms in Wadsworth, just west of the park, shows featuring Lipizzan stallions—bred from horses of the famous Spanish Riding School in

Vienna—take place over the summer. Just south lies Waukegan, probably the only place where an audience walked out on one of Lincoln's speeches (a fire interrupted the proceedings), and the hometown of comedian Jack Benny and of science fiction writer Ray Bradbury, who in some of his books portrayed the city as Green Town. On Waukegan's near north side—between Madison, Glen Flora and Ash streets—stands a group of nineteenth-century buildings, some listed on the National Register. At Deerfield, to the south, you can visit the Kitchens of Sara Lee where the huge bakery churns out an endless stream of pastries, many stored in the four-story freezer that holds eight million cakes— countless calories ready to challenge weight watchers across the country. At Glenview, still closer to Chicago, is The Grove, an eighty-two-acre nature preserve, listed on the National Register, where the Redfield mansion, also listed on the Register, and two other historic houses stand; while southwest of Glenview, at Des Plains, you'll find on the travel menu for the area another famous food company, McDonald's, which receives visitors at its hamburger museum. Back to the north, west of Waukegan, lie two towns filled with antique shops—Long Grove, an 1840s German settlement where an 1846 covered bridge, sections of a nineteenth-century tavern and other venerable buildings, many housing the village's eighty or so shops, lend an old-time atmosphere to the place, and Richmond, whose antique stores occupy century-old brick buildings. Iron hitching rings around town in Richmond recall the horse and buggy era there.

More antique stores tempt the traveler at Woodstock, southwest of Richmond. Many shops stand near the town square, an attractive enclave with cobblestone streets and an ornate gazebo surrounded by a pleasant lawn. The old Woodstock courthouse and jail building once held labor leader Eugene Debs, imprisoned here for his involvement in the

1894 Pullman strike, and also a n'er-do-well named "Red" McGee who politely left his jailer a Christmas card when the inmate escaped over the holiday. These days the courthouse delivers not justice but merchandise, sold in the shops that now occupy the restored structure. Across from the courthouse stands the 1889 Opera House, where Paul Newman and Woodstock native Orson Welles performed at the beginning of their careers. Performances still take place at the theater, whose interior—topped by an old stencil-decorated ceiling—resembles the salon of a Mississippi River steamboat. Little Union, a town of six hundred or so inhabitants southwest of Woodstock, boasts three museums: the rather commercial Seven Acres Antique Village and Museum, with a mixed bag of attractions, including an antique photograph collection, replicas of old buildings and a "necktie machine" (gallows) with a thirteen-coil noose built for use after the 1886 Haymarket Riot in Chicago; the Illinois Railway Museum, featuring one hundred and seventy vintage trolley and train cars and engines, some which carry passengers on short rides; and the McHenry County Historical Museum, housed in an 1870 schoolhouse. From Union you might want to swing out to the southwest via Sycamore—the town boasts an attractive county courthouse and hosts the annual Pumpkin Festival the last full weekend of October—to De Kalb, where barbed wire was invented in 1874. After timber grew scarce a need developed in the farm regions for a new type of fencing that animals couldn't breach. A number of people—among them De Kalb's Joseph F. Glidden and E. L. Elwood—filed patents for the idea of a barbed fence; only nearly twenty years later, in 1892, did the U.S. Supreme Court finally uphold Glidden's claims. Glidden Hospital memorializes the inventor, while the Elwood House Museum, an opulent Victorian mansion, recalls one of the product's early manufacturers. In downtown De Kalb stands the old

Egyptian Theater, listed on the National Register, a funky art deco structure.

Back to the east, but still west of Chicago, lies the lovely Fox River Valley, along which nestle historic old towns such as Elgin, St. Charles, Geneva and Aurora. Although the valley here is fewer than fifty miles from Chicago, the big city scarcely intrudes on the area's suburban, and occasionally country, atmosphere. The famous Elgin watch, first produced in 1867, is the product most closely associated with the city of that name, but Elgin also produced butter tubs, religious publications, craftsmen (graduates of the Watchmakers College) and condensed milk, developed soon after the Civil War by the town's Gail Borden, who gave his name to the now widely known dairy and food products company. Present-day attractions in Elgin include the Fox River Trolley Museum, with train and tram cars that run along the river, and the Leewards Creative Crafts Center, said to be the world's largest craft supply house. East of the central business area lies the historic district with nearly seven hundred old structures, three of them listed on the National Register: the Greek Revival-style "Old Main" (1856), a typical old cottage and the Universalist Church which—designed by the Elgin Watch Company's superintendent—sports a configuration resembling the shape of a pocket watch enclosed in a case. One house (155 South Gifford) belonged to a banker and a railroad magnate with the redoubtable name of Increase Child Bosworth, while at the residence of George Cook—son of David Cook, who founded what became the nation's largest interdenominational religious publishing house—the owner installed in his garage a turntable to avoid having to back his car out. St. Charles, farther south in the valley, is the antique capital of Illinois, also of the Midwest, perhaps of the U.S. and—who knows?—maybe even of the world. The town claims that the Kane County flea market, held the first

Sunday of every month, is the world's largest such event. The town also boasts more than a hundred antique dealers, many installed in old buildings near the Fox River, which runs through the center of town. Dozens of other boutiques and shops—one advertises with the temptingly sinister phrase "chocolate is our specialty"—dot the town, which also has more than fifty restaurants, one occupying an 1851 church converted into an eatery (old pews serve as seats) and another at the historic 1928 Baker Hotel. Geneva, just to the south, offers more antiques and boutiques, as well as dozens of specimens of late nineteenth- and early twentieth-century architecture which embellish the city's National Historic District. The town, nestled on the banks of the Fox, also specializes in specialty stores: more than a hundred independent (non-chain) shops clustered in Geneva purvey a wide range of merchandise. In late June every year Geneva celebrates its Swedish Days Festival. At La Fox, due west of Geneva, you'll find the Garfield Farm Museum, listed on the National Register, which features a working 1840s-era farm and an 1846 brick stagecoach inn. Continuing south in the valley, at Batavia you can visit the Fermilab, the world's largest (four miles long) and highest-energy nuclear particle accelerator, a device that smashes subatomic particles to produce even more infinitesimal fragments of matter. The complex includes a geodesic dome made from one hundred and twenty thousand soft-drink cans, perhaps the world's biggest atrium and a herd of buffalo that roam part of the lab's sixty-eight-hundred-acre grounds. To revert from the atomic age to antebellum times, the Batavia Depot Museum, which occupies the restored 1855 Gothic-style train station, includes a Mary Todd Lincoln Room, filled with Mrs. Lincoln's furniture. The last stop in the Fox River Valley is Aurora ("dawn"), so called, according to legend, because it was the first town in Illinois to install electric lights (1881); the name, however, predated the illuminations. Among the exhibits at the history museum, installed in an 1857 house, is the clock built over many years by local resident William Blanford, a nine-by-three-foot carved console with the Roman forum and other scenes depicted and a generous display of temporal and astronomical information. If you fancy recalling other sorts of stars, Aurora's art deco Paramount Theater, an old movie house, is worth a visit.

East of the Fox River, between the valley and Chicago, you'll find some additional attractions on the western fringes of the big city. East of Aurora lies Naperville, an attractive "down home" sort of town where old-time Illinois seems to live again at the Naper Settlement, a restored and re-created nineteenth-century pioneer village with twenty or so historical structures, among them a Victorian mansion listed on the National Register. To move from history to natural history, head for the Morton Arboretum, a fifteen-hundred-acre plant preserve just north of Lisle, the town adjacent to Naperville. At the Arboretum—established in 1922 by Morton Salt Company founder Joy Morton, whose father, agriculture secretary J. Sterling Morton, originated Arbor Day—you can tour the well-garnished grounds on an eight-mile drive, and on one of the park's six trails you can also catch a glimpse of the now rare Illinois prairie. Another rustic attraction lies nearby at Oak Brook, where the Old Graue Mill, established in 1849, still functions, the last antique grist mill in Illinois that continues to operate. The stately three-story brick mill building nestles among trees along Salt Creek where an eighteen-foot water wheel, dam and mill pond combine to create a picture-perfect scene. Inside, a miller explains the operation as he goes about his daily grind, while rooms on the upper floors house a museum of nineteenth-century Americana. Until 1916 water ran the mill, then steam power served up to 1924 when the facility closed. Now electricity turns the grinders, so the mill wheel remains only as a symbol of the old days and ways.

On the way to Wheaton, back to the northwest, you'll pass Stacy's Tavern Museum, listed on the National Register, an authentically furnished 1846 country inn stagecoach stop at Glen Ellyn, which also boasts some historic century-old houses, many between the 300 and 800 blocks of Main Street. At Wheaton, just west of Glen Ellyn, lies Cantigny, the five-hundred-acre country estate of Colonel Robert R. McCormick, one time editor and publisher of the *Chicago Tribune*. The colonel's grandfather, Joesph Medill, a founder of the Republican party, built the Georgian-style mansion—now a museum crammed with furniture and artifacts—in 1896. McCormick later added two wings and two porticos, the eastern side modeled after the one at Jefferson's Monticello. The former stables house a military museum, while ten acres of gardens enhance the grounds of the property, named after the French village where the American army undertook its first World War I offensive. Other famous Wheatonians are recalled at the Heritage Gallery, with exhibits on Illinois football star Red Grange, U.S. Steel Corporation head Judge Elbert Gary (after whom Gary, Indiana, is named) and evangelist Billy Graham, also commemorated in a museum on the campus of his alma mater, Wheaton College, whose library contains the Wade Collection of books and papers of such British authors as G.K. Chesterton, C.S. Lewis, Dorothy L. Sayers and J.R R. Tolkien. An 1891 Romanesque-style limestone building listed on the National Register houses the DuPage County Historical Museum, which might have been at Naperville, DuPage's first county seat. But in 1868 a band of Wheaton men, determined to carry out the mandate of a county election, descended on the courthouse then at Naperville and carried the public records back to Wheaton in a wagon. Thus was the county seat transferred.

Before leaving the Chicago area it's well worth visiting two historic enclaves that form part of the big city but somehow seem separate from it. English journalist James H. Morris, who visited the U.S. in 1953, observed in his book *As I Saw the U.S.A.:* "The Middle West is full of intense local patriotisms, but when a small frontier settlement blossoms into a metropolis Americans demand some more intimate loyalty, and are inclined to scuttle some of their fervor for Detroit or Chicago, let us say, in favor of such desirable suburbs as Grosse Pointe, Michigan, or Lake Forest, Illinois." One such "well-fed" (as Morris calls them) community is Oak Park, ten miles due west of downtown Chicago. Oak Park boasts a large number of sites recalling two local residents of great renown—Ernest Hemingway, born there in 1899, and Frank Lloyd Wright, a twenty-year resident. Hemingway, who lived in the leafy Chicago suburb until age eighteen, was born in the frame house embellished with a distinctive conical-roofed corner tower at 339 North Oak Park Avenue where the family lived until 1906 when they moved a few blocks north to a fifteen-room stucco structure at 600 North Kenilworth. On the stairway landing of this house stood a large mirror where young Ernest used to shadow box, and in the spacious music room (now removed to reduce heating costs) Grace Hemingway gave lessons to her son Ernie, who later avowed: "I was absolutely without talent. That cello—I played it worse than anyone on earth." A plaque on the lawn of the residence reads: "In this house Ernest Hemingway, novelist and journalist, lived his boyhood years and created his first literary efforts." Fully twenty-five Frank Lloyd Wright-designed structures still stand in Oak Park to mark the famous architect's years there. The first house he built in the town was his own, a Prairie School-type structure with typical horizontal lines, geometric forms and use of natural materials. Registered as a National Historic Landmark, the house, along with the architect's studio there, is the only Wright residence in Oak

Park open to the public. But you can see other Wright structures—including Unity Temple Unitarian Church, also listed on the National Register and also open to visitors—in the seventy-five square block area, a National Historic District, in the center of Oak Park where the buildings nestle among "the heavy trees of the small town that are a part of your heart if it is your town," as Hemingway wrote in a short story. The other Chicagoland enclave worth seeing is the Pullman Historic District, a National Historic Landmark, on the city's far south side. The model town was built in the 1880s for workers at the Pullman Palace (sleeping) Car Company. George Pullman's refusal to lower rent for houses in the company town after the depression that started in 1893 led the following year to the Pullman Strike, a renowned labor uprising. Almost all the original buildings—many still used—remain, among them the 1880 executive offices topped by a clock tower, workers' cottages, the stables, row houses and the venerable Hotel Florence, in operation from 1881 to 1975, now a museum (lunch is served in the old restaurant) and headquarters of the Historic Pullman Foundation, an organization engaged in preserving the century-old settlement.

Heading downstate you can proceed—perhaps via Lemont, which boasts a cookie jar museum—to Lockport, founded in 1836 as headquarters of the Illinois-Michigan Canal, a ninety-six-mile waterway, which functioned from 1848 to 1933, connecting Lake Michigan with the Illinois River. Installed in the original headquarters building, located in Lockport's National Historic District area, is a ten-room museum with displays relating to the canal's construction and operation. Also at Lockport, one of the country's best preserved canal towns (for another, Indiana's Metamora, see Chapter II, section 7) is the Pioneer Settlement, a collection of fifteen old structures—including a jail, a schoolhouse and a privy—which recall the nineteenth century. Through Lockport passes the unusual hundred-and-twenty-mile-long, ribbon narrow, cultural park, designated a National Heritage Corridor in 1984, that runs between Chicago and Peru. You can travel along the Corridor by foot, bike, horseback or canoe, while by car you can reach the sixty-foot-wide canal—which facilitated the growth of Chicago and led to the development of northeastern Illinois—at various access points along the way.

At Joliet, a few miles south of Lockport, a National Historic District filled with old houses recalls the days when boat traffic thronged the canal. In addition to that area, which lies just southeast of downtown, venerable Second Empire-style and limestone residences line North Broadway and Hickory Streets, while turn-of-the-century Victorian mansions rise along Western Avenue. The city also boasts the nation's first junior college, founded as the Joliet Township High School Central Campus, and the splendid old Rialto, a restored 1926 vaudeville and movie theater, listed on the National Register, with a block-long lobby reminiscent of the Hall of Mirrors gallery at Versailles Palace near Paris, an ornately decorated auditorium and a twenty-foot-long eight-arm chandelier bearing two hundred and fifty lights. To the southwest of Joliet lies Goose Lake Prairie State Park (no lake there; it was drained years ago), Illinois's only surviving extended stretch of original prairieland (for a brief summary of the Prairie State's prairieland history, see section 4). Farther south the little town of Dwight offers the 1857 Carpenter Gothic Church and an 1891 train depot, both restored and listed on the National Register. You can both visit and stay overnight in another landmark building, the Frank Lloyd Wright-designed Yesteryear Inn in Kankakee. Created by Wright in 1900 as a private house, the building was later converted into an inn with nine rooms and a restaurant. The large veranda overlooking the Kankakee River offers a pleasant place to relax and laze away the day after you've roamed the open road near and far to visit the many out-of-the-way attractions around the vast Chicagoland area.

9. The River Road Back to the Beginning:

The Life and Death of Mormons at Nauvoo and at Carthage
The River Towns of Warsaw and Quincy
Calhoun County: Living in the Past
Endearing, Enduring Elsah
Alton
Lewis and Clark Where the Mississippi and Missouri Meet

Mormon prophet Joseph Smith, who in 1839 led his followers from Missouri to Nauvoo in western Illinois, was the sort of person people reacted to with strong opinions—so strong that one day a mob of men murdered him. Peter Cartwright—a circuit-riding Illinois Methodist preacher, founder of McKendree College (see section 4) and, in 1832, winner of an Illinois General Assembly seat over a young New Salem store clerk and surveyor named Abe Lincoln—adjudged Smith "to be a very illiterate and imprudent desperado in morals but at the same time he had a vast fund of low cunning." In April 1844 Josiah Quincy, son of the President of Harvard University, and Charles Francis Adams, son of ex-president John Quincy Adams, visited Nauvoo where they enjoyed an unusually warm reception, thanks to confusion created by their names, which led locals to suppose the former chief executive himself was in the party. Young Adams found Smith clad in "striped pantaloons, a linen jacket, which had not lately seen the washtub, and a beard of some three days' growth." The cunning, slovenly Smith, as

Cartwright and Adams described him, established the town of Nauvoo ("beautiful place") at a bend overlooking the Mississippi River. There his followers built a thriving community which soon grew to become Illinois's largest city, with some twenty-five thousand inhabitants. (For the Mormon's departure from their settlements in Missouri to Nauvoo, see Chapter V, section 5.) During the early 1840s Smith turned the town into a kind of state within a state, a quasi-sovereign area with a militia called the Legion. Alarmed by the rise of this powerful kingdom of God and man, an armed mob took advantage of Smith's presence in June 1844 in Carthage, twenty-two miles southeast of Nauvoo, to storm the jail where the Mormon patriarch was lodged to protect him. As the crowd advanced toward the building two shots suddenly rang out, both hitting Smith's brother Hyrum, who fell to the floor groaning, "I am a dead man." Moments later, he was. Smith fired at the assailants, but the assault continued. When he finally moved to a window and prepared to jump from the second-floor room two shots exploded into his chest and the Mormon leader fell to the ground, where four additional bullets quickly riddled his body. Further attacks on the settlers at Nauvoo persuaded Brigham Young, the new prophet, to leave the area, and in February 1846 he led the first group of Mormons west across the frozen Mississippi River. Before long, others followed and Nauvoo soon became deserted. In 1849 a small band of French communists called the Icarians settled in the town but the utopian experiment eventually failed and Nauvoo languished until a handful of German settlers arrived in the late 1850s. Preserved in the village, now inhabited by eleven hundred people, are twenty or so buildings that date from the Mormon presence there a century and a half ago. The structures you'll see in old Nauvoo include the Joseph Smith Homestead, an 1803 log house—the town's oldest structure—the Prophet occupied on arriving in the area, and the lovely two-story wood mansion, filled with period furnishings, that Smith occupied from 1843 until his death the following year. Other original old structures include Brigham Young's house, its stair-step roof facade recalling Dutch architecture, as well as such commercial establishments as the *Times and Seasons* printing office, the Webb wagon shop that constructed vehicles for the 1846 Mormon exodus from Nauvoo, and the workshop of Jonathan Browning, a gunsmith whose son invented the Browning automatic machine gun. Behind the Homestead lie the graves of the Smith brothers, while atop a hill on the east side of town stands the site once occupied by the classic-style limestone temple, said to have been the largest and most impressive building in the entire west, outside of St. Louis. The day after the temple was dedicated on May 1, 1846, after more than five years of construction, the Mormons stripped the building of whatever they could remove and carried the pieces west with them to Salt Lake City. During the night of October 8, 1848, a fire destroyed virtually the entire building, leaving only the walls standing, and a year and a half later after a cyclone blew down one of the walls the others were razed. So today nothing remains of the great temple except the ground it once occupied. If you're in Nauvoo the second week in August, the *City of Joseph Pageant* presents a musical play that reviews the town's history, while the venerable Hotel Nauvoo, installed in a restored 1840 Mormon residence, will also give you the feel of the old days. A winery established during the Icarian period in the 1850s recalls the town's early days as well, and nearby stands a creamery that makes the tangy Nauvoo Blue Cheese, a delicacy that recalls the boast of an Illinois newspaper back in the late nineteenth century, when the state's dairy industry was booming, that at one establishment there operated a "500-cow-power cheese factory."

The River Road, south out of Nauvoo to Hamilton, twelve miles away, follows the Mississippi and offers some splendid views. At Carthage—inland, to the east—stands the old two-story stone block jail (open for tours) in which Joseph and Hyrum Smith were killed, while just west of Hamilton lies the river town of Warsaw, where Captain (later President) Zachary Taylor established a fort. The town later took the name Spunky Point, as Indians in the area procured there "spunk water" ("firewater"). At the corner of Second and Clay Streets stands the boyhood home of John Hay, lawyer, poet, novelist, short story and essay writer, private secretary to President Lincoln, ambassador to England and secretary of state under Presidents Teddy Roosevelt and William McKinley, the latter the second chief executive Hay served who died by an assassin's bullet. Hay campaigned for Lincoln and, as private secretary, lived in the White House. When the president died, Hay was at his bedside. Hay—who co-authored a biography of Lincoln considered by some the best until Carl Sandburg's volumes—is perhaps the only secretary of state whose poetry appears in anthologies. His verse is a rather rough-hewn version of Edgar Lee Masters-type tales of local characters, one being Jim Bludso, an engineer on the *Prairie Belle* steamer who saved passengers from the burning boat: "And, sure's you're born, they all got off/ Afore the smokestacks fell,—/ And Bludso's ghost went up alone/ In the smoke of the Prairie Belle."

The Federal architecture and laid-back old-time ambiance of Quincy, down river, recall those nineteenth-century steamboat days. Quincy, Adams County seat—the names honor President John Quincy Adams—was for twenty years in the mid-nineteenth century Illinois's second largest city, thanks in part to the thriving steamboat traffic of the era when as many as twenty-five hundred ships a year docked there. A few never made it. In 1827 Quincy merchant Asher Anderson ordered from St. Louis three thousand dollars worth of woolens, calico, muslins, cottons and ribbons that submerged when the boat sank, but after the store owner retrieved the water-soaked materials they immediately sold out because of the unusual patterns formed when the colors all ran together under water. Quincy's heritage from those prosperous times includes an unusually large stock of old buildings in a wide range of styles—even a Moorish-type castle, Villa Katherine, listed on the National Register. Stained-glass windows and ornamental pieces from some of those early structures are on display at the Gardner Museum of Architecture and Design, while the 1835 seventeen-room John Wood Mansion—a magnificent Greek Revival residence (listed on the National Register) owned by Wood, Quincy's founder and an early governor of Illinois—contains period furnishings and personal items, such as his Civil War pistols and the medical books Wood's father, a surgeon, used during the Revolutionary War. Displays on those and other wars fill the ambitiously named All Wars Museum, on the grounds of the Illinois Veteran's Home, one of the nation's largest and oldest residences for former military men. You'll find two other unusual collections at the Pharmacy Museum, crammed with antique bottles and apothecary items displayed in a century-old drug store, and the Lincoln-Douglas Valentine Museum, with unusual vintage valentines. The name of the latter museum recalls Quincy's Lincoln-Douglas debate, sixth in the series, commemorated by a Lorado Taft relief, the Illinois sculptor's last completed work (1935), which stands in Washington Park, formerly called John's Square to round out the John Quincy Adams trio of names honored in Quincy.

As the Mississippi flows south, the Illinois wanders west and finally the two rivers draw near to form the borders of Calhoun County, an oddly shaped peninsula-like tongue of land some fifty miles south of Quincy. "Every man and woman is in love with Calhoun county," claimed Mary Hartwell Catherwood in her booklet *Lower Illinois Valley Local*

Sketches of Long Ago. Indeed, it's hard not to like the tranquil rural region secluded there between the rivers. Only one bridge and four ferries connect Calhoun with Missouri (across the Mississippi) and with the Illinois "mainland," making the county—inhabited by less than six thousand people—one of the state's most isolated areas. For that reason, it's a true "getaway" sort of place—away from cities, from shopping centers, from fast food establishments (only slow food is served in the sleepy county) and from the twentieth century, for in Calhoun County you could well be back in 1847, or thereabouts, the year the Wittmond Hotel, a former stagecoach stop, was built. The red brick Wittmond in Brussels is a true period piece. At one side nestles a long narrow bar crammed with a chaos of objects, including a gold thread embroidered sombrero, while the next room serves as a general store with the emphasis on "general," for the items on offer seem as if Goodwill has just made a delivery there rather than a pick up. Plates, hats, doo-dads, gizmos, knickknacks litter the area. On one shelf stand bottles of wine—definitely non-vintage, although the dust on them no doubt is. In the old-fashioned dining room family-style meals—six hundred on a typical summer Sunday—stuff visitors from near and far. The Wittmond takes overnight guests in its eight rooms on the second floor, but even if you don't stay the night or dine there, you might want to try some apple pie, the local specialty. Calhoun County is apple country and, during the fall season, any number of farms or roadside stands offer pick-'em-yourself or freshly picked apples, as well as pumpkins, squash, cider, jellies, jams, apple butter and other treats.

Before leaving Calhoun to rejoin the outside world and contemporary life it's worth visiting Kampsville in the northern part of the county. If Calhoun's ambiance takes you back a century and a half, then the archeological museum at Kampsville will transport you ten thousand years back, for there you'll see artifacts excavated in the area at digs that unearthed prehistoric Indian cultures. Thousands of such sites have been identified in Illinois's Mississippi River Valley, among them Cahokia Mounds (see section 2) and Dickson Mounds (section 6). At the famous Koster site (now filled in, the dig was named after the farmer who owned the land) across the Illinois from Kampsville more than a dozen strata of early American Indian life—the earliest dating back to 8000 B.C.— were discovered. The Koster site yielded evidences of some of the earliest civilizations yet found anywhere in the world. The Kampsville Archeological Center, run by Northwestern University, offers tours of the area and operates research and dig programs. To leave Calhoun County it's fun to take one of the area's four ferries (all carry cars). *The Winfield* and the *Golden Eagle* crossings take you to Missouri; the *Golden Eagle*, one of the few ferries that crosses the Mississippi, is perhaps the nation's only remaining paddle-wheel ferry; while the Kampsville and Brussels boats cross the Illinois. On one early Illinois River ferry the enterprising owner connected to the steam engine a pair of millstones, which ground two hundred bushels of meal a day during the ship's trips back and forth.

The Brussels ferry drops you just by Pere Marquette State Park, Illinois's largest, with nearly eight thousand acres. The park commemorates Jesuit Jacques Marquette's exploration of the area (along with Louis Joliet) in 1673. A large white cross on highway 100 just east of the park entrance marks the spot where the two men, the first Europeans to enter what is now Illinois, landed. Pere Marquette Park includes a rustic stone and timber lodge with fifty rooms as well as seven stone guest houses, along with what's believed to be the world's biggest chess set, a twelve-foot-square board and pieces as tall as six-year-olds. Downstream a few miles lies the endearing village of Elsah, whose two hundred or so inhabitants (not including the faculty and students at the town's Principia College) occupy lovely old houses tucked into a narrow mile-long limestone ravine. Virtually all the homes in Elsah—the first entire community to be listed on the National Register—date from the Civil War era and earlier, making the hamlet one of the least spoiled and most photogenic places in the Midwest. The Elsah Landing Restaurant serves tasty meals and tempting pastries (also on sale at the bakery next door), while a few of the old homes in town house bed and breakfast establishments. The riverside road between Elsah and Alton takes you through a magnificent stretch of scenery: on one side flows the mighty Mississippi while to the east rise high tree-topped bluffs. A few miles before reaching Alton you'll pass on the left a modern reproduction of the Piasa bird, a fierce looking creature which, according to Indian legend, feasted on humans. Marquette mentioned in his journal having seen an early representation of the bird, said to be the greatest Indian painting ever found in North America. Alton is a hilly old river town crammed with antique stores, many installed in nineteenth-century buildings that line Broadway, a block from the Mississippi. A stone monument in a small park on Broadway marks the spot where the seventh and last Lincoln-Douglas debate took place on October 15, 1858. After Douglas spoke, a Democrat in the audience shouted, "Now let old long legs come out," whereupon Lincoln took the floor and said, among other things, that Douglas's arguments had as little substance as the soup made by boiling the shadow of a pigeon that had been starved to death. Just inside the door of the Alton *Telegraph* office a block up Broadway stands a horse-collar-shaped section of the press thrown into the Mississippi on November 7, 1837, to prevent Elijah Lovejoy from publishing his abolitionist newspaper in Alton. Shortly before,

Lovejoy had given up his St. Louis newspaper to move across the river from Missouri, where slavery was legal, to the free state of Illinois. Between July 24, 1836, and September 21, 1837, three presses he ordered delivered to Alton had been destroyed by local pro-slavery agitators. On the night of November 7 the anti-abolitionists not only destroyed Lovejoy's new press but also killed the young editor, who was buried the next day, his thirty-fifth birthday. The base of the slim ninety-three-foot-high granite pillar topped by a winged figure of Victory—the state's tallest monument—that marks Lovejoy's grave in the Alton Cemetery bears a portrayal of the printing press and the editor's stirring words: "But, gentlemen, as long as I am an American Citizen, and as long as American blood runs in these veins, I shall hold myself at liberty to speak, to write, to publish whatever I please on any subject—being amenable to the laws of my country for the same." Displays at the Alton Museum of History and Art next to the *Telegraph* office recall the Lovejoy affair (as does the National Register-listed homestead of his brother Owen Lovejoy, a leading abolitionist, at Princeton, Illinois: see section 7) and other local history, such as a duel involving Lincoln, and the life of Alton resident Robert Wadlow, who grew to be the world's tallest known human, topping out at eight feet eleven inches when he died in 1940, at age twenty-two. A lifesize statue of the "Gentle Giant," as he was called, stands on the College Avenue campus of the Southern Illinois University dental school, while his body lies buried at Upper Alton Cemetery. (The world's heaviest known human, one-thousand-and-sixty-five-pound Robert Earl Hughes, reposes in a pianocase-shaped, seven-foot-long, four-and-a-half-foot-wide casket in the hamlet of Benville, near Mt. Sterling east of Quincy. Hughes, who made his living as an exhibit with a traveling carnival, contracted measles in Indiana in July 1958 and died a few days later, having been too large to pass through the door of the local hospital to receive treatment. A moving van carried his corpse to the cemetery where a crane lowered Hughes's coffin into the grave.)

Two miles south of Hartford, below Alton, you'll come to a short spur road west to the Mississippi where a monument by the river commemorates the famous Lewis and Clark Expedition. William Clark, one of the leaders, was the younger brother of George Rogers Clark, who took Kaskaskia and Cahokia (see section 2) on his way to capture Vincennes, Indiana (Chapter II, section 3), from the British during the Revolutionary War. Eleven plaques, one for each state the expedition visited, relate a brief summary of the party's progress across each area, while in the center of the circular pavilion another inscription summarizes the undertaking: "Near here at Camp Dubois the Lewis and Clark detachment spent the winter of 1803–04. They left on May 14, 1804, and ascended the Missouri River to its source, crossed the Great Divide reaching the Pacific on November 7, 1805. They returned to Illinois on September 23, 1806, having concluded one of the most dramatic and significant episodes in our history." This site is the only easily accessible place where you can see the confluence of the Missouri and the Mississippi Rivers. Off to your right, across the wide Mississippi, the mouth of the Missouri gapes open as the waterway ends its long journey from the far reaches of the continent. This is truly the very heart of the heartland, for here merge the two watery arteries that drain the vast central section of the nation. Past this point Marquette and Joliet, the first white men to have visited the region, floated in 1673, and from here Lewis and Clark trekked west to explore the huge unknown continent beyond the great river. Here hunted Indians of old and by this spot once chugged steamboats and now glide mile-long freight barges. Lincoln and Lovejoy, Masters and Sandburg haunt the area, as do countless other figures—rivermen, prairie farmers, the renowned, the obscure—who populated the nearby prairie or floated the fast-flowing waters. And here at this isolated spot—near Cahokia (section 2) where the ancient Indian mounds rise and where the first French settlers founded what became Illinois—we can end our tour of the state, watching the great Missouri and Mississippi as they stream together and thinking of the past, of time and the rivers.

IV

Iowa

1. Iowa:

Land of the Land

In Iowa the land dominates as in no other state. Even as the state was being organized awareness of the land's importance remained deeply rooted in peoples' minds. During a discussion of the proposed banking system at the October 1844 Constitutional Convention in Iowa City a delegate delivered an impassioned speech asserting that "a Bank of earth is the best Bank, and the best share, a Plough share." Iowans have had an almost mystic, primitive view of their land. *Iowa: The Home for Immigrants,* published in 1870 by the Iowa Board of Immigration, personified the soil as a kind of earth mother: the land "is always true to the confidence reposed in her, she has never failed at the harvest to give her people bread."

This confidence in the soil's fertility is not misplaced. As early as 1840 Iowa was producing a surplus of food, and for years the state has ranked second only to California—nearly three times as large—in the value of farm products sold. Iowa

IOWA

Decorah
Guttenberg
Dubuque
Cedar Rapids
Amana
Iowa City
Davenport
Mississippi River
Keokuk
Waterloo
Mason City
Britt
Fort Dodge
Boone
Grinnell
Des Moines
Pella
Winterset
Mt. Pleasant
Burlington
Keosauqua
Le Mars
Sioux City
Council Bluffs
Missouri River

produces about 10 percent of the nation's food. It is the largest corn producer in the U.S., and, for that matter, in the world. The state ranks first or second every year in oat and soybean production. Iowa supplies 20 percent of the nation's soybeans and the same proportion of the country's corn. In Iowa reside a quarter of the country's hogs and, measured by income, the state leads the U.S. in livestock. All but about 6 percent of the state's thirty-six million acres is devoted to agriculture. Iowa occupies fully 26 percent of the nation's grade I ("excellent") land. Iowa's terrain is divided into five categories that encapsulate the state's agricultural activity: Western and Eastern Livestock, Northeast Dairy, Southern Pasture and North Central Grain. That grain area, which occupies the stretch of soil in the center part of the state from near Des Moines to the Minnesota line, is said to be the finest corn land in Iowa and thus, no doubt, in the world.

Corn is Iowa's most pervasive image. In *Portrait of Iowa,* Iowa writer Paul Engle noted: "If one symbol to represent the state had to be chosen, it should be the tough corn plant." In *Ioway to Iowa,* Irving Berdine Richman recounted the typical diet consumed by mid-nineteenth settlers in the state: "Corn bread and corn mush! Corn mush and corn bread! Corn bread and corn mush! Morning, noon, and night—corn bread and corn mush! Day in and day out, week in and week out, corn bread and corn mush!" Nor was that the eating cycle only for humans. G. Smith Stanton, a New Yorker who in the 1860s moved to "the breezy West," as he called it, described in *When the Wildwood Was in Flower* the transition from grass-fed to corn-fed cattle: "Thousands of acres of prairie were broken up, corn planted, and the cattle yarded to be fattened and shipped to the Eastern markets. Absolutely nothing but corn was fed. . . . The droppings from the cattle were as yellow as corn meal; in fact, it was ground corn, so to speak. In all feed-yards there were twice the number of hogs as of cattle; the hogs were fattened from the droppings of the steers. We calculated what passed through one steer would fatten two hogs. The cattle ate the corn, the hogs the droppings, and we ate the hogs."

Like the regularity of the seasons, this sort of food cycle seems to symbolize the regularity and stability—the sense of permanence—that prevails in Iowa. In an agricultural state, everything comes around—and around again, thus lending life a certain symmetry. In an introduction to *Iowa The American Heartland,* Hugh Sidey notes: "Towns and cities have not grown too big in Iowa so that they are more problem than pleasure. They form, instead, by some magic a network of people that has symmetry." This symmetry extends even to the state's rank in the union—Iowa was for a time twenty-fifth in both size and population (now twenty-ninth in inhabitants)—and to its arrangement, the counties being so regular and symmetrical that, as G. Smith Stanton (quoted above) notes: "One could have a good game of checkers on a map of the State of Iowa."

Iowans' connection with their land is a constant in the state's history. An essay on "The Iowans" by Rollin Lynde Hartt, referring to an attempt to put Scotland into five words (Scott, Burns, heather, whiskey, religion) maintains that "In Iowa you pack the thing tighter. Three nouns are enough: corn, cow, and hog!" Iowa is an especially nonurban state: its largest city, Des Moines, does not rank in the top hundred, by size, of American cities. Only as late as 1960 did the state's urban population exceed the rural, but Iowa still has the nation's largest number of farm residents, measured both by percentage and by numbers.

Perhaps only in such an agriculturally intensive state as Iowa could there have arisen controversies dubbed the "Honey War," an 1839 boundary dispute with Missouri (you'll read about it in section 2), or the 1931 "Cow War" when farmers refused to allow their animals to be inoculated by veternarians, arguing, "They can't punch holes in our cows." This agricultural orientation gives the Iowans an earthy, practical view of the world. Well grounded in their rural ways, the people of Iowa, whose culture flourishes along with their agriculture—Iowans enjoy the nation's highest literacy rate—sometimes seem a throwback to earlier times when life was less removed from the land. In *Reminiscences of New Castle, Iowa,* Sarah Brewer-Bonebright referred to that intimate connection with the land, which is perhaps Iowa's most distinguishing feature. As a farm child, she wrote, she "developed an acuteness of vision and hearing that rarely is acquired except through contact" with nature. She goes on: "We were instructed to be alert, vigilant, active; to listen and look for the bee, birds or other field-game; to note the peculiar call or cry and observe the habits of small forest-varmints."

Iowa's land-locked mentality extends even to manmade artifacts. *A Handbook of Iowa,* published in 1893, described the Sioux City Corn Palace, built in 1887, as "decorated with corn, all varieties of that cereal in size, color and tint being used in happy combination of form and shade which made the Corn Palace to the beholder, when the rich autumn sun light shone upon it, a thing of surprising grandeur" that "enraptured" visitors. In other countries and cultures, such glowing terms might be used to describe architectural gems like the chateaus of the Loire Valley, castles on the Rhine or the stately homes of England, but in Iowa—true to its roots—it is a corn building, a crop-covered structure, that elicits such rapturous praise.

As you wander the back roads and byways of Iowa you'll see the endless fields of corn and the neat white farmhouses tucked into the green landscape—picturesque scenes that seem out of a painting by Grant Wood, the Cedar Rapids artist who captured on canvas the state's essence (see section 5). The landscape, and Iowans awareness of and dependence on it, defines the state and its people. In *Prairie City, Iowa,*

Douglas Bauer refers to a southern woman who maintained that "the Midwestern sensibility must surely be the most finely tuned of any region's, because of the landscape that nourishes it. Plain, squarely sectioned, altered only by its seasons, it has none of the easy majesty of oceans, mountains, forests. A Midwesterner must look hard for his natural variety, must grow an appreciation for the hummocky roll of hillsides, the imperceptibly varying line of land to sky."

The land has shaped Iowans as much as the people of Iowa have shaped the land. No poet or professor, novelist or journalist ever gave a better testimony to the land than did Elmer G. Powers, a Boone County farmer who wrote in *Years of Struggle,* a diary he kept from 1931 to 1936:

> Personally I still think the farm is by far the best place of all. . . . It is life itself. First of all, the soil, the feel of the earth. . . . The weather and the changing seasons. All life itself comes from these several things. Then there is the plant life. The crops, the trees. The livestock and poultry and all of their young things to be cared for. The responsibility of growing the food and flesh for a distant and often unappreciative city. Just to be close to and work with nature is one of life's greatest opportunities.

2. Valley Villages, Pleasant Places:

The Des Moines River Country Towns of Bonaparte,
Farmington, Bentonsport and Keosauqua
American Gothic at Eldon
Ottumwa
Fairfield
Old Threshers at Mount Pleasant
Salem

Tucked away in the rolling hills of southeastern Iowa is the delightful village-filled Des Moines River valley as well as pleasant places like Mount Pleasant and other rustic areas typical of the state. Mount Pleasant's old-time agricultural museum, along with the small-town and rural atmosphere in the area, offers a good introduction to Iowa, a state rich in out-of-the-way hamlets and off-the-beaten-track attractions.

A good place to start a tour of this secluded corner of Iowa is Bonaparte, one of the many peaceful little villages perched beside the Des Moines, which meanders through the green, hilly countryside. Settled in 1836, Bonaparte was named for the French emperor by William Meek, who built a dam and a grain mill there on the Des Moines River. Like the other riverside towns in the valley, Bonaparte presents a picture out of the past. Lining First Street, the sleepy settlement's main artery, are such old-fashioned establishments as the Bonaparte Territorial Saloon, the historic White's Shopping Center buildings (1886) and the tin-facaded Haney Opera House (1894). You'll also find there the headquarters of the Bonaparte Navy, not a remnant of one of Napoleon's far-flung military units but a canoeing club where you can get information on arranging a "float trip"—as canoe excursions are called in the Midwest—on the Des Moines River, a popular float stream. The 1844 Aunty Green Hotel, once a famous hostelry for riverboat passengers, now houses the Bonaparte Museum. The old Aunty Green is listed on the National Register, as are the nineteenth-century lock walls on the river behind the town's old-time restored mill, which occupies the site of the original grist mill built by town founder William Meek in the 1830s.

Much of Bonaparte's history has swirled around the mill and through the locks. Mill towns were always important and Bonaparte is a good place to see a surviving example of those now scarce symbols of old Iowa. As Jacob A. Swisher noted in his 1940 book *Iowa, Land of Many Mills,* "The water of Iowa streams has turned hundreds of mill wheels and ground the grist for thousands of pioneers. More than seven hundred flour mills, driven by water power, have been erected along Iowa streams. Only a very few are left, and those are slowly passing." Back in the old days, farmers came from miles around—their crop-laden wagons pulled by pack horses—to get grain ground into flour at the mill in Bonaparte, then a lively town crowded with hotels, taverns and trading posts. After William Meek died, his sons took over the property—the Meek inherited the mill, if not the earth—and added various improvements, including carding machines that saved pioneer women from the time-consuming hand-carding process. When the Meeks refused to alter their dam to improve the fishing in the Des Moines River there, locals promoted a bill in the state legislature in 1902 providing for construction of a fishway. The petition for the proposal was in verse (of sorts), the first stanza—representative of the poem-petition's other fourteen stanzas—stating:

> Said the Pickerel to the Catfish:
> "I heard rare news today;
> That the dam down here at Bonaparte
> Will have a good fish-way!"

After listening to the rest of the poem the legislature—perhaps to avoid a second reading—passed the bill, a result the *Chicago Tribune* noted as based on "arguments in doggerel."

A decade before the Bonaparte pickerel confided in the catfish, the dam was the scene of unusual traffic when an army of the unemployed passed through the village on the way from California to Washington. After the Panic of 1893, a band of unemployed joined together to march on the nation's capital in a force called Coxey's Army, named after Jacob S. Coxey, an Ohio businessman who formed the movement. When one unit of some fifteen hundred men, called Kelly's Industrial Army, arrived in twenty-four boxcars at Council Bluffs in western Iowa on April 15, 1894, the railroads refused to carry the men onward, so the band made its way on foot halfway across the state to the Des Moines area. There the group assembled one hundred and thirty-four scows that the men used to float down the Des Moines River. One of the "foot soldiers" in this army of the unemployed was Jack London, then a San Francisco coal heaver and later the famous author of *White Fang* and other adventure tales. In his pencilled diary of the march, London noted on May 17 in Bonaparte: "The first boat of the Kelly fleet slid over the dam at 3 o'clock this afternoon, and by 8:30 all were over, with no damage beyond wetting a few men." The restored historic old mill by the dam these days houses a restaurant called Bonaparte's Retreat and an antique store.

A few miles downstream from Bonaparte lies Farmington, Van Buren County's oldest settlement (1833) and once a major trading center. The 1848 Congregational Church, the oldest west of the Mississippi, houses the village museum, while the nearby Burg Building, a stone structure where a thriving carriage factory once operated, is listed on the National Register. One of those nineteenth-century utopian settlements common in the Midwest once functioned in the Farmington area. In the spring of 1839 a liberal thinker and religious dissident named Abner Kneeland, the last person ever imprisoned in Boston for blasphemous writings, left Massachusetts at the age of sixty-five to establish in Iowa the colony of Salubria, the "First Society of Free Inquirers." To his friends in the East the transplanted New Englander well described the valley's beguiling landscape: "Even aside from the persecution I have endured in my native state, I know of no place in Boston that could afford one half the pleasure, as to the beauty and grandeur of the scenery, as it does to sit in my front door here and look across the Des Moines River; to see the large branching trees on the nearest bank and the beautiful green forest on the opposite side—this wonderful country which is destined to outvie everything which can be even imagined in the East." After Kneeland's death in 1844, the colony disbanded, but a turn-of-the-century visitor discovered the agnostic's granddaughter teaching Sunday school at Farmington's Congregational Church, built on land given by the Kneeland family.

Upstream from Bonaparte is the lovely little town of Bentonsport, a settlement of thirty or forty or so souls—maybe even fifty if you include dogs and cats. Founded in 1839 and named after Missouri's Senator Thomas Hart Benton, the village was (along with Vernon just across the Des Moines River) designated a National Historic District in 1972—and justifiably so, for Bentonsport is one of the best preserved and least spoiled nineteenth-century settlements in the Midwest. Bentonsport is truly a delightful place to linger. Perhaps nowhere else in Iowa can you so well get the feel for how the state appeared a century and more ago. A scattering of some twenty historic houses and buildings along the Des Moines recall the days when Bentonsport was a thriving river town of fifteen hundred people. Among the residents in the mid-nineteenth century was Albert Bigelow Paine, one of Mark Twain's most respected biographers. Paine no doubt met Twain when the young man from Hannibal, Missouri

was working in Iowa's Mississippi River towns in the 1850s
(see section 9). In pioneer days Bentonsport served as a port
of call for flatboats plying freight between the Mississippi
(into which the Des Moines River flows) and the interior of
Iowa. After the Civil War Bentonsport's whirring mills
churned out paper, flour, wool and linseed oil, while the
town's two hotels, three hardware stores, four general stores
and five churches catered to other needs.

Some of the buildings that housed those activities survive
to this day. The narrow, one-story 1853 Greef Commercial
Building—now housing a small museum and an antique
shop—served through the years as a bank, post office, general store and town hall. Nearby stands the 1852 post office,
which operated for ninety-five years until closing in 1947.
The interior—crank phone on the wall, old fixtures and a
posted admonition "Be thrifty, invest in postal savings"—
recalls the old days when locals gathered in the room to
collect the latest news by mail and by gossip. The old-
fashioned country store next door—complete with original
furnishings, antiques, "penny" candy and other typical old-
time items—also presents a picture out of the past.

In a town as small as Bentonsport, the general store offered
not only a place to shop; it also served as a meeting place
where people came to socialize. News, as well as merchandise, was traded there. Phil Strong, an Iowan who often
wrote about his native state—he grew up in Keosauqua, a few
miles up river from Bentonsport—recalled in *Hawkeyes: A
Biography of the State of Iowa,* a place like the Bentonsport
shop:

> Now the general store is not peculiarly Iowan . . . but they are
> particularly well developed in the Midwest and, in the Midwest,
> in Iowa. . . . As a substitute for the theater, the forum, state
> banquets, grand opera, the Union League or any other club, and
> a multitude of other urbane metropolitan activities, the Iowa
> country store is second to no country store in the United States.

Next to the general store rises Mason House, built in 1846 as a hotel for steamboat passengers and other travelers. Operated by the Mason family for ninety-nine years, the hotel—one of the few Des Moines River steamboat hostelries still functioning—contains many of its original furnishings. Mason House is now run as an inn which, the establishment's brochure states, is "worthy of special note because of the stout determination of the hosts to give visitors a place to stay that is quiet, charming and memorable."

Before leaving Bentonsport it's worth stopping in at the Odd Fellows Hall, an 1840s-vintage building that once served as a furniture factory. Installed in the hall these days is a cooperative arts and crafts shop. Nearby stand most of the town's few remaining residences, many of them attractive and stately red brick structures in Georgian style.

A rickety, single-lane 1882 iron bridge, the oldest span still in use on the Des Moines, takes you across the river to the village of Vernon, part of the Bentonsport National Historic District. Vernon's main building of historical interest is the 1868 Federal-style structure used as a schoolhouse until 1960. In 1968 artist Wendell Mohr and his wife, Betty, bought the building, which they restored and remodeled. The schoolhouse and Mohr's studio, which occupies a spacious room where teachers once taught readin', writin' and 'rithmetic to grades one through eight, are open to visitors by chance or by appointment.

A few miles up river you'll arrive at Keosauqua, seat of Van Buren County. The quiet settlement of a thousand people retains its nineteenth-century river town atmosphere. When the *Science*—laden with flour, meat and pork—reached Keosauqua in the autumn of 1837 the steamboat era began for the town. Soon some forty sternwheelers, mostly light-draft craft, plied the Des Moines. The story was told that when the *Michigan,* an especially small ship, put in at Keosauqua in 1856 a local said to the captain, "My wife's never seen a steamboat. Can't you let me put your boat on my wagon and take it home to show her? I'll return your ship in an hour or two, then you can be on your way."

Phil Strong, Iowa native and perhaps the leading author of the lore and traditions that typify the state, was a local boy (born at Keosauqua in 1899) who wrote some forty books, the most famous of them *State Fair,* which inspired the Rodgers and Hammerstein musical of the same name. In a reminiscence entitled "Christmas in Iowa," Strong recalled the old days in Keosauqua: "We have climbed the high hill above the Des Moines River, and there is my hometown, a crescent of red and green and yellow lights spooning around the river bend where, a hundred years ago, the little steamboats connecting the Mississippi with the center of Iowa would have been discharging passengers for the town's two over-size hotels—one gone now, gone with the boats."

The remaining hotel—Keosauqua's most striking relic of those early riverboat days—is the delightful old Manning, built in 1854 on the site of a log cabin trading post Edwin Manning constructed in 1837. At first the structure served as a general store and a bank, then later it was converted into a hotel and the two upper stories added. Listed on the National Register, the Manning offers a true picture out of the past. Outside, a long two-tier gallery runs along the facade, while within old fixtures and furnishings recall the days of a century and more ago. Summers, dinner theater shows enliven the dining room of the Manning, which has continuously operated as a hotel for nearly a hundred years. Near the hotel rises the handsome Van Buren County courthouse, the oldest (1840) in Iowa, and the 1845 Pearson House, one of the earliest surviving residences in the state.

That great crescent Strong referred to describes the sweeping horseshoe bend curve the Des Moines River makes as it snakes past Keosauqua which, appropriately enough, means in Indian language "great bend." The ripples in the bend there led to the 1839 Missouri-Iowa boundary dispute which became known as the Honey War. A controversy arose over the location of the Des Moines River "rapids," fixed by Congress in 1820 as the border between the two states. Iowa claimed the "rapids" lay farther south, where the Des Moines joins the Mississippi. In the disputed territory grew groves of so-called honey trees—trees in which bees produced honey, the only sweetener available on the frontier and thus coveted by both states. When a Missouri sheriff tried to collect taxes in Van Buren County, Iowans arrested him, whereupon the governor of Missouri called out the troops. Robert Lucas, territorial governor of Iowa, then mustered a rather motley band of twelve hundred Iowans—armed with pitchforks, dashers from churns, crude swords cut from sheet iron—to form a militia to repel the expected invasion. One captain carried six wagonloads of supplies for his men: five of the vehicles transported liquor. A woman who owned property in the border area hoped the land would remain part of Iowa as she'd heard the Missouri climate was not as good for crops. A Missouri poet derisively wrote:

> Three bee-trees stand about the line
>   Between our state and Lucas;
> Be ready all these trees to fall,
>   And bring things to a focus.
> We'll show old Lucas how to brag,
>   And seize our precious honey!
> He also claims, I understand,
>   Of us three bits in money.

But no blood—or honey—was shed, as the two states opted to decide the dispute peacefully, as if in confirmation of Shakespeare's observation in *Henry V*: "So work the honey-bees,/Creatures that by a rule in Nature teach/The act of order to a peopled kingdom"—and in 1849 the U.S. Supreme Court decided the matter in favor of Iowa.

Perhaps this legal rather than martial method of handling the conflict reflects that down-to-earth practicality and realism which typifies the Midwestern mentality. An illustration of those characteristics appears in what Phil Strong describes as a remark "now a part of legend in Keosauqua—the answer made by Thad Shewd when, just after his restaurant burned down without insurance, someone asked him with clumsy sympathy, 'How are things?' 'O.K.,' said Thad. 'I had a good breakfast, and it ain't time for dinner yet.'"

Still farther up the Des Moines, twenty-five miles (by road) northwest of Keosauqua, you'll come to Eldon, a small farm town that boasts one of America's most famous houses. At the northwest corner of Gothic and Burton streets stands the old Dibble residence, a simple one-and-a-half-story, 1860s-vintage, white modern house with a gothic-style window on the upper facade. In 1930 Iowa artist Grant Wood, inspired by the archetypical Midwestern small-town house, posed his sister Nan and his dentist, a man named Byron McKeeby, in front of the residence. That house and their visages are now world famous, for the resulting painting was "American Gothic," a work acquired for three hundred dollars by the Chicago Art Institute, which still owns the picture.

Ottumwa, which straddles the Des Moines River a few miles up from Eldon, reflects Iowa's agricultural activity, with its John Deere farm implement factory (open for tours) and the John Morrell packing plant that formerly functioned there. It was purely by chance that the Morrell operation located in Ottumwa. On his way home from England in the 1870s Joseph G. Hutchison, Ottumwa lawyer and businessman, happened to meet Thomas D. Foster, nephew of English meat packer John Morrell. Foster was traveling to the U.S. to find a site for his uncle's packing plant. Hutchison convinced Foster to establish the operation in Ottumwa, where it began in 1876. Edna Ferber, author of *Show Boat, So*

Big, Cimarron and other well-received novels, lived in Ottumwa from 1890 to 1897 when her father operated a store there. When she returned in the late 1920s she wrote, "I found Ottumwa a tree-shaded, sightly, modern American town of its size; clean and progressive." Another famous local resident was a young lieutenant (j.g.) named Richard M. Nixon, who was stationed at the Ottumwa naval air base for seven months during World War II. He and his wife, Pat, who worked as a teller at Union Bank and Trust Company, lived in a fifty-five-dollar-a-month apartment at the Hillside, East Fourth and Green Streets.

At Agency, a hamlet of six hundred people seven miles east of Ottumwa, reposes Chief Wapello of the Fox tribe. The tribe's campground was located at the present site of Ottumwa High School. Joseph Street, a federal Indian agent, befriended the redskins and smoked the peace pipe with Chief Wapello, who requested that he be interred next to Street. When the Indian died in 1842, two years after the white man's death, he was laid to rest near Street in the small cemetery at Agency, and there the two repose today, one grave marked by a boulder with a metal plaque, the other by a small obelisk.

Although the first Iowa State Fair was held (in 1854) in Fairfield, eleven miles east of Agency, the town was named not for that event but for the fair fields that embellish the area. After moving around the state for twenty-five years, the Fair in 1879 received a permanent home in Des Moines where it's held every August for eleven days. The Iowa Fair—which Phil Strong romanticized in his novel *State Fair*—is perhaps the nation's quintessential state fair, much of Iowa's culture being based on agriculture. At the very first fair there in Fairfield, which boasts the first Carnegie Library west of the Mississippi, ten girls mounted on horses vied for a gold watch. Disputing the judges' decision, the spectators in protest collected one hundred and sixty-five dollars for the favorite, whom they sent to the Fairfield Female Academy. Another local educational institution was Parsons College, founded in 1875. In 1974, after the college closed, Maharishi Mahesh Yogi's Universal Field Based Civilization movement bought the one-hundred-and-forty-acre campus and buildings for two million dollars and moved from cramped quarters at Santa Barbara, California, into the Fairfield facilities, renamed Maharishi International University. Followers of the Transcendental Movement now constitute 10 percent or so of the Iowa town's nine thousand residents, a touch of California exotic there in the small Midwestern settlement of Fairfield.

A more typical Midwestern ambiance prevails at Mount Pleasant, twenty-two miles east of Fairfield. Recollections, and collections, of old-time rural and small-town America abound in Mount Pleasant. The Thresher's Museum offers dozens of antique steam-driven farm vehicles, some a century old, while the unusual Museum of Repertoire Americana contains displays of memorabilia from early stage productions, including medicine shows, showboats, minstrel revues, Chautauqua and Lyceum companies, musicals, stock companies, touring troupes and other such theater ensembles. The museum boasts an especially large collection of antique stage drops and front curtains. Also on the grounds of the Thresher's display stands a nineteenth-century Midwestern village with a blacksmith shop, saloon, jail, bank, post office and other old establishments, many of them originals moved from elsewhere.

In those old days of the last century, threshing time was a major event on the farm. In *Memories of Fourscore Years,* Charles August Ficke, a Davenport lawyer who grew up on an Iowa farm, recalled: "Threshing week was an outstanding event in pioneer days. . . . Threshing week was the barometer that was to indicate whether joy or disappointment was to be the reward for the year's labor and worry." Every year for five days ending on Labor Day those old times are recalled at the annual Midwest Old Settlers and Threshers Reunion at Mount Pleasant. The event started in 1950 when a group of Henry County farmers assembled to fire up their old steam threshers. The Reunion is a splendid, nostalgia-rich celebration, with demonstrations of the old steam-driven farm equipment, displays of antique vehicles, craft demonstrations, musical performances, tent theater shows and plentiful down-home country cooking. A passage from a 1958 *Popular Mechanics* magazine article by Clifford B. Hicks captures the allure of the lumbering old machines: "The chuff-chuff, toot-toot of a restored engine is an irresistible call to the soul of the old-time iron man or farmhand who once sweated beside such a behemoth. The ponderous hulk of iron is a magnet. Spot a restored steamer and you'll find a gang of old-time threshers threshing over the good old days."

If you overnight in Mount Pleasant, the most atmospheric place to stay is the historic old Harland House, a boxy brick pile built in 1857 by James Harlan, a friend of Abraham Lincoln. Harlan was the first president of Mount Pleasant's Iowa Wesleyan College, which in 1866 graduated the first woman lawyer in the U.S., Harlan also served as U.S. senator and secretary of the interior. He built in addition to the brick mansion a smaller house, a handsome white frame residence where he lived for sixteen years. In 1868 Lincoln's son Robert married Harlan's daughter Mary, and the couple and (later) their three children spent many summers at the house, which Mrs. Robert Todd Lincoln donated to Iowa Wesleyan in 1907. In the residence, restored and outfitted with period furnishings and open to visitors, is preserved a door bearing the names, ages and height measurements of the three grandchildren of Abraham Lincoln—a poignant reminder, there in serene and pleasant Mount Pleasant in the American heartland, of the martyred president and his time, an era recalled in Salem, ten miles south, beyond the Skunk River.

In 1835 Aaron Street founded Salem, Iowa's first Quaker settlement and, in fact, the first Quaker village west of the Mississippi. Like their co-religionists in Wayne County, Indiana, where the Levi Coffin house offered escaped slaves a haven (see Chapter II, section 7), the Quakers in Iowa were active in the abolitionist movement. In Salem stands the old Lewelling homestead, an imposing stone house that served as a stop on the Underground Railroad. Furnished with authentic frontier pieces from the 1830s, the house, combed with hideaways and tunnels where runaway slaves sought refuge, is open to visitors. If you're in the area in late August, the weekend before the Mount Pleasant Reunion, you can drop in to share the food, music, dancing and other festivities at the annual reunion of descendants of the Salem pioneers.

There you can experience the Midwestern tradition of community and hospitality that often includes strangers. Because distances in the Midwest are long, outsiders have of necessity traveled a far piece to get there—wherever the "there" might be. In addition, a newcomer might arrive with some information or gossip or news from the wider world beyond. Far from the coasts, the Middle West cannot be a landfall at which travelers automatically arrive, and bicoastal jetsters who view middle America from afar (from above) find the heartland a fly-over region unless they contrive to land on its broad land. A visitor to the Midwest must thus want to get there. So, likely as not, visitors will be well received in those little towns that dot the Midwestern landscape. Less taciturn than the New Englander and less saccharine than the southerner, the matter-of-fact Midwesterner will often run the risk of being taken by taking in strangers and offering them hospitality. In *Hawkeyes: A Biography of the State of Iowa* Phil Strong tells of the gathering at Kilbourne: "Once a year hundreds of people came to eat a picnic under the oaks and maples of a field outside this hamlet, listen to a brief, homemade program, and talk to each other." It seems that outsiders, people from nearby counties, tended to drop "in for a moment—the moment was always 11:59—lunch was at 12:00." But all comers, from near and far, were served, as you too will be if you "drop in for a moment" at the annual Salem reunion—a typical heartland get-together where you can enjoy the flavor and taste of small-town Midwestern life.

3. May Festival and Maytags, "Go West" and Wild West:

Iowa's Dutch Town of Pella
Oskaloosa
What Cheer
Josiah ("Go West, Young Man") Grinnell's Grinnell
Newton, Home of Maytag
A Wild West Remnant at the Mesquakie Indian Settlement

Something about Iowa—the land, the space, the freedom, the frontier—attracted to the state in the nineteenth century a wide variety of Europeans. Czechs, Hungarians, English, French, Swiss, Luxemburgers, Norwegians, Dutch, Germans and others settled in the state in the early days. In 1870 more than one out of five Iowans were foreign born, and as late as 1918 so many German speakers still populated Iowa that Governor William Harding issued a proclamation forbidding the use of any foreign language in the state. Although the decree was much ignored, during the First World War Iowans did take to calling German measles "liberty measles." Languages in which the 1870 promotional handbook *Iowa: The Home for Immigrants* appeared indicate the range of nationalities sought: thirty-five thousand copies in English, fifteen thousand in German, six thousand in Norwegian, five thousand in Dutch, four thousand in Swedish.

Many of the early European colonies—Hungarian, English, French—failed to endure, but the Dutch town of Pella, founded in 1847 by nearly eight hundred Hollanders, not only survived but thrived. In the aftermath of the Napoleonic wars in Europe a state church was established in Holland. When the church harassed certain Calvinistic sects, members decided to emigrate to the New World. One group established the town of Holland, Michigan. Another smaller group traveled west from Baltimore by rail and stagecoach to the Ohio River, then by boat to St. Louis and north to Keokuk, Iowa, where they exchanged gold carried in an iron chest for wagons, oxen and horses. Finally they reached the eighteen thousand acres of land in Marion County they'd acquired for a dollar twenty-five cents an acre and there the Dutch settled. So eager were they to put Europe behind them, the Hollanders requested a special commissioner to administer the oath of citizenship to the entire populace collectively. Since the newcomers spent the first winter in sod houses with straw roofs, the settlement became known as Strawtown. Before long, log cabins and brick and stone houses sprung up, and by 1850 Quaker missionaries praised the town as the best-kept village on the prairies.

These days the tidy, sparkling clean town may still be Iowa's best-kept village. The Dutch heritage permeates the settlement of eight thousand, whose residents bear names such as Vermeer, Kuyper and Van Zee. Among the local attractions are the Historical Village, with eleven restored buildings, and the home of Dominie Scholte, who led the first settlers from Holland to the heart of the New World. The twenty-two-room Scholte house contains furniture from the old country, paintings and drawings by early Pella residents and the iron chest that held the horde of gold the emigrants carried with them. Another historic residence—

the Van Spankeren House—was the boyhood home of Wyatt
Earp, the frontier lawman who lived in Pella from 1850 until
1864 when he and his family joined a wagon train headed
west. (Earp was born in Monmouth, Illinois: see Chapter III,
section 6.) This handsome 1850s-era residence (actually two
houses side by side) bears on its facade fully fifteen windows
that lend the boxy building an open, light look. Other Dutch
touches in Pella include a huge windmill, a "klokkenspel"
animated by Dutch figures that perform to the accompani-
ment of a carillon, architecture reminiscent of Holland and
everywhere windows dripping with fancy lace. Many of
those windows are the famous Pella brand, made at the
town's Rolscreen Company factory. A museum installed in a
renovated railroad depot traces the development of the company's products.

The second week in May every year is "Tulip Time"—first
celebrated in 1935—when the locals wear Dutch dress, including wooden shoes. Parades, concerts, music from a
Dutch street organ and dancing enliven the town. Residents
scrub down the streets with brooms, cleaning the town to a
gleam before the Tulip Queen parades through Pella in the
coronation procession. Further local color stems from some
quarter of a million blooming tulips that blaze out their
brightness all around town during the festival.

Two motels in Pella offer accommodations, but for atmosphere the best place to stay is the Strawtown Inn, an
attractive old house with seven antique-furnished guest
rooms. One room seems straight out of the old country: the
"Bedstee Kamer" sports Dutch beds built into the wall. Rates
include a traditional Dutch breakfast of cold meat, cheeses,
boiled egg, breads and tea or coffee. In an 1855 residence next
to the inn is the Strawtown restaurant, which specializes in
such Dutch delicacies as pea soup, spiced beef and "uitsmi-
jter," a sandwich of roast beef or ham topped by fried eggs.
The nearby Strawtown country store, which occupies the

original buildings of Central College, founded in 1853, offers items made by Iowa artists and craftspeople.

From Pella it's thirty miles southeast to Oskaloosa, an old Quaker town and seat of Mahaska County. William Penn College, a Society of Friends (Quaker) institution, occupies a pleasant campus in the northern part of town. Two miles east of the college is the Nelson Pioneer Farm and Craft Museum, an unusually well-preserved pioneer farm virtually unchanged from its beginnings a century and a half ago. The property, continuously worked from 1844 to 1958, was given to the Mahaska County Historical Society in 1958 by Roy and Lillian Nelson. The house, built in 1852 of native timber and bricks fired in a local kiln, and the barn, constructed in 1856 from lumber cut on the farm, are both listed on the National Register. Outfitted with period pieces and with family photos and furnishings, the house appears as if the Nelsons of a half century ago will return home at any moment.

Other buildings at the site include a so-called voting house, believed to be the first room west of the Mississippi built specifically for voting (and still so used by Spring Creek township voters); the old Mott country store, restored to its 1910 appearance; an 1867 log cabin located on the site of the original 1844 Nelson cabin; and the 1861 Prine School, a one-room schoolhouse furnished with double desks, books, dinner pails, slates, *McGuffey Readers* and a dunce stool. Near the farm's museum, which includes exhibits on the history of the county and the state, is Iowa's only mule cemetery, last resting place of Becky and Jennie, two four-leggers that served in the U.S. Artillery during the Civil War and which later lived and died on the Nelson farm. On the third Saturday in September the old Nelson homestead comes alive with the annual pioneer craft day festival, featuring demonstrations of old-time skills and other traditional activities.

The Nelson farm is a good place to get a feel for how mid-nineteenth century rural life in Iowa unfolded through the days and years. That way of life is gone forever, but back then youngsters revelled in the freedom, the simplicity, the essential naturalness of frontier farm life. "Oh, what a joy to be a frontier youngster!" exclaimed Nancy Henderson Call in *Early Algona, The Story of Our Pioneers 1854–1874*. Half a century after she lived her mid-1800s farm days, Call recalled them for her grandchildren:

> We ran out and dug a few potatoes for dinner with the hoe, cutting many of them in two in our enthusiasm. We picked the currants and the gooseberries, scratching our arms and getting well bitten by mosquitoes. We hunted the eggs, drove home the turkey hen and her chickens when she wandered away. We carried the milk pail to the hired man, hunted in the new melon patch for cut worms, knocked the potato bugs off the vines in an old pan with a stick, washed our hands in a tin wash basin, wiped on a common towel and drank out of a common dipper at the pump and knew no germs. We churned the butter and drank real buttermilk.

And she frolicked on the prairie, its rich black soil "teeming with millions and millions of flowers! Just see the acres of violet and mauve and purple fall asters—the scattered red lilies, the heavenly blue gentians, the black-eyed susans, the feathery goldenrod and the tall, billowy waving grass reaching on and on until it met the sky with fleecy clouds." Such was the sort of idyllic life on a Midwestern mid-nineteenth-century farm like the Nelson homestead—a vanished world whose remnants you can see and whose delights you might imagine when visiting the Nelson Pioneer Farm and Craft Museum.

Another relic of the nineteenth-century way of life is the hamlet of What Cheer, which lies fifteen miles northeast of Oskaloosa. When Roger Williams encountered the Indians of what is now Rhode Island he greeted (and perhaps puzzled) them with the expression "What cheer," a salutation common in the coal country of England. After coal was discovered near the Iowa town, local resident Major Joseph Andrews, recalling Williams's greeting, proposed it as a name for the settlement. Although Iowa isn't considered a coal state, mines operated in the south-central part of Iowa from the late nineteenth to the early twentieth centuries. Famous labor leader John L. Lewis, for forty years president of the United Mine Workers, was born in Chariton (a town fifty-two miles southwest of Oskaloosa) where the Lucas County Historical Museum contains exhibits recalling coal-mining activity in that area. In What Cheer, a village of nine hundred or so people, it's worth visiting the brick museum, installed in a century-old brick schoolhouse, with displays on the terra-cotta products once produced from the white clay found in the area. Also in What Cheer is a delightful old-time opera house, built in 1893, with a horseshoe-shaped balcony and excellent acoustics. The theater, listed on the National Register in 1973, is open to visitors.

From What Cheer you can make your way on the back roads some fifty miles northwest up to the college town of Grinnell. Back in 1853 when Josiah Bushnell Grinnell, a Congregational minister in New York City, went to Horace Greeley for advice, the publisher of *The Tribune* responded, "Go West, young man, go West and grow up with the country." West Grinnell went, and on the prairie between the Iowa and the Skunk River he established the settlement named after him. Grinnell sold lots to the early settlers with the stipulation that the land would be forfeited if liquor was ever sold on the property. An abolitionist as well as a prohibitionist, Grinnell became an active supporter of the anti-slavery cause. John Brown, who crossed Iowa a number of times on his way to Kansas where he promoted the abolitionist movement, stayed at Grinnell's house in February 1859 on his way back east, where, later that year, Brown carried out his famous raid at Harper's Ferry, West Virginia. Brown so impressed Grinnell that the clergyman described him as looking like Andrew Jackson and compared Brown to Michelangelo's Moses.

Grinnell College, established in 1846 as the first four-year coeducational liberal arts school west of the Mississippi, occupies a pleasant tree-shaded ninety-acre campus in the center of town. Graduates of the college include actor Gary Cooper, former Des Moines *Register* publisher Gardner Cowles and Harry Hopkins, Franklin Roosevelt's assistant. The thirty-five college buildings are relatively new, for an 1882 tornado destroyed the school and much of the town. On June 17 that year one tornado spun toward Grinnell from Kellogg, about ten miles to the southwest, while another whirled southeast toward the town where they met to form a fearsome twister that swept away the college and killed thirty-nine people.

Among the exhibits at the Grinnell Historical Museum, installed in a late-Victorian-style ten-room house near the college, is Josiah Grinnell's desk, a fascinating elaborate piece whose niches, cubbyholes, drawers and compartments compose virtually an entire office. Not far from the museum stands the Poweshiek County National Bank building, a creation of the renowned architect Louis Sullivan. Sullivan was the leader of the late-nineteenth- and early twentieth-century "Chicago School" of architecture that included Frank Lloyd Wright. When Sullivan came to Grinnell in 1914 he bought a pencil and pad of yellow paper at a local drugstore on Broad Street and proceeded to sketch out the first drawings of the proposed bank. Listed on the National Register in 1976, the building is a fortress-like brick cube embellished with friezes, a terra-cotta cornice, heraldic griffin statues and an elaborately decorated square ornament around a round stained-glass window above the doorway. The interior—with a gold frieze, eleven stained-glass windows, oak chandeliers, a skylight and other well-worked decor—is no less elaborate.

At Newton, eighteen miles west of Grinnell, stands another National Register structure, St. Stephen's Episcopal Church, an 1874 building in the "Carpenter Gothic" style. Cleanliness being next to Godliness, you'll find not far from the church the Maytag washer factory, for Newton is the home of Maytag appliances. Maytag so dominates the city that Iowa writer Phil Strong once described Newton as "principally a washing-machine factory with dormitories." The washing machine industry began there in 1898 when a local firm later called One Minute Manufacturing Company, which remained in business until 1957, made simple washers distributed around the countryside on one-horse wagons and sold for five dollars each. In 1907 Fred Maytag's company produced its first washer, a wooden tub with an agitator on top, and in 1909 the firm introduced a hand-operated wringer model, two years later adding a motor to the device. Even after the automatic model made its appearance in 1949 the company continued to manufacture the wringer washers until 1983. At one time Iowa produced half of all the washers made in the U.S., many at Newton's huge Maytag factory which still today churns out the appliances.

Some of the lore and history of the washing machine industry is recalled at the Jasper County Historical Museum, which contains on the second floor a large exhibit moved there from the Maytag Company. Among the displays are samples of the old Maytag appliances, including the 1907 "Pastime" model, the 1909 Model 40, the 1914 Model 44 and the 1922 Model 80 with a "gyrafoam," an underwater agitator so popular that in the two years following its introduction Maytag leaped from twenty-sixth to first in industry sales. A few of the 1920s and 1930s models on display included a device to connect the agitator to a butter churn or a meat grinder, thus enabling the washing movement to perform two household chores at once. Other exhibits at the museum include a completely furnished one-room country school, rooms from a Victorian home, old tools and farm implements and other memorabilia from the early days.

Before leaving Newton it's worth visiting the Maytag Dairy Farms, three miles north of town. This affords you the rather unusual opportunity to see an operating Iowa dairy farm. Gleaming white buildings house the herd of contented cows—at least they should be contented, so comfortable is their bovine existence—which produce torrents of milk every day. The best time to visit the farm is in the morning when the dairymen and maids make the tangy Maytag Blue Cheese. Iowa dairy products are renowned, and the state is proud of them. At a speech in 1898, Iowa Congressman Robert Gordon Cousins opined, "The Iowa cow has slowly and painfully yet gradually and grandly worked her way upward to a shining eminence in the eyes of the world." Such praise of the cow has seldom sounded in the lecture halls of our fair land: not for nothing was Cousins once described as "the finest orator in Congress." In 1900 Iowa politicians promoted the Grout Bill, a proposal introduced in Congress to tax "every article colored in imitation of butter." In support of the bill, which passed the House but failed in the Senate, Cousins, who represented Iowa in Congress sixteen years, railed against oleomargarine, calling it a "fraudulent product" which "greases our bread, when we [wish] to butter it." Even back in the nineteenth century Iowa cows were great producers. Dining on succulent clover grown in the rich Iowa soil, the animals emitted great floods of milk. The problem of what to do with the surplus was solved in 1872 when the state's first creamery started up at Spring Branch in Delaware County. John G. Cherry, an itinerant mender, invented a can with an ingenious top to carry the milk from the farm to the creamery. Four years later, when Iowa butter won first prize at the Centennial Exposition in Philadelphia, the product became coveted on the east coast and elsewhere. At Maytag Dairy Farms you can get an idea how milk from that "shining eminence," the Iowa cow, is processed into dairy products consumed the land over.

Ten miles west of Newton at the old coal town of Colfax— named for U.S. Grant's vice-president, Schuyler Colfax, passenger on the first train through the village—stands the venerable Hotel Colfax, the last survivor of the time around the turn of the century when the town was a popular mineral water spa. At Marshalltown, north of Newton, the Fisher Community Center boasts an art collection featuring works by Utrillo, Cassatt and other famous painters. The center was given by the Fisher family, which owned Fisher Controls, the town's main industry, until Monsanto Company acquired the firm. William Fisher, superintendent of the Marshalltown waterworks, founded the company in 1880 when he devised a constant-pressure pump governor he contrived while struggling to maintain water pressure during a raging fire.

Back in that era of the 1880s two other Marshalltowners became well-known figures. Adrian "Cap" Anson, baseball's first superstar, was born there in 1852 and was taught the game by his father, Henry Anson, who founded the town in 1851. After leaving Notre Dame University, Cap Anson returned to Marshalltown where he played on the local baseball club before hiring on with the Chicago White Stockings in 1876. Chicago poet and sportswriter Eugene Field, best known for his poem "Little Boy Blue," wrote of Anson, a big boy in white, "Lo! from the tribunes on the bleachers comes a shout,/Beseeching bold Ansonius to line 'em out." Late in his career, when the press urged him to retire, Anson responded by wearing false whiskers at bat. When a pitch grazed his beard in the second inning Anson started toward first base but umpire Tom Lynch, doubting the whiskers were touched, called the star back, holding that "even if the ball had hit them, they aren't really yours and you couldn't take first base just because somebody else's whiskers got hit."

Anson, the first player to make three thousand hits and whose average was .300 or better in twenty-five of the twenty-seven seasons he played, recruited for the White Stockings in 1883 fellow Iowan Billy Sunday, who had been working at a Marshalltown furniture store. One day, after staggering out of a saloon in Chicago, Sunday happened on a gospel meeting where he was converted to the cause of temperance. Sunday refused to play ball on Sunday, and in 1890 he finally left the team and started religious work at one-sixth his baseball salary at the YMCA in Chicago. Sunday later became a nationally known firebrand revivalist preacher. In 1909 he returned to Marshalltown to deliver seventy-four sermons during a six-week revival session, trying to persuade the locals to close the twenty or so saloons in town.

Long before Anson and Sunday ran the bases Indians roamed the area, and they still do, their horsepower now in the form of car and truck engines. In the countryside about twenty miles east of Marshalltown you can visit the Mesquakie Indian Settlement, a remnant of the early Wild West days in Iowa. The area is designated "settlement" rather than "reservation" as the land was not reserved to the Indians by the government but is owned by them. Between 1836 and 1851 the complexion of Iowa changed from red to white as settlers poured into the state and the Indians moved farther west. By 1845 most of the Sac (or Sauk) and Fox, as the Mesquakie are also called, had left Iowa for Kansas, but in the mid-1850s tribe members began to return to their native soil along the Iowa River in Tama County. The story goes that one day three Foxes visited Governor James W. Grimes in the Old State Capitol Building in Iowa City. Asked the purpose of the visit, the chief pulled from beneath his blanket a bag of money which he directed the governor to count. Grimes tallied the total, then announced, "Seven hundred and fifty." The Indian replied, "White man count seven hundred and fifty. Indian count seven fifty." As the chief swept the money back into the bag, the governor asked what they planned to do with the funds. "Buy land," came the curt reply. "What do you want to buy land for?" the governor asked. "White man buy land, white man business. Indian buy land, Indian business." After obtaining the consent of the state in 1856, the Foxes bought eighty acres for one thousand dollars. Through the years they added more land until now the Indians own more than three thousand acres on which some fifteen hundred Sac and Fox Indians live.

A visit to the settlement will give you a feel for the nineteenth-century days when Indians inhabited Iowa. The "wickiups" (teepees) you'll see aren't occupied as in the old days and are kept only for special occasions. But even if some of the sights are there just for show, it's still interesting to see Iowa's only Indian town. The very best time to visit the area is during the annual pow-wow, held in mid-August at a lovely site along the Iowa River. Leather goods, beadwork, weavings and other craft items are on offer and Indian dances as well as other colorful performances and activities take place. An advertising poster from 1918, three years after the first pow-wow, suggests the festival's flavor: Indians "will appear in tribal dances, Indian songs, foot races, shooting matches, la Crosse games and other tribal customs. Music by Indian band. Only chance to see real Indians living tribal life of old. Worth driving miles to see." Among the committee members listed on the poster were Peter Old Bear, John Bear and Sam Slick.

The chief of another tribe in another state, Sioux leader Red Cloud, once mourned the end of the era of the Indian and the emerging dominance of white settlers. "The white children have surrounded me and left me nothing but an island," the great chief lamented. "We are melting like snow on a hillside, while you are grown like spring grass." At the Mesquakie Settlement there remains a last remnant—a small patch of snow, as Red Cloud put it—of the Indian era in Iowa when the state was a frontier area out in the Wild West. All the rest has melted away.

4. "Amana That Was and Amana That Is":
The Seven Amana Villages

The Amana Colony is Iowa's most popular tourist attraction. Some one million visitors a year stop in at the colony's seven villages, whose population nearly doubles during the summer to about four thousand when waitresses, sales clerks and other workers arrive to serve the flood of tourists that roll in during the high season. Amana's picture-perfect nineteenth-century villages—each a few miles apart, an hour or so's journey by ox cart (that's a relic of the early days: you'll travel by car, not by cart)—seem made for tourists and, perhaps inevitably, the area has become somewhat commercialized. You can find in a few of the towns, filled with shops, restaurants and retail establishments, nearly everything but a parking place. But unlike such manufactured tourist attractions as Disneyland, Williamsburg, theme parks or Florida porpoise shows and parrot jungles, the Amana Colony evolved as an organic, living community. So if you go there off season or if you explore some of the nooks and crannies or linger to chat with the locals, perhaps you'll discover the settlement's basic simplicity and allure, as described in idyllic terms by Bertha M.H. Shambaugh in her 1936 article "Amana That Was and Amana That Is":

> In one of the garden spots of Iowa there is a charming little valley from which the surrounding hills recede like the steps of a Greek theater. Through this valley the historic Iowa River flows peacefully to the eastward. A closer view reveals seven old-fashioned

villages nestling among the trees or sleeping in the hillsides. About these seven villages stretch twenty-six thousand goodly acres clothed with fields of corn, pastures, meadows, vineyards, and seas of waving grain. Beyond and above, surrounding the little valley are richly timbered hills, forming as though by design a frame for this quaint picture of Amana—the Iowa home of the historic Community of True Inspiration.

The term "Inspiration" refers to the True Inspirationists, an early eighteenth-century sect that split away from what the dissenters felt was the overly dogmatic Lutheran Church in Germany. To escape persecution, fines and imprisonment, the Inspirationists established in Germany their own settlements where they set up communal societies. In 1842 four members of the sect traveled to America and bought five thousand acres of land in the Seneca Indian Reservation near Buffalo, New York. Soon more than eight hundred Inspirationists arrived to found the Ebenezer Community on the property. After about ten years the Community wanted to expand, but land in the area had become too expensive so four Ebenezer members traveled west to look for a place to settle in Kansas or Iowa. In May 1855 they acquired eighteen thousand acres in east central Iowa and later that year the initial wave of settlers moved west and built the first village, named Amana ("remain faithful") from the Song of Solomon. Five more villages soon developed—Middle, High, West, South and East Amana—and in 1861 the community purchased Homestead to gain access to the train that passed through that town.

Although the seven Amana villages are close to one another, it takes at least a full day to visit the community. Perhaps the best place to start is Amana, the largest settlement and one whose museums, shops and other attractions provide a good introduction to the community's culture and history. The Museum of Amana History, installed in the 1864

Noe family house, contains informative displays of early Inspirationist documents, writings, heirlooms and lithographs that trace the early years of the movement from its beginnings in Germany in 1714 to the era when Amana was settled. Next to the museum stand an old washhouse and a school building furnished as it was when children attended classes there from 1870 to 1955. Near the history museum—distance has virtually been banished in the Amana Colony: nothing is far away there except the outside world, seemingly an age and a world apart—stands the woolen mill, in operation continuously on the same site since 1859. The entire production process from raw wool to finished fabric unravels (or, rather, ravels) at the mill. The kinds of products you'll see being turned out as you tour the factory are on display at the mill's salesroom, piled high with well-nigh irresistible woolen goods. Steps away from the mill stands the Amana furniture factory, the brick section of which originally housed a calico operation that functioned from the early days of the colony to the First World War when indigo dye from Germany became unavailable. A tour of the factory will show you how the simple yet elegant traditional furniture is made and finished by hand using walnut, cherry and oak wood from a ten-thousand-acre spread of timberland owned by the Amana Society. Desks, cabinets, tables, chairs and clocks embellish the showroom. Timepieces account for fully a quarter of the firm's sales. Crating and shipping are available if an item catches your fancy.

Amana suffers from no shortage of souvenir shops: some bear rather resistible names, such as Tick Tock Antiques, Antique Tower Haus and The Kitchen Sink. Places to eat and food stores featuring locally made bread, wine, meats and sausages also abound. Two of the most popular restaurants are the Colony Inn, which serves family-style meals and features an especially bountiful breakfast (a bowl of mixed fruit, orange juice, pancakes, toast, eggs, bacon, sausage, hash browns; seconds encouraged, even if improbable), and the Ox Yoke Inn, installed in a mid-nineteenth-century building that once served as a community kitchen where the people of Amana would gather to eat.

As an antidote to the somewhat unrelieved commercial atmosphere of Amana you might want to proceed on to East Amana, the only colony village without shops or any other business establishments. Here you can get the true flavor of how the Colony used to be, for this tiny town of a few streets and a handful of houses no doubt resembles the Amana of old, when the settlement was an isolated and self-contained enclave that functioned for its own members rather than catering to visitors from the outside world. East Amana presents a picture of tranquility. Boxy barns, with appropriate barnyard odors, stand behind simple houses garnished with flowers that lend touches of color to the neatly tailored green lawns. Cornfields surround the town, and overhead, perched on spindly legs, towers an aquamarine-hued water tank. In East Amana time has not simply stood still, it seems never to have moved from the day the hamlet was established nearly a century and a half ago.

If you return to Amana, the road west will take you to Middle Amana. The route runs by Lily Lake, which in July and August glistens with bright white water lilies. You'll also see on the left the large Amana Refrigeration factory where some of the famous Amana appliances are manufactured. Founded in 1934, the company was later acquired by the Amana Society and then in 1965 sold to the Raytheon Company. This is a far cry from the nearly century-long communal way of life—all working and all sharing—the people of Amana practiced until June 1932 when "the Great Change," as the colonists call the restructuring, took place. That year the Amana people, separating church and state, established the Amana Society which privatized the community's property by issuing shares of stock to the residents, who for the first time received wages, owned their own houses and ate at home rather than at one of the Colony's fifty-two communal kitchens.

Middle Amana boasts the colony's only surviving community kitchen. There you can get an idea of the pre-June 1932 way of feeding. Enticing fragrances from the nearby Hahn's Hearth Oven Bakery invite you to taste the bread and coffee cake baked in the shop's original wood-fired oven. Baking begins at 3:30 A.M.; the store opens at 8; it closes, a sign states, "after day's baking is sold." Middle Amana is a pleasant place to linger. The town, built on a high point with long views onto the surrounding countryside, enjoys a better balanced mix of commercial and residential elements than does the busier metropolis of Amana up the road.

Two miles west of Middle Amana you'll come to High Amana, a tiny and tranquil town whose only commercial establishment is an old-fashioned general store little changed since its founding more than a century ago. This is the most unspoiled and truly genuine old-time store in the colony. Inside the 1858 stone building are antique display cases, the original tin ceiling, a venerable wall clock, vintage bottles and containers, a period vending machine for Zeno chewing gum, and many other relics of yesteryear. From High Amana you can enjoy a lovely view onto the seven-mile-long canal built in 1860 to bring water from the Iowa River to power the woolen mill and other industries.

Continuing on for a mile down the same road, you'll reach West Amana. Like all the other Amanas, the town is laid out with a single main street, side streets that branch off at right angles and a central church. At one end of the village sits the communal barn, while at the other were workshops and small factories. The idea was to make each village self-sufficient so that every town would have its own sawmill, bakery, dairy, blacksmith, wagon shop and other facilities. In accordance with the Amana de-emphasis of embellishment, the

Colony's simple stone churches lacked altars, steeples or other decorations or appendages.

Built on a knoll, West Amana is a pleasantly peaceful village with a scattering of large boxy barns. The West Amana Store, installed in a restored 1863 yellow-brown sandstone structure with a lone gas pump out front, tempts the visitor with an appealing selection of merchandise, including handmade rag rugs, sunbonnets, quilts, craft items and paintings of Amana scenes. Down the hill from the store stands the Old Broom and Basket Shop, whose slogan is "broom corn is sweeping the country." At the shop a broom maker, clad in bib overalls and working next to an old-fashioned iron stove, uses original hand-operated machinery to turn out the product. The store's walls bristle with displays of unusual brooms, one a double device with each part attached to the forks of a branch. According to an attractive and whimsical brochure available at the shop, Ben Franklin planted the first broom corn seed, which he obtained from Hungary, and made the first brooms. Witches' brooms, explains the leaflet, come in three sizes and "have plural functions. . . . Before witches ride them on Hallowe'en they may have been seen as scarecrows, and later they may show up in children's snowmen."

From West Amana you head south, perhaps now by airborne broom, to South Amana, where you'll find some of the colony's more tasteful stores. An especially tasteful place is the Ackerman Winery, one of the various wineries scattered throughout the area, where you can taste the wide variety of fruit wines on offer. Chateau Mouton Rothschild has nothing to fear from the selection, but nevertheless you may enjoy sampling wines made from rhubarb, cherries, cranberries, elderberries, watermelon, strawberries, dandelions, blueberries, wild mulberries, red clover, blackberries, apples and even grapes. At Bramwell's Flour Mill, slightly east of town, Amana jellies, preserves and honey are available, as well as stone-ground wheat, corn, rye, oat and buckwheat flour which you can see being processed beyond a plate-glass window separating the shop from the factory at the back of the store. Next door to the mini-mill stands the Schanz Furniture Shop, where the sixth generation continues the family woodworking tradition. Among the pieces for sale are walnut reproductions of chairs and desks made by the shop in 1977—based on the 1839 originals—to furnish the restored House Chamber in the Old Stone Capitol building at Iowa City.

Also in South Amana is a museum installed in a 1913 barn, with a large collection of miniature scenes including old Amana, an 1890s California logging camp and Lincoln's New Salem, Illinois—all carved by Henry Moore, a retired Amana farmer who allows, "I'll be one hundred and eighty-two and a half when this entire project is completed." The nearby general store witnessed what was probably sleepy South Amana's most exciting episode when, on the rainy night of April 27, 1877, Jesse James and his gang lifted two thousand dollars from the establishment's safe. The gang escaped the next morning on an early train out of Marengo, a few miles away.

That line's train tracks pass through Upper South Amana (a mile south of South Amana) where the Amana Society Bakery turns out some of the breads and pastries sold at the Colony's shops and restaurants. Tracks also pass by Homestead (about six miles east of Upper South Amana), a one-street town that the colony purchased in 1861 to gain access to the railroad, then the Mississippi and Missouri line. At Homestead you can visit Ehrle Brothers Winery, the oldest (1934) in the colony and, next door, the eight-room Amana "Heim" (home), a mid-nineteenth-century house outfitted with period furnishings and with blue walls, the color chosen to suggest heaven. The "Heim" is probably the best place in Amana to see how the colonists lived in the old days. The old blacksmith shop, with a plank floor, antique implements hanging from the walls and a pleasantly musty smell, also presents an atmospheric picture out of the past.

Homestead boasts the colony's only place to stay: the attractive Die Heimat Motor Hotel, which occupies a modernized 1858 building. German sayings decorate the walls and the pleasant owners add to the friendly atmosphere. There are only two other places convenient to Amana to stay, neither with Die Heimat's old-time Old World feeling—the Holiday Inn and the Best Western, on Interstate 80. So if you prefer the old-fashioned Heimat it's strongly recommended you make reservations there as far ahead as possible, especially during the tourist season. Two blocks from Die Heimat stands Bill Zuber's Restaurant, installed in the 1862 Homestead Hotel building. Decorating the four dining rooms are antiques and dozens of baseball photos that recall Zuber's eleven-season major league pitching career. Zuber, born in Middle Amana, threw a fast ball reputed to be as blazing as that hurled by his fellow Iowan Bob Feller from Van Meter, a hamlet near Des Moines. When baseball scout Cy Slapnicka arrived at Middle Amana to size up young Zuber, no baseball was available so the scout handed the seventeen-year-old prospect a baseball-sized onion, which the boy pitched well enough to impress Slapnicka. The restaurant hands out cards listing "The Ten Commandments of Baseball," among which are: "Keep your head up and you may not have to keep it down" and "Do not find too much fault with the umpires: You cannot expect them to be as perfect as you are."

Having toured the seven Amana villages and visited their tourist attractions, you may be left with the feeling that the real Amana has escaped you. Truth to tell, if you want to experience the genuine Amana atmosphere you have to linger in the colony, taking time to immerse yourself a little deeper than is possible visiting only the tourist places. Pick up a copy of the local newsletter called *Amana Society Bulletin,* for example, and you can read about the doings of the colonists and perhaps join some of the get-togethers announced in the *Bulletin*. Or maybe you can watch the comings and goings or perhaps even attend a Sunday morning church service (some are still given in German) held at Middle Amana, South Amana, Amana and Homestead, where you'll see the women clad in the traditional black cap, shawl and apron. Fall and winter visitors might enjoy the slow-paced horse-drawn hayrides and bobsled rides available, while visitors at any season can get a more complete and intensive understanding of the colony by taking a guided tour to the villages. Those are just a few of the ways you may be able to enhance your visit to the community. In Amana's Noe House, which houses the Museum of Amana History, appears the inscription "Let your heritage not be lost, but bequeath it as a memory, treasure and blessing. . . . Gather the lost and the hidden and preserve it in thy children." Beneath the tourist's Amana—Amana as it is—lies that hidden heritage, a picture out of the past, frozen in time: Amana as it was a long time ago.

5. A College Town, A President's Hamlet:

The University at Iowa City
Herbert Hoover National Historic Site
Kalona's Amish
Cedar Rapids
Grundy Center
Waterloo

About twenty miles east of the Amana Colony lies Iowa City, an attractive Midwestern college town scattered across low hills and riven by the Iowa River. Iowa City is very much a town of middle America; it's located a few hundred miles from the center point between the coasts and was founded about midway in time between settlement of the Atlantic coast and the present. In the mid-nineteenth century, Iowa City boasted not only Iowa's university but its state capital as well. The town also served as the terminus of Iowa's first railroad. An incentive plan encouraged the Mississippi and Missouri line (an extension of the Chicago and Rock Island) to reach Iowa City before January 1, 1856. At nine o'clock the night before, the tracks still fell short of the station by a thousand feet. By eleven o'clock two hundred feet remained unfinished. The workmen feverishly toiled by the light and heat of large bonfires, and just before midnight the train reached the Iowa City station, enabling the Mississippi and Missouri to collect its bonus with a full sixty seconds to spare.

Like the other small college towns in the Midwest, Iowa City is dominated by the university, whose buildings cluster along the banks of the Iowa River. In addition to strolling around the pleasant, tree-shaded campus, it's worth visiting a few of the university's buildings. The Art Museum, which contains more than five thousand works, was, in effect, built around a collection of European paintings. In 1965 Owen and Leone Elliott of Cedar Rapids gave their collection to the university with the stipulation that a museum be built to house the works. The museum, which opened in 1969, includes not only the Elliott canvases—with paintings by such artists as Matisse, Braque, Bonnard, Dufy, Chagall and Soutine—but also large collections of jade, old silver and African sculpture. Crowning the crest of a hill near the center of the campus is the Old Capitol Building, a National Historic Landmark. The lovely classic-style structure, built in the early 1840s of limestone and topped by a small gold dome, is one of the most elegant and well-proportioned buildings in the state. The Old Capitol served as the first permanent seat of Iowa's territorial and state governments until Des Moines became the capital city in 1857, after which the building housed university offices. Inside the restored structure a splendidly graceful stairway leads from the ground floor—where you can see the old Supreme Court room, the one-time offices of the governor and of the state treasurer, and the former territorial library—upstairs to the House and the Senate chambers. Dating from the same era is Plum Grove, home of Robert Lucas, Iowa's first territorial governor. Built by Lucas (he of Honey War fame: see section 2) in 1844, the restored two-story brick house occupies a spacious lot once filled with plum trees, a mile or so south of the campus.

In 1832 Lucas presided in Baltimore over the first Democratic National Convention ever held, where Andrew Jackson was nominated for the presidency. A century after that convention the first president born west of the Mississippi, Iowan Herbert Hoover, ended his single term in office. Hoover's early years in Iowa and his later career as a mining engineer and politician are recalled at the nearly two-hundred-acre Herbert Hoover National Historic Site, a beautifully maintained enclave in the quiet little town of West Branch twelve miles east of Iowa City. Many of the early settlers who migrated to the fertile prairie farmlands in the region were Quakers. Encouraged by area Quakers John Brown, the famous abolitionist who led the attack on the U.S. Arsenal at Harper's Ferry, West Virginia, in 1859 (see section 3 for Brown's visit to Grinnell, Iowa) set up headquarters in February of that year near Springfield (purported birthplace of actress Sarah Bernhardt), a Quaker town five miles east of West Branch. There he drilled his troops and made final plans for the raid.

Among the early West Branch Quaker settlers were the parents of Jesse Hoover and Huldah Minthorn, who married in 1870 and whose second son, Herbert, was born in a two-room cottage in the village on August 10, 1874. That now restored tiny residence, which housed the three Hoover children and their parents, is one of the dozen or so century-old buildings at the Hoover National Historic Site, an evocative re-creation of the mid-nineteenth-century Iowa farm village where Herbert Hoover spent the first eleven years of his life. In the low-ceiling white-washed wood cottage are the original walnut wood cradle in which baby Herbert was rocked, a trundle bed and other original furnishings. Steps away from the house stands a reconstruction of the blacksmith shop that Jesse Hoover operated from 1871 to 1879. An ad for the shop in the *West Branch Times* promised "Prices to suit the times." In his memoirs the former president recalled a boyhood visit to his father's establishment: "Playing barefoot around the blacksmith shop, I stepped on a chip of hot iron and carry the brand of Iowa on my foot to this day." These days a smith at the shop shapes iron items in a kiln stoked by a huge bellows that huffs and wheezes as it fans the blazing fire. By the shop stands the 1853 one-story frame schoolhouse furnished with old-fashioned desks and an old-time metal stove. On the wall hang pictures of Hoover's predecessors, Washington and Lincoln.

From the schoolhouse you can make your way along Poplar and Downey streets, lovely tree-lined ways with nineteenth-century houses, also part of the National Historic Site, on each side. In these houses, many fronted by white picket fences, lived acquaintances of the Hoover family. Opposite the delightful 1874 Gothic Revival Garvin Cottage on Downey street stands the house of Hoover's uncle, Laban Miles, whom the eight-year-old Herbert visited for eight months in 1882 when Miles was serving as Indian agent at the Osage Reservation in Oklahoma. Just across the footbridge over the West Branch of Wapsinonoc Creek you'll come to the starkly simple 1857 Friends Meetinghouse where the Quakers gathered to meditate and to listen to any of their number who felt like sharing with the congregation an insight or spiritual message. The north side of the sanctuary includes a "cry room" where babies and children were taken if they threatened to disturb the services. Still today a handful of Quakers, part of Iowa's community of five thousand or so Friends, meet every Sunday in West Branch.

Beyond the Meetinghouse stands the Herbert Hoover Presidential Library-Museum, built of Iowa limestone quarried at Stone City near Cedar Rapids. The Library-Museum houses books, documents (more than five million items) and displays relating to the native son's long and busy life, starting with his boyhood in West Branch and continuing on with his college days as a member of Stanford University's first class (1891), his career as a mining engineer and later government service as secretary of commerce for seven years and then as president. Among the exhibits are the device used on April 7, 1927, when Hoover participated in the first long-distance demonstration of television, a transmission from Washington to New York; some one hundred embroidered flour sacks presented to Hoover by Belgians in gratitude for his work on food programs for Europe in World War I; and a telegram Hoover sent on October 14, 1964, to ex-president Truman after the Missourian had suffered a broken bone in a bathtub fall: "Bathtubs are a menace to ex-presidents for, as you may recall, a bathtub rose up and fractured my vertebrae when I was in Venezuela on your world famine mission in 1946. My warmest sympathy and best wishes for your speedy recovery." Less than a week later, Hoover, age ninety, died.

Hoover and his wife, Lou, an Iowan whom he met at Stanford, lie buried in graves a short walk beyond the Library-Museum, marked by two utterly unembellished white stone slabs. On the way to the impressively simple gravesite you'll pass an overlook with a view onto part of a seventy-six-acre site of restored tall grass prairieland. In the mid-nineteenth century, about the time West Branch was settled, some 85 percent of Iowa was prairie: rolling land covered with grass and other low vegetation. Looking out onto this rare surviving example of the once common Iowa prairie enables one better to appreciate the rigors of those early days when hardy pioneers moved out from the more hospitable wooded areas to brave the challenges of the open spaces, a movement recalled by a reminiscence of Iowa in 1837 by Charles Mason, the state's first chief justice: "Occasionally, someone more adventurous than the rest had launched boldly out from the shore . . . into the open ocean prairie, and had fixed his home where the storms of summer and the wintry winds might approach him on all sides, and in defiance, also, of the distance whence the materials for fire and shelter and fences were to be procured." Hoover, too, once recalled the fields and the natural delights of his native Iowa: "I prefer to think of Iowa as I saw it through the eyes of a ten-year-old boy—and the eyes of all ten-year-old Iowa boys are or should be filled with the wonders of Iowa's streams and woods, of the mystery of growing crops. His days should be filled with adventure and great undertakings, with participation in good and comforting things." Hoover also fondly remembered his West Branch native ground: "The most formative years of my boyhood were spent here. My roots are in this soil." Now the native son has come home to his roots forever: Hoover's adventures and great undertakings are at an end and he reposes near where he first saw the light of day, in the eternal soil of his beloved home state of Iowa.

Before leaving the Iowa City-West Branch area it's worth heading down to Kalona, eighteen miles southwest of Iowa City, to visit the Amish settlement there. The Amish are distinct from and not to be confused with the Amana people. Rather, the Amish are to be confused only with themselves, for the sect's variants include Old Order Amish (they use no cars, telephones, electricity or other modern conveniences), New Order Amish (permitted to use rubber-tired farm equipment), Beachy Amish (they can drive cars—dark colors only—and use certain modern equipment), not to mention Old Mennonite Conference members and Conservative Mennonites. The ancestors of those various branches arrived in Iowa in 1846 from Lancaster County in Pennsylvania and from Ohio and settled in Washington County. Following the biblical admonition in Romans 12:2 not to conform, the Amish dress differently and simply, the women wearing bonnets and plain brown or blue dresses, the bearded men garbed in black hats and trousers with suspenders over their white shirts. Of all the rural folk in Iowa, a huge category, the Amish are perhaps the quintessential farmers for their very religion requires that they work the land, an occupation which both affords them self-sufficiency and enables members of the sect to remain distanced from the outside world.

As you drive the back roads of Washington County you'll see families wearing the typical Amish outfits and you will pass tidy farms cultivated only with horse-drawn equipment and no machines. Washington, the county seat, is a lovely little town with an abundance of well-preserved old homes, including the Conger House, crammed with memorabilia of old Iowa. But a better place to see the local culture is in and about Kalona, which, with seven Amish congregations totalling about seven hundred members and seventeen Mennonite churches (the Amish don't worship in churches: they gather in homes, a tradition resulting from the sect's persecution in Europe two centuries ago) is the largest Amish settlement west of the Mississippi. Try to visit the town on a Saturday, the liveliest time of the week, for Kalona is a typical Saturday-shop-and-gossip Iowa farm town, except that instead of cars and parking meters you'll find there horse-drawn wagons and hitchrails. While visiting Kalona, named after the registered sire of a once-famous herd of shorthorn breeding bulls, you might want to stop in at the Mennonite-run Unto Others shop that sells imported handicrafts and at the Mennonite Museum and Archives, with old records, genealogical information and artifacts used by the early settlers. For a more vivid view of how the early Amish lived, it's worth visiting the Historical Village which includes eight old buildings, among them a general store, a one-room schoolhouse, a buggy shop, a museum and a Grandpa House—a residence with a wing added for the retired older generation. The annual Kalona Fall Festival, held the last weekend of September, presents demonstrations of weaving, quilt making, apple butter churning, spinning and other such homey activities.

From Kalona you can head back to Iowa City on highway 1—paved only in the mid-'50s, prior to which the town remained rather isolated—and from there continue on to Cedar Rapids, another twenty-five miles or so north. Iowa is for the most part a state of rural areas and towns (nine hundred and fifty-five in all), many already described in this chapter. With a population of more than one hundred thousand, Cedar Rapids is the first place included on this Iowa tour with the feel of a city. Even so, the typical Iowa rustic country touch exists there at such places as the City Market, a farmer's market where home-grown produce and baked goods are sold; at Seminole Valley Farm, a restored late nineteenth-century Iowa farmstead listed on the National Register, with the original farmhouse, barn, smokehouse, summer kitchen and old equipment; and, next to the farm, at Usher's Ferry Pioneer Village, a re-creation of a turn-of-the-century Iowa hamlet with twenty-five restored buildings.

But it is the more urban-type attractions at Cedar Rapids that make a visit to the city worthwhile. These include such industrial operations as the Collins telecommunications factory and the huge Quaker Oats cereal mill, largest such installation in the world. These factories help Cedar Rapids rank first in the nation in exports per capita. Another city sort of sight is the Brucemore Mansion, a twenty-one-room Queen Anne-style house on a twenty-six-acre estate lush with rolling lawns and a formal garden. The 1885 Mansion, warmed by fully thirteen fireplaces, is the only property in Iowa belonging to the National Trust for Historic Preservation.

An unusual and perhaps unique Cedar Rapids attraction is the Iowa Masonic Library, a gleaming white marble building that houses what is believed to be the world's most complete collection of Masonic books, documents and artifacts. The library was established in 1844 by Theodore S. Parvin, secretary to Robert Lucas, Iowa's first territorial governor. Finally, Cedar Rapids boasts one of those Old World ethnic enclaves so typical of the large industrial cities of the east and the Upper Midwest. Along the Cedar River, near downtown, you'll find the Czech Village, a delightful mixture of shops, markets, cafes and people that recall the days when the city had the highest per capita population of Czechs in the country. The Czechs first came to Linn County in 1852 to work in the T.M. Sinclair (later Wilson Company) packing plant. Some of the newcomers arrived the hard way: one early community leader, Joseph Sosel, a revolutionary in the old country, was smuggled out of his homeland in a barrel. The Czech Museum and Library contains a large collection of national costumes, Bohemian glass and porcelain and other native artifacts. A stroll through the village will make you feel like you're in Prague: on 16th Avenue the street signs bear Czech as well as English writings, while at the Old World Sykora bakery you can enjoy such traditional treats as "kolaches" (a stuffed tart). The Cedar Rapids Czech community celebrates its heritage in the spring (Houby Days in mid-May), summer (the early June Kolache Festival) and fall (Village Festival, early September).

Cedar Rapids's most renowned resident was Grant Wood, the painter of typical Iowa rural scenes such as the famous "American Gothic," which portrays a farm couple standing in front of a Gothic Revival-style house that still exists in Eldon,

Iowa (see section 2). Wood was born in 1892 at Anamosa, twenty-five miles northeast of Cedar Rapids and just east of Stone City, where the painter later founded an artist's colony. At Stone City, which in early June celebrates a Grant Wood Art Festival, stands the Inn, an attractive hostelry in a restored stone manor house. The cozy inn is a pleasant place to overnight or to dine, or both. Wood once painted a picture entitled "Stone City," which included a view of some prime Iowa farmland. The artist recalled observing a farmer carefully studying the rural landscape at an exhibition of Wood's works. The painter eagerly awaited the farmer's aesthetic judgment. After further detailed inspection the man finally shook his head and said, "I wouldn't give thirty-five cents an acre for that land."

Wood, who died in 1942 at age fifty and is buried at Anamosa's Riverside Cemetery, painted his most famous works in the 1930s during the eleven years he occupied a studio in the loft of an old carriage house provided by a Cedar Rapids undertaker named David Turner. It was there the artist turned out "American Gothic," "Stone City," "Fall Plowing" and other masterpieces of Americana. In Turner's Alley—next to Turner's East, a renovated 1880s house listed on the National Register—stands the coach house where Wood lived and kept his studio, now open (by appointment only) to visitors. The Cedar Rapids Museum of Art contains what is said to be the largest collection of Grant Wood works anywhere. One of the artist's largest creations is the twenty-by-twenty-four-foot stained-glass window, believed to be the biggest such glass work in the world, portraying a large female figure symbolizing Victory with a row of six soldiers below. The window decorates the Veteran's Memorial Building on ship-shaped Municipal Island where the Linn County courthouse also stands. Cedar Rapids claims to be the only city, other than Paris, with its government buildings situated on an island.

Cedar Rapids's final claim to fame is as hometown of the Cherry Sisters, Linn County farm girls who, in the late nineteenth century, toured the country with one of the worst acts ever to darken America's stages. One critic wrote: "They never missed a note, or found one either." When the girls played at Oscar Hammerstein's Olympia Music Hall in November 1896 the Big Apple's produce retailers suffered a shortage of fruits and vegetables, for wholesalers peddled them directly to patrons of the Olympia who used the food to pelt the stage. One sample of the Sisters' jeer-provoking repertoire is their theme song: "Cherries ripe, Cherries red, Cherry Sisters still ahead." The Cherrys lived most of their lives in Cedar Rapids. One sister, Effie, ran for mayor twice, campaigning in 1926 on a platform of opposition to "high taxes, high skirts, high life, high utility rates." In their later years Effie and her sister Addie ran a Cedar Rapids bakery specializing in cherry pies. Effie, the last Cherry plucked from life, died in 1944 and was planted in Linwood Cemetery in Cedar Rapids.

Between Cedar Rapids and Waterloo, some fifty miles north, runs the Cedar Valley Parkway, a long hiking and biking trail. Near the trail, at the hamlet of Garrison, stands the Old Creamery Theater, a boxy brick building where stage productions are presented. A detour to the west as you head to Waterloo will take you to the irresistibly named town of Grundy Center, where the schoolhouse attended by Herbert Quick stands as a memorial to the novelist who captured the flavor of pioneer times in the state in his Iowa trilogy *Vandermark's Folly*, *The Hawkeye* and *The Invisible Woman*. Born near Grundy Center in 1861, Quick saw covered wagons rolling west, prairie fires lighting up the night sky and German settlers breaking the virgin sod, all of which, and more, his trilogy relates. First in his class at District School Number 9, Quick devoured the *McGuffey Reader* and any other book he could get his hands and his mind on. He later moved to Sioux City in western Iowa where he served as mayor and practiced law. Later Quick settled in West Virginia, far from the world he wrote about in what is considered one of the best fictional accounts of pioneer life on the great Midwestern prairies.

Waterloo, with its John Deere tractor factory and Rath packing plant, reflects the agricultural hinterland that surrounds the town, as does the week-long National Dairy Cattle Congress held every year in late September and early October, bringing to an end for the year the Iowa fair and exposition season. Although in Iowa corn is king, cattle were courted. In the early years of animal husbandry Iowans fanned out over the world to procure the leading breeds, acquiring Holsteins in Holland, Brown cows in Switzerland, and Jerseys and Guernseys from the English Channel Islands, as well as horses in Belgium, France and England. A WPA mural in Waterloo's main post office depicts a typical scene from the Congress, showing a crate of chickens, a basket of corn and a horse and cow being groomed. Waterloo almost served as the model for that quintessential Midwestern town described in Sinclair Lewis's novel *Main Street*. After graduating from Yale, Lewis worked as a reporter on the Waterloo *Daily Courier* in 1908 and 1909. When he returned to the town in 1919, by which time he'd published five books, Lewis mentioned to a friend there that he wanted to use Waterloo as the setting for his new novel. Alarmed by the possibility of the keen-eyed sharp-penned Lewis's scrutiny, the locals tried to discourage the idea by distracting the novelist with plentiful liquid refreshments and nonstop hospitality to prevent him from gathering information about the town. Lewis finally left Waterloo and proceeded north to his hometown of Sauk Center in Minnesota, which he used for *Main Street,* published in 1920. But Lewis was on the right track, for there is something archetypical about a place like Waterloo, as well as Cedar Rapids and many of the other towns and villages scattered across the Iowa landscape. Each of them has a main street, if not a Main Street; an ingrained mood of conservatism typical in the Midwest; a certain time-lessness; and an air of continuity and permanency—all qualities that have become scarce in a land and a time perhaps too oriented to change and novelty.

6. New World Symphony, Old World Settlers:

Dvorak and Spillville
The Norwegian–American Museum at Decorah
Fort Atkinson
Festina's Mini-Chapel
Little Brown Church in the Vale

Not long after the famous Czech composer Antonin Dvorak arrived in New York City in 1892 he found that the noise and distractions of the big city interfered with his efforts to compose. When Dvorak decided he needed a quieter setting the composer's assistant, J.J. Kovarik, a native of the Czech settlement of Spillville in Iowa, suggested they move out to the tranquil village, so in June 1893 Dvorak, his wife, their six children, his sister, a maid and Kovarik transferred to the small Midwestern town. Originally called Spielville after Joseph Spielman, who in 1850 established a mill on a creek near the Turkey River, Spillville soon attracted Czech set-tlers, the first arriving in 1854. Before long some fifty Czech families had moved there, so by the time Dvorak arrived he found an Old World settlement with people from his native country in the heartland of the New World.

That peaceful corner of mid-America was conducive to creation: within three days of his arrival there Dvorak sketched out the *String Quartet in F Major,* Opus 96, which he finished in less than two weeks. During his stay in Spillville that summer Dvorak also finished his *String Quartet in E Flat,* Opus 97, and embellished the *New World Symphony,* adding to the final movement its trombone parts. While in the Midwest the Czech composer became intrigued by Indian melodies. When he was visiting Minnehaha Falls in Minnesota one day, inspiration struck the composer. Lacking paper, Dvorak jotted down a few notes on his starched shirt cuff. Back in Spillville a few days later Dvorak discovered his wife had sent the noteworthy shirt to the laundry. The composer rushed over to retrieve the garment just before suds washed away the notations, which inspired him to write the well-known *Sonata in G Major,* popularly called *The Indian Lament,* Opus 100.

While in Spillville Dvorak joined St. Wenceslaus Church, completed September 18, 1860, that saint's feast day, when the Czech colony celebrated its first mass in the sanctuary. The composer frequently played the organ during mass at St. Wenceslaus, one of the heartland's most unusual churches. Modeled after the Church of St. Barbara in Kuta Hora, Czechoslovakia, a place of pilgrimage, the Spillville sanctuary is crowned by a spire that recalls the architecture of middle Europe rather than the Middle West. The churchyard is reached through a wrought-iron arch erected in 1910 to commemorate the building's fiftieth anniversary. Beyond the arch a long stairway rises toward the church at an angle, lending a sense of drama to the approach. With the low round ceiling and lack of high Gothic arches or soaring vaults, the interior has an intimate feeling to it. The Gothic windows bear Czech inscriptions, while the flag of Czechoslovakia hangs along with that of the U.S. and the papal banner. Outside, on the east side of the church, is an old Czech cemetery with some unusual grave markers.

During the three months Dvorak stayed in Spillville in the

summer of 1893 he and his family occupied a forty-year-old sandstone and brick house, now a museum with one room devoted to photos, sheet music and other memorabilia pertaining to the composer. The rest of the house contains an extensive display of wooden carvings, clocks and figures crafted by Frank and Joseph Bily, sons of a Czech immigrant. The Bily brothers, who as youths practiced their carving on school desks, never sold a piece of their work, all of which they willed to Spillville. As for Dvorak, one day toward the end of the summer his oldest daughter revealed she planned to elope with a local boy. Dvorak ordered his wife, sister and six children to pack their bags and the entourage left Spillville the next day for New York, and in 1895 the family returned to the composer's native Bohemia. Near Dvorak's favorite resting place on the banks of the Turkey River at Spillville stands a monument to the musician, an irregularly shaped stone with a metal plaque commemorating his visit and the name of one of his compositions on each face of the octagonal base.

About ten miles north of Spillville lies another Iowa ethnic settlement, the Norwegian town of Decorah. Writing of Decorah and the upper Iowa River region, former TV newsman Eric Sevareid evoked the area with a lyrical description:

> There is a corner of America here where the spring is lovely beyond belief, the land rolling and intensely green like the center of France, the rivers small between oak-covered bluffs and crossed by quiet bridges where boys still sit with pole and line, hook and worm. . . . Of course, generation after generation, the young mature and go away to the big and crowded cities. But their hearts never seem to leave this place and today, they tell me, more and more drift back here in their older years, trying—I hope not vainly—to find the magic talisman of peace.

To this lush and lovely land, around the middle of the nineteenth century, came Norwegian settlers whose culture and

traditions are remembered in Decorah's Vesterheim, a Norwegian-American Museum said to be one of the country's
oldest and largest immigrant ethnic museums. The founders
of the Vesterheim, established in 1877, decided to make it a
folk museum with displays of everyday objects used by ordinary settlers rather than a collection of artworks. As a result,
the exhibits include many items the early Norwegians
brought in chests and trunks from the old country—traditional clothes, household objects, furniture, tools, jewelry
and other such items of daily use. These occupy an unusual
and rather distinguished looking three-story structure, once a
Norwegian-language publishing house, embellished with
balconies, decorated windows, pillars and other details. In
addition to the main museum, the Vesterheim features on the
campus of nearby Luther College eight restored old buildings, including the 1852 Erik Egge cabin, which served as a
residence and as the first Norwegian Lutheran parsonage
west of the Mississippi, and also a restored four-story stone
and wood mill (1853) operated by the Bernatz family for
more than fifty years. In late July every year the Norwegian
community celebrates its heritage with a Nordic Fest, featuring smorgasbords, folk dancing and other ethnic events.

The hamlet of Festina, thirteen miles south of Decorah,
boasts what is supposedly the world's smallest church. In
1846 Johann Gaertner, who served as a soldier under Napoleon, arrived in Iowa from Europe and in 1885 he built the
twelve-by-sixteen-foot St. Anthony of Padua chapel to give
thanks for his safe return from the disastrous winter retreat of
Napoleon's army from Moscow. A forty-foot belfry was
added later to the garage-sized structure, while in 1903 the
miniature altar and stained-glass windows were installed in
the tiny church whose pews seat eight people. In the Old
Mission Cemetery behind the chapel repose Gaertner, his
wife and sister-in-law. On June 13 every year the feast of St.
Anthony is celebrated at the chapel. It is perhaps passing

strange that a memorial to an episode of the long-ago, faraway Napoleonic wars stands in an obscure corner of the American Midwest, but there it is.

At Clermont (originally named Norway), to the southwest of Festina, stands Montauk, an elegant 1874 mansion of native limestone and brick where William Larabee, Iowa's twelfth governor and a substantial landowner (some two hundred thousand acres) lived; while just west of Festina, and a few miles south of Spillville, stands restored old Fort Atkinson. Built in 1840, the fort was unusual for it served not to protect the settlers but to keep one Indian tribe from harassing another. The federal government built the installation, which occupies a high bluff overlooking the Turkey River, to protect the Winnebago from the fierce Sioux. After the Winnebago moved to a new reservation in 1848 the fort was abandoned and its buildings sold at public auction for thirty-five hundred and twenty-one dollars in 1853. The blockhouses and other structures on the grounds eventually fell into disrepair, but in 1921 the state acquired the property and eventually restored many of the buildings. The frontier era at Fort Atkinson is recalled at the history museum, housed in one of the original barracks, and also at the annual old-time military rendezvous held in late September. The fort affords one of the best places in Iowa to get a feel for the time a century and a half ago when isolated fortified outposts were thrown up in the empty spaces of the vast prairies. As Jacob A. Swisher noted in his book *Iowa in Times of War:*

> Running through the warp and woof of Iowa history there is a thread of interesting data concerning these military posts. Some were erected to quell Indian disturbances and to promote and foster trade relations with the Indians. Some were built to protect the natives against more hostile and warlike tribes, and to maintain order among them. In some instances forts were built to promote explorations and aid the settlers in seeking new

homes. Some forts were erected to protect surveyors and early settlers from Indian attacks in the northwest.

After the fort was abandoned, settlers, many of them Czechs from Spillville, gradually moved into the area. In 1873 they decided to build a church, which not without difficulty was completed two years later. It seems that the money ran out after the four walls had been put up but before workmen could add the roof. A Czech farmer, Joseph Sluka, mortgaged his property to raise money for the roof. When his crops failed, the lender threatened to foreclose but a priest from nearby St. Lucas came to the rescue, traveling from farm to farm to collect funds, thus saving both the Sluka property and the roof. Some of the three hundred or so present-day inhabitants of the hamlet of Fort Atkinson still attend St. John Nepomucepe, whose exterior bears brick decor, contrasting with the stone facade, and tall graceful windows topped by pointed Gothic arches. Inside stand three original Gothic altars and a rounded ceiling not unlike that at St. Wenceslaus in nearby Spillville.

Northern Iowa seems to be the land of churches. Apart from the two Czech churches at Spillville and at Fort Atkinson, and the St. Anthony Chapel at Festina, the town of Nashua, about thirty-five miles southwest of Fort Atkinson, boasts the Little Brown Church in the Vale. A Wisconsin doctor named William Pitts, traveling through the area in 1857, came upon a beguiling grove nestling in a valley which he envisioned as a perfect setting for a chapel. That scene near Nashua (then called Bradford) inspired him to write a poem, which he later set to music, about an imaginary *Little Brown Church in the Vale*. In the early 1860s the locals built a church at the very spot that had inspired Dr. Pitts. When he returned in 1864 he found a small brown-hued sanctuary, as if his very vision had become incarnate. The severe rather plain Gothic Revival-style exterior seems a bit formal in contrast to the more cozy confines of the interior, with its wallpaper, dark stained woodwork and pews, oil lamps, and walls that curve gracefully as they flow into the pressed metal ceiling. A popular wedding chapel, the church holds an annual reunion the first Sunday in August for couples married there. When Dr. Pitts returned to the wooded valley in 1864 and beheld his imaginary church that had materialized there he sang his song in the chapel, the first public performance of the work. Through the sanctuary rang out the words:

> There's a church in the valley by the wild wood,
> No lovlier place in the dale.
> No spot is so dear to my childhood,
> As the little brown church in the vale.

And ever since, all around the land and through the long years, has echoed the song recalling the little chapel nestled there in the woods in the heartland of America.

7. Northern Iowa:

Old Homes and Seventy-Six Trombones in Mason City
National Historic Landmarks at Grafton and Carpenter
The Fertile Mill
Winnebagos at Forest City
Hobohemia: The Hobo Convention at Britt

Until the 1957 Broadway musical *The Music Man* starred Mason City as the home of a seventy-six trombone band, perhaps the town's most memorable performance unfolded on March 13, 1934, when John Dillinger, "Baby Face" Nelson and their gang robbed the First National Bank of more than fifty-two thousand dollars. But the hit men were upstaged when the hit show opened and River City—Mason City's stage name—became famous as the setting for *The Music Man,* the show's title character being based on a band instrument salesman of the sort that used to travel for the C.G. Conn Company of Elkhart, Indiana (see Chapter II, section 9). Native son Meredith Willson, who lived in Iowa until he was a teenager, set his period-piece musical in Mason City in 1912, the year he was a boy of ten there. Mason City commemorates its fame as a music city with the annual North Iowa Band Festival in early June featuring thousands of musicians. Perhaps the most exciting festival blared forth in 1958 six months after *The Music Man,* a smash success, had opened on Broadway. Willson returned home for that twentieth annual festival, which included eighty-seven bands, five thousand players and a "Seventy Six Trombones" ensemble of two hundred and eight musicians who strutted and tooted down Federal Avenue, led by the composer himself. The Mason City native, Iowa's "music laureate," composed the *Iowa Fight Song* for the University of Iowa in 1951 and, to even the score, *For I for S Forever* for Iowa State in 1953. Willson's 1946 composition *Iowa,* which became the state's centennial song, evokes sumac in September, shoes in the snow, songs after dark on the porch and "a memory of long ago."

Another well-known Mason City show business figure was puppeteer Bil Baird. Perhaps Baird transferred to Willson that extra "l" which the puppet-master dropped from his given "Bill" supposedly to qualify for a club for people whose first names contained three letters or less. Baird's father gave his son a homemade puppet when the boy was seven and later, after a five-year apprenticeship with puppeteers, he introduced his marionettes in Chicago in 1934. Eventually Baird and his wife, Cora, brought to their popular CBS TV show such characters as Whistling Wizard, Flannel Mouse, Bubbles La Rue (a stripper) and Slug O'Brien (a honky-tonk pianist). At the Charles H. MacNider Museum in Mason City you can see a collection of Bil and Cora Baird puppets, and, not to forget Mason City's favorite composer, near the museum stands the Meredith Willson footbridge.

Mason City also boasts some architectural attractions rather more elaborate than the Willson footbridge. Some thirteen Prairie School-style buildings in the tradition of Frank Lloyd Wright embellish the northern Iowa town. Wright himself designed the 1910 City National Bank (now Van Duyn's clothing store) and the adjoining Park Inn Hotel in the center of town. A few years later some local businessmen commissioned Wright associate Walter Burley Griffin—perhaps best known as the master architect for Canberra, Australia's capital—to design two adjacent residential subdivisions, Rock Crest and Rock Glen, that stand above Willow Creek. Griffin's success in securing the assignment incensed Wright, even though the latter was hardly in a position to take on a new commission, having left his wife and children, given up his practice and eloped from his Oak Park, Illinois, house (see Chapter III, section 8) with his neighbor's wife. Griffin designed five houses in the new subdivisions, which include such striking Prairie School-style structures as the 1913 J.G. Melson residence, a fortress-like affair considered one of the first modern houses of the twentieth century, built of sharp-edged stone blocks with fan-like devices over the upper windows; the 1913 square, boxy Arthur Rule house; and the Page residence, truly a tribute to Griffin's salesmanship in that the structure is built of reinforced concrete although Page operated a lumber business.

North of Mason City, up toward the Minnesota state line, lie two small towns with buildings listed on the National Register. At Grafton stands the turn-of-the-century train depot, while a few miles farther north at Carpenter is the so-called Fort Severson, an 1867 limestone structure built by a

Norwegian immigrant not as a fort but to serve as an agriculture building. Heading southwest from Carpenter you'll reach the village of Fertile where the ten-acre Fertile Mill Park, on an island on the Winnebago River, includes the mid-nineteenth-century mill built by William Rhodes. Originally used to grind flour, the mill today turns out feeds. The relic is one of eighteen or so grist and flour mills remaining out of the seven hundred and twelve such old installations that once dotted the Iowa landscape. At Forest City, ten miles west of Fertile, you can tour the factory that turns out the well-known Winnebago motor homes. When the town's economy started to decline in the early 1950s the local leaders established a commission to develop new industry for the area. Visiting California, one member of the commission, furniture dealer Jim Hanson, devised the idea of motor homes and thus was born Winnebago Industries. By 1968 the town of three thousand boasted more millionaires per capita, thanks to the company's soaring shares, than any other town in the Middle West. In at least one place in Iowa, stock other than livestock had made people wealthy.

Southwest of Forest City, beyond the hamlet of Hayfield, lies the town of Britt. Britt is one of those typical Iowa farm towns scattered across the great prairies of the state. Dozens of them dream away the years in a kind of timeless reverie out there in the open endless spaces—invariable small clusters of stores and houses and people like the town described by Douglas Bauer in *Prairie City, Iowa, Three Seasons at Home:*

> Prairie City lasts no more than a few blocks in any direction before the fields resume. Crop rows run to the edge of town, crowding it all around, like an ocean eating resolutely at its shore. Immaculate frame houses fill the city blocks, laid out in a strict grid of straight, flat streets, and there is an overwhelming dominance of sky, swooping down, uninterrupted by trees or buildings, to the horizon.

Britt, then, is like all the other small farm towns—peaceful, permanent, unchanging, tied to the ever-recurring cycle of the seasons. But once a year, in early August, things are different. Then the place bustles with activity when some twenty thousand visitors descend on Britt to attend one of the Midwest's most colorful events—the National Hobo Convention.

The hobo jungle, in those hot early August days, spreads out hard by the Milwaukee Road tracks in the shadow of the grey grain elevator that towers above Britt, named, appropriately enough, after a brakeman on the Milwaukee line. The grub—canned beans, stew, Iowa corn—simmers over the flickering campfire. Perhaps one of the hoboes dozes, maybe dreaming of the open road, while another tends the pails in which the meal cooks. Others lounge about, waiting to eat. The hoboes—some twenty of them, the last of a dying breed—are in Britt, a town of two thousand, hoping to be coronated as the new Hobo King and Queen.

On the Friday of the festivities a flea market and the midway with rides, craft booths, food stalls and a souvenir stand selling hobo-imprinted items are open, but the main events take place on Saturday. Things get under way in mid-morning with a Hobo Day parade featuring antique cars, fire engines and floats, the latter carrying bands, corn country politicians and, most likely, a crew or two of boys eagerly squirting water pistols at the crowd. Starting at noon free mulligan stew is dished out of twenty-gallon metal drums in which the grub, more than four hundred gallons of it, has been cooked. Back in 1974 some prankster dumped cinnamon instead of chili powder into the stew but people devoured it anyway. In the afternoon each of the twenty or so candidates who are pretenders to the throne delivers a two-minute presentation—a talk, a song, a tune on the harmonica. The crowd's applause determines the winners. In recent years the competitors included Slow Motion Shorty, Mountain Dew, Fry Pan Jack and Long Looker Mic, so named for her practice of taking a long look down the tracks while awaiting the next fast freight.

After the coronation, with crowns cut from coffee cans, visitors can chat with the hoboes and listen to their tales of the open road. You can also shop at the flea market, wander the midway and tour the Hancock County Museum. On view at the museum, installed in a three-story Victorian-style 1896 banker's house, are period furniture, old glassware and household objects that give an idea how a well-to-do Iowa prairie family lived at the turn of the century. One item, a dinner bell, bears the inscription: "That all softening/O'er powering knell,/The tocsin of the soul—/The dinner bell." It was back in those days, in 1900, when Britt hosted the first Hobo Convention. As an archetypical Iowa farm village, Britt would seem an unlikely place for hoboes to gather. Surrounded by cornfields, the hamlet presents a picture of rural peace and isolation, a far cry from the urban hobo jungles of the great rail centers. Parked around the village are green John Deere tractors and combines, their color a visual echo of the cornstalks that bend and ripple as an occasional breeze passes by. White frame houses line the wide, tree-shaded streets, and a generous scattering of churches, eight of them, proclaim the town's piety. It all seems like a scene out of a Grant Wood painting. Yet, once a year, the hoboes repair to this little Iowa farm town for their annual conclave.

The tradition started back in 1900 when a group of Britt citizens invited Tourist Union No. 63, a small hobo club that had previously met in Illinois, to gather in Britt for the next meeting. The program for the first convention advertised that "all the good fellows for a hundred miles around will be here. . . . all Tourists, Printers, Bindlestifts (can cook anywhere), Nestocrats (can sleep anywhere) and Society Tramps are invited." On August 22, 1900, the hoboes arrived. Greeting them was a banner that read "Hobo Headquarters," while nearby hung a sign proclaiming "Hobo Hindquarters." That afternoon a short-distance hobo foot race, first prize a bottle of beer and second a five-dollar bill, lasted for two hours before a halt was called to the laid-back competition. For a time the convention lapsed but in 1933 the townfolks of Britt revived the event and through the years a series of hobo royalty reigned, among them Hairbreadth Harry (the first king), Scoopshovel Scotty, the Hardrock Kid (the four-time hobo monarch reposes in Britt's Evergreen Cemetery), Slow Motion Shorty and Steamtrain Maury Graham.

These days only a few of those hoboes of old are left, men (and a few women) who found the long lonesome whistle of a passing freight sounding in the night to be an irresistible summons to the life of the open road. One of the best-known hoboes in American history was author Jack London, who traveled across Iowa with Kelly's Army in 1894 (see section 2). In his story "Hoboes That Pass in the Night" London wrote "of the wanderlust in my blood that would not let me rest." Similar restless blood coursed through the veins of other old-timers, freight hoppers with "nom-de-rails," as London put it, like Ohio Fatty, Cleveland Mushy, Poison Face Slim, Adam Ydobon ("nobody" spelled backwards) and Slim Jim from Vinegar Hill "who never worked and never will."

Every year in early August some of the few remaining hoboes make their way to Britt for the annual festivities. Late in the day when the shadows begin to fall across the Iowa cornfields and the heat of the August day starts to drain away, the wanderers gather at Britt's hobo jungle by the grain elevator. The newly crowned Hobo King and Queen hold court there, attended by the other vagabonds who traveled from afar to the little Iowa village to carry on the long-standing Hobo Convention tradition. The old-timers will swap a tall tale or short story or two—reminiscences of the open road and of the now vanished golden days of the

hobo—and soon, perhaps, a rail rider will pick up his guitar
and start to strum a song of the wandering life, and in the soft
August dusk, brightened by the flickering camp fire, he'll
sing:

> Hear the mighty rush of the engine, hear those
> Lonesome hoboes squall,
> While traveling through the jungle
> on the Wabash Cannonball.

It's enough to make you want to jump the next fast freight
that passes by.

8. Covered Wagons and Covered Bridges:

*The Old Frontier Towns of Algona, Dakota City and Fort
Dodge
Boone, Home of Mamie Doud Eisenhower
Iowa State at Ames
Covered Bridges at Winterset
The Western Frontier Towns of Council Bluffs and Sioux City*

Western Iowa somehow takes on the tone of the frontier. The
towns seem farther apart and more isolated, the prairies and
the sky grander and more dominating. In the western half of
Iowa, that half of the state west of Interstate 35, lie a number
of historic towns and attractions recalling the frontier days of
the nineteenth century.

Twenty-three miles west of hobo haven Britt is Algona,
where the old days seem revived at the Pioneer Drug Store
Museum—a re-creation of a turn-of-the-century pharmacy
with display cases filled with old bottles, false teeth and other
wares—and the Kossuth County Historical Museum, with

three floors of exhibits housed in Algona's first schoolhouse, built in 1867. At Dakota City, twenty-four miles south of Algona, the Humboldt County Historical Museum occupies a stately 1879 brick house listed on the National Register, which has been restored and furnished with period pieces. Also on the grounds of the property, the former Mill farm, are a schoolhouse, barn, log cabin and jail. At Clarion, due east of Dakota City, you can visit the 4-H Historical Museum which traces the development of the famous farm club. As might be expected, Iowa being the quintessential agricultural state, the 4-H organization for young farm people originated there. The same year that Jessie Field Shambaugh was elected Page County superintendent of schools at age twenty-four (1906), she established at each of the county's hundred and thirty schools a Boys Corn Club and a Girls Home Club. Those groups evolved into the now internationally active 4-H Clubs, the H's standing for Head, Hands, Heart and Health.

Southwest of Clarion lies Fort Dodge, one of the old Iowa frontier fort towns like Fort Atkinson and Fort Madison that recalls the time when the Midwest was the Wild West. Recapturing those days is the Fort Museum, an exact replica of the outpost the army built to protect area settlers from Sioux Indians. The museum includes displays on the region's history as well as a country schoolhouse, jail, newspaper office, blacksmith shop and general store. At Frontier Days, held the first weekend of June every year, the Fort comes alive with music, a rodeo and other activities. Fort Dodge, which became the seat of Webster County when local John Duncombe won the honor for his hometown by defeating a resident of rival Homer in a wrestling match in 1856, played a role in one of the most amusing hoaxes of the nineteenth century. In October 1869 workmen digging a well at Cardiff, New York, near Syracuse, happened upon a ten-foot-tall stone human figure that astonished the nation. *Scientific American* magazine adjudged the find a petrified giant that was "the most extraordinary and gigantic wonder ever presented to the eye of man." Local entrepreneurs bought the body and put it on display. Showman P.T. Barnum offered to lease the giant for three months for sixty thousand dollars. Then someone remembered that in the year before a Binghamton, New York, man named George Hull had carted away from the gypsum deposits near Fort Dodge a ten-foot-long slab, and soon after the statue surfaced so did the truth: Hull had commissioned a Chicago stonecutter to carve the block into the shape of a man and then "age" the material by coating the figure in sulfuric acid. Hull then buried the supposed relic at Cardiff where well diggers "discovered" it the following year. The Cardiff Giant today reposes in the Farmers Museum not in farm-filled Iowa but at Cooperstown, New York, which acquired the figure in 1948.

About halfway between Fort Dodge and Des Moines, to the south, lies Boone, hometown of Mamie Doud who in 1915 met and later married a young army second lieutenant named Dwight Eisenhower. The simple one-story frame house where she was born in 1896 is now a museum with the original furnishings and a collection of items relating to Mamie's life and Ike's military and political career. From a Mamie-era vintage depot in Boone runs the Boone and Scenic Valley Railroad excursion train, which follows the ten-and-a-half-mile route of the former Fort Dodge, Des Moines and Southern line. The train of old-time cars passes across a one-hundred-and-fifty-six-foot-high bridge—the highest single-track interurban bridge in the country—that spans the Des Moines River valley. During Boone's annual Pufferbilly Days festival, held in mid-September, a special steam train crosses the Kate Shelley High Bridge, said to be the world's longest and highest double-track span. Built in 1901 and listed on the National Register in 1978, the High Bridge commemorates the bravery of fifteen-year-old Kate who crawled across an earlier Des Moines River span one stormy night in 1881 to warn the station operator at Moingona about some washed-out tracks, enabling him to halt an approaching train. The Kate Shelley Railroad Museum, installed in a restored depot at Moingona, five miles southwest of Boone, contains exhibits relating to Kate's exploit.

A few miles east of Boone lies Ames, site of Iowa State University, arch rival of the University of Iowa in Iowa City (see section 5). Iowa humorist Ellis Parker Butler, author of an amusing narrative entitled *Pigs Is Pigs,* encapsulated that rivalry in his complaint about how the legislature favored the agriculturally oriented State school over the University's liberal arts programs: "Millions annually for manure but not one cent for literature." Iowa State, established in 1858 as the country's first land-grant college, is perhaps the nation's leading agricultural university. Three U.S. Secretaries of Agriculture—James Wilson and Henry C. and Henry A. Wallace (father and son)—graduated from the school, and famous black scientist George Washington Carver, a protege of Wilson and a mentor to the younger Wallace, attended Iowa State between 1891 and 1896. (For Carver's early years in southwestern Missouri, see Chapter V, section 8.) In the early days the undergraduates confronted some unusual demands: an 1876 report noted that "The law requires that all students shall engage in manual labor an average of 2½ hours each day (except Sundays)." The students received credit on their bills at a rate of three to nine cents an hour for the work. Those early days are recalled at the Farm House, a National Register-listed residence built in 1860 at the Iowa Agricultural College and Model Farm, as the university was originally named. Grant Wood murals in the university library also recall the institution's farm orientation; the scenes portrayed illustrate Daniel Webster's observation, "When tillage begins, other arts follow."

If the culture of rural life interests you, then you might want to visit the Living History Farms complex, a six-hundred-acre agricultural museum at the northwest edge of Des Moines which includes four functioning farms—an 1840 pioneer farm, a 1900 horse farm, plus farms of today and of the future. Also on view is Walnut Hill, a reconstructed typical village of the 1870s. It was at the Farms complex where Pope John Paul II delivered a major agricultural address in 1979. Baseball fans might enjoy staying overnight at Walden Acres in the town of Adel, twelve miles west of the Living History Farms, a bed and breakfast house where speedball pitcher Bob Feller, from nearby Van Meter, once lived.

Twenty miles south of Adel lies Winterset, seat of Madison county where six old covered bridges take you back in time to the old days when covered wagons, as well as covered bridges, evidenced a now long-vanished way of life. "My grandparents and my parents came here in a covered wagon," wrote Herbert Hoover of his forebears' arrival at West Branch, Iowa (see section 5), and Nancy Henderson recalled for her grandchildren, a half century after the experience, traveling to Iowa by covered wagon in 1850 as a girl of fourteen. In *Early Algona, The Story of Our Pioneers* she wrote: "I can't imagine anything more thrilling than sleeping outdoors under the stars and listening to the queer sounds at night. It was such fun to watch mother cook our food outdoors and to ride over the immense prairies and ford the rivers. . . . The woods were full of ferns and flowers and birds and animals and we never knew what we might see next. The prairies were just one great flower garden." It was back in those covered wagon days between 1855 and 1885 when Madison County's sixteen covered bridges were built. Six now remain, all listed on the National Register. Why were the bridges covered? One builder explained, "Our bridges were covered, my dear Sir, for the same reason that our belles wore hoop skirts and crinolines—to protect the structural beauty that is seldom seen but nevertheless appreciated." Every fall, the second full weekend in October, Winterset celebrates its Covered Bridge Festival with craft demonstrations, food galore, a spelling bee, music and other activities—all much as at the annual Parke County, Indiana, autumn covered bridge festival (see Chapter II, section 2).

Other attractions in Winterset, one of the most interesting towns of its size (four thousand inhabitants) in the Midwest, include the Art Center, installed in an 1854 brick house and featuring an exhibit dedicated to George Washington Carver, who lived in Winterset before attending Iowa State University in the 1890s; the birth house of movie actor John Wayne, with period furnishings and such Wayne memorabilia as the black eye-patch the actor wore in his Oscar-winning performance in the 1969 movie *True Grit;* the Madison County Historical Complex, with two National Register-listed structures, a limestone barn and the 1856 Bevington House, as well as other old buildings; the county courthouse and St. Patrick's Catholic Church, both also listed on the National Register; and the one-hundred-and-fifteen-acre City Park, which includes an inscribed boulder commemorating the discovery in 1881 on a farm near East Peru (southeast of Winterset) of the original "Delicious" apple tree. Around the county you'll find more National Register buildings—two in East Peru, one in Macksburg and an old stone schoolhouse near the Hogback covered bridge—as well as other scenes and sights that make Madison County a pleasant place to linger.

After savoring the many delights of the Winterset area you can head toward the western part of the state. Near Adair, just off Interstate 80, occurred what is said to be the first train robbery in the West, an 1873 escapade by Jesse James and his gang who derailed a five-car train and then relieved the passengers of their worldly goods. Farther west, six miles north of I-80, lies the town of Elk Horn where you'll see a genuine Danish windmill built in 1848 in Denmark and reassembled in one of America's largest settlement of Danes. At nearby Kimballton a replica of Hans Christian Andersen's

Little Mermaid statue in Copenhagen stands in the town
square. Farther west, at the Missouri River, which separates
Iowa from Nebraska, lies Council Bluffs.

For many years Council Bluffs served as a way station for
travelers and visitors to what was once the Far West. As early
as 1804 the Lewis and Clark Expedition (see Chapter III,
section 9) passed by the site on its way up the Mississippi. In
the middle of the century a group of Mormons led by Brigham Young arrived at Council Bluffs where they settled for a
few years on their way from Nauvoo, Illinois (Chapter III,
section 9), out to Utah. Council Bluffs also served as an
outfitting post for the "forty-niners" heading to California
for the 1848–1849 gold rush—"yellow fever," the Keokuk,
Iowa *Register* called it. Other travelers came and went on
Missouri River steamboats bearing such evocative names as
Time and Tide, Creole Belle, West Wind and *Western Belle.* In
1859 Abe Lincoln, who arrived in Council Bluffs by riverboat from St. Joseph, Missouri, met Grenville Dodge, an
engineer and surveyor who promoted a transcontinental railroad with Council Bluffs to serve as the eastern terminus.
The city has commemorated much of that early history with
monuments scattered all around town. You'll find in Council
Bluffs historical markers dedicated to Lewis and Clark, to the
Mormon Trail, to Lincoln's visit, and to the city's role as
eastern terminus of the transcontinental line. Although one
of the town's early renowned residents—Amelia Bloomer,
who gave her name to the then (1855) scandalous garment
she popularized—remains uncommemorated, the lavish
Grenville Dodge home, a fourteen-room residence built in
1869 and listed on the National Register, recalls one of Council Bluffs' leading citizens of a century ago. Furniture, photos, portraits, bric-a-brac, old-fashioned light fixtures dripping with crystals and other Victorian-era items cram the
house. Council Bluffs also boasts one of the six remaining
lazy susan or squirrel cage jails, the 1855 Pottawattamie

County Jail, which sports revolving cell blocks that enabled one jailer to keep an eye on all the prisoners. (You'll find another such turning jail at Crawfordsville, Indiana: see Chapter II, section 9.)

Heading north from Council Bluffs to Sioux City you'll pass near the DeSoto National Wildlife Refuge. The refuge lies along the so-called Missouri Flyway, a migratory route that some quarter of a million waterfowl follow in the spring and the fall. The peak viewing months are March and April and October and November. Also at the refuge is a visitors center with a display of artifacts salvaged after more than a century from the steamer *Bertrand,* which sank in the Missouri River in 1865. The craft's cargo remained perfectly preserved beneath the river's silt and sand, and the recovered (or, rather, uncovered) objects—clothes, glassware, tools and much else—now comprise one of the best collections of Civil War-era items in existence. Those wreck remnants recall the vicissitudes of the Missouri, perhaps the country's most dangerous and unpredictable major river. An estimated four hundred and forty-one ships were sunk or damaged on the muddy Missouri, which some Iowans describe as too thick to drink and too thin to plow. A Sioux City editor once wrote: "Of all the variable things in creation the most uncertain are the action of a jury, the state of a woman's mind, and the condition of the Missouri River."

Like Council Bluffs to the south, Sioux City bears a name that recalls the early days when Indians dominated the area. The city's site once formed part of the Sioux Indian nation. In August 1804 white men in the person of the Lewis and Clark Expedition appeared there along that remote stretch of the Missouri. On August 19, Clark, whom the Indians called "the big blue eyes," wrote in his journal: "Sergeant Floyd is taken very bad all at once with a bilious colic. We attempt to revive him without much success as yet. He gets worse and we are much alarmed at his situation." The next day Charles

Floyd died—the only person on the nearly two-and-a-half-year, five-thousand-mile-long expedition to expire—and "We buried him on the top of the bluff a half mile below a small river to which we gave his name." The restless Missouri later encroached on the burial site, so Floyd's remains were reburied higher on the same bluff. In 1901 the present stone obelisk was erected and in 1960 the grave became the nation's first National Historic Landmark. At the opposite edge of Sioux City repose the remains of the other end of the paleface-redskin spectrum—the body of War Eagle, which rests on a high bluff from which the great chief used to watch the approach of friends, or sometimes foes, from out of the west. Forty-four years after Floyd's death, pioneers began settling in the area and Sioux City soon prospered as a steamboat and railroad center, one popular passenger hotel bearing the alluring name "The Terrific." The 1887 Corn Palace, a huge frame building embellished with corncobs of all shapes and colors arranged in elaborate designs, is long gone, but one unusual carryover from the days when extensive stockyards and meat-packing plants (the first opened in 1860) dominated the city is the K.D. Stockyards Station, a shopping center installed in the massive old Swift packing plant in the heart of the stockyards.

Heading northeast out of Sioux City you'll pass through Le Mars, near which a colony of English gentlemen established in 1877 a mini-English settlement, complete with polo matches, golf (perhaps the earliest example of that game in America), horse races and the Prairie Club, modeled after the genteel clubs of London. Unlike the artificial Camelot town of North Webster, Indiana (see Chapter II, section 9), Le Mars was a true English outpost in the New World. The dandies frequented such local establishments as Albion House Hotel as well as pubs named House of Lords and Windsor Castle. Founded by Cambridge graduate William Close, the Close Colony thrived between 1879 and 1885. St. George's Anglican Church, built by the settlers in 1881, still stands, a wooden replica of an English stone country church, and is listed on the National Register. (For another early English prairie settlement—Albion, Illinois—see Chapter III, section 4.) About twenty miles north of Le Mars lies Orange City, another European settlement, founded by Dutch settlers in 1869 and named for Prince William of Orange. Orange City is a smaller and lesser known version of the Iowa Dutch settlement of Pella (see section 3). The town boasts a replica of a Dutch mill, while craftsmen at The Old Factory carve and decorate wooden shoes fashioned in the old-country style.

To travel from the civilized European communities of Le Mars and Orange City to the so-called Iowa Great Lakes in the north-central part of the state near the Minnesota border is to revert to the natural delights and raw history of the American West. At Cayler Prairie, west of West Okoboji Lake, lies a stretch of native prairie, brilliant with wildflowers from spring to fall and never touched by plow or progress, while in Arnolds Park on the south edge of that lake stands the Gardner Log Cabin and a stone obelisk, memorials to the 1857 Spirit Lake massacre when a band of Sioux, their skins smeared with black, the tribe's war color, killed forty settlers. Iowa native Mackinlay Kantor's novel *Spirit Lake* recounts the story of the massacre, which epitomizes the frontier atmosphere that seems still to linger there in western Iowa where the prairies meet the great plains.

9. The Great River Road:

Following the Mississippi to Keokuk, Burlington, Muscatine
and Davenport
Buffalo Bill House
North Along the River to Dubuque, Guttenberg, McGregor
and the Effigy Mounds National Monument

The Great River Road, now skirting the Mississippi and now wandering inland, runs along the eastern edge of Iowa, passing on its winding way through scenic farm country and old river towns rich in historical and cultural sights. By the great river nestles a series of cities that were once enclaves of culture and prosperity on the eastern edge of the vast Iowa prairieland. "Dubuque, Davenport, Burlington, Keokuk, or Muscatine [where you] find yourself in the very heart of civilization and refinement," a traveler in the area noted in *Iowa As It Is in 1854.* "You see magnificent churches, and gorgeous dwellings, and large wide streets. Everything has an air of neatness and purity. And then too you see indications of life and animation—you see the large stores and warehouses groaning under the weight of their valuable commodities—you hear the puffing of the steam-engine, hear the cheerful ringing of the anvil." Apart from those old-time sounds—the engine's puff and the anvil's ring—Iowa's Mississippi River cities still boast a certain nineteenth-century atmosphere of understated well-being and underlying tranquillity.

Tucked away in the far southeastern corner of Iowa, where the Des Moines River that demarks the border with Missouri flows into the Mississippi, is the town of Keokuk. Keokuk's attractions typify many of the themes and scenes—Indians, steamboats and other Mississippi memorabilia, as well as memories of prominent personalities—found along Iowa's Great River Road. In Rand Park stands a bronze statue marking the grave of Chief Keokuk, the Sac leader, while installed in the nineteenth-century paddle wheeler *George M. Verity* is a steamboat museum filled with memories of the Mississippi in the olden days when showboats and passenger craft plied the waterway. A more recent river attraction is Lock Number 19 and the adjacent dam, which when completed in 1913 was the world's largest hydroelectric station. Fifteen, sixty-five-ton turbines at the dam, open for tours, whirr the water's currrent into electricity, most of it transmitted to St. Louis. The locks, the Mississippi's largest, can raise or lower boats thirty-eight feet, more than any other lock on the river. A few old houses scattered around Keokuk recall the town's famous residents. At one nineteenth-century home (629 High Street) resided Jane Clemens, Mark Twain's mother. In the 1850s Twain himself lived in Keokuk, where his brother Orion owned a job-printing shop. At a January 1856 banquet in Keokuk Twain delivered his first known public speech, an effort the local paper adjudged as "replete with wit and humor, being interrupted by long bursts of applause." One day Twain found on a Keokuk street a fifty-dollar bill. The honest young man advertised the find in the paper and, as he later revealed, "suffered more than a thousand dollars worth of solicitude and fear and distress in the next few days lest the owner see the advertisement and come and take my fortune away." After four days of torment Twain left Keokuk with his new fortune intact. Also still standing is the house (318 N. 4th) where Elsa Maxwell, who rose to fame as an international hostess and society figure, was born in 1887. Nearby stands the 1858 homestead of Samuel Freeman Miller, appointed by Lincoln in 1862 to the U.S. Supreme Court. Listed on the National Register, the restored residence now houses the Lee County Historical Society Museum. Also listed on the National Register is the 1890 Lee County courthouse, successor to the court building where *Star Spangled Banner* composer Francis Scott Key, a lawyer for the New York Land Company, once appeared during a visit to Keokuk on a matter involving local land title disputes.

On the Great River Road just north of Keokuk stands the Galland School, a rough-hewn one-room log cabin replica of the first school in Iowa, built in 1830 and named for Dr. Isaac Galland. Galland, supposedly a counterfeiter who gave up the trade because there was too much competition, also served as secretary to Mormon Prophet Joseph Smith. A mile or two north of the school is the ferry that crosses the Mississippi to Nauvoo, Illinois, where the Mormons headquartered in the early 1840s (see Chapter III, section 9). This spot in Iowa marks the beginning of the trail over which thousands of Mormons, led by Brigham Young, began their trek west to Utah a year and a half after Smith was murdered at Carthage near Nauvoo in June 1844. Farther on you'll come to Fort Madison, home to both pen and penitentiary. At the north end of town rise the forbidding walls of the Iowa State Penitentiary, while in the center of the city stands the Sheaffer pen factory. After local jeweler W.A. Sheaffer saw an ad in 1908 for a pen that had to be filled with an eyedropper he invented a self-filling lever pen. He patented the device, then began producing it, with seven employees, in 1913. The present factory, built in 1951, offers tours of the writing instrument manufacturing operation.

Sixteen miles north of Fort Madison lies Burlington where, in 1805, Zebulon Pike, of Pike's Peak fame, established a small fort, one of the first outposts along the new frontier. Mark Twain found hilly Burlington a "beautiful" town but he complained that the place was too sober, thanks (or no thanks) to a temperance bill forbidding "the manufacture, exportation, importation, purchase, sale, borrowing, lending, stealing, drinking, smelling, or possession, by conquest, inheritance, intent, accident, or otherwise, in the State of Iowa, of each and every deleterious beverage known to the human race, except water." However, you may feel as if you've over-imbibed the forbidden elixir as you weave your way down Snake Alley, which Ripley's "Believe It or Not" called "the crookedest street in the world." It is great fun to drive down the gas lamp-lined brick street, built in 1894, which bends seven times as it descends one block from Heritage Hill down to the center of town. Heritage Hill, a twenty-block residential area listed on the National Register in 1982, encompasses some one hundred and sixty nineteenth-century houses, many of architectural interest. At the edge of the historic area nestles tiny Mosquito Park, which perches on a bluff that affords a splendid view of the Mississippi, here dotted with verdant islands that seem earthy green counterparts to clumps of clouds that often clot the Midwestern sky. Near the waterfront stand old brick factories, stores and warehouses for a variety of goods from baskets (Burlington Basket Company) to caskets (Embalming Burial Case Company).

Leaving Burlington you'll pass at the north edge of town a reminder of Iowa's agriculture hinterland, the huge J.I. Case farm implement factory where a sign proudly proclaims, "Backhoe Capital of the World." The River Road winds its way through a rolling green landscape dotted with red barns and white farmhouses as it takes you north toward Muscatine. On the way you'll pass Toolesboro, a National Historic Landmark, where some one hundred pre-Columbian Indian mounds dot the landscape. Dioramas at the Toolesboro visitor center and a marker recall that the site was where French explorers Marquette and Joliet became the first Europeans, in 1673, to set foot on the soil of what is now Iowa. As you continue north, a detour to the west will take you to Columbus Junction where an unusual old wooden "Swinging Bridge" spans a gulch between Third and Fourth Streets.

It is definitely a moving experience: you'll sway your way over as you cross the bridge, restored in 1954 as a successor to the original 1886 barrel-stave and wire construction.

Muscatine—originally named Casey's Woodpile for the stacks of logs stored there that fueled the steamships—is, like Burlington, a hilly, sleepy river town with a scattering of old Victorian residences. One, the 1855 Octagon, now houses a restaurant. There should be no problem getting a corner table in the eight-sided building. Muscatine has a colorful history. Because the great bend in the river there made the town an ideal place to land logs shipped downstream from the northern forests, an extensive lumber industry developed. The city also became the nation's leading manufacturer of buttons, originally cut from shells of the once abundant clams in the river and now produced from artificial materials. One of the first sawmill magnates, Ben Hershey, savored roasted geese that had been fed corn soaked in whiskey to improve the taste of the birds. The 1908 Musser Mansion, which houses part of the art center, belonged to another of the early lumber barons. A number of Muscatine patriarchs served during the Civil War in Iowa's "Greybeard Regiment," a unit of more than a thousand senior citizens, some very senior, the most venerable being an eighty-year-old named Curtis King. Mark Twain, who surfaced in towns all up and down the river, remembered Muscatine, where he worked on the *Journal* newspaper, "for its summer sunsets. I have never seen any, on either side of the ocean, that equaled them. They used the broad smooth river as a canvas, and painted on it every imaginable dream of color; from the mottled daintiness and delicacies of the opal, all the way up, through cumulative intensities, to blinding purple and crimson conflagrations which were enchanting to the eye." To this paean to sunsets Twain added, "The sunrises are also said to be exceedingly fine. I do not know." Sun shows and the river in Muscatine can best be seen from the Mark Twain Overlook, a hill just north of downtown where the city's first radio station operated. KTNT—named for the slogan "Know The Naked Truth"—belonged to Norman Baker, a local character who, perhaps influenced by the florid Muscatine sunsets, fancied purple shirts and orchid-hued cars. Baker, who in the 1930s lured people to Muscatine with his supposed cure for cancer, displayed over the door of his building the slogan "A quack is one who thinks and does things others can't do." Baker eventually moved to Mexico.

At Muscatine the Mississippi bends sharply to make an eccentric sort of contortion that puts Davenport to the east more than to the north. With a population of a hundred thousand, Davenport is the first place along Iowa's Great River Road that has the feel of a city. The settlement took its name from Colonel George Davenport whose 1833 house stands on Rock Island, which lies between Iowa and Illinois just across the river (for Rock Island, see Chapter III, section 7). In the Iowa part of the so-called Quad Cities the Davenport Art Gallery contains a display of "Midwest Regionalist" painters, including Missouri's Thomas Hart Benton and works by Iowa's Grant Wood. A self-portrait pictures the Iowa painter with a serious expression, his steel-rim spectacles finding a visual echo in the round windmills in the background. On display are Wood's wooden sketch box that holds a color-smeared palette, the cameo broach used as the model for the one worn by the woman in "American Gothic" and a Carl Sandburg book autographed by the author for Wood with the inscription, "As between fellow strugglers." The nearby Putnam Museum, one of the oldest museum's west of the Mississippi, houses exhibits on the area's history, including more than a thousand artifacts and hundreds of photos tracing the past from prehistoric times up to the era of local jazz great Bix Beiderbecke, born in Davenport in 1903. Beiderbecke lived in a homey old-fashioned sort of house at

1934 Grand Avenue and lies buried in Oakland cemetery where his friends held a jam session by his grave in 1971 on the fortieth anniversary of the musician's death. In late July every year Davenport celebrates its local boy made good with the Bix Beiderbecke Jazz Festival.

As you continue up the Mississippi or over, for the river maintains its eastwardly path, you'll pass through the village of East Davenport, which appears much as it did a century and more ago when the town served as a logging center and a steamboat port. Listed on the National Register, East Davenport hosts on the third weekend of September every year a Civil War Muster and Mercantile Exposition, featuring re-enactment of a battle complete with cannons, cavalry and infantry, and a ball with music and dances of the 1880s. Nearby Le Claire is another old town rich in history. During the mid-nineteenth century, when steamboat traffic was at its peak, a special and perhaps even unique occupation developed in Le Claire—that of rapids pilot. Le Claire rivermen would hire on to guide ships through the treacherous nearly fourteen-mile-long Rock Island Rapids. Fourteen old Le Claire homes once occupied by the town's pilots, boat builders and ship captains, are listed on the National Register under the evocative designation "Houses of Mississippi Rivermen." Some of the old river history, with photos of nineteenth-century pilots and other Mississippi lore, is recalled at Le Claire's Buffalo Bill Museum. Buffalo Bill in Iowa? It's true, for William F. Cody, once described by Massachusetts governor Curtis Guild as "from spur to sombrero one of the finest types of manhood this continent has ever produced," was born in 1846 not in the Wild West but in the mild Midwest in Scott County, near Le Claire. Exhibits trace the Cody family's Iowa roots and Buffalo Bill's later career as a Pony Express rider, Union Army soldier and Wild West show impresario and performer.

Just past Princeton, five miles north of Le Claire, county

road F 33 takes you five miles west to the Cody Homestead, built in 1847 by Buffalo Bill's father, Isaac. The house occupies a lovely, lonely spot on a slight rise with a view across the nearby fields. A certain sense of isolation prevails, and even today in this mechanized, computerized and televised age one can well imagine, out there at the Cody Homestead, the pioneer times of old when houses were few and far between and families dwelled alone in the endless spaces of the great American heartland. Young Bill lived in the house, listed on the National Register, until his family moved to Kansas when he was eight. Inside the residence, furnished with antiques of the period, hangs a tintype photo picturing "Little Billy Cody at the age of two."

Back on the River Road you'll pass through Clinton—birthplace of turn-of-the-century glamour girl Lillian Russell and site of a river museum in an old-time showboat where stage shows are presented in the summer—on the way to Bellevue, home of a butterfly garden, where some sixty species flutter, and of the nearby century-and-a-half-old Potter's Mill. Tucked between limestone cliffs near the Mississippi, the old mill, listed on the National Register, now houses a restaurant. Between Bellevue and Dubuque, twenty-four miles north, the River Road abandons the river but winds through some especially scenic rolling countryside.

Dubuque's paddle wheelers moored at the levee, cobblestone streets near the waterfront, and nineteenth-century brick warehouses lend the city the flavor of an old-time river town. Although the *New Yorker* avowed on February 21, 1925, that the magazine "is not edited for the old lady in Dubuque," the Iowa city is no provincial backwater, even if its old ladies are not all engrossed in the most recent issue of the east coast's last word in sophistication. Author Richard Bissell, Dubuque born and bred, recounted how big-time New York theater impresario Harold Prince, who produced

The Pajama Game, a Broadway musical based on the Iowan's novel *7½ Cents,* once visited the Midwestern river city: "Dubuque is pretty far from Sardi's and I don't think he had a very good time. Dubuque can be very strong medicine for an outsider especially from New York City." Bissell even "took Hal to the Dubuque Golf and Country Club and . . . introduced him to the bartender. This is one of the highest honors that can come to any visitor to Dubuque." Prince, however, for some reason remained unimpressed.

Admittedly, Dubuque is not the Big Apple or even Iowa's Big Corncob but you'll find there some worthwhile reminders of the city's long and colorful history. Julien Dubuque, a French Canadian who came to the area about 1785 to work the lead deposits, is considered Iowa's first permanent white settler. A limestone tower on the Mississippi River bluffs at the mouth of Catfish Creek south of town marks Dubuque's grave. Downtown, the Civil War-era Old Jail, listed on the National Register and said to be country's last example of Egyptian Revival-style architecture, houses an art gallery, the dungeon serving as a pottery studio and the prisoner's exercise yard as a sculpture court. Also dating from the Civil War time is the Old Shot Tower out by the colorful old Dubuque Star Brewery, open to visitors, where workmen produced pellets by dropping molten lead from the local mines through sieves that formed the metal into beads. In the same area stands the Riverboat Museum, installed in an old brick warehouse building, while back downtown the Silver Dollar Bar occupies another venerable structure, the turn-of-the-century German Bank Building, listed on the National Register. Also listed on the National Register is the unusual Fenelon Place Elevator, described as "the world's steepest, shortest scenic railway." To cope with the problem of getting from his bluff-top house to the town below, banker J.K. Graves in 1882 built a cable car to connect the two areas. Located in Cable Car Square, a revitalized nineteenth-century area of shops, boutiques and eating places, the funicular still operates. Steps away stands the Redstone Inn, an antique-crammed bed and breakfast establishment built in 1894 by A.A. Cooper, manufacturer of many of the "prairie schooner" wagons used for the westward trek. According to legend, when Henry Ford proposed building his horseless carriage in Dubuque, Cooper refused, predicting that the newfangled machine would never last.

For a truly unusual place to stay you might consider the New Melleray Abbey, a Trappist monastery a few miles southwest of town. Monks from Ireland founded the monastery in 1849 and now some forty Trappists, "totally dedicated to contemplation," states an abbey brochure, live and farm on the well-wooded thirty-four-hundred-acre grounds. In accordance with the Benedictine's long tradition of hospitality, the monks graciously receive overnight guests at no charge, although offerings are appreciated. Please do not expect at the cell-like but comfortable rooms Hilton, Hyatt or Holiday-type amenities. "New Melleray is a quiet place. No blare of radio or TV here," says the brochure. Even if you don't overnight there it's worth visiting New Melleray to see the 1870 abbey church, magnificent in its stark simplicity, an umembellished long and narrow sanctuary built of locally quarried limestone.

Buildings constructed of that attractive honey-colored Iowa limestone abound in Guttenberg, a river town forty miles north of Dubuque named (with an extra "t") after movable-type inventor Johannes Gutenberg. Among the nineteenth-century limestone structures in the downtown area listed on the National Register are the Diamond Jo warehouse, once operated as a branch hide-purchasing office by the family of Ulysses S. Grant, who lived in nearby Galena, Illinois (see Chapter III, section 7), and the Gutten-berg *Press* building where a reproduction of the Gutenberg

Bible is on display. The quiet town's mile-long riverside park affords a pleasant place to linger and watch the Mississippi roll by. The Mississippi also dominates McGregor, thirty miles north, site of the world's first pontoon bridge (1874). Main Street, lined with nineteenth-century store fronts, appears little changed from 1860 when August Ringling moved to the village and opened a harness shop. There, four of his sons, born in McGregor, held their first circuses, early versions of what became "The Greatest Show on Earth."

Out of McGregor the River Road north is sandwiched between high limestone bluffs, railway tracks and the Mississippi. It was nearby bluffs like these that the French explorers Marquette and Joliet referred to in the *Narrative* of their 1673 journey down the Wisconsin River and into the Mississippi at the site where McGregor now stands: "On the right is a large chain of very high mountains," not peaks but the rugged nearly six-hundred-foot-high bluffs. At Effigy Mounds National Monument, five miles north of McGregor, you can climb up onto the bluffs high above the river. The nearly fifteen-hundred-acre Monument area contains a hundred and ninety-one known two-thousand-year-old Indian mounds, twenty-nine of them in the form of bear and bird effigies.

After making your way up the steep path to the top of the bluff, Fire Point Trail will take you past Little Bear Mound and out to Fire Point, an observation terrace overlooking the Mississippi. There, perhaps, is an appropriate place to end your tour of Iowa. Behind you, scattered across the landscape, rise the ancient Indian mounds where early dwellers of the region have reposed for hundreds of years, while far below flows the eternal river, its surface now and again rippled by a breeze as the great waterway rolls its way south, past the history-filled land where men's dreams and dramas have played out over the centuries. The river that flows before you flows forever. Sometimes a bit of stray matter, borne along by the restless current, spins and bobs for a moment in the rush of water, and then is carried onward by the great river on its long journey through the heartland down to the distant sea.

V

Missouri

1. Missouri:

The United State of America

Missouri unites in one state the traits of many. It is the most eastern place in the west and the most western corner of the east, the southern edge of the north and the northern tier of the south. Missouri entered the Union paired with Maine as part of the "Missouri Compromise," and a compromise of a state it is. During the Civil War Missouri was a border state and it still is, bordering various regions of the nation from its position smack in the middle of the country: two states from Canada and the Gulf, five states from each coast. Southwestern Missouri lies equidistant from Maine and California, and the nation's population center is located in the state.

This central position has contributed to Missouri's diversity. As a publication of the state government described it in a paragraph headed "Missouri: Not middle America, but the middle of America":

MISSOURI

Mississippi

River

Hannibal

Marceline

Columbia

Fulton   St. Charles

St. Louis

Washington

Jefferson City

Osage Beach

Rolla

Ste. Genevieve

Ironton

Cape Girardeau

Springfield

Branson

Lexington

Kansas City

St. Joseph

Joplin

Missouri River

Few states can match the diversity of Missouri. Missouri is the state where the four major regions of the United States come together. The terms "back East," "out West," "up North," and "down South" have greater meaning if you're standing in Missouri than almost anywhere else. Each of the major regions either begins or ends here, depending on your point of view. The Corn Belt, with its commercial farms and small towns, dips down to the Missouri River, but the South, with its hills, timber, small farms and the recent Sun Belt growth of industry, retirement and population, comes as far north as the Missouri River. The West begins either at St. Louis or St. Joseph, depending on which period of history you choose.

The cultures of the disparate regions that meet in Missouri flavor the state, making it a kind of "united state of America." After his 1969 driving trip through the state, Mackinlay Kantor wrote in *Missouri Bittersweet* that Missouri "was neither east nor west, north nor south . . . Missouri was the true keystone of Central States . . . the Show-Me State—old Mizzou, a puzzling commonwealth which partook of the characteristics of all adjacent states and still resembled none of them in essence." And Irving Dilliard wrote in *I'm From Missouri!* that "Missouri is *all* America in one place. It is the [fifty] states of the Union joined together, superimposed on one another, fused into a composite of many outlooks and moods and experiences and ways of thinking and speaking and doing things."

The state's economy reflects its diversity. From the very early days two utterly different products, pelts and lead, attracted settlers. Fur trading began not long after the French explorers Marquette and Joliet floated down the Mississippi in 1673. The fur traders brought back from Missouri tales of the area's mineral deposits, and a survey by a French minerologist in 1700 led to development of the extensive lead mines in the eastern part of the state, starting about 1720. The two trades, lead and fur, developed in tandem. Moses Austin, father of "Father of Texas" Stephen Austin, established the Mississippi River town of Herculaneum in 1808 as a lead shipping point, while in 1809 entrepreneurs founded in St. Louis the Missouri Fur Company. Still today a portion of the state's economy is based on both organic and mineral products as if Missouri were an amalgam of agricultural Iowa and coal-rich West Virginia. Pasture, prairie, orchard, field and plantation grow a diversity of crops, including cotton and tobacco. The nearly three quarters of Missouri's forty-four million acres devoted to agriculture are cultivated such that the state ranks in the top three nationally in number of cows and feeder pigs, in hay and soybean production and in the number of farms—one hundred and fourteen thousand. The state boasts a similar number of nonfarm businesses, one hundred thousand, which produce everything from corncob pipes and barrels to cars and beer; as for mineral production, Missouri ranks among the top five states in lead, fire clay, lime, barite, zinc, cement and copper. The state's official musical instrument, as designated by the legislature in 1987, is the fiddle—an appropriate choice, for it has various strings.

This rather curious mixture of a rural, mining, industrial, all-points-of-the-compass culture and economy has made Missouri "a bewildering blend . . . [of] extraordinary variety," as Paul C. Nagel put it in *Missouri, A Bicentennial History*. Missourian Tom Sawyer teased his chum Huck Finn for supposing Illinois was actually green and Indiana pink, the colors those neighboring Midwestern states carried on maps; based on its diversity, the boys' own state might well have been shown as a swirl of hues. Huck and Tom lived on the Mississippi, which back in the mid-nineteenth century marked where the East ended and the West began. But Missouri served not only as a place of demarcation but also as a point of embarcation, for the Santa Fe and Oregon Trails originated in the state. Missouri thus acted as a link between the two parts of the country and from them experienced their turmoils. Even a Revolutionary War skirmish reached Missouri, a combined British and Indian attack on St. Louis in 1780; while the 1846 Mexican War, for which Missouri furnished more troops than any other state, agitated settlers in the western part of the state. The North-South split also greatly influenced Missouri: although admitted to the Union as a slave state, the majority of Missourians favored the north and more than one hundred thousand citizens served in the Union Army whereas a third as many joined the Confederates. This sort of split personality recalled the earlier days when the state couldn't make up its mind if it wanted to be German or French. The land of milk and honey, as it was portrayed to entice early settlers, alternated between becoming the land of beer or of wine. A saintly series of eighteenth-century settlements—Ste. Genevieve, St. Louis, St. Charles—reflected Missouri's French leanings, but mid-nineteenth-century German towns such as Holstein, Rhineland, Wittenberg and Altenburg suggested a Teutonic tone. In the end the state cultivated both beer—Anheuser-Busch calls St. Louis home—and wine, Missouri today boasting more than thirty wineries.

The geography of Missouri seems to contribute to its representative nature. The state—larger in size than any east of the Mississippi and its population third, after California and Texas, of the states west of the river—borders on eight other states (only Tennessee touches as many) and partakes of each of their environments. Add to Missouri's middleness a touch of Tennessee's, Kentucky's and Arkansas's south, the flavor of Illinois on the east, Iowa's and Nebraska's country culture, the Kansas plains and the west of Oklahoma and the resulting mixture creates if not a state of confusion as least a state of many characteristics. The large number of Missouri counties—more than any states except Texas, Georgia and Kentucky: a hundred and fourteen (plus the independent city of St. Louis)—perhaps symbolizes the state's pluralism. And the state's very shape, an oddly aligned semi-square, seems to be a keystone holding together the very core of the Union at the point where so many corners of the country converge. Remote from the coasts, from the ocean, from foreign lands, Missouri is the opposite of extremes; it is, rather, the quintessential center section of the country and a mixture of all sections.

Perhaps that balanced central position in the Union has contributed to the middle-of-the-road practical skepticism that gave to Missouri the nickname the "Show Me" state. The people of Missouri enjoy neither the sunny optimism of the Californian or Texan nor do they suffer from the flinty caution of the New Englander. Rather, the Missouri resident views the world with a certain healthy yet wary "show me" attitude. Back in the mid-nineteenth century the Bank of the State of Missouri, established in 1837, became famous for its policy of specie payment—redeeming paper money in gold, a practice possible because, unlike other financial institutions of the time, the bank retained its reserves in precious metal assets. This strain of practical conservatism has run through the state's history as forcefully as the Missouri River runs through its terrain. A late nineteenth-century promotional book published by the Missouri Pacific Railway Company left no language unturned to extoll the state's virtues, a "garden spot of the West," but the text admits that "she has perhaps been retarded in development by the too conservative spirit heretofore displayed by her citizens." Emblematic of this conservative bent and of the state's somewhat nondescript nature are the writings of Missourian Reinhold Niebuhr, the famous theologian, born in Wright City (near St. Louis) in 1892 and a student at St. Louis's Eden Theological Seminary. Perhaps growing up in Missouri influenced Niebuhr's beliefs. "Tamed cynic," part of the title of one of his autobiographical books, fairly well describes the "show me" mentality, while Niebuhr's view of man as an ambiguous sort of creature—"free and bound, both limited and limitless," as he wrote in *The Nature and Destiny of Man*—conforms to the theologian's home state: an ambiguous kind of place, Midwestern and American, both unique and every state.

2. Missouri's Missouri River Valley:

St. Charles, the First State Capital
The Daniel Boone House
The Hamlet of Femme Osage, the Village of Augusta
Winston Churchill at Fulton
Jefferson City, the State Capital
Old German Villages: Westphalia, Frankenstein and Hermann
Corncob Pipes at Washington

Just west of St. Louis, a few miles upstream from where the Missouri River joins the Mississippi, lies the historic old town of St. Charles. Scattered across hills that rise gently above the Missouri's north bank, St. Charles in the early nineteenth century served as the state's first capital and for a time as the last enclave of civilization for explorers, pioneers and travelers before they headed out to the vast West. Lewis and Clark (see Chapter III, section 9) paused in St. Charles from May 16 to May 21, 1804, to make final preparations for their expedition, and in 1806 Zebulon Pike started from the town—the first permanent European settlement on the Missouri River—on his exploration trip to the west country where, in Colorado, he discovered the peak which now bears his name. A lesser known early day traveler, Henry Marie Brackenridge, accompanied fur trader Manuel Lisa on a trip up the Missouri River. Brackenridge's journal of the journey

vividly evokes the sense of anxiety and doubt those early
adventurers felt as the last glimpses of civilization faded from
view. Published in 1814, a few weeks before the Lewis and
Clark journals appeared, his account was the first widely
available description of the region. Upriver, not long after
leaving St. Charles on April 2, 1811, Brackenridge noted:
"We have now passed the last settlement of whites, and
probably will not re-visit them for several months. This
reflection caused us all to think seriously of our situation. . . . I heaved a sigh when I reflected that I might never
see [home] or my friends again, that my bones might be
deposited on some dreary spot, far from my home, and the
haunts of civilized man."

St. Charles these days still retains the atmosphere of a
nineteenth-century Missouri River town, thanks to the well-
preserved nine-block area, listed on the National Historic
Register, just by the great waterway. It's well to start your
visit to the historic area at the visitors center, installed in a
restored 1892 M-K-T line depot where a "Wild West"-era
type of escapade occurred in the twentieth century when in
1921 five bandits kidnapped a U.S. Mail messenger carrying
registered packages with more than one hundred and twelve
thousand dollars in cash. The depot lies between the Missouri
River and South Main, the main street in the historic district.
Along the cobblestone streets, lined with old-fashioned gas
lamps, stands a stretch of nineteenth-century structures that
evoke St. Charles of a century and a half ago. The buildings
include 1815 Stone Row, a series of houses (one served as
Missouri's first state jail); the 1789 Blanchette-Chouteau
Grist Mill, the town's oldest building, which now houses a
restaurant; Eckert's Tavern (number 515, now a candy store),
where in 1827 the three men appointed by President John
Quincy Adams to survey the route for the Santa Fe Trail met
to write their report; the 1799 house (number 301, now a
print shop), where a mob attacked abolitionist newspaper

editor Elijah Lovejoy in October 1837 after he preached an anti-slavery sermon in St. Charles (Lovejoy had moved to nearby Alton, Illinois, where, in November 1837, a pro-slavery gang murdered him: see Chapter III, section 9); the "Mother-in-Law" house (number 500), a double residence built in 1860 so the mother of the owner's homesick wife could move into her own quarters there; and (at numbers 208–216) Missouri's first capitol building (open for tours), the state's seat of government from 1821 to 1836 when the capital moved to Jefferson City, a Missouri River town a hundred and seventeen miles upriver (west) of St. Charles. Period furnishings outfit the nine rooms in the Capitol complex where, in 1821, Governor Alexander McNair first heard the news that Missouri had been admitted to the Union. Although the governor back then wore civilized clothes, in keeping with the state's frontier character most members of the legislature dressed in more primitive garb—homespun shirts, buckskin leggings, moccasins and raccoon-skin hats.

At the far south end of South Main you'll find the 1860 Swiss chalet-style St. Charles Vintage House Restaurant and Wine Garden. It's a local tradition to linger there of a balmy summer night, sitting at the tables on the terrace overlooking the river while savoring Missouri wine and a plate of tangy cheese. The rise on which the wine garden perches recalls the town's first name, Les Petites Cotes—"the little hills"—which Louis Blanchette gave to the settlement when he founded it in 1769. In *Missourian Lays and Other Western Ditties,* the first book of original poems published west of the Mississippi (1821), Angus Umphraville referred to the town's "little hills": "Near where Missouri vast in its mighty tide/Pours by St. Charles, a young state's rising pride,/Two gently swelling hills, in nature's green/By every passing trav'ller may be seen." Such was the state of Missouri and the state of poesy on the early frontier—definitely nothing to cause such later Missouri poets as T. S. Eliot, Sara Teasdale, Eugene Field and

Marianne Moore to fear that their verse mightn't maintain the state's literary standards. Up on the hills, on North Second Street in the higher precincts of St. Charles, lies the antique shop area known as Frenchtown. The neighborhood took its name when the French moved to their own corner of town after German settlers began arriving in St. Charles in the 1830s. During that era Germans settled in many areas of the lower Missouri River valley, many of the immigrants drawn there by the idyllic description of the region proffered by Gottfried Duden, who lived in Missouri for three years before returning home to Germany, where in 1829 he published his *Report* on the Rhine-like valley he'd found in the New World. "There are two varieties of deer here in Missouri and they are for the most part very fat. The meat is savoury," reported Duden in a passage that typifies his rather Edenic view of the state. Game, land, crops, space—all was to be had by any German bold enough to venture across the Atlantic to the Rhineland of Missouri. German villages founded by those newcomers from the Old World a century and a half ago still dot the landscape along the north shore of the Missouri west of St. Charles—typical mid-America places bearing such old country names as Augusta, Dutzow, Holstein and, yes, even a settlement called Rhineland.

Highway 94, the road near the Missouri out to those old German villages, takes you on one of the Midwest's most attractive routes. In fact, this rustic road that winds, rises and dips its way along the upland just north of the river was once deservedly ranked among the country's fifteen most scenic drives. About ten miles west of St. Charles you'll pass along the edge of the August A. Busch Wildlife Area, a nature preserve often teeming with waterfowl, songbirds and other animal life. Shortly before you reach Defiance, little-traveled highway F will take you north five miles to one of the area's most famous and most attractive historic attractions, the Daniel Boone House. Seeking "more elbow room," as Boone put it, the renowned frontiersman left Kentucky in the fall of 1799 at the age of sixty-five leading fifty pioneer families up the Ohio River by dugout canoe and then by horseback and on foot into the Spanish-controlled Femme Osage district in Missouri. This then-remote area was, indeed, the "Boonedocks." Boone and his wife, Rebecca, moved into a log cabin on the six-hundred-eighty-acre farm of their son Nathan and his wife, Olive. Between 1803 and 1810 Boone and his son built the imposing limestone structure, which graces the property now listed on the National Register. On the grounds—a delightful wooded hillside site—stands the trunk of "the judgment tree," the remnant of a huge elm thought to have been more than three hundred years old when it succumbed to Dutch Elm disease in 1971. According to tradition, Boone held court under the tree as "syndic," or judge, for the Femme Osage District when the Spanish controlled the area. On display in the house is a photocopy of an 1804 trial report, in Boone's hand, regarding two men who "had some difference which came to blows and in the scuffle the said James Meek bit off a piece of Bery Vinzant's left ear." Boone's judgment is not recorded, but such was the type of case that came before him during those early frontier days. Boone apparently exuded a magisterial presence even when he wasn't sitting in judgment under the great tree. In *Views of Louisiana,* Henry Marie Brackenridge, mentioned above as one of the area's earliest travelers, described the back-woodsman in 1820, the year he died: "This respectable old man, in the eighty-fifth year of his age, resides on Salt river, up the Missouri. . . . He is surrounded by about forty families, who respect him as a father, and who live under a kind of patriarchal government, ruled by his advice and example." By then the great frontiersman's reputation had spread far and wide—even to the fashionable literary salons of Europe, for Lord Byron devoted seven stanzas in his poem *Don Juan* to the pioneer, telling of "The General Boon" who "Enjoy'd the lonely, vigorous, harmless days/Of his old age in wilds of deepest maze." Although Missouri these days is no maze, back in Boone's time the unmapped land could confuse even the most seasoned of travelers. Once asked if he'd ever been lost in the wilderness, Boone replied, "No, I can't say as ever I was lost, but I was bewildered once for three days." Byron continues: " 'Tis true he shrank from men even of his nation,/ When they built up unto his darling trees,—/He moved some hundred miles off, for a station/Where there were fewer houses and more ease."

Boone's own substantial four-story house, there in the Missouri countryside—those one-time "wilds of deepest maze"—contains period furnishings, many of them original items once owned by the family. It's believed that Boone himself crafted the home's five delicately carved walnut fireplaces. Over the stone fireplace in the dining room hang an old rifle and a powder horn, while on each side of the front door, gun-port openings to help defend against Indian raids recall the early frontier days. You can best get an idea of the house's two-and-a-half-foot-thick walls and its hand-hewn woodwork in the dining area on the ground floor. Perhaps Boone himself cut some of the nicks in the room's thick ceiling beams. The home's most evocative area is the small bedroom where Boone died on September 26, 1820. It was the end of an era. Missouri was by then civilized enough to be admitted to the Union, which took place less than a year later, and within a decade or so new settlers, many of them German, flooded into the Missouri River valley.

One of the valley villages the German immigrants established was Femme Osage, hidden away in the nearby hills. Tiny Femme Osage, in fact, is less a village than a hamlet. Too small to appear on Missouri's official highway map, Femme Osage lies a few miles beyond the Boone homestead and is reached by a remote back road (ask directions at the Boone house). Behind the one-time general store (now an antique shop) stands a lovely tree-shaded house: *the* house, for it's the only residence of any size there. Beyond the bridge over the little creek rises the century-old church, successor to the original 1834 sanctuary that housed the first Evangelical congregation west of the Mississippi. Behind the tidy white church climbs a steep hill lined with neat rows of gravestones marking the final resting places of members of the old German families. One could do worse on a warmish May day in the bud of spring or an autumn afternoon tinged with the chill of fall than to climb the hill and there pause among the graves to enjoy the view onto the snug little settlement that nestles in the valley below. There is something timeless about this scene: the seasons alter but not the graves, the hills, the creek, or the vista. All present a picture of permanence. A strange sort of dreamy other-world ambiance seems to pervade the place, as if a certain enchantment had frozen Femme Osage in place and in time, never to change. But the hours press, the day ages and the traveler must hurry on. Down in the town—the village, the hamlet—stands a one-room schoolhouse built in 1887 with stone from an 1841 church. Old desks and other antiques furnish the interior of the school, where classes were once taught in German. Of this structure Paul C. Nagel notes in *Missouri, A Bicentennial History,* "Long abandoned, this old building and the graves surrounding it impart something of the diversity of these Germans who brought their Evangelical faith and their determination to take up farming near Femme Osage, Dutzow, Marthasville, and New Melle."

Before proceeding to nearby Marthasville via highway 94 it's worth backtracking slightly on that road to visit Augusta, a few miles back to the east. Compared to Femme Osage, Augusta (population about three hundred) is a metropolis. Craft, antique and art shops occupy many of the old buildings in Augusta, founded in 1836 by Leonard Harold, one of the settlers who followed Daniel Boone from Kentucky to St.

Charles County. By the middle of the century German settlers, attracted by Gottfried Duden's glowing descriptions of the area, predominated in the town. An inscription over the door of the white brick United Church of Christ, "Evangelische Ebenezer Kirche 1861–1902," recalls that era, as do the old tombstones bearing German names and inscriptions in the cemetery out by highway 94. Among the markers is one for John Fuhr, director of the local "Harmonie Verein" (music club) with one string on the gravestone's harp emblem broken to symbolize the musician's demise. Back in the mid-nineteenth century the settlement was called Mount Pleasant, a name that survives today as the designation of a winery in town. In June 1980 the federal government named the fifteen-square-mile area around Augusta America's first "controlled appellation" wine district, a designation based on the French practice of labeling better wines as originating from specific regions. In the nineteenth century, when Missouri ranked as the nation's second largest wine-producing state, a dozen or so wineries thrived in the area. Today only a few survive, among them Mount Pleasant, which occupies a delightful old building on a high point not far from the Missouri River, and Montelle and Osage Ridge, both in the countryside near Augusta.

From Augusta, highway 94 takes you west for seven miles to Dutzow, another Missouri River valley German village, this one founded in 1832 by members of the Berlin Emigration Society. Before continuing a few miles west to Marthasville, cast a glance or two at Dutzow's old buildings sided with pressed tin and at the turn-of-the-century country store where until recently a sign "Der Landstadt Schrank" (The Village Cupboard) hung. Farther west on a knoll in a wooded area just east of Marthasville nestles a small cemetery where Daniel Boone reposes, or reposed. When Rebecca Boone died in 1813 the frontiersman buried his wife there and requested that on his demise his survivors inter him beside her.

In 1845, twenty-five years after Boone's death, a delegation visited the tiny cemetery to dig up the pioneer's remains and transfer them to Kentucky, where he lived between 1767 and 1799. It seems, however, that the Kentucky group excavated the wrong bones, for Boone was apparently buried at the head or foot of his wife's grave rather than beside her, the spot the Kentuckians dug. So it's likely the famous man's remains do remain there at the Missouri grave site, marked by a metal relief portraying fur cap-clad Boone as a vigorous young man.

Following the Missouri, highway 94 west from Marthasville will take you past Holstein, through Rhineland and on to Steedman where highway CC to the north leads to the Union Electric Company Callaway Nuclear Plant. A visitors center there explains the workings of the three-billion-dollar plant (open for tours) completed in December 1984 after nine years of construction. Ten miles northwest of the plant lies Fulton, an easygoing town of eleven thousand people, "a healthy and pleasant village" with no "ruinous temptations," as the 1854 catalog of Fulton's Westminster College described the place. The pleasant, tree-shaded Westminster campus boasts an unusual attraction—an entire Christopher Wren-designed church, transported to Fulton from London—and some evocative history, for it was at that remote Midwestern college, in the middle of the supposedly isolationist heartland of the U.S., where Winston Churchill delivered his famous "Iron Curtain" speech on March 5, 1946. At the bottom of the invitation letter sent by the head of the college to Churchill, Missourian Harry Truman, then president, added: "This is a wonderful school in my home state. Hope you can do it. I'll introduce you." And so it happened that there in the American heartland, far from the coasts and even farther from Europe, the British statesman warned the New World of dangers threatening the Old: "From Stettin in the Baltic to Trieste in the Adriatic, an iron curtain has descended across the Continent." Churchill spoke not in the Wren church, St. Mary Aldermanbury, but in the nearby nondescript beige brick college gymnasium. The church arrived in Fulton only later, twenty years after the speech, as a gift of the British government to commemorate Churchill's visit. After German bombs destroyed the building on December 29, 1940, the sanctuary lay in ruins. The church's remnants, weighing seven hundred tons, were sent to Westminster—not the one in London, but the college in far-off Missouri—and the building reconstructed, stone by stone, on the campus.

Built of soft white Portland limestone, St. Mary Aldermanbury, no doubt the only English building listed on America's National Register, fairly glows in the sun. It is perhaps curious that Shakespeare, so it's believed, worshiped in a church now in the American heartland, and that English poet John Milton married in the sanctuary. The building's oldest section is the belfry stairway, twenty-four rough stone steps that survive from the original twelfth-century church of St. Mary. When you tread those steps you'll be walking on nearly nine hundred years of English history. A few of the ancient steps bear dark patches, possibly scars left by the Great Fire that destroyed most of London in 1666. When King Charles II commissioned Wren to rebuild the city after the fire one of the fifty-one churches the architect designed was St. Mary Aldermanbury, completed in 1676. The church's interior enjoys a cheerful brightness, thanks to the eight tall clear windows that allow great showers of light to flow in. The twelve stately columns along the nave are non-supporting, for Wren added the pillars only for symmetry, not for strength. Over the vestry door appear limewood carvings by Grinling Gibbons, the famous seventeenth-century English woodworker, while overhead hang glistening brass chandeliers.

The church undercroft now houses a museum, with such items as the lectern Churchill used to deliver the "Iron Curtain" speech; a black leather dispatch case stamped with the impersonal but evocative words "Prime Minister"; and a personalized six-inch-long La Corona Habana cigar, its gold crown label bearing the name "Winston Churchill." One of the various Churchill letters on display—dated April 12, 1945, to his daughter Mary, on 10 Downing Street stationery—bears a handwritten note added at the bottom: "Since I dictated this the news has come of President Roosevelt's sudden death. You know how this hits me." By the museum nestles the wood-paneled Clementine Spencer-Churchill Reading Room, a cozy space, much as might be found in a stately home of England, with a collection of more than a thousand books by and about the English statesman and his era. It's a bit of transition to step out of the little enclave of old England and back into the streets of a present-day Midwestern American town. Before you leave Fulton you might want to visit the courthouse of Callaway County, an area which became known during the Civil War as the "Kingdom of Callaway" after it seceded, in spirit if not in law, from both Missouri and then the Confederacy. A rough stone on the courthouse lawn bears the name "D. Boone 1801," a relic of the frontiersman's days in old Missouri, while inside the building a large mural portrays the county's history. Disparate figures populate the picture—an Osage Indian, Boone, Confederate President Jefferson Davis (who addressed twelve thousand people in Fulton in September 1875), members of the Lewis and Clark expedition, bank robbers Frank and Jesse James—all figures of pure Americana. And there in the foreground, among all those legendary Yankees, stands the rotund John Bull image of none other than Winston Churchill.

By the Missouri River, twenty-five miles southwest of Fulton, perches Jefferson City, which became the seat of government when the state capital moved there from St. Charles in 1826. The capitol building, with its majestic dome, fully a hundred and thirty-four columns and boxy build, fits the classical image of U.S. statehouses. Inside you'll find exhibits on Missouri history as well as the delightful four-wall mural by Thomas Hart Benton entitled "A Social History of the State of Missouri." Missouri native Benton (see section 8) completed the work, which decorates the House lounge on the third floor in the capitol's west wing, in 1936. In the room hangs a whimsical letter the artist posted "To the Visitors" who came when he was painting the mural: "I would like to answer the questions and I am appreciative of all information but I cannot give time to the first and it is too late for the second to operate on this work," the notice said in part. One question posed to Benton at a meeting of upstanding citizens held in a Kansas City church was why he included a portrayal of such a scantily clad female dancer in a scene picturing a gathering of businessmen, to which the artist replied: "I've been to many businessmen's parties here and in St. Louis and I want to tell you I put considerable clothes on her." Alongside the Missouri below the capitol lies Jefferson Landing, a state historic site with three old buildings—a store, a hotel and a house—dating from the mid-nineteenth century when the town served as a river port, while nearby stands the rather spooky 1871 governor's mansion (tours by reservation). Two other state structures merit a glance. With its huge atrium the interior of the modernistic 1984 Harry S Truman Office Building (on High Street just west of the capitol) is rather striking, while at the east side of town near the river rise the forbidding stone walls of the State Penitentiary, which over the years has hosted such characters as former heavyweight boxing champion "Sonny" Liston, 1930s-era gangster "Pretty Boy" Floyd and James Earl Ray, convicted killer of Martin Luther King.

The Missouri River country east of Jefferson City south of the waterway contains more of those tiny towns founded by the German settlers who arrived in the area a century and a half ago. Westphalia, seven miles east of the capital, typifies those towns. The first German settlement in Osage County (1835), the village stretches along the crest of a hill overlooking gently rolling countryside and neatly cultivated fields dotted with white farmhouses. Red geraniums embellish window boxes on the brick, stone and wood houses that line the main—and virtually the only—street. Westphalia's most prominent structure is St. Joseph's Church, built in 1848. Below its sharply pointed silvery one-hundred-and-sixty-foot-high steeple are four clocks, seemingly redundant in a village where time seems to linger if not to stand still. Elaborate metal strapping designs decorate the building's front and side doors, while inside the church, listed on the National Register, twenty stained-glass windows from Germany brighten the sanctuary. From Westphalia, where the Westphalia Inn serves family-style fried chicken and country ham dinners, you can proceed along the back roads toward the Missouri through Frankenstein, no monster here but just another of those German hamlets, and on to Bonnots Mill, an attractive settlement with frame structures scattered across hills that form a tiny hollow. Two churches serve the village's one hundred and seventy-five residents, and Krautman's Korner—a cafe and tavern installed in a nineteenth-century building where a general store and saloon once operated—offers meals in an old-fashioned setting. Bonnots Mill's restored Dauphine Hotel, which has operated as a hostelry since 1875, still takes guests, although the establishment opens only for parties of eight or more.

Farther downriver lies Chamois, a longtime steamboat stop, founded in 1818 and named for the antelope found in the Alpine regions of the settlers' homeland. Water tower hill affords a view down onto the seemingly devout village— seven churches minister to its five hundred and forty-six residents—and across the Missouri to the huge volcano-like concrete chimney of Union Electric's Callaway County nuclear plant that emits great clouds of steam. After passing through Gasconade, fourteen miles east, you'll reach route J, a rather deserted back road that leads to the meandering Gasconade River. On a hill off to the right, about a mile before you reach the river, rises century-old St. John's church. Set in a small grove of trees and surrounded by a cemetery (many grave markers bear German inscriptions) this isolated church and its grounds comprise one of Missouri's most delightful spots. In 1978 the West German Broadcasting Company chose St. John's and its congregation for a film on Missouri's German heritage. Over the entrance of the church, whose tawny-colored stone contrasts with its green shutters, white wood trim and tin roof, an inscription recalls that heritage, "Deutsche Evan. St. Johannis Kirche 1884," as does a German inscription above the altar inside the small, cozy sanctuary, just large enough for a few pews and a mini-organ. After leaving the church, continue down route J to the tree-lined Gasconade where you ring a bell to summon *The Roy J* to carry you across the river on Missouri's only in-state (as opposed to interstate) car ferry. You can then connect with highway 100, which takes you to Hermann, a Missouri River town whose name recalls its German origins.

With more than a hundred buildings listed on the National Register and two National Historic Districts, Hermann offers a treasure trove of old architecture and ambiance. The town started up a century and a half ago when members of the German Settlement Society of Philadelphia, a group organized to locate and settle in an area on the then western fringes of the country, chose the Rhine River valley-like region. In the spring of 1838 two hundred and three people arrived at the site, and within a year the new town boasted ninety houses—all brick or frame, as the German settlers disdained less sturdy log structures—five stores, two hotels and a post office. Because so many of the early buildings survive, Hermann presents a more German appearance and it also adheres more closely to customs of the old country than perhaps any other town in the nation. As for the nearby countryside, no less an authority than the *Frankfurter Allgemeine Zeitung* observed in a 1981 article on Hermann that "the little place on the Missouri sits in a landscape that recalls the Rhine." The 1871 German School building, where classes continued until 1955 and whose design Philadelphia's Independence Hall inspired, now houses the tourist office as well as museums that trace the venerable town's history. Craft and antique shops, restaurants and fourteen or so bed and breakfast establishments now occupy many of the old buildings in Hermann, named after a Germanic hero who in A.D. 9 helped defeat a Roman army. Among the especially atmospheric corners of town are Hermann's two old wineries. At one time Missouri ranked as the nation's second largest wine state, producing fully one-third of the country's supply. Around the turn of the century Hermann bottled more wine than any other town in the U.S. Stone Hill Winery, which crowns the crest of a hill at the south end of town, was once the nation's second largest winery and the third largest in the world. Beneath the winery (founded in 1847) extends a vast network of underground cellars used during Prohibition for the cultivation of mushrooms. The winery, a National Historic District, operates the Vintage 1847 Restaurant, installed in an old carriage house and horse barn. Both Stone Hill and the colorful Hermannhof winery across town are open for tours and tastings.

About thirty miles east of Hermann on highway 100 lies Washington, corncob pipe capital of the world. Two factories in town produce the world's entire supply of commercially made cob pipes—some twelve to fourteen million of them a year. The industry began more than a century ago when someone asked Henry Tibbe, a Dutch woodworker who'd arrived in Washington from Holland in the late 1860s, to carve a cool, sweet-smoking pipe. Tibbe whittled a corncob to fashion a pipe, and by 1872 business so thrived that he founded the Missouri Meerschaum Company, which to this day produces cob pipes in a century-old red brick building on Front Street. Wooden file cabinets, a century-old walk-in safe, early cob pipe ads and framed original company documents, photos and awards lend the firm's office a nineteenth-century air. The creaky old factory with its 1870s-vintage brick walls and worn wooden floors is also a period piece. Until recently Buescher Industries, founded in 1939, churned out fifteen thousand or so cob pipes a day at its more modern factory across town at Walnut and Eighth. Buescher's supplied the product to two famous Douglases, MacArthur and Fairbanks, Jr., who favored cob pipes. Other Americans who smoked them include H. L. Mencken, Herbert Hoover, Fiorello La Guardia and Mark Twain, said to have remarked, "If you grow corn to get the cob, you're smart." The Buescher's operation has shrunk to a mere kernel of its formerly full-fledged production line, so the best place to see the manufacturing operation is at Missouri Meerschaum (by appointment only). The company favors hybrid corn with high wood content and large cobs, more than twice the diameter of regular ones, developed especially for the pipe industry. After aging for two years the cobs are sawed into pieces—a single cob yields up to four pipe bowls—and then the sections are hollowed, sanded, coated with plaster of paris, dried, resanded and shellacked. The stem hole is bored and finally a stem and plastic mouthpiece are affixed.

A smattering of old buildings scattered around Washington recall the town's early days. Across from Buescher's, which now occupies a small part of its original new building, stands the brewery and residence of John B. Busch, who started his beer company thirteen years before the more famous firm, Anheuser-Busch, co-founded by his younger brother, Adolphus, began in St. Louis in 1862. A row of nineteenth-century buildings on Front Street near the Missouri Meerschaum factory and facing the Missouri River—the old Hirschl and Bendheim cob pipe factory, a tavern, a one-time hotel, an inn, a former boarding house—combine to give the Washington waterfront the flavor of the Civil War era. Two old houses on Front—the 1846-vintage Zachariah Foss residence, listed on the National Register, and the Schwegmann residence—offer bed and breakfast accommodations; while farther west on Front a hilltop mansion houses Elijah Mclean's, a restaurant in an elegant setting overlooking the river. At the north end of Walnut stands the Franz Schwarzer house, listed on the National Register, where in 1864 the Austrian immigrant started his zither business. Later, in 1871, Schwarzer built a factory east of the house, and by the time the operation closed in the 1920s the firm had sold more than eleven thousand zithers, mandolins and guitars.

Washington today, snug by the wide ribbon of river there in the middle of the country, seems a typical American town, as its very name symbolizes. But its early businessmen— Dutchman Henry Tibbe of corncob pipe fame, brewer John Busch from Germany, zither master Franz Schwarzer of Austria—recall the settlement's European origins. From the arrival in 1833 of the first settlers from Germany, the town took on a distinctly German flavor. By the middle of the century *Turnvereins* (athletic societies) and a *Theaterverein* (dramatic society) had been formed and the German-language Washington *Post* (a resonant name for a newspaper, that) established, and as late as the 1930s some of the locals used German in everyday life. So even Washington—like Femme Osage, Augusta, Dutzow, Rhineland, Westphalia and Hermann—is a legacy of that great wave of mid-nineteenth-century German immigration that flooded into the lower Missouri River valley, there to establish those tidy towns and villages which seem Old World enclaves tucked away in the great American heartland.

3. Mark Twain Country:

To Hannibal via Clarksville, Bowling Green and Louisiana
Twain's Hannibal and Clemens's Florida
The Nineteenth-Century Utopian Settlement at Bethel

In the novel *Dandelion Wine* Ray Bradbury recalls the Midwestern settlement of Green Town (thought to be Waukegan, Illinois: see Chapter III, section 8): "There were a million small towns like this all over the world. Each as dark, as lonely, each as removed, as full of shuddering and wonder." Perhaps the archetypical such small town of the American Midwest is Hannibal, or at least the legendary Hannibal portrayed by native son Mark Twain. The famous writer once noted that his birth had been "postponed—postponed to Missouri. Missouri was an unknown new state and needed attractions." Hannibal has indeed made of the famous author a great attraction, for Twain-related sights abound in the town. The roads north from the St. Louis-St. Charles area, highway 79 and highway 61, follow the gradual and rather graceful curves of the Mississippi, Twain's beloved river. On the way to Hannibal you'll pass through a few of those self-contained Midwestern small towns, townlets removed and seemingly remote from the greater world beyond. The River Road, highway 79, runs north via Clarksville (named for William Clark of the Lewis and Clark expedition) where a chairlift to the top of the Mississippi's highest bluff south of St. Paul, Minnesota, presents you with a panorama over eight hundred square miles of the river valley. At Clarksville's rustic Apple Shed, concerts, theater performances and craft shows take place throughout the year. Ten miles upriver lies Louisiana, an attractive town filled with antebellum and Victorian-era houses, many of them on Georgia Street. At 1401 Georgia stands the spacious old mansion of one-time

(1937–1941) Missouri governor Lloyd Stark, a member of the family, now at least the sixth generation, which founded and owns Stark Brothers Nursery, believed to be the oldest nursery in America and the largest in the world. Founded in 1816 and located on the western edge of Louisiana, the nursery developed the renowned red "Delicious" apple (discovered in Iowa's Madison County: see Chapter IV, section 8) and has sold more than ten million Delicious trees. On the nursery grounds stands the original log cabin of James Stark, who in 1816 arrived in Missouri with cuttings from apple trees on his father's Kentucky farm. Grafting the scions to wild crab apple trees, young Stark started the first cultivated fruit west of the Mississippi. Stark Brothers doesn't sell fruit or produce but the firm does operate a garden center in the old Stark-Burbank building, half named for famous plant wizard Luther Burbank who worked with the company. Before leaving Louisiana you might want to take some time to browse in the town's dozen or so antique stores. A few miles west of Louisiana at Bowling Green, seat of Pike County, stands "Honey Shuck," a typical homey Midwestern small-town house where Champ Clark, Speaker of the U.S. House of Representatives and father of U.S. Senator Bennett Champ Clark, lived.

But those places are just preludes to the Midwest's most famous small town—Hannibal. "There ain't anything that is so interesting to look at as a place that a book has talked about," Huck Finn commented in one of Mark Twain's lesser-known books, *Tom Sawyer Abroad*. So artfully did Twain capture Hannibal on the printed page that the Mississippi River settlement has come to represent the quintessential American small town, a place peopled by freckle-faced boys, pigtailed girls, old Aunt Sallys and other colorful local characters, residents of a friendly laid-back town nestled on tree-shaded streets lined with white frame houses. Some of that old-time down-home small town ambiance still shows through in Hannibal if you can somehow look beyond the commercialism and the somewhat overdone exploitation of the Twain connection—Tom & Huck's Go-Carts, the Huck Finn Shopping Center, the Mark Twain Dinette, the Hotel Clemens and many, too many, others—which threatens to smother the town's underlying appeal. A good place to start your visit is atop Cardiff Hill, where the view you'll enjoy is much like what young Sam Clemens saw a century and a half ago when he was a boy in Hannibal—a "white town drowsing in the sunshine," with "the great Mississippi, the majestic, the magnificent Mississippi, rolling its mile-wide tide along, shining in the sun" as it slides by the city and braids its way between a cluster of islands downstream, one of them Jackson's Island where long ago Tom Sawyer, Huck Finn and their chums enjoyed many adventures. From Cardiff Hill—a "boy-paradise," Twain called it—Hannibal stretches before you, neat and snug in the mile-and-a-half-wide fan-shaped valley where the town rises gradually from the river up to residential areas in the low hills and knolls a mile or two off to the west. Near the cobblestone levee just by the river, run downtown's grid-like streets, Main Street stretching toward Lover's Leap, the high bluff that overlooks the river to the south. At the bottom of the long flight of steps on Cardiff Hill stand statues of Tom and Huck, while two blocks away lies Hill Street, the heart of Twainland, lined with restored mid-nineteenth-century houses from the era of Sam Clemens's boyhood in Hannibal. In 1839 when Sam was four, John M. and Jane Clemens moved there from Florida, Missouri, a hamlet twenty-seven miles southwest of Hannibal.

On Hill Street stands the Clemens home, a two-story white clapboard house built in 1844. By the residence runs a wooden fence similar to the one Tom Sawyer tricked his pals into whitewashing: "Does a boy get to whitewash a fence every day?" Tom teasingly temped his friends. Today's youngsters need less coaxing, for during Hannibal's annual

Tom Sawyer Days, held over Fourth of July weekend, children from around the country avidly—and messily—compete in the national fence-painting contest. Inside the Clemens house the small low-ceilinged rooms are furnished as in the days when young Sam lived there. The kitchen, dining room and parlor occupy the first floor, while upstairs nestle two cramped bedrooms. Sam occupied the back room, from which he used to sneak out the window to join Tom Blankenship, the model for Huck Finn, for their devilish nighttime escapades. Adjoining the house is the Mark Twain Museum, with Twain memorabilia and items from the Hannibal of a century and more ago. You'll find there such evocative displays as the cherry wood table on which Twain wrote part of *Tom Sawyer,* the first known photo of Clemens, taken when he was about fifteen and working as a printer's devil, and a copy of the certificate issued April 9, 1859, to one Samuel Clemens licensing him as a pilot of steamboats on the Mississippi River. For ten cents you can set into motion and sound the mahogany-encased orchestrelle, a large mechanical music box. On Christmas night 1909 Twain's biographer, Albert Bigelow Paine, played three rolls of music on the orchestrelle while Twain peered through falling snow from a window at Stormfield, his Redding, Connecticut, house, to watch the body of his just-deceased daughter Jean being carried away for burial in Elmira, New York. Twain, who died April 21, 1910, also reposes in Elmira.

Across Hill Street from the museum stands the law office where John Clemens presided as justice of the peace in the 1840s. A cast-iron stove, a large jug with a corncob stopper, a quill pen, Franklin spectacles and a corncob pipe resting on a crate that serves as a desk recall those early days of frontier justice. It was there where young Sam, playing hooky from school one day in 1843, stumbled onto the corpse of a man who had been stabbed in the chest, a sight that propelled the boy out the window. Financial reverses forced the Clemens family to leave their house, so in late 1846 they moved to the second floor, over Dr. Orville Grant's drugstore, in the Greek revival-style house that stands at the corner of Hill and Main. The living area upstairs—where Judge Clemens died March 24, 1847—contains old furnishings, while on the ground floor remains Dr. Grant's mid-nineteenth-century medical office, with its "fearsome" physician's instruments, and the old-time apothecary whose shelves hold jars of medicinal herbs. Along North Main stretch a group of antique, craft and curio shops installed in a row of old buildings that housed during Sam's childhood such old-time Hannibal establishments as the Baltimore Cheap Cash store and the Leer and Arrowgast tobacco shop. That shop is long gone, but over at 308 Broadway still survives Schaffer's Smoke House, a venerable tobacco emporium all but unknown to most visitors, which is one of the town's most evocative places, for it is here where past and present meet in Hannibal. Virtually unchanged from the time of its founding more than a century ago—tin-pressed walls and ceiling, a penny match machine and an 1899 photo of a local band lend antique touches—the store today serves as a lively gathering place for residents who, in a smoke-filled room in the rear, trade small talk and tall tales as they play pinochle at round tables where, so tradition holds, Samuel Clemens used to play cards.

On the south side of town is the Mark Twain Cave (open for tours), which is featured in a number of passages in the author's works, while out to the west stands the 1871 Victorian-style Garth Woodside Mansion, listed on the National Register. The Mansion takes overnight guests, as do the 1895 Victorian Guest House and The Bordello, a bed and breakfast establishment ("a reputation built on satisfaction" is its motto) installed in a 1917 building where once a house of ill repute functioned. Steps from The Bordello is the Molly Brown Dinner Theater, named for Hannibal native Margaret Tobin Brown, who became known after her heroic acts during the sinking of the *Titanic* as the "Unsinkable Molly Brown." But it is for unforgettable Mark rather than unsinkable Molly that Hannibal is known. Twain and his enduring characters haunt every nook and cranny and corner of the old river town. The author made his last visit to his beloved hometown in 1902 when he addressed three hundred guests assembled in the main entrance hall of Rockcliffe Mansion, an imposing residence listed on the National Register and open for tours, built at the turn of the century by lumber magnate John J. Cruikshank. That final visit of Twain to Hannibal was an exercise in nostalgia for him as, in fact, was much of his writing career. "I was profoundly moved and saddened to think that this was the last time, perhaps, that I would ever behold those kind old faces and dear old scenes of childhood," he said at the time. Elsewhere, Twain recalled his nostalgic visit to Hannibal—"a heartbreaking delight, full of pathos, laughter, and tears, all mixed together." He mused on "the boys and girls that we picnicked and sweethearted with so many years ago, and there were hardly half a dozen of them left; the rest were in their graves." Up to Cardiff Hill (called Holliday's Hill in Twain's time) he went "and looked out again over that magnificent panorama of the Mississippi River, sweeping along league after league, a level green paradise on one side, and retreating capes and promontories as far as you could see on the other, fading away in the soft, rich lights of the remote distance."

In Riverview Park just north of Cardiff Hill stands a statue of Twain, now forever gazing out onto his favorite view—the Mississippi, rolling its mile-wide tide along below the bluffs where the park perches. It is pleasant to finish a visit to Hannibal out there in Riverview Park, perhaps in early evening after a day in Twain's town, as dusk drifts across the scene. The vanished day, the monument, the setting serve to recall the words of the old song Twain remembered in *Villagers 1840–3,* a time-haunted reminiscence of his vanished youth in Hannibal: "The day goes by like a shadow on the wall, with sorrow where all was delight." It is that sort of bittersweet sense of the slow flow of time, of time passing and passed, that a visit to Mark Twain's Hannibal leaves with you as you linger there in the twilight stillness on the bluffs high above the great rolling river.

Twain—or, rather, Sam Clemens—began his life in Florida, a hamlet (back then) of a hundred people southwest of Hannibal. "I increased the population by 1 percent . . . more than many of the best men in history could have done for a town," the author later wrote. Were Clemens to be born today, he'd swell the settlement's population by two percent, as only fifty people live there—truly "almost invisible," as Twain put it. At the hamlet a plaque proclaims: "In this village was born November Thirteenth 1835 Samuel Langhorne Clemens—Mark Twain. He cheered and comforted a tired world." Twain arrived in a rather rude two-room rented cabin now exhibited in the Mark Twain Birthplace Museum just up the road. Later in life Twain referred to the humble slightly sway-backed shack: "Recently someone in Missouri has sent me a picture of the house I was born in. Heretofore I have always stated that it was a palace, but I shall be more guarded now." Other exhibits at the museum include family photos, foreign-language editions (among them Burmese, Russian, Chinese and Japanese) of the author's works and a self-portrait "done with the best ink," Twain noted on the picture. Not far from the museum lies the small cemetery where some of Twain's relatives repose: his sister, Margaret Clemens; Benjamin Lampton, his grandfather; and John and Martha Quarles, his uncle and aunt, who owned a nearby farm, "a heavenly place for a boy," Twain recalled, which young Sam often visited and where he met country characters and absorbed impressions he later included in his books.

A few other attractions enhance the Mark Twain region. If you've driven west from Hannibal to visit Florida you might

want to continue on to Paris, near where you'll find the
Union Covered Bridge, one of four such spans remaining in
Missouri. (To reach the bridge, drive three miles south of
highway 24 on route C, then one-fourth mile west on the
unmarked asphalt road.) Built in 1871, the one-hundred-and-
twenty-five-foot-long oak timber bridge lasted for a century
before it was closed to vehicular traffic. According to local
lore the barnlike appearance of the covered bridge helped
coax timid farm animals across the rushing waters of the Elk
Fork. In the office of the Monroe County *Appeal* at Paris
hangs a reproduction of "The Country Editor" by Norman
Rockwell, who visited the newspaper and used its office and
staff as models for his painting. If you're heading north out of
Hannibal you'll reach nearby Palmyra, a sleepy old town not
far from the Mississippi River. Palmyra's restored early nineteenth-century Gardner House, listed on the National Register, once served as an inn on the stagecoach line between St.
Louis and eastern Iowa, while on the Marion County courthouse lawn stands a monument to the execution of ten Confederate hostages in 1862, the so-called Palmyra Massacre.
Other historic buildings that embellish the town include the
1857 Hanley Opera House and the 1858 jail, still used, which
held the ill-fated ten Confederate soldiers, while out in
Greenwood Cemetery reposes Pony Express founder
William H. Russell. A marker at his grave bears the "Pony
Rider's Oath" and a map of the Express route. A mural on
the post office wall in Palmyra recalls Marion City, a gran-
diose scheme promoted in the 1830s to build a "golden city"
destined to be a future metropolis of the Midwest. But the
Mississippi washed away the site of the city, located five miles
east of Palmyra near highway 168, thought by some to be the
highly touted but in fact desolate "Eden" in Charles Dickens's
novel *Martin Chuzzlewit.* "There were not above a score of
cabins in the whole; half of these appeared untenanted; all
were rotten and decayed," Martin discovered when he visited

the development. The book's un-edenic Eden might also have been based on a similar promotion, in which Dickens, to his regret, invested at Cairo, Illinois (see Chapter III, section 3). Farther north along the river lies the tiny town of LaGrange, with a dilapidated two-story frame house where Woodrow Wilson's vice-president Thomas Riley Marshall once lived. Marshall, who later moved to Indiana (see Chapter II, section 1), was the man who advised the nation: "What this country needs is a really good five-cent cigar." Canton, a few miles north, is the home of 1853 Culver-Stockton College, listed on the National Register, and of the Golden Eagle Showboat, a dinner theater where musical performances are presented from late May to early September. In Missouri's far north, at the town of Kahoka, the huge Gregory's antique emporium, with six buildings, bulges with old furniture, artifacts and other orphaned objects from the Midwest of yesteryear.

Inland, west of Palmyra, lies the hamlet of Bethel, one of those mid-nineteenth-century Midwestern utopian settlements that sprung up across the region. Like the mythical musical village of Brigadoon, those communal colonies lie wrapped in the mists of time and hidden in secluded corners of the countryside. Surviving examples of century-old Midwestern communal societies include New Harmony, Indiana (Chapter II, section 3), Bishop Hill, Illinois (Chapter III, section 6), the Amana Colony in Iowa (Chapter IV, section 4), and, in Missouri, the Bethel German Colony, listed on the National Register. As at the other utopian settlements, the air at Bethel somehow seems perfumed with idealism and the town presents a picture out of the past, for the village appears little changed from the time nearly a century and a half ago when William Keil, a religious leader born in Germany, attracted some six hundred and fifty colonists to Bethel. Today, thirty or so structures from the colony period still stand, among them the Bain residence, the settlement's oldest house (1845), with such ingenious features as plaster walls with horse and cow hair added as binding agents and a chimney bent so smoke would linger longer to better heat the home. The nearby Miller house, another early residence, boasts what are said to be the earliest built-in cabinets west of the Mississippi.

When writer Charles Nordhoff—best known as co-author of *Mutiny On the Bounty*—visited Bethel in 1870 he found a bustling community with "a saw-mill and grist-mill, a tannery, a few looms, a general store, and a drug-store, and shops for carpenters, blacksmiths, coopers, tinners, tailors, shoemakers and hatters." Nordhoff further noted: "The young people have a band of music, but no other amusement that I could hear of. Tobacco they used freely, and strong drink is allowed; but they have no drunkards." These days the village of one hundred and thirty-two residents is less lively. Only a few shops line sleepy Main Street and traffic is sparse. But the band survives: At one corner stands a Victorian-era bandstand where the fifteen-piece Bethel German Band, said to be one of America's last such community ensembles, holds forth on Tuesday or Wednesday evenings over the summer and during Bethel's various festivals. Those celebrations include spring antique and craft shows, fiddling contests in the summer, a Labor Day weekend sheep fest, and a Harvest Fest the first weekend in October. Next to the bandstand stands the old Fest Hall, which offers meals and accommodations in basic but rather delightful rooms with quilt-covered beds, wood floors and rustic touches. In one room a cornhusk doll on a string serves as a fan-pull.

A mile or so east of town rises Elim, William Keil's imposing mansion, which dominates the countryside from its hilltop spot. But even this showplace failed to keep the leader at Bethel, for Keil, fearing the colony had become too subject to outside influences, headed west in 1855 over the Oregon Trail with some two hundred followers to establish a new communal settlement. Shortly before the wagon train departed Keil's son Willie died of malaria. Unwilling to leave the boy behind, Keil stored the body in a lead-lined box filled with Bethel-distilled Golden Rule whiskey, and he carried the coffin on the six-month, two-thousand-mile trek west. After riding in what was no doubt the longest funeral cortege in history, Willie was buried at Willapa, Washington. Keil never returned to Bethel and the communal settlement finally disbanded in 1877. Still today, more than a century later, Bethel survives, a living remnant of those olden days and simpler times when people banded together to experiment in communal living in small colonies in the vast spaces of the American heartland.

4. From Mickey Mouse to Pony Express:

Walt Disney of Marceline, John J. Pershing of Laclede
J.C. Penney of Hamilton
The Amish at Jamesport
St. Joseph and the Pony Express

Once upon a barn in the remote northern Missouri town of Marceline a farm boy scrawled in tar animal pictures. The family sold the forty-eight-acre farm in 1909 and moved to Kansas City, where the boy delivered newspapers, worked at odd jobs, took baby portraits, sketched newspaper ad layouts and produced seven animated fairy-tale movies under the label Laugh-O-Gram Films. None of this led to fame or fortune, so in 1923 at age twenty-one the young man set off for California with forty dollars in his pocket along with memories of Missouri and dozens of ideas in his head. Now fast forward—forward across the blur of years to 1956 when the Missouri native returned to his boyhood home in Marceline for the first time in nearly half a century. "More things of importance happened to me in Marceline than happened since or are likely to happen in the future," the local boy fifty years removed said. "Things like experiencing my first country life, seeing my first circus parade, attending my first school, seeing my first motion picture." Thus did Walt Disney recall his early years in the small Missouri farm town.

Marceline lies just south of highway 36, which stretches across northern Missouri from Hannibal to St. Joseph, home of the Pony Express. The road more or less follows the route taken by the old Hannibal and St. Joseph postal train that hauled mail the two hundred and six miles between those far eastern and far western Missouri cities for delivery to Pony Express riders who carried the letters onward to the west. On the initial train trip, April 3, 1860, ran the first mail car used in the U.S. There must be something in the air or in the soil in that highway 36 country that nourishes over-achievers, for in addition to Walt Disney, other notables grew up in villages along that route: John J. Pershing, general of the armies; and store magnate J. C. Penney.

In Marceline you'll find a few places that evidence Disney's connection with the town. When the Walt Disney grade school opened in 1960 the cartoon king sent a few of his artists to Marceline to decorate the school's interior with portraits of Disney characters, while a glass case just inside the door holds a small desk on which young Walt carved his initials, twice. During his 1956 visit Disney recalled that "when I was a kid here in Marceline, we swam in a cow pasture pond after we chased the cows out," a way of life that led him to present to the town a more elegant place to swim, the Walt Disney Pool. He also gave his hometown a park with a jungle gym designed to resemble the boat Mickey Mouse piloted in the 1929 "Steamboat Willie" cartoon. But perhaps there is more of Marceline in Disney than of Disney in Marceline, for his interest in animal characters might well have stemmed from his farm years, and he supposedly modeled Disneyland's Main Street USA on Marceline's Main Street as it looked in the early twentieth century when young Walt grew up there. Like fellow Missourian Mark Twain, Walt Disney tried to capture in his life's work his lost past in a small town in the American Midwest. It is perhaps passing strange that two small-town boys from the same neck of the woods, northeastern Missouri, grew up to give people everywhere such universally beloved visions of a certain sort of old-fashioned world, a world long gone, but thanks to Twain and Disney, still remembered.

Thirteen miles west on highway 36 you'll reach Laclede, home of another famous native son, John J. Pershing, born September 13, 1860, half a mile west of town in a small section house (no longer standing) of the old Hannibal and St. Joseph Railroad, his father's employer. The future general of the armies first encountered war when a band of Confederate irregulars attacked Laclede on June 18, 1864. In 1866 the family moved to a two-story nine-room white frame residence, listed on the National Register, which now houses period furnishings and exhibits relating to Pershing's career in the Indian wars, in the Philippines, and as commander-in-chief of the World War I American Expeditionary Forces. On the grounds of the house, which Pershing left in 1882 to enter West Point, stands a one-and-a-half-times-life-size statue of the general. About two miles west of Laclede on an unmarked gravel road parallel to and one mile north of highway 36 survives another of Missouri's four remaining covered bridges, the 1868 Locust Covered Bridge, a one-hundred-and-fifty-foot span, listed on the National Register, across the old channel of Locust Creek, which flows south to what is now Pershing State Park. In bygone days young John and his boyhood chums used to frolic in the old swimming hole there.

A few miles south of Laclede lies Sumner, self-proclaimed "Wild Goose Capital of the World," so called for the esti-

mated two hundred thousand Canadian geese who winter at
the Swan Lake National Wildlife Refuge there. Sumner
boasts a mascot named Maxie, a five-thousand-pound fi-
berglass goose that perches in a park at the edge of town near
Main Street. Sumner was the birthplace of former U.S. Senator from Arkansas J. William Fulbright, commemorated in
the town museum where displays recall the politician's career.
Farther west on highway 36 you'll pass through Chillicothe
where in the early 1870s the brothers Earl and Foreman Sloan
concocted a potion to relieve sprains and bruises in horses, a
nostrum they later marketed to humans as Sloan's Liniment,
which became world famous.

On a three-hundred-and-ninety-acre farm near Hamilton,
farther along on 36, a household word was born when J. C.
Penney arrived on September 16, 1875. Like the Pershings in
Laclede, the Penney family moved from farm to town, settling in Hamilton in an attractive white frame house that still
stands at 201 East Bird Street. At the James Cash Penney
Memorial Museum a block west, exhibits recall Penney's
early life in Hamilton and his career as founder and head of
the nationwide retail chain that bears his name. Penney's
career began in Hamilton in 1894 at the J. M. Hale Dry
Goods Store on Davis Street. The nineteen-year-old budding
businessman worked there as a clerk for less than ten cents a
day. After Hale retired in 1924 Penney, by then head of a four-
hundred-and-ninety-nine-store chain, bought the establishment, making it store number five hundred. Until 1981 the
historic store, located on the very site where the famous
merchant learned his trade, remained open for business, but
the J. C. Penney Company closed the outlet in June of that
year. Perhaps recalling the inbred skepticism of the residents
of his native Missouri, the "Show Me State," Penney once
assigned a company trainee to the store in Moberly (southeast of Marceline) with the observation: "If you can sell
merchandise to a Missourian, you can sell anyone." The

neophyte, Albert Hughes, must have satisfied the "Show Me" mentality, for he later served as J. C. Penney president and board chairman.

In an obscure corner of Missouri called Far West, located southwest of Hamilton, a marker designates the site of the temple Mormons hoped to build in 1837 when they moved there after having been driven out of Jackson County (the Kansas City area: see section 5). Mormon leaders Joseph Smith and Brigham Young laid out a spacious city at Far West, seat of Caldwell County, which the Missouri legislature established in December 1836 as a refuge for the persecuted sect. The Mormons also settled at a place they called Adam-Ondi-Ahman near Gallatin, north of Hamilton (an unusual rotary jail at Gallatin was the site of the last public hanging in Missouri) but Missourians continued to harass the Latter Day Saints, so in the winter of 1838–39 they left for Nauvoo, Illinois (see Chapter III, section 9), establishing there a new settlement. Another religious group, the Amish, enjoyed better luck in northwestern Missouri, for some hundred and fifty Amish families live near Jamesport, eleven miles east of Gallatin. Attracted by cheap land prices, the Amish settled in the Jamesport area in 1963. A total of about thirty-five hundred Amish live in Missouri, scattered about the state in a dozen or so rural settlements, one near Bowling Green (section 3) in eastern Missouri south of Hannibal. The Amish do without such newfangled conveniences as cars, telephones, electricity and engine-powered farm machinery, so as you drive around the Jamesport area you'll see them cultivating their fields with horse-drawn equipment and traveling to town in buggies. In town are nearly thirty antique and craft shops (closed Thursdays as well as Sundays if Amish-owned) and the log cabin Jesse Harris, the area's first European settler, built in 1836. Those old-fashioned buggies parked around Jamesport and the "plain" people, as the Amish are called (they call outsiders "English") with wide-

brimmed hats, dark clothes and thick beards worn by the
men and long dresses and bonnets favored by the ladies lend
the town a photogenic touch, but the Amish prefer that no
pictures be taken of them. At the Cedarwood Restaurant you
can sample an Amish meal, including kettle roast (roast beef),
gingersnap gravy and shoofly pie, and also arrange for tours
of the Amish country.

To proceed from Jamestown directly on to St. Joseph, the
Pony Express town on the western edge of Missouri, it's well
to return south to highway 36. But if you have time, the
roundabout way to St. Joseph will take you to some sights
scattered through the northwestern corner of the state. At
Princeton, north of Jamestown, Martha Canary was born in
1850. She's better known as "Calamity Jane," a nickname
given her when she rode as a U.S. Army scout, clad in the
buckskins, chaps and spurs of her male colleagues, during the
1872 Sioux Indian conflict in the Black Hills. One admirer
noted that "Her profanity . . . was so rich in metaphor, and
so varied, that it was a source of delight to discriminating
audiences." Off to the west near Bethany (highway W north
to highway F, then four miles west on F) lies the Fitzgerald
Buffalo Ranch, a one-hundred-and-sixty-acre spread where
buffalo are bred and raised. At Grant City, to the northwest,
young Glenn Miller learned to play the horn and joined the
local town band, the first step on a career which made him
one of America's most famous orchestra leaders. Farther west
are two small religious communities. In Clyde (population:
sixty-one) stands the 1881 Benedictine Convent of Perpetual
Adoration, established in 1875 by three nuns from Switzerland. The Romanesque-style stone chapel, built in 1909, contains richly colored mosaics and stained-glass windows. At
Conception, a mile away, rises mural-rich Conception Abbey, also a Benedictine community of Swiss origin. The
Benedictines began the red brick church in 1882, nine years
after they arrived in the area, and the monks completed the

solid-looking Romanesque-style structure in 1888. A few years later they added the abbey's twin towers, one designed to conceal a water tank. Still farther west lies Maryville, where motivational speaker and writer Dale Carnegie was born on November 24, 1888. Carnegie grew up on a Nodaway County farm near Pumpkin Center, about seventeen miles from Maryville, where he rose at three every morning to study by oil lamp and to feed his father's pedigreed hogs. In 1911 Carnegie left Missouri and moved to New York to "win friends and influence people."

Tucked away in the far northwestern corner of the state is Tarkio (Indian for "walnut"), home of Tarkio College, which got its start in 1883 when local citizens founded the school to make use of an empty courthouse building they'd constructed in the thwarted hope of attracting the county seat. Tarkio boasts the Mule Barn Theater, an unusual octagonal brick structure built in 1892 by David Rankin, whose thirty-thousand-or-so-acre Atchison County spread was considered the largest corn farm in the world around the turn of the century. The mule barn originally sported four stories—the first used to house some two hundred and fifty mules, the second providing living quarters for hired hands—but a fire destroyed the upper area so the structure, listed on the National Register, now includes only three floors. In 1965, long after it had fallen into disrepair, Tarkio College bought the building and converted it into a theater, which in 1968 began to present musical shows. So if perchance you ever hankered to see a Broadway musical in a mule barn, Tarkio is definitely the place to go. On the way south to St. Joseph you'll pass near Squaw Creek National Wildlife Refuge, where hundreds of thousands of ducks, geese, pelicans, heron, sandpipers and bald eagles pause each spring and fall during their twice-a-year migrations. From a high point on the Loess Bluff Trail, hikers can enjoy a panorama over the Missouri River floodplain and much of the Refuge.

The Missouri marks the end of the Midwest. Beyond the river begins the West. In the nineteenth century the city of St. Joseph, downriver from the Squaw Creek Refuge, served as a link between the two parts of the country. It was in 1860 that the following ad appeared in newspapers in the mid- and far-west: "WANTED: Young skinny wiry fellows, not over eighteen. Must be expert riders willing to risk death daily. Orphans preferred. Wages $25 per week. Apply Central Overland Express." The thirty or so young men hired took an oath: "I do hereby swear, before the great and living God, that during my employment as a Pony Express rider, I will under no circumstances use profane language, drink intoxicating liquors, abuse my mount, quarrel or fight with any other riders and that in every respect I will conduct myself honestly, be faithful to my duties and so direct my acts as to win the confidence of everyone." On April 3, 1860, the Hannibal and St. Joseph mail train arrived in St. Joseph, the letter pouch was passed to the waiting rider, J. W. Richardson, and then off he galloped on the first leg of the two-thousand-mile trip to Sacramento, California. So began the Pony Express.

Landmarks recalling the legendary Pony Express and other aspects of the settlement's early days abound in "St. Jo," as the town is affectionately called, which still today retains a certain frontier feel to it. The Pony Express Museum, installed in the original stables building, contains exhibits that trace the history of the famous mail service. Opposite the stable stands a stone marker designating the place where the Pony Express began. Buffalo Bill, one of the Express riders, attended the monument's dedication ceremony on April 3, 1913. A few blocks up the street you'll find Patee House Museum, which occupies the old one-hundred-and-fifty-room hotel opened in 1858 by John Patee. When Patee ran short of cash in 1865 he held a lottery to dispose of the property. In order to get the entire issue sold, he bought in the last hundred tickets and when the drawing took place

Patee won his own hotel back. Russell, Majors and Waddell, the firm that founded the Pony Express, established the operation's headquarters in the hotel, which today contains the restored Express office, an 1860 wood-burning steam locomotive used on the Hannibal and St. Joseph line and other exhibits which recall nineteenth-century St. Jo. St. Joseph is the town where, on an April 3 (in 1860) the Pony Express began and Jesse James ended (1882). Next door to Patee House stands the residence where the famous outlaw was shot dead by Bob Ford, a member of his gang, while James was living there with his wife and two children under the assumed name of Tom Howard. Using a .44 caliber Smith and Wesson his victim had given him a few days before, Ford killed his colleague in crime to collect a ten-thousand-dollar reward. "Oh, the dirty little coward/That shot Mr. Howard,/And laid poor Jesse in his grave," goes the famous ballad that recalls the episode. The hole from the fatal bullet that passed through Jesse's head can still be seen in the wall.

Historic old St. Jo offers other worthwhile museums, including two installed in nineteenth-century mansions: the Albrecht Art Museum, with a group of works by such American artists as Thomas Hart Benton, George Inness and Mary Cassatt; and the St. Joseph Museum, which boasts an exceptionally large (five thousand items) collection of Indian items and what is believed to be the first glass installed by the New York firm of Louis Comfort Tiffany outside that company's home state. The State Hospital on the east side of town houses a psychiatric museum, with seventeen rooms filled with exhibits covering the last four centuries of mental care. Also at the east side of town is a firm that recalls the western flavor of old St. Jo: the Stetson Hat Company. Stetsons crowned the heads of all manner of frontier figures: Buffalo Bill wore the hat as did his sidekick Annie Oakley, and such latter-day cowboys as Tom Mix, Gene Autry and Roy Rogers also favored the ten-gallon headgear. New Yorker John B. Stetson worked in St. Jo in the 1850s before heading west with a wagon train to the Pike's Peak area to look for gold. During his trek to Colorado, the story goes, Stetson invented the broad-brimmed, high-crown hat that eventually put his name on the top of everybody's head, if not on the tip of everybody's tongue, and made his bank account as good as gold. In 1971 the Stevens Hat Company of St. Joseph acquired the Stetson operation and moved it out to the Missouri city. At the factory outlet store you can buy ten-gallon models at five-gallon prices.

Before leaving St. Jo it's pleasant to drive around the quiet tree-shaded town to see some of the old buildings, more than twenty of them listed on the National Register. These include Robidoux Row, a strip of seven apartments built about 1850 by Joseph Robidoux, St. Joseph's founder; the 1863 Bank of the State of Missouri, believed the oldest building west of the Mississippi continuously occupied by a bank (deerskin bags of gold dust once changed hands in the banking hall, little changed from the nineteenth century); the 1889 German American Bank, featuring elaborate terra-cotta decor; Wholesale Row, a block of commercial structures which once served as wholesale houses; the stately neo-classical-style Buchanan County courthouse, second largest in the state when completed in 1876; and the Hill Street Historic District, filled with late nineteenth-century mansions built by St. Jo's merchant princes who operated stores and warehouses that provisioned travelers passing through town on their way west. To complete your visit, wander along leafy Lovers Lane, an attractive residential street commemorated in the 1889 poem "Lover's Lane, Saint Jo" written in London by one-time St. Joseph resident Eugene Field, who courted his wife in the Missouri town:

Saint Jo, Buchanan County,
    Is leagues and leagues away;
And I sit in the gloom of this rented room,
And pine to be there today.
Yes, with London fog around me,
    And the bustling to and fro,
I am fretting to be across the sea
    In Lover's Lane, Saint Jo.

5. Missouri's Wild West:

Whiskey at Weston
The James Brothers at Liberty and at Kearney
Old Watkins Mill and the Victorian Spa Town of
Excelsior Springs
Independence: Home of Harry Truman, the Oregon and Santa
Fe Trails, and of the Mormon Zion
History at Fort Osage, at Missouri Town 1855 and at Lone
Jack's Civil War Museum
Civil War Era Lexington
Warrensburg's Old Drum: Dog of Dogs

Ben Holladay was a legendary figure in the old West. They called him the "king of wheels." Holladay built a transportation empire, a freight and stagecoach colossus that boasted fifteen thousand employees, twenty thousand vehicles and a hundred and fifty thousand animals. Holladay owned a share of the Pony Express and at one time the businessman controlled more than five thousand miles of stagecoach lines. The great entrepreneur sold his empire to Wells Fargo for some two and a third million dollars in 1868, only months before the "Golden Spike" ceremony at Promontory Point,

Utah, marked the opening of the first transcontinental rail-road and the closing of the stagecoach era. A decade before, in 1856, Holladay established another sort of business, a distillery, in the Missouri River port town of Weston. The distillery used water from a limestone spring discovered by the Lewis and Clark expedition when it passed through the area in 1804. Holladay's bourbon spread like wild firewater. Conestoga freight wagons carried "the whiskey that opened the West" out to thirsty pioneers in Colorado and miners in California, and many a stagecoach passenger took a swig, and maybe three or four or more, to warm himself during bone-chilling nights on the ride through the endless open spaces on the way west. The McCormick Distillery at Weston still operates, the nation's oldest and smallest distillery and one of only two listed on the National Register (the other is the Jack Daniels installation in Lynchburg, Tennessee). Located just outside the delightful little town of Weston, which lies halfway between St. Joseph and Kansas City, the McCormick Distillery offers tours that take you to the limestone spring, which still bubbles forth some twenty-two thousand gallons of crystal-clear water every day; to the still house where the bourbon is made—just twenty-four barrels a day; to the rick house, which holds twenty-five thousand barrels of aging bourbon; to the bottling department; and to the office building, a replica of the original house Ben Holladay built more than a century and a quarter ago.

A visit to the 1856 McCormick Distillery provides a good introduction to picturesque Weston, whose more than one hundred pre-Civil War buildings lend the town a pronounced mid-nineteenth-century ambiance. Founded in 1837, Weston, a town of thirteen hundred, more or less froze in time about the middle of the nineteenth century as unfavorable economic conditions kept the town from growing or changing. Dozens of old buildings cluster along Main, Spring and other streets that comprise the Weston Historic District, a twenty-two block area listed on the National Register in 1972. Many of the old structures serve new functions: the Historical Museum, which stands on the site of Benjamin Holladay's 1848 International Hotel, occupies a former church (built in 1900) as does Pirtle's Winery, installed in the one-time German Lutheran Evangelical church (1867), while the American Bowman Keeping Room Restaurant includes an 1842 wine cellar, and the 1898 Benner House offers bed and breakfast accommodations. A bit beyond the central Historic District stands the New Deal Tobacco Warehouse, where six million pounds of burley leaf change hands at the only tobacco market west of the Mississippi. The proceedings are open to the public during the auction season from early November to late January.

Once you manage to pull yourself away from Weston, where it's so tempting to linger and savor the old-time atmosphere, you can head east toward Jesse James country at Kearney and Liberty, perhaps on the way passing through Platte City. The 1866 county courthouse there is listed on the National Register, and the local historical museum occupies an 1882 reduced version of Jefferson City's governor's mansion, a house which so fascinated German immigrant Frederick Krause that he built a two-story facsimile of the chief executive's residence. At Kearney began Jesse James and there he lies buried. East of town stands the forty-acre farmstead listed on the National Register, where he and his brother and partner in crime Frank were born; Jesse in 1847, Frank in 1843. Now restored, the house contains personal effects owned by the brothers, family furniture and such other items as a piece of the bomb Pinkerton detectives hunting for the outlaws tossed through a window in 1875, killing Jesse's half brother and causing his mother to lose an arm. Jesse was shot dead in St. Joseph, Missouri, in 1882 (see section 4), and reposes in Kearney's Mt. Olivet cemetery (highway 92, a half mile east of I-95). Frank, acquitted of all charges against him, lived on the farm (except for four years in Oklahoma) from 1901 until his death in 1915. His widow, Annie, continued to reside there until she died in 1944, not all that long ago, so a living connection with the James era survived until relatively recent times. Weekend evenings during the last week in July through Labor Day "The Life and Times of Jesse James" show is performed at the farm. Opposite the James farm stands the Claybrook House, a restored residence listed on the National Register, where Jesse's daughter, Mary James Barr, once lived. George Claybrook of Virginia built the residence (1858), which somewhat resembles a southern plantation house, perhaps the westernmost example of such style.

More Jesse James lore lingers in Liberty, south of Kearney, where you'll find the Jesse James Bank Museum, installed in an 1858 bank the hold-up artist supposedly robbed on February 13, 1866, in what is said to be the first successful daylight bank robbery on record. Antique walnut office furniture, a wood stove, oil lamps, scales for weighing gold, and old-time bank forms recall the era. The Clay County Historical Museum across courthouse square occupies an 1877 apothecary building, which houses a nineteenth-century drugstore and area heirlooms, while upstairs is preserved the vintage office of a local doctor. Housed in a modern visitors center a block away is the stone and timber 1833 jail, cut away to show its innards, where Mormon leader Joseph Smith and his brother Hyrum were imprisoned for more than four months over the winter of 1838–39. Shortly thereafter they left Missouri and led their people to Nauvoo, Illinois (see section 4 for the Mormons' Missouri settlements at Far West and Gallatin, and Chapter III, section 9 for Nauvoo). Liberty's William Jewell College, established in 1850, occupies an attractive campus filled with low-rise red brick Georgian and classic revival-style buildings, one of which—three-story William Jewell Hall—served Federal troops in 1861 as a hospital, installed on the upper two floors, and as a horse stable.

Before heading into Independence, on the eastern edge of Kansas City south of the Missouri River, you may want to detour back north to visit the historic Watkins Woolen Mill, listed on the National Register, said to be the only nineteenth-century textile factory in America with its original machinery still intact. After Waltus Watkins, a native of Kentucky, settled on the land there in 1839 he gradually developed the thirty-six-hundred-acre Bethany Plantation, which included his Greek Revival-style house, built in 1850, and the three-story mill, constructed of brick handmade at the site and timber cut from the property. The mill contained more than fifty machines, shipped from the east by steamboat on the Ohio, Mississippi and Missouri Rivers, then hauled by ox teams some twenty miles to the factory, which Watkins established in 1861 at age fifty-five. Although the mill closed nearly a century ago, it still looks unchanged from the times when the machines, using forty to sixty thousand pounds of wool a year, spun thousands of yards of finished fabric. In addition to the mill and the manor house, the nearby octagonal Franklin school (1856) and Mt. Vernon church (1871) are open to visitors. (Another of those rare old octagonal school buildings stands near Schuline, Illinois; see Chapter III, section 2.)

A few miles south of Watkins Mill lies Excelsior Springs, an old spa town that remained fashionable until the late 1950s when the place started to decline. In recent years, however, Excelsior Springs has revived, and you can enjoy there such liquid pleasures as four different types of mineral water, available at the forty-two-foot counter, "the world's longest water bar," so it's billed (perhaps it's the world's only one as well), in the striking art deco Hall of Waters, or bathe in the local saline waters at the swimming pool or in a bath house.

A particularly alluring reminder of the town's former popularity as a spa is the late nineteenth-century Elms Hotel, a handsome stone and half-timber resort on twenty-three lushly landscaped acres, which offers a state-of-the-art spa and other amenities. The hotel has hosted such celebrities as John D. Rockefeller and Al Capone, as well as two presidents, Franklin Roosevelt and Harry Truman, who spent election night 1948 at the Elms. "Dewey Defeats Truman," screamed the now-famous banner headline in the Chicago *Tribune,* so the president went to bed believing he'd lost the race. But the next morning Truman awoke at the Elms to learn that he'd been reelected and would continue to serve as president of the United States.

Independence, south of Excelsior Springs, is Truman country. The Truman Library and Museum contain exhibits recalling the Missourian's political career: a reproduction of the White House Oval Office, the table on which the United Nations charter was signed, displays relating to the 1948 campaign, presidential letters and documents and much else. At the railroad station in Independence another display recalls Truman's famous 1948 "whistle stop" campaign, the one in which, as he put it, he didn't give the Republicans hell, he just told the truth and they thought it was hell. But no less interesting are the places in Independence that give you a feel for Truman's way of life and character as a down-home rather basic middle-class Middle Western citizen. Plain-spoken, outspoken, simple in the best sense of the word, without pretentions but with convictions, Truman well represents the typical Midwestern temperament and personality. Moreover, he valued that sense of place, the rooted feeling that typifies the Midwesterner: Truman was born in Missouri, lived there all his life—although he was known to spend time in Washington, where the Missouri boy managed to find work—died there and reposes in the soil of his native state. The very name is one long established in the state. In 1852 Missouri author

Sally Rochester Ford published *Grace Truman,* a didactic novel about the attempt of Grace's father-in-law to convert her from the Baptist to the Presbyterian faith, an effort the stubborn Truman resisted. Truman, stubborn Grace and feisty Harry, both exemplify the "show me" mentality.

A good place to start an excursion to sites that show plain old Harry Truman's pre-presidential way of life is at the family home, 219 North Delaware, a typical Midwestern late nineteenth-century Victorian-style residence built by George P. Gates, Bess Truman's grandfather. Four generations of the family called the fourteen-room house home. The residence remains furnished as it was when Harry and Bess lived there, starting in 1919 when they married. A stroll through the neighborhood, listed on the National Register, will take you along the same streets Truman walked on his famous brisk early morning constitutionals. Along Delaware rise other old homes; at the northwest corner of Waldo and Delaware stands the birthplace of Charles S. Thomas, President Eisenhower's secretary of the navy, while at 909 West Waldo is the house where Truman lived as a boy. "We had wonderful times in that neighborhood from 1896 to 1902," he recalled in his *Memoirs.* "There was a wonderful barn with a hayloft in which all the kids met and cooked up plans for all sorts of adventures." Farther out, on Pleasant Street, is Palmer Junior High, which occupies the site of the old Central High School from which Truman and his future wife Bess Wallace graduated in 1901, and over on Maple Avenue stands the First Presbyterian Church where they attended Sunday school in the 1890s. The Memorial Building across the street served through the years as Truman's voting place, most notably in the 1948 presidential election. Truman began his political career in 1921 as an executive for Jackson County; at the courthouse, a few blocks east of the Truman home, you can see his working quarters from those days. The central section of the courthouse, listed on the National Register and modeled after Philadelphia's Independence Hall, encompasses the 1836 brick courthouse built when Independence served as an important jumping-off point for the West. A stone marker on the square recalls that the Oregon Trail began there in the early 1840s, as did the Santa Fe Trail, whose starting point moved in 1830 to Independence from Franklin, Missouri, about a hundred miles to the east.

In *The Oregon Trail* historian Francis Parkman describes bustling Independence as it appeared in the 1840s: "A multitude of shops had sprung up to furnish the emigrants and Santa Fe traders with necessaries for their journey; and there was an incessant hammering and banging from a dozen blacksmiths' sheds, where the heavy wagons were being repaired, and the horses and oxen shod." The wild old days in Independence—"Wild Bill" Hickok received his nickname there—are recalled at the 1859 jail where Frank James, Jesse's brother and crime partner, and Civil War guerrilla leader William Quantrill, among others, were held. The marshal's home and office, now a historical museum, adjoin the jail. During the Civil War, Union General Thomas Ewing issued in 1863 his infamous "Order Number Eleven," a security measure that forced thousands of supposed southern sympathizers in Jackson and neighboring counties to vacate their homes. Missouri artist George Caleb Bingham painted his famous work "Martial Law," popularly known as "Order Number Eleven," in a studio at the Bingham-Waggoner house, his mid-1850s mansion, listed on the National Register, built just by the Santa Fe Trail at Independence. In 1883 the two Waggoner brothers, millers from Pennsylvania who purchased the Bingham residence and its nineteen acres in 1879, founded with George P. Gates, Bess Wallace Truman's grandfather, the Waggoner-Gates Milling Company. Across town stands another old house, the 1881 Vaile Mansion, also listed on the National Register, an opulent and rather spooky-looking place with pointy roofs and dripping with gingerbread and metal trim.

In 1831, half a century before the Vaile house was built, Joseph Smith designated Independence as the site of the city of Zion, the new Mormon headquarters. Church members from Ohio and New York moved to the frontier town, and by 1833 they comprised a third of Jackson County's population of thirty-six hundred. Southern sympathizers, fearing the anti-slavery newcomers would soon dominate the area, harassed the Mormons, eventually forcing them to resettle elsewhere in Missouri (see section 4 for the Mormon communities at Far West and Gallatin). The Mormon visitors center in Independence contains exhibits that trace the history of the church in Missouri. Early Missouri history of a secular sort haunts some other sites in Jackson County. On a high promontory overlooking the Missouri River fourteen miles northeast of Independence stands Fort Osage, a restoration of the first outpost of the United States in the Louisiana Purchase Territory. William Clark built the fort in 1808 a few years after he returned from his Lewis and Clark expedition. Missouri Town 1855, at Lake Jacomo south of Independence, contains twenty or so old buildings moved to the site from various places in western Missouri and arranged to give the flavor of a mid-nineteenth-century settlement. At Lone Jack to the southwest a Civil War museum houses displays on the conflict as it played out in western Missouri. Two Union cannons near the museum entrance recall the bloody Battle of Lone Jack (August 16, 1862), while exhibits inside relate the story of the Confederate capture of Independence; of Order Number Eleven, the evacuation decree issued by Union General Ewing (see above); and of the Battle of Westport (October 23, 1864), the largest Civil War battle fought west of the Mississippi, with twelve thousand Confederate troops facing twenty thousand Union soldiers.

At Grandview, twenty miles south of Independence, is the 1894 Truman Farm Home where from 1906 to 1917, during his twenties, Harry Truman lived, worked and acquired the earthy style for which he later became famous. "It was on the farm that Harry got his common sense. He didn't get it in town," his mother, Martha Ellen Truman, once observed. In nearby Belton, just beyond the Jackson County line, lies the grave of the hatchet-wielding prohibitionist Carry Nation, buried in Belton cemetery in 1911. Her monument bears the sentiment: "She hath done what she could." A museum in Belton's original city hall building contains Nation memorabilia, a collection of Harry Truman's masonic items, and displays devoted to Missourian Dale Carnegie (see section 4).

Much of Missouri's early history is encapsulated in the attractions at Lexington, an attractive Missouri River town about twenty-five miles northeast of Independence. More than a hundred pre-Civil War houses embellish Lexington, which boasts four districts listed on the National Register, one encompassing Wentworth Military Academy, founded in 1880; a second that includes old houses along Highland Avenue; another called the Old Neighborhoods District; and, finally, the Commercial Community section. In the latter district stands the handsome white 1847 Lafayette County courthouse, believed to be the oldest courthouse west of the Mississippi in continuous use. Embedded at the top of one of the building's four columns is a projectile supposedly fired during the three-day Civil War Battle of Lexington in September 1861. The one-hundred-and-five-acre battlefield site at the edge of town still bears scars of the engagement (trenches and earthworks), which became known as the "Battle of the Hemp Bales" as Confederate troops used the bales as shields while the soldiers advanced on Union positions that the Southerners took. The nearby 1853 Anderson house (now a museum), which served both sides as a hospital (it changed hands three times during the fierce fighting), is to this day disfigured by bullet holes and blood stains. The local history museum, installed in the 1846 Presbyterian church building, contains a collection of Civil War items, as well as displays on the Pony Express, owned by the firm of Russell, Majors and Waddell, headquartered in a building that stood at the corner of Main and North 10th. Lexington in its day was a major, as well as a Majors, transportation center. Apart from the Pony Express owners' home office, the town served as a river port and as a flourishing supply stop where army units, wagon trains and other travelers outfitted themselves for the trek west. U.S. highway 24, which passes just by Lexington, is essentially the old Santa Fe Trail paved over. One of the twelve "Madonna of the Trails" statues erected in the U.S. by the DAR to commemorate the country's early road network overlooks the Missouri River at Lexington. Harry Truman dedicated the monument in 1928.(Another such statue stands in Vandalia, Illinois; see Chapter III, section 4.)

At Warrensburg, about thirty miles south of Lexington, another sort of statue commemorates a different kind of historical happening. On the Johnson County courthouse lawn stands a bronze of Old Drum, a dog whose death in 1859 occasioned a famous trial. It seems that Leonidas Hornsby, upset by all the sheep he'd lost to dogs, vowed to kill the next hound that entered his property. One night Old Drum wandered onto the farm and, true to his threat, Hornsby ordered the animal shot. Charles Burden, the dog's owner and Hornsby's brother-in-law, sued for damages. George Graham Vest, who served in the Missouri House, the Confederate States Senate and for twenty-four years in the U.S. Senate, represented the plaintiff. After the case made its way through the courts, the final trial took place in Warrensburg on September 23, 1870. During the proceedings Vest delivered his now famous "A Tribute to a Dog":

The one absolutely unselfish friend that a man can have in this selfish world, the one that never deserts him and the one that never proves ungrateful or treacherous is his dog. . . . If fortune drives the master forth an outcast in the world, friendless and homeless, the faithful dog asks no higher privilege than that of accompanying him to guard against danger, to fight against his enemies, and when the last scene of all comes, and death takes the master in its embrace and his body is laid away in the cold ground, no matter if all other friends pursue their way, there by his graveside will the noble dog be found, his head between his paws, his eyes sad but open in alert watchfulness, faithful and true even to death.

The oration brought tears to the eyes of the jury members and money to the pocketbook of Charles Burden: the jury delivered a verdict awarding Old Drum's owner fifty dollars.

The trial took place at Warrensburg's old court house, now on the west edge of the city but then located on the town square. The restored two-story yellow-brown structure, built in 1838 and listed on the National Register, offers a rare example of Federal-style architecture of the time this far west. The Johnson County Historical Museum next door houses local antiques and artifacts. The dog isn't the only animal that figured in Warrensburg's past. The building now occupied by Cassingham's hardware store, at College and Railroad Streets, once housed the Jones Brothers Sale Barn, a mule market. The first mules arrived in Missouri by way of the Santa Fe Trail, after the Trail opened in 1821, when traders obtained the animals at the Mexican settlement of Santa Fe and brought them back to the Midwest. Between 1870 and 1900 the mule population in Missouri exceeded that of any other state. During World War I the state furnished thousands of the animals to the British Army for use as beasts of burden, the Jones Brothers firm in Warrensburg being one of the major suppliers. The famous Missouri mule seems a fitting symbol for the state, for the animal reflects the character of Missouri's inhabitants. Known for stubbornness and basic common sense, the renowned Missouri mule exemplifies the "Show Me" state's skeptical but practical outlook. Lions, eagles and other such imposing fauna embellish the insignias of many places, but the seal of the city of Independence portrays four Missouri mules pulling a covered wagon. Other states have produced presidents, poets, painters and desperadoes, so characters like Truman, Eugene Field, George Caleb Bingham and Jesse James are hardly unique. But only the "Show Me" state has given the world the Missouri mule—a singular, if perhaps unenviable, distinction. Such is what passes for pride out there in the American Midwest.

6. Mid-Missouri:

Sedalia
Burger's Ham Smokehouse
Boonville
Nineteenth-Century Arrow Rock
Picture-Perfect Fayette
The Old Port of Rocheport
The University and Colleges at Columbia
Omar Bradley in Moberly, Centralia's Chance Gardens,
Mexico's Saddle Horse Museum

Back in the late nineteenth century a young black piano player arrived in Sedalia, a mid-Missouri town eighty-eight miles east of Kansas City, from Texarkana, Texas. The musician managed to get a job in Sedalia's tenderloin district, a group of raucous saloons, gambling clubs and honky-tonk night spots at the east end of Main Street. While playing piano in the back room of the Maple Leaf Club the young man began to experiment with a new, lively type of music called "ragtime," and in 1898 he set down on paper a piece called "The Maple Leaf Rag," which John Stark, a Sedalia music store owner, published. Thus did renowned ragtime composer Scott Joplin's career begin. A plaque at 121 East Main in Sedalia marks the site of the Maple Leaf Club where Joplin played and composed the ragtime music that later made him famous. The Maple Leaf Room in Yeater Library at State Fair Community College houses a ragtime archive that also recalls Joplin's time in the town, where a Scott Joplin Festival, with ragtime performers from around the country, takes place every year in June. As the name of the college suggests, Sedalia hosts in late August every year the Missouri State Fair, held on a three-hundred-and-thirty-six-acre site a few blocks from the school. The fair, with its agricultural orientation, reflects central Missouri's farm economy and Sedalia's long participation in the cattle industry. Starting just after the Civil War, the town served as a major link between the livestock-rich ranches of Texas and beef-hungry bellies in the eastern states. Cattle drivers herded the animals north from Texas to the nearest western railhead, at Sedalia, from where the Texas longhorns were shipped onward to packing plants in Chicago, East St. Louis and elsewhere. On Marshall Avenue and East Highway 50 stand the turn-of-the-century Missouri Pacific repair shops, believed to be the largest west of the Mississippi back then, and the holding pens that mark the end of the so-called Rawhide Trail from Texas to Sedalia. It was that trail and the Sedalia terminal which suggested the theme for the 1960s television series "Rawhide."

As you head east on highway 50 you'll pass near some truly back road off-the-beaten-track attractions. A few miles north on highway A, which branches off from 50 about nine miles east of the center of Sedalia, is New Lebanon, too small and remote to appear on Missouri's official highway map. Three remnants of the early days in New Lebanon, settled in 1819, remain: the school (1889) and the Presbyterian church (1860), both listed on the National Register, and Abe's Country Store, a restored version of the general store Abe Rothgeb operated in the settlement for sixty-two years until his death in 1959 at age ninety-four. A few miles away are two more National Register places, both open to visitors. On highway 135 lies Pleasant Green Plantation House, dating from the 1820s, and on highway 5 to the east stands stately Ravenswood, an early 1880s red brick country mansion with huge white columns above which rises a castellated tower. For at least six generations, starting with Nathan Leonard in 1824, members of the Leonard family have lived on the property. Highway 5 will lead you back to 50 which takes you to California, three miles south of which is the ham-processing operation at Burger's Smokehouse.

Ham from the heart of Missouri has delighted taste buds far and wide. Even Winston Churchill came to appreciate that "Show Me" state treat. On sampling some Callaway County ham when he visited Fulton in 1946 to deliver his "Iron Curtain" speech (see section 2), the British statesman proclaimed, "The pig has reached its highest point of evolution in this ham." Burger's Smokehouse, believed to be the largest processor of naturally cured hams in the United States, is tucked away on the century-old three-hundred-and-seventy-acre family farm overlooking the bluffs of the Moreau River. The Smokehouse processes a quarter of a million hams a year, as well as about half a million pounds each of hickory-smoked bacon and summer sausage. Before touring the operation it's worth browsing at the small museum where old photos and Burger family lore trace the history of the company and the early days of country ham curing. "It was early on a clear frosty November morning, the moon was on the wane, and it was a perfect time for butchering," evocatively reads a caption to pictures showing butchering day in 1905. An antique hog scraper, scalding hook, boning knife and butcher's saw recall that turn-of-the-century late autumn ritual. Not to be outdone by Churchill, Dwight Eisenhower, in a letter on display, thanked Burger in September 1955 for "the prize ham from the Missouri State Fair," a treat the president adjudged delicious.

The factory tour starts in the original smokehouse, with an old iron stove that burned hickory wood to smoke the meat. These days dampened sawdust, which affords more smoke with less heat, is used in the three ham smokehouses, each containing five to six hundred hams. Contrary to popular belief, smoking doesn't affect the ham's taste; it simply speeds up the aging process. Burger's processes both artificially and naturally aged hams. The artificially aged hams remain for four to six months in a series of season-simulating temperature-controlled rooms. In the winter room the refrigerated hams are stored to absorb the salt, brown sugar and pepper cure applied to them. In the spring room hams hang from poles to dry, while in the summer room the meats sweat off a fifth of their weight. You'll also visit the four-story white stone-block curing house where twenty-five thousand hams hang in thirteen tiers for a year or so to age naturally. After the tour you can sample some of Burger's ham at the snack bar, there enjoying that down home central Missouri delicacy—what might be called Missouri "ham Burger."

From California, highway 87 will take you north to the Missouri River and Boonville. (Or you can head east to Jefferson City, the state capital, and pick up the tour covered in section 2.) Antebellum and Victorian-era homes line the streets of Boonville, established in 1817 and named after Daniel Boone (see section 2). Other old buildings include the 1848 Cooper County jailhouse (open to visitors), used for one hundred and thirty years, and 1857 Thespian Hall, a handsome classical-style brick structure, listed on the National Register, believed to be the oldest surviving continuously used theater west of the Alleghenies. The Boonville Library, Reading Room, and Thespian Association built the hall, which became a stop on the mid-nineteenth-century play circuit that applauded such alluring works as *The Loan of a Lover, Mischief Making, The Married Rake* and *The Spectre Bridegroom*. At the cornerstone ceremony on July 25, 1855, Boonville's mayor lauded the project as one which would help deter "ardent and impulsive youth from debauchery and vice."

At nearby Arrow Rock—a delightful Missouri River hamlet of eighty-two souls—stands another old playhouse, the Lyceum Theatre, installed in a Gothic Revival-style 1872 Baptist church. Shows take the stage in June, July and August. Like Elsah in Illinois (Chapter III, section 9) and Iowa's Bentonsport on the Des Moines (Chapter IV, section 2), Arrow Rock, listed on the National Register, is one of those endearing and rare old river hamlets preserved virtually unchanged from a century and a half ago. A stroll through unspoiled Arrow Rock, so nineteenth century that the movie musical "Tom Sawyer" was filmed there, will take you to such old-time establishments as a blacksmith shop, gunsmith store, newspaper office, the 1871 one-room stone "calaboose" (the jail was never used, legend has it) and the still-functioning 1834 Tavern where you can get a country-style meal in a setting where travelers in the western territory dined a century and a half ago. The old log courthouse (1839) served as a model for the building portrayed in the famous painting "County Election" by George Caleb Bingham, whose cottage, built by the artist in 1837, survives in Arrow Rock. Other well-known early Missourians lived in the village, among them Dr. John Sappington, who discovered the effectiveness of quinine in the treatment of malaria. Four of Sappington's daughters married Missouri governors—three of them the same one, Claiborne Fox Jackson. After Jackson's first two wives—Sappington's offspring—died in childbirth, he asked the doctor for the hand of yet a third daughter. The governor's already twice father-in-law replied, "You can have her, Claib, but don't come back for the old lady."

Arrow Rock rose and declined because of the river. When Lewis and Clark were returning from their exploration of the Northwest, Clark observed that the site, which Arrow Rock eventually occupied, would make a "handsome spot for a town." In 1817 a ferry began operations there and the following year an inn, later acquired by David Todd, uncle of Abraham Lincoln's wife, Mary Todd, started up. On the morning of September 1, 1821, William Becknell, who the night before had crossed the Missouri from Franklin, a short distance downstream from Arrow Rock, set off on a trading trip to Santa Fe, the first trek on what was to become the Santa Fe Trail. The Trail survived—even today traces of the famous route can be seen at Arrow Rock—but the town of Franklin, the Trail's true starting point, disappeared when the Missouri washed the settlement away, an episode that recalls humorist George Fitch's comment: "There is only one river with a personality, a sense of humor, and a woman's caprice; a river that goes traveling sidewise, that interferes in politics, rearranges geography and dabbles at real estate; a river that plays hide-and-seek with you today, and tomorrow follows you around like a pet dog with a dynamite cracker tied to his tail. That river is the Missouri." Arrow Rock thrived from the Trail traffic and later as a river port, but when a bridge spanned the Missouri at Glasgow, upstream, in 1923 the village remained frozen in time as the delightful backwater it is today. So it's by way of Glasgow, which boasts the state's oldest library building still in use (1866; listed on the National Register), that you cross to the Missouri's east bank. Yes, east, for true to Fitch's description, the river here rearranges its normal alignment and runs north to south. The road leads on to Fayette, whose pre-Civil War houses and century-old storefronts preserve it as a photogenic example of those small town nineteenth-century county seats found throughout the Midwest. Many of Fayette's vintage structures lie within a few blocks of courthouse square, including the delightful little Gothic-style St. Mary's Episcopal Church (1848) and buildings in the National Historic District that encompasses the campus of Central Methodist College, whose 1874 Morrison Observatory is the oldest such facility west of Chicago. The Stephens Museum on campus houses a natural history section as well as exhibits devoted to painter George Caleb Bingham and to Daniel Boone, whose tombstone is on display. To the west of Fayette by the Missouri River is Boonslick State Park, listed on the National Register, where a salt-water spring furnished the mineral to pioneers. Nathan and Daniel M. Boone, the frontiersman's sons, established a salt processing operation here in the early years of the nineteenth century, boiling the water off to produce the coveted product.

Also on the Missouri, farther east, nestles the tiny river town of Rocheport, listed on the National Register. Like Arrow Rock, but with all of two hundred and seventy-two inhabitants, a true metropolis compared to that hamlet's eighty-two, Rocheport is a beguiling little river village out of the nineteenth century. The settlement seems little changed from the days when settlers first arrived in the area back in the 1820s. Old houses, churches and commercial buildings line the grid of streets tucked between Moniteau Creek and the Missouri River. Antique stores occupy a few of the old buildings. Installed in an 1840s house on Moniteau Street is a museum that recalls the old days of steamboat traffic a century and more ago when Rocheport served as a flourishing port.

Columbia, a few miles east, boasts the oldest state university (1839) west of the Mississippi. In Francis Quadrangle on the campus stand six starkly isolated Ionic columns, the only surviving part of the original Academic Hall destroyed by fire in 1892. Among the eighteen buildings around the Quadrangle (all listed on the National Register) are Neff and Williams Halls, part of the world's first journalism school (1908), and the 1869 chancellor's residence by which stands the stone obelisk that served as Thomas Jefferson's original grave marker. It is a true curiosity to find a founding father's monument out there in a mid-Missouri college town: Jefferson's heirs presented the stone to the university in 1883 to commemorate the president's interest in Missouri, the first state carved out of the Louisiana Territory, acquired under Jefferson's administration. The State Historic Society, installed in the east wing of Ellis Library, contains paintings by such Missourians as Thomas Hart Benton and George Caleb Bingham. Other museums at the university include those devoted to art and archeology, to geology and to anthropology. Two other schools help enliven the college town of Columbia: Columbia College (1851), the first four-year state college for women west of the Mississippi; and Stephens (1851), whose campus includes the Firestone Baars Chapel, designed by renowned architect Eero Saarinen, which features entrances on all four sides to symbolize that religion can be approached from different directions. Two places removed from the bustle of the trio of campuses which dominate Columbia are the tranquil gardens tucked behind the Shelter Insurance building and Maplewood, listed on the National Register, an 1877 mansion filled with period furnishings set in sixty-acre Nifong Park.

A few scattered attractions lie in central Missouri north of Columbia. Highway 63 takes you up to Moberly where the historical museum, installed in an old railroad building, contains displays on General Omar Bradley, who grew up in the town. Bradley was born in 1893 on a farm south of Moberly near Higbee where his mother worked as a switchboard operator at the Mutual Telephone Company. Higbee boasts the A & K Cooperage factory, believed to be the nation's only operation specializing in oak barrels for the wine industry. Over in Centralia, to the southeast, you'll find the nine-room A. B. Chance house and gardens, both listed on the National Register. The residence houses historical exhibits while the half-acre garden includes a Japanese-like harmonic arrangement of flowers, shrubs, trees, wood, rocks and water. At Mexico, fifteen miles east, stands the Register-listed 1857 Ross house, a spacious old place where various episodes of history unfolded over the years. In 1861 Colonel Ulysses S. Grant received word there, by reading the newspaper, that he'd been nominated for promotion to brigadier general, while the home's second owner, Colby T. Quisenberry, brought to the area the first Kentucky thoroughbreds. From its earliest days, Mexico favored fine horseflesh and the town became an important saddle horse center. The American Saddle Horse Museum at the Ross house contains paintings, trophies, photos, documents, saddles and other horsy items. Mexico is also the center of the firebrick industry, the A. P. Green factory there turning out refractory materials from the area's extensive clay deposits. Before leaving town cast a glance at the Mexico *Ledger* newspaper building on Washington Street. Reversing Missouri's usual "show me" attitude, the building sports a "show you" appearance, proclaiming its function with a facade designed as a newspaper's front page.

7. Kicks on 66 and Float Trips on Pristine Streams:

Old Route 66 to New Wineries
Maramec Spring
Dillard Mill
Ozark National Scenic Riverways
Big Spring and Small Towns
Mingo Wildlife Refuge

A century and a half ago a band of Shawnee Indians, their faces decorated with bright red paint, arrived at the Ohio house of pioneer businessman Thomas James, banker and owner of iron furnaces. Even back then it wasn't every day that a tribe of painted redskins showed up on one's doorstep, so it took the startled James a while to realize the paint the Indians wore was hematite, an iron ore. Asked where they'd mined the substance the Shawnees replied, "Miaramigoua," their name for "catfish." Not long afterwards James accompanied the Indians on a trek west to a remote spot in the Ozark foothills of Missouri where he found a natural spring and a large deposit of hematite ore. In 1826 the businessman bought the Catfish Spring property and established an ironworks at the site. With remnants of the historic ironworks and the delightful ninety-six-million-gallon-a-day spring, Maramec Spring Park (sometimes spelled Meramec; "Maramec" is a corruption of "Miaramigoua") is one of the various pleasant places to visit near Interstate 44, which follows the route of old highway 66 as it cuts along south central Missouri on its way from St. Louis to Oklahoma.

After you break free of the St. Louis metropolitan area via the interstate or more rustic highway 30, head for St. Clair, about forty miles west. Villagers chose that name in 1859 after finally tiring of the town they previously called Traveler's Repose being mistaken for a pioneer cemetery. Back in the mid-nineteenth century a local school teacher named Phoebe Apperson was courted by a neighbor from Sullivan, just down the road, who moved away to California, amassed a fortune in gold mining and later became a U.S. Senator. When the former Missourian returned to the state to do business with the Maramec Iron Works, located at what is now Maramec Spring Park, he resumed his courtship of Miss Apperson and the couple married at nearby Steelville in 1862. The groom was George Hearst and their only child, born in 1863, grew up to become the famous publisher William Randolph Hearst. Five miles out road PP from St. Clair stands a memento of the days when the renowned publisher's parents lived in Missouri, a one-room log cabin replica of the old Salem schoolhouse Phoebe Apperson attended in the late 1840s. Rough-hewn benches and tables furnish the primitive classroom, while on the wall hang Hearst family photos. It is somehow curious to see in a log cabin on that remote road in an obscure corner of Missouri pictures of the sophisticated and powerful Hearst clan of California.

Return on PP to highway 30 to connect with K, one mile south, which winds its way wildly through sparsely inhabited heavily wooded back country and then connects with 185, the road that leads through Maramec State Forest back to I-44. The interstate follows the path of famous Route 66 which, in turn, was built along a stagecoach line established in the early 1840s. During the Civil War when the artery was a military thoroughfare the federal government strung a telegraph line along the highway, which became known as the Wire Road. I-44 takes one past Bourbon, whose water towers labeled with the town's name have given rise to the local tale that wayward travelers occasionally stop off to photograph what they take to be huge containers of spirits. Nostalgia buffs can take Old Highway 66, which parallels I-44, south-

west out of Bourbon toward Cuba. You'll pass near Onondaga Cave, a National Natural Landmark, one of Missouri's
nearly five thousand or so known caverns (more than any
other state). First explored a century ago, Onondaga—along
with twenty-two other Missouri show caves, among them
Meramec Caverns at nearby Stanton—is open for tours. At
Rosati, a few miles down I-44, you'll come to one of the
many wineries that dot the area. Founded in 1934, Rosati
Winery greets visitors with wine and grape cluster-draped
trellises. A self-guided tour takes you to the press room
where grapes are crushed, the fermenting vats and down to
the dark damp cellar where dust-covered bottles age. North
of I-44 you'll find three more wineries: Heinrichshaus,
nestled in a secluded corner off road U; Ferrigno (reached
from U via county 108, a gravel road), which occupies a
rustic barn-like building; and back down by I-44, St. James
Winery, located on terrain where Charles Lindbergh landed
on June 25, 1926, to offer airplane rides to locals. In addition
to wine, St. James sells such regional taste treats as Missouri
ham, sorghum, molasses, cheeses and Ozark mustard.

Just south of I-44 lies the pleasant tree-shaded town of St.
James, gateway to Maramec Spring Park six miles south. The
park is unusual in that it's privately owned but maintained for
public use. When she died in 1938, Lucy Wortham James,
great-granddaughter of Thomas James, who founded the
Maramec Iron Works in 1826, left behind her expressed hope
that what she deemed "the most beautiful spot in Missouri"
would be set aside "and open to the enjoyment of the people." Her fortune stemmed not from the ironworks, which
eventually went bankrupt, but from the Dun and Bradstreet
Company, founded by Robert G. Dun, brother of Lucy
James's grandmother. Maramec Spring Park is indeed one of
the state's most beautiful spots. A scenic road takes you along
a ridge with a view onto the wooded valley below and to the
Ozark foothills beyond. Another road leads to the old mine

where workers extracted hematite ore, then taken by mule-drawn wagons down still used Stringtown Road—so called for the string of miners' houses that lined the thoroughfare—to the furnace, which still stands in a delightful wooded glen criss-crossed by streams and rivulets. In that part of the park Maramec Spring, sixth largest in Missouri, bubbles out its nearly hundred million gallons a day from a pleasant nook beneath a moss-covered bluff. Exhibits at the park museum just across the way trace the area's history, while the nearby Ozark Agricultural Museum houses old farm implements and equipment. Back in St. James I-44 takes you to Rolla where Memoryville, U.S.A., a commercial museum, contains an eccentrically eclectic collection of old time Americana objects. At the nearby village of Newburg stands historic Houston House, constructed in 1884 as the town's first building and originally called The Railroad Eating House, as "Frisco" line workers frequented the restaurant, which still serves meals. A few doors away stands the nineteenth-century Old Opera House where the Regional Opera Company presents stage plays and musicals on summer weekends.

The area south of I-44 offers miles of unspoiled and sparsely inhabited country. The million-and-a-half-acre Mark Twain National Forest greens much of the terrain and pristine streams vein the landscape. Missouri's rivers are one of the state's most characteristic and, along with the springs and old mills that feed and feed off of streams, most attractive features. In *An Artist in America* Thomas Hart Benton described with his artist's eye the state's picturesque streams:

The rivers of Missouri are often very beautiful. Many of them have their sources in immense hill springs which pour out of the limestone bluffs at the rate of thousands of gallons a minute. . . . Great sycamores hang over their banks and in the summer when the current moves slowly these are duplicated in the stream below. . . . Missouri's summer moon is big and white and cuts out vivid and clear edges. . . . There is over these summer night waters and on the shadowed lands that border them an ineffable peace, an immense quiet, which puts all ambitious effort in its futile place and makes of a simple drift of sense and feeling the ultimate and proper end of life.

Delightful old Dillard Mill, off highway 49, seems to epitomize the rustic character of the country in and near the Twain National Forest. Dillard is one of the best preserved of Missouri's seventy or so known old mills. The early settlements in the remote corners of the Ozarks were isolated from both the outside world and each other, necessitating a self-dependence that led to the proliferation of water mills in the area. Although the present barn-red Dillard building, which perches at the junction of Indian and Huzzah Creeks, dates only from 1904, it includes timbers from the original pre-Civil War grist mill that stood on the site. Another old grist mill, built in 1896, stands beside the Current River in Montauk State Park to the southwest of Dillard. Pioneers in the area in the early 1800s named the settlement after their former home at Montauk at the far tip of Long Island in New York. Seven springs feed the headwaters of the one-hundred-and-thirty-nine-mile Current which, together with its forty-four-mile-long tributary, the Jacks Fork, forms the Ozark National Scenic Railways, the nation's first such preserve, a protected and unspoiled stretch of streams swelled by the gush of crystal-clear water from dozens of springs. One of the traditional activities in the area is a "float trip," a canoe excursion, on one of the many rivers that flow through the region. On the Jacks Fork you'll pass through a narrow canyon-like stretch, then by high bluffs, some towering as much as four hundred feet above the river, on to Jam-up Cave, where car-sized boulders block the entrance, to Slanting Rock, a house-sized boulder split from the cliff and tipped into the stream, and to rich red Alley Mill at Alley Springs, one of those picturesque old (1894) riverside grist grinders. The upper Current flows by Akers, where still today, as for years, a ferry operates, then on to Troublesome Hollow and to Pulltite, so-called as horses stretched their harnesses taut when pulling grain wagons up the steep west bank. The lower Current's main attraction is renowned Big Spring, said to be one of the two largest springs in the nation (the other is Silver Springs in Florida). A vast system of caves and underground conduits feed into Big Spring an average daily flow of two hundred and seventy-six million gallons. At Big Spring the National Park Service operates rustic cabins and a dining lodge built of logs, rocks and cut stone in the 1930s by Civilian Conservation Corps workers. Missouri outdoor writer Leonard Hall's classic account of a Current River float trip, *Stars Upstream,* suggests the pleasures of drifting down the serene stream:

> There is always a thrill about being afloat again. The canoes follow the current, slipping through the dappled shade and sunlight of the late afternoon with only an occasional stroke of the paddle. . . . I maintain steerage-way and keep a sharp eye out for the gravel bar that will make the ideal camp site. We aren't concerned about how far we travel this afternoon, and life is reduced, at least for this golden moment, to its real essentials—a tasty bass or goggle-eye for the meal just ahead and a lodging for the night.

Like Thomas Hart Benton, Hall found on the river a certain elemental simplicity—a return to the basics; there is something free and easy and fine about a float trip on a remote Ozark stream.

Other outdoor excursions and exertions can be enjoyed on the Ozark Trail, a partially completed projected seven-hundred-dred-mile-long walkway through well-wooded areas in

southern Missouri and northern Arkansas. It's anticipated
that the Ozark Trail when finished will join the Pacific Crest
and Appalachian Trails as a National Scenic Trail. The thirty-
mile Current River section of the Ozark walkway begins at
the river near Owls Bend. Owls Bend is just one of the places
in the area dubbed with those rather delightful names that
seem to hint at a special charm or at the presence of an offbeat
curiosity or two. Other such dots on the map and on the road
in and around Mark Twain National Forest include Fairdeal-
ing, Wilderness, Gypsy, Des Arc and Mill Spring: total population—six hundred and eighty-five. Such hamlets typify the
sparsely settled area. East of Big Spring back roads cross the
National Forest, taking you through great stretches of unin-
habited countryside on the way to Lake Wappapello, named
after a Shawnee Indian chief, and then to Mingo National
Wildlife Refuge, one of the nation's more than four hundred
such nature preserves. The Mississippi River once flowed
through the area the refuge now occupies. After the river
shifted forty miles to the east eighteen thousand years ago the
abandoned channel gradually evolved into a dense swamp
which attracted wildlife. Three centuries ago southeast Missouri, called "swampeast" by the locals, contained some two
and a half million acres of swampland. As recently as 1861 a
Civil War Union Army officer compared the area to the
Florida Everglades. By now, however, all but fifty thousand
acres have been drained and converted to farmland, and of
that remaining swampland Mingo and the adjacent Duck
Creek State Wildlife Area preserve nearly sixty percent. The
native trees and plants that fill the refuge provide food and
shelter for migratory waterfowl traveling the so-called Mississippi Flyway, one of North America's four major migra-
tion pathways. The best time to see the birds is Sunday
afternoons during October and November when a special
seasonal twenty-five-mile self-guided driving tour can be
taken. Some fifty thousand Canadian geese and more than a

hundred thousand ducks usually enliven the refuge in the fall, while in the spring wildflowers and other blooms brighten the terrain. But Mingo is worth visiting at any time of year. Five short (one mile or less) hiking trails there offer a variety of contacts with the area's natural features. Boardwalk Nature Trail, the longest (at one mile), takes you on a "forest primeval" walk through the swamp, past thick vines, gossamer stretches of spiderwebs and stately trees, then across a floating bridge out to an observation tower to see a splendid sea of white lotus flowers nestling in large green leaves that cover the marshland. The buzz of insects, bird calls and the rustle of leaves add to your encounter with the unspoiled natural world from long ago as you return along the trail back to your car, the highways, civilization and the world of the twentieth century.

8. The Hills 'n' Hollows of Missouri's Ozarks:

Lake of the Ozarks Area
West to Hermitage, El Dorado Springs and Nevada
Laura Ingalls Wilder Home at Mansfield
Springfield, Capital of the Ozarks
The Branson Area of the Ozarks
West to the George Washington Carver Farmstead near Joplin, Thomas Hart Benton's Neosho, Noel and the Truman House at Lamar

In the early part of the century the Missouri Ozarks hamlet of Zebra, perched at the confluence of the Osage and Grand Glaize Rivers, consisted of a few houses, a feed store, a gas station and a general store and a post office. Summer Saturday evenings the locals, joined by country folk from the surrounding Ozark hills, would swing and sway the balmy night away under a mellow moon on the large wooden dance floor at the north end of town. In 1911 or 1912 the idea of damming the Osage River originated, but it wasn't until July 27, 1929, that the Union Electric Company of St. Louis received authorization to construct Bagnell Dam. Work on the dam, which cost thirty-six million dollars, began ten days later and within eighteen months the project was completed, the largest and the last dam in the nation built solely with private capital. Over the next three months the reservoir filled to form fifty-eight thousand-acre Lake of the Ozarks, at the time the world's biggest manmade lake. In the late 1930s the name Zebra was changed to Osage Beach, now the center of the highly developed Lake of the Ozarks vacation area in south-central Missouri. The Lake of the Ozarks region comprises one of the two main tourist areas in the Missouri Ozarks; the other, in and around Branson, lies at the southern edge of Missouri below Springfield.

Dragon-shaped Lake of the Ozarks boasts eleven hundred and fifty miles of shoreline, more than the California coast, most of it privately owned. Motels, resort hotels, condominiums, private homes, marinas, houseboats, souvenir shops, restaurants, country music theaters and other attractions, or distractions, abound in and around Osage Beach, definitely not a back road off-the-beaten-track sort of place. But the area does offer a few places of interest. A good starting point is the installation that stimulated all the development—Bagnell Dam, where Union Electric conducts free tours through the two-hundred-and-fifteen-thousand-kilowatt-capacity power generating facility. Before the dam rose, local residents made their livings largely in agriculture and forestry. In 1923 engineers carried out a preliminary study of the Osage River; then the power company optioned fifty thousand acres of land and on August 6, 1929, work began. Crews relocated more than three thousand old graves and topped or chopped down thousands of trees that stood above the full reservoir level of the projected lake. The denuded terrain looked desolate but before long water flowed in to form the new lake and the hydroelectric plant became operational on October 19, 1931. The region soon began to develop, the old days and ways of isolated hamlets and back country simplicity gave way to progress, and the area was never the same again.

To find the less contemporary and more country corners of the Ozarks, it's necessary to leave the Osage Beach area and wander some of the back roads. You can get the flavor of the Ozarks of long ago over at Tuscumbia, a hamlet of two hundred and forty-one people ten miles northeast of Bagnell Dam. The tiny town, seat of Miller County, was bypassed by the tourist boom and left high and dry after completion of the dam in 1931. Perched on one-hundred-seventy-five-foot-high bluffs above the Osage River, the century-and-a-half-old hamlet seems as frozen in time as the painted hands on the courthouse clock, which always shows the hour as eight. Across from the courthouse, a period piece, stands the old jail, which now houses a small historical museum. Around the other side of the lake, on route O a mile from highway 5 at Laurie, you'll find another relic of the old pre-dam days— St. Patrick's, listed on the National Register, the area's first Catholic church, built in 1870 of native stone with split-log pews. Around the southeast branch, or tentacle, of the lake spreads Lake of the Ozarks State Park, Missouri's largest (seventeen thousand acres), which offers wildlife, caves, camping facilities and a network of trails with such evocative names as Lazy Hollow, Squaw's Revenge, Fawn's Ridge and Swinging Bridge. By the lake's southwestern branch nestles Ha Ha Tonka State Park, an unspoiled corner of Missouri filled with bluffs, caves, a forty-eight-million-gallon-a-day spring (one of the state's fifteen largest) and many other natural features. Trails take you to such formations as the hundred-foot-high Natural Bridge and the adjacent Colosseum, a theater-like pit where, legend has it, Indians used to gather for tribal meetings. In 1801 Daniel Boone and his son Nathan spent the winter at Lake Ha Ha Tonka ("laughing water") trapping beaver, which the Osage Indians proceeded to wrest away from the white pioneers. A century later the area attracted another paleface, Robert M. Snyder, who purchased the property and then commissioned a three-story-high castle. Stone masons imported from Scotland constructed the castle with sandstone quarried on the land and hauled up the hill by a miniature railroad built for the purpose. Wood for the oak timbers and walnut interior used in the castle also came from the property. Work on the project stopped in 1906 after Snyder died in an automobile accident, but in 1922 his family completed the sixty-room castle that served as a residence and then, in 1937, became a resort that operated until 1943 when sparks from a kitchen stove touched off a fire, gutting the mansion. The tall walls still stand as silent but eloquent witnesses to Robert Snyder's grandly conceived but ill-fated dream castle.

The area south of Lake of the Ozarks is covered in the next paragraph, but off to the west lie a few attractions worth a visit if you're heading that way. North and south of highway 54 lie Truman Lake and Stockton Lake, sinuous bodies of water that offer fishing, boating, camping and other outdoor activities. A visitor center by Truman Dam near Warsaw contains exhibits about the area and offers a view of the lake and dam. At tiny Hermitage (less than four hundred people), Hickory County seat, stands the 1896 red brick courthouse topped by a shiny metal-roofed cupola, while behind the building perches the old pale yellow jailhouse out of the last century. Through the county, from 1858 to 1861, ran the Butterfield Overland Mail stagecoach and in the county at Bone Spring near Pomme de Terre River were found in the late 1830s mastodon bones, one assembled set being acquired in 1844 by the British Museum. Farther west on 54 lies the pleasant town of El Dorado Springs, established in 1879 when a couple on their way to Arkansas camped by the spring and decided to settle there. In the center of town nestles a delightful terraced park where the spring still bubbles forth and where, since 1888 except during World War I, summer band concerts have been held (Friday and Saturday evenings and Sunday afternoons in June, July and August). Old buildings ring the park. Across the street to the north is the Wayside Inn, a nineteenth-century hotel (no longer in operation) with displays of antique household objects, and at the corner of Main and Spring stands the 1884 Cruce Brothers Bank Building, now the Red Bull Exchange rummage shop. The 1915 Opera House across the street bulges with antiques on sale in an antique atmosphere created by lazy fans that twirl away the day, a pressed tin ceiling and old fixtures.

At Nevada (pronounced Na-VAY-dah in these parts), eighteen miles west, you'll find installed in the former Vernon County jail, whose cellroom of "medieval malevolence" was used for a hundred years ending in 1960, the Bushwacker Museum (listed on the National Register) that recalls the outlaws who terrorized western Missouri during the Civil War. To destroy the headquarters of the pesky Bushwackers who supported the Confederate cause, Union troops burned Nevada to the ground in 1863.

Returning now to the Lake of the Ozarks area, highway 5 takes you south from near Ha Ha Tonka State Park to Lebanon—home of prize-winning Broadway playwright Lanford Wilson, who captured the tone of his native Ozarks in such works as *Talley's Folly* and *5th of July*—and then on to Mansfield where the Laura Ingalls Wilder House and Museum recall the author of *Little House on the Prairie, The Little Town on the Prairie* and other "little" books. The author lived more than sixty of her ninety years at the house, left unchanged from the time of her death in 1957, and she wrote all of her nine books there. At the museum next to the two-story frame house, listed on the National Register, is Mrs. Wilder's writing desk and other family memorabilia. West of Mansfield lies Springfield, the Ozarks principal city, which boasts two buildings on the National Register—the restored 1909 Landers Theatre and the 1892 Bentley House, a twenty-two-room Queen Anne-style residence that contains the Museum of Ozarks History. Springfield claims what is believed to be the nation's largest redbud tree, at 1745 South National, and what is supposedly the world's largest sporting goods store, the Bass Pro Shops Outdoor World. The store sports huge aquariums, an indoor Ozark stream and waterfall and nearly one hundred and fifty thousand square feet crammed with goods for camping, hunting, fishing, athletics, boating and other such outdoor activities. There's even a taxidermy studio at the huge emporium. Before heading south to the Branson area of the Ozarks it's worth visiting the well-documented and marked Wilson's Creek National Battlefield site ten miles southwest of Springfield. The Battle of Wilson's Creek on August 10, 1861—one of the first major encounters of the Civil War—marked the beginning of the conflict in Missouri, whose four hundred skirmishes and battles, exceeded only by those in Virginia and Tennessee, made it the nation's third most fought-over state. A fiber-optic relief map and other displays at the Visitor Center trace the story of the bloody battle, where some thirteen hundred soldiers on each side were killed, wounded or missing, while a five-mile drive around the park shows you the lay of the land where the fighting took place. You'll see on the way to the Ray house, from 1858 to 1860 a mail stop on the Butterfield Overland Stage route and used by the Confederates as a field hospital, the positions occupied by Union and Southern forces as well as Bloody Hill, the high ground held by the men of Northern General Nathaniel Lyon. Lyon, the first Union general felled in battle during the Civil War, died from a musket shot that hit his heart. The battle finally ended when the outnumbered Northern troops withdrew to Springfield.

About thirty miles south of Springfield lies the Branson area of the Ozarks. Like the Lake of the Ozarks region, Branson has become overdeveloped and, like Lake of the Ozarks, the local lake—Table Rock—originated from a dammed river, the White. Local tourist attractions, many of them clustered along highway 76 west of Branson, include more than a dozen country music shows and such other lures as Hound Dawg Hollar ("hollow" in city English) Miniature Golf, Sammy Lane Pirate Cruise, Wilderness Safari, Mutton Hollow Craft Village, and the Waltzing Waters fountain display. If these are not to your taste you might prefer a few somewhat less garish places like the Stone Hill Winery, a branch of the nearly century-and-a-half-old wine firm in Hermann (section 2), the 1880s mining village theme park Silver Dollar City, and the "Shepherd of the Hills" show based on the 1907 novel of that name set in the Ozarks by local Harold Bell Wright, a minister whose nearby farm is open for tours.

Just south of Branson lies the town of Hollister, modeled after an English village, whose central section, the Downing Street Business District, was listed on the National Register in 1979. A stone's throw away is the School of the Ozarks, which occupies a nine-hundred-and-thirty-acre campus that includes a working farm. Each of the twelve hundred students, most of them from the Ozarks, is obligated to work nine hundred and sixty hours a year to pay a portion of his or her college costs. The main attraction on the spacious campus is the Ralph Foster Museum, named after the owner of a Springfield radio station with the call letters KWTO, "Keep Watching The Ozarks." Foster donated his collection of Indian artifacts to the museum, which also houses collections of firearms, cars, wildlife, coins, artwork and "Kewpie" dolls,

created in 1909 by Branson resident Rose O'Neill, said to
have inspired the song "Rose of Washington Square" when
she lived in New York's Greenwich Village near the Square.

In order to get a taste of the Ozarks back country you have
to break away from the tourist-thronged Branson area. Just
about any side road will take you to unspoiled corners of the
hilly well-wooded countryside, little changed from the time
the Osage Indians inhabited the region. The low rises and
valleys—no towering peaks or steep slopes—recall the local
saying, a paraphrase of a comment on the Ozarks by Carl
Sandburg, that "the hills ain't high but the hollers sure are
deep." One rather atmospheric and little-visited Ozark village, to take just a single example, is Pierce City off to the
west near Joplin. Now a bit of a ghost town, the settlement
once bustled with activity when the railroad maintenance
shops operated there, but when they moved away the town
declined. An old brick building labeled "Opera Hall" and a
nineteenth-century hardware store with antique fixtures recall Pierce City's early days. Near Diamond, to the west, the
George Washington Carver National Monument memorializes where the future famous black scientist was born in the
early 1860s. In a short sketch of his life Carver, once described as the man who had the worst start in life and the best
finish, relates how "my sister, mother and myself were
kuckluckled [kidnapped], and sold in Arkansas. . . . Mr.
Carver, the gentleman who owned my mother, sent a man
for us, but only I was brought back, nearly dead with
whooping cough." As a teenager, Carver, who'd taken the
last name of the family at the farm, moved to nearby Neosho
to begin school. After a series of jobs as a cook, laundryman
and farm worker Carver made his way to Winterset, Iowa,
and then moved on to Iowa Agricultural College, now Iowa
State, from which he graduated in 1894 (see Chapter IV,
section 8). Two years later Carver moved to Tuskegee Institute in Alabama where he did the research and agricultural

studies promoting the peanut plant as a restorative for cotton-exhausted soil which eventually made him famous. The Visitor Center at the Monument contains displays that recall the scientist's early years and his career, and a pleasant path around the site takes you to a statue of young Carver, a half-clad lad shown cradling a plant in his left palm; to the 1881 house of farm owner Moses Carver and to other sights on the property.

In 1889, thirteen years after young George Washington Carver left the Lincoln School for Colored Children in Neosho, Thomas Hart Benton was born in that southwestern Missouri town. Neosho back then still retained the atmosphere of the frontier west. The town lay only a few miles from the Indian Territory that only later became the state of Oklahoma. The famous Missouri artist and great-nephew of the equally renowned nineteenth-century Missouri Senator Thomas Hart Benton recalled in his autobiography *An Artist in America* those early years in Neosho: "My recollections of the Missouri of my childhood present a very rustic and backwoods atmosphere. The country was isolated, self-sufficient. Corn and wheat were readily grown in the bottoms. Game and fish were plentiful. Life was easy and, although perpetually secure, had very much of a pioneer flavor." Fish are still plentiful at Neosho, but in a civilized, scientific setting these days for the town—known as "Flower-Box City" for its floral clock and the many blooms which embellish its business district—boasts the nation's oldest National Fish Hatchery (1888), which raises rainbow trout to stock Ozark lakes.

Highway 71 leads you south to 59, a road that passes through some especially scenic Ozark country on its way to Noel. Four miles north of Noel is the Ginger Blue Resort, established in 1915 and named for an Indian chief supposedly buried on the grounds. A rustic antique-filled lodge, seventeen cozy cottages and other accommodations nestle by the

Elk River on the resort's forty-acre grounds. On 59 just north
of Noel the road passes beneath overhanging bluffs, limestone formations that extend out over the highway. Noel is a
quiet Ozark town of twelve hundred people, ringed by
wooded hills and watered by the Elk River as it curves
through the town after being fed by nearby Indian, Sugar and
Little Sugar Creeks. At Christmas every year Noel, like Santa
Claus, Indiana (Chapter II, section 4), receives for remail and
the affixing of a special cachet thousands of pieces of holiday
mail. Just past the descriptively named Southwest City—the
town lies in the very southwestern corner of the state—rises
the Tri-State Marker that designates the point where Missouri, Oklahoma and Arkansas meet. If you "collect" states,
a walk around the cornerstone that marks the western boundary of the original Mason-Dixon survey will take you to two
new ones in a few moments.

Head back north on highway 43 to Joplin, where Thomas
Hart Benton from nearby Neosho started his art career as a
cartoonist on the Joplin *American*. In his autobiography Benton relates how he used to frequent the House of Lords, turn-
of-the-century Joplin's main saloon where a painting of an
unclad woman transfixed the young man. Benton maintained
at the time that he "wasn't particularly interested in the naked
girl but that I was studying the picture because I was an artist
and wanted to see how it was done." Such was the beginning,
and end, of Benton's career in fiction. A fourteen-foot-long
mural by Benton in the Joplin Municipal Building, 303 East
3d Street, illustrates scenes from the town's past, while the
Dorothea B. Hoover Museum in Schifferdecker Park contains late nineteenth-century period rooms and other historical displays. Near the Municipal Building at 300 Main stands
the Post Memorial Art Reference Library, a delightful enclave
furnished with English antiques, fixtures and paintings. A
seven-century-old Gothic-style stone head of King Edward II
hangs over the door leading into the room where a beamed

ceiling, fireplace and pictures such as "Portrait of a Lady in a Pink Gown" and "Portrait of a Gentleman in a Wig" create the atmosphere of a library in an old English house. Just east of Joplin lies the attractive city of Carthage, whose large Romanesque-style Jasper County courthouse (1895), listed on the National Register, is built of the locally quarried marble for which the town is known. Among the many buildings constructed of the stone is the Missouri State Capitol in Jefferson City. The City Council Room in the courthouse retains its turn-of-the-century appearance and a mural in the building portrays the history of Carthage and Jasper County.

Due north of Carthage lies Lamar, seat of Barton County whose spacious red brick courthouse stands on one of Missouri's largest squares. The town was named after Mirabeau G. Lamar, president of the Republic of Texas, and the county after David Barton, Missouri's first U.S. Senator, so perhaps it's appropriate that yet another famous politician is associated with the place. On May 8, 1884, a local livestock dealer and his wife, John and Martha Ellen Truman, became parents of a boy they named Harry. So elated was the father that he nailed a mule shoe over the front door of his modest home and planted a pine tree in the yard. Both tree and shoe still decorate the yard and the one-and-a-half-story white frame Lamar house, listed on the National Register, where Harry Truman was born. John Truman bought the six-room house in 1882 for six hundred and eighty-five dollars, but eleven months after baby Harry arrived the family moved back to the Kansas City area, finally settling in Independence (section 5) in 1890. Small-town boy Truman, the last U.S. President not to have attended college, returned to Lamar in 1944 to deliver a speech accepting his nomination by Franklin Roosevelt as candidate for vice-president. Less than a year later Truman became president of the United States. On April 19, 1959, the former chief executive spoke at the dedication ceremony of the house, acquired in 1957 from descendants of early western lawman Wyatt Earp, who once served as a constable in Lamar and whose first wife lies buried in the town's East Cemetery. At the dedication Truman observed: "They don't do this for a former president until he's been dead fifty years. I feel like I've been buried and dug up while I'm still alive and I'm glad they've done it to me today."

The former President lies buried on the grounds of the Harry S Truman Library and Museum in Independence, so the one-time chief executive is now spending his death where he spent his life—in his beloved Missouri. The Trumans never left their home state. Both his father and mother were Missouri born (in 1851 and 1852, respectively) and bred (on Jackson County farms), and although after marrying they moved, the senior Trumans always stayed in the state: Lamar, Harrisonville, Belton, Grandview and, finally, Independence, where Harry grew up, married (a hometown girl), and to which he always returned, and where he now reposes forever. It is perhaps out of date to remain so close to home, so rooted to the land of one's clan—a quaintly old-fashoined trait that in a way typifies the conservative down-home way of life that still exists in the American Midwest.

9. The River Road South:

The Frozen-in-Time Mississippi River Hamlet of Kimmswick
De Soto, Population Center of the U.S.
The Lead District: Old Mines, Potosi, Bonne Terre and
Ironton
The Old French Town of Sainte Genevieve and Old German
Settlements at Wittenberg and Altenburg
Bollinger Mill
River Towns: Cape Girardeau and New Madrid
Across the Mississippi and A Farewell to the Midwest

In the middle part of the country all rivers, if not all roads, lead to the Mississippi, a watery artery that drains the nation's heartland. Waters from the Des Moines in Iowa, from the Wabash in Indiana, from Missouri's Missouri and Illinois's Illinois eventually merge into the mighty Mississippi, patriarch of rivers—"Father of Waters," "Old Man River." An excursion on the River Road along the Mississippi furnishes a fitting conclusion to our long journey through the Midwest from east to west to south through Indiana and Illinois to Iowa and, finally, across Missouri. The northern half of Missouri's River Road, above St. Louis, is covered in section 3; here we'll wander down the Mississippi, starting at the riverside village of Kimmswick, twenty-five miles south of St. Louis.

Kimmswick isn't a particularly old town: Theodore Kimm, a native of Germany who'd worked in St. Louis, laid out the village in 1859. After the Civil War Kimmswick prospered, with both train and riverboat traffic stopping there. But when the auto age arrived highways bypassed the town and Kimmswick fell into decay. In 1970 Lucianna Gladney Ross, daughter of a founder of the Seven-Up soft-drink company, spearheaded the town's restoration and now Kimmswick, whose central section fits neatly into a four-square-block grid, offers a freshly painted but frozen-in-time picture of a late nineteenth-century Mississippi River village. Four or so antique buildings have been moved to the town from elsewhere in Missouri, among them the pre-Revolutionary War log Old House, now a restaurant and once a roadside stagecoach stop and tavern frequented by Ulysses S. Grant when he was stationed at Jefferson Barracks in south St. Louis. Kimmswick's oldest indigenous buildings, which date from the 1860s and 1870s, now house antique and craft shops. The post office, still outfitted with old fixtures, retains the atmosphere of the last century. By Rock Creek south of town stands a red granite boulder which marks "El Camino Real," the King's Road which ran along the route of an old Indian trail linking St. Louis with New Madrid, a Mississippi River town in the southern part of Missouri near the so-called "bootheel," the state's heel-shaped far southeastern corner.

Before continuing south you might want to stop at the new Mastodon State Park Museum, a mile or two from Kimmswick, where a ten-foot-tall replica of a mastodon skeleton portrays the prehistoric animals whose twelve-thousand-year-old remains were discovered at the site. Also on view are other exhibits and dioramas as well as an excavation pit. At the British Museum in London stands a mastodon reconstructed from bones believed to have originated in the area. Highway 21 swings away from the river and leads you south to the century-old (1872) Sandy Creek covered bridge, one of four such spans in Missouri, which sits in a rustic niche below a wooded hill and above the winding stream. Twelve miles south of the bridge turn left off 21 and onto road N to De Soto where, at least until the next census, a red, white and blue billboard proclaims the place as "Population Center of the United States." At this spot you find yourself in the heart of the heartland, the very center of the United

States, based on geographic distribution of the nation's nearly two hundred and fifty million people. Since 1790, when the country's first census put the population center just east of Baltimore, the center point has moved about seven hundred and fifty miles west and eighty miles south, finally crossing the Mississippi River to De Soto, a town of six thousand, in 1980. In 1890 the center reached Indiana, where it remained until 1950 when Illinois claimed the honor for three decades. Demographic experts estimate that the point should remain in Missouri until 2030 when it will cross into Oklahoma.

Highway 21 passes through Washington State Park, where thousand-year-old rock carvings evidence the early presence in the area of Indians, on the way to the world's largest lead district. Towns with names such as Mine La Motte (site of the first mine: 1720), Valles Mines, Mineral Point, Leadwood and Leadington recall the area's long connection with lead mining. Missouri's lead land—which even boasts its own flower: *Amorpha canescens,* a two- to four-foot-high blue-flowered shrub that grows in the ore-rich soil there—was first exploited when Frenchman Philippe François Renault, whose last name survives at the Illinois town across the Mississippi (see Chapter III, section 2), arrived to extract the mineral for France's Company of the Indies. The lead mines, Missouri's first industry, attracted to the state its first permanent settlers. Still today the deposits yield some 90 percent, more than five hundred thousand tons, of the lead mined in the United States. At one of the earliest mining settlements, Old Mines, which one commentary says "was accumulated rather than founded," the early French influence survived until well into the twentieth century, with residents of the rural town speaking French, or at least a dialect of the language, until as late as the 1970s. The interior of Old Mines' St. Joachim church, which dates from 1828, has been modernized, but the outside retains its original appearance and the nearby cemetery also recalls the old days. A few miles down 21 at Potosi, named for the Mexican silver mining city of San Luis Potosí, you'll find the grave of Moses Austin, father of Stephen Austin, whose name designates the capital city of Texas. In 1796 Moses Austin, one of Missouri's first entrepreneurs, expanded his interests from his lead mines in Virginia to the lead deposits near Potosi that he founded. But he's better known as the pioneer who in 1819 devised a plan to form an American colony in the then-Spanish territory of Texas. In 1820 Austin rode by horseback to San Antonio where the Spanish authorities gave him permission to settle three hundred Americans in the area. On the trip back to Missouri Austin died in 1821 near Potosi where he lies buried in a simple whitewashed tomb (wrongly dated 1820) behind the century-and-a-half-old Presbyterian church. After Moses Austin's death his son Stephen carried out their plans to colonize Texas.

The Missouri Mines State Historic Site at Flat River includes a mining museum installed in a milling complex once used by the St. Joe Minerals Company, but the best place to get a "hands on" impression of the area's mining industry is at Bonne Terre, French for "good earth," just east of Potosi. At Bonne Terre Mine, listed on the National Register and said to be the world's largest manmade caverns, a tour through the netherworld of huge rock rooms of the abandoned mine shows you where and how the lead was extracted. When the operation closed down in 1962 the water pumps that had functioned around the clock were shut off, after which the mine's lower levels filled with water to create nearly three-hundred-foot-deep lakes now used for scuba diving.

Before returning east to the River Road it's worth continuing south to the Ironton area. Two oddly named state parks recall the region's age-old geological history: Elephant Rocks, whose huge boulders (hefty Dumbo, the largest, measures twenty-seven feet long and seventeen feet wide and tips the scales at nearly seven hundred tons) originated in the

pre-Cambrian period a billion years ago, while Johnson's
Shut-Ins includes a series of canyon-like gorges formed by
rhyolite, some of the world's oldest exposed rock. A mile or
two from the shut-ins, but reached by a roundabout route, is
the Union Electric Taum Sauk hydroelectric plant (open to
visitors) which generates power for customer use during
peak daytime periods, then consumes power at night and on
weekends by pumping the water back to the upper reservoir
atop Proffit Mountain. This fifteen-hundred-and-ninety-
foot-high hill is what passes for a mountain in Missouri,
whose highest point is nearby seventeen-hundred-and-sev-
enty-two-foot-tall Taum Sauk, where a lookout tower affords a far-ranging panorama. Back down in the lowland
nestle Arcadia, Ironton and Pilot Knob, three contiguous
towns. On the grounds of Ironton's 1858 Iron County courthouse, which still bears scars of Confederate gunfire, stands a
delightful gazebo (1899) with elaborate "gingerbread" wood
trim. Both the courthouse and the gazebo are listed on the
National Register of Historic Places. Nearby St. Paul's Episcopal church (1870), its wood painted a bright white, offers a
splendid example of the American Gothic style. Over in Pilot
Knob, a mile or so north, you'll find another reminder of the
Civil War—Fort Davidson, the first command post Ulysses
S. Grant received after his promotion to general in August
1861, and a fort where one of the most decisive battles in
Missouri later took place. On September 27, 1864, some
twelve thousand Confederate troops under General Sterling
Price attacked the installation, defended by a thousand or so
Union soldiers. Although the federal troops retreated to
Rolla, their resistance managed to deter Price from con-
tinuing his advance north toward St. Louis. Price instead
turned west, engaging the enemy at Boonville, Glasgow and
Lexington, all three along the Missouri River (see sections 5
and 6), before finally meeting defeat at the Battle of Westport
(Kansas City) on October 23, 1864. Detailed signs recount

the story of the battle at Fort Davidson, where the moat and raised earthen perimeter still survive.

From Ironton you can return east toward the river via highway 72, which passes through the scenic Arcadia Valley, then head north to the old French town of Sainte Genevieve. The rich river bottomland and the lead deposits west of Ste. Genevieve attracted settlers to the area—some from Kaskaskia, the French town then just across the Mississippi in Illinois (see Chapter III, section 2)—in the mid-eighteenth century, and by about 1750 a village sprang up along the banks of the river. This was the nation's earliest permanent settlement west of the Mississippi. After the flood of 1785 Ste. Genevieve residents moved the town to higher ground, there constructing a French-style village that essentially survives to this day. When Timothy Flint, an early traveler in the middle part of the country, visited Ste. Genevieve in 1816 he found "a considerable village, almost wholly French," he recounted in *Reflections of the Last Ten Years in the Valley of the Mississippi*. "In this place we were introduced to amiable and polished people; and saw a town evidencing the possession of a considerable degree of refinement. Here we first see the French mode of constructing houses, and forming a village. . . . Their modes of building, enclosing, and managing, are very unlike those of the Americans. Here the French is the predominant language." That French-type architecture Flint found still dominates the quiet photogenic town, a National Historic District. Houses bearing such names as Amoureaux, Beauvais and Guibourd-Valle, all built in the late eighteenth century and all with galleries and other French architectural features, abound. The Felix Valle House, a State Historic Site, is open to visitors, as are half a dozen or so other old buildings (more during the annual Jour de Fete held the second weekend in August). The new Great River Road Interpretive Center, installed in a French Creole-style structure at the corner of Main and Market Streets, houses the tourist office and offers exhibits on the Mississippi River as well as sketches of local historic sights. The Ste. Genevieve museum on Du Bourg Place contains collections of local memorabilia, including a town safe supposedly looted by Jesse James in 1873 and ten birds said to have been mounted by ornithologist John James Audubon who lived in the village in 1811. Along the south side of Du Bourg Place, on which stands the solid brick Catholic church (successor to the original 1790s log sanctuary on the site), ran Missouri's first European-built road. Used to transport lead from the mines west of town, the route was later (in 1851) converted to a forty-two-mile plank road, the longest such highway of its type in the U.S. In the nearby cemetery, the state's oldest (used from 1787 to 1833), repose many of Ste. Genevieve's founding fathers and mothers, their graves marked with French-inscribed tombstones. Those early settlers brought to the area "La Guignolée," a festive New Year's Eve celebration still practiced at Ste. Genevieve. A mural in the town's post office portrays the event.

The French weren't the only Europeans to settle along the west bank of the Mississippi and bring to the area their customs and religion. South of Ste. Genevieve beyond Kaskaskia (Chapter III, section 2), a spur of Illinois located on the west side of the Mississippi at a site you'll pass heading south on highway 61, lie the old German villages of Altenburg, Wittenberg and Frohna. Before proceeding on to those tiny towns (four people live in Wittenberg, less than three hundred in each of the other two) it's worth stopping in Perryville to see the imposing red brick courthouse (1904), the National Register-listed stone (dating from 1828) and brick (added in 1855) Faherty House, which contains the Perry County Museum, and St. Mary's of the Barrens, the first Catholic seminary in the Louisiana Territory (1818) and the fourth in the U.S.

The seminary's Tuscan-style Church of the Assumption,

begun in 1827, was planned as an exact reproduction of the Vincentians' mother church in Rome but the brothers reduced the building's Missouri version to a scale one-third the size of the Italian original. From the seminary, believed to be the oldest institution of higher learning west of the Mississippi, went missionaries to the Far East as well as the first bishops of St. Louis, Pittsburgh, Buffalo, Galveston and New Orleans. Buildings on the campus house richly endowed museums, with large collections of porcelain, paperweights and Oriental objects brought back from the East by missionaries a century and a half ago. The rare book room contains manuscripts and books ranging from the twelfth to the nineteenth century and also some eight hundred first editions of American authors.

The cluster of German villages south of Perryville recalls the area's Lutheran heritage. In 1839 Pastor Martin Stephan led a group of some seven hundred Lutherans from Saxony to America to seek religious freedom. Most of the families settled in Perry County in and around Altenburg, one of the country's earliest settlements established for purely religious reasons. At Altenburg stand relics of those early days—the 1839 Log Cabin Concordia Seminary, listed on the National Register, and two Trinity Lutheran churches, an 1844 limestone sanctuary with a bell from a Spanish monastery, which later served as the area's so-called "Big" school, and the 1867 white-steepled structure whose interior sports a barrel-vaulted ceiling and long lateral balconies. Altenburg also boasts the Oldtimers Agricultural Museum and Park, with a collection of more than six hundred pieces of antique farm equipment including tractors, buggies, sleighs and implements. At nearby Frohna you'll find further reminders of the early Lutheran presence in the area. The Saxon Lutheran Memorial, also listed on the National Register, comprises an eleven-and-a-half-acre park with old buildings constructed by the pioneers. The relics include early log structures, the red brick 1898 "Little" school (a bit smaller than Altenburg's "Big" school), and the white frame 1839 Concordia Lutheran church, as well as what's said to be the country's largest boxwood bush. Wittenberg, just down the road, is virtually a ghost town, but you can see there the historic Mississippi River Tower Rock formation (Chapter III, section 3) and the world's second largest pipeline suspension bridge. Nearby Appleton is a picturesque nineteenth-century settlement with a grist mill, dam and waterfall, while at Brazeau stands the 1819 Presbyterian church and museum.

As you continue south on highway 61 you'll be following the route of the old "Camino Real," the late eighteenth-century Spanish King's Highway between New Madrid and St. Louis, once an ancient Indian trail, later a trace and trade route, then (in 1805) a designated public road and in 1812 a postal route. At Jackson rise the 1819 hand-hewn log Old McKendree Chapel, believed the oldest Protestant church still standing west of the Mississippi—services continued there until 1902—and the 1840s-vintage nine-room Oliver House, a Federal-style structure listed on the National Register, which houses antiques and local memorabilia.

On weekends the St. Louis, Iron Mountain and Southern Railway runs an old-time steam-drawn excursion train from Jackson south to Gordonville and to Delta. On the banks of the Whitewater River a few miles west of Jackson stands Bollinger Mill and Covered Bridge, listed on the National Register. The combination of the 1867 four-story stone and brick mill and the 1868 one-hundred-and-forty-foot-long covered bridge, below which extends a waterfall with gleaming strands of gossamer-like rivulets, presents one of the state's most picturesque scenes. George Frederick Bollinger, who came to the area in 1797 from North Carolina, built the first two mills on the site, part of a six-hundred-and-forty-acre land grant he received from Don Luis Lorimier, the Spanish commandant at nearby Cape Girardeau. The mill soon ground out substantial profits for Bollinger, who served as one of Missouri's original senators in the legislature that met at the first state capital in St. Charles (section 2). The covered bridge by the mill is one of Missouri's four such surviving spans. In 1942 eleven such bridges still existed in the state but most of them disappeared before the Missouri legislature finally passed a bill in 1967 to preserve the four which then remained.

The above-mentioned Luis Lorimier of nearby Cape Girardeau established that town about 1793 near a rocky promontory overlooking the Mississippi River, said to be the world's only inland cape. Sixty years earlier Frenchman Jean Baptiste Girardot had set up on the promontory a trading post, now commemorated by a marker in Cape Rock Park. As the first high point above the confluence of the Ohio and Mississippi Rivers, Cape Girardot—so spelled on early maps—enjoyed a strategic position which, during the Civil War, attracted Union troops to the town. The old brick riverfront building that now houses Port Cape Girardeau restaurant served as headquarters for General Ulysses S. Grant during his stay in the city. Atop a terraced hill a few blocks west of the river stands the 1854 Common Pleas Courthouse with a splendid view of the Mississippi from its steps. Scattered around the center of town are other historic structures, including 1853 Gothic-style pointy-spired St. Vincent's church and the Glenn House on South Spanish Street, both listed on the National Register. The River Heritage Museum contains exhibits relating to the Mississippi, while the Southeast Missouri State University museum features a collection of pre-Columbian effigies, Indian artifacts and statues from the 1904 Louisiana Purchase Exhibition (World's Fair) in St. Louis.

Thomas Jefferson's purchase of the Louisiana Territory from France in 1803 ended the trading of the area back and forth between France and Spain, exchanges based on European power politics. The French originally claimed the area but the 1762 Treaty of Fontainbleu transferred Louisiana to Spain. Then, in 1800, the Treaty of San Ildefonso conveyed the Louisiana Territory back to France. Cape Girardeau's Spanish Street, the El Camino Real route (now highway 61) and the name New Madrid, a Mississippi River town some sixty miles south of Cape Girardeau, all recall Spain's dominion over the region in the late eighteenth century. The first Spaniard who visited New Madrid is said to have been Hernando de Soto, who in 1540 supposedly held the earliest European religious service west of the Mississippi, near an Indian mound that rises by the south interchange of highway 61 and Interstate 55. In 1789 former Revolutionary War colonel George Morgan, representing the Spanish government, selected the site of New Madrid as capital of the colony Spain hoped to establish in the Louisiana Territory. After the United States acquired the Territory fourteen years later the designation "New Madrid" was a misnomer, one that became famous in December 1811 when the first of a series of tremors known as the New Madrid earthquake shook the area. Shook? "Rearranged" would be a more appropriate word: the quake opened huge fissures in the ground, twisted the Mississippi into flowing backwards for a time, created lakes, leveled buildings, felled thousands of trees, raised and lowered the earth and caused cascades of landslides. The tremors, felt over two-thirds of the United States, are the most severe on record. Eliza Bryan, a resident of New Madrid back then, wrote that "Until the 4th of February the earth was in continual agitation, visibly waving as a gentle sea," thus perhaps making people in the American Midwest, far from the oceans, seasick. These days somnolent New Madrid is definitely a place that doesn't move very much. The sleepy river town offers a scattering of nineteenth-century houses, including the fifteen-room 1860 Hunter-

Dawson mansion, a State Historic Site. Downtown, just by the Mississippi, stands the century-old Kendall Saloon building that now houses the local museum. The tavern once sported signs "Last Chance" (on the city side) and "First Chance" (on the river side) to entice departing and arriving packet-boat passengers to stop in for a drink. The museum contains little on the famous earthquake, displaying instead a miscellaneous collection of old furniture, toys and household objects such as might be found in granny's long-forgotten attic. From the museum you can drive up onto the levee to gain a view of the Mississippi at one of the river's widest points.

But the only way truly to experience the great river—the river that our trips through the Midwest have constantly encountered—is to pass across it. Due east of New Madrid—across from Hickman, Kentucky, where the Mississippi curls back to the north after its contortions every which way—you can catch a car ferry that carries you across the waterway. The ferry is a catch-as-catch-can proposition: unlike the Mississippi, the boat runs erratically. But it's worth taking a chance, for the ride across the Mississippi, "rolling, like a destiny, through its realms of solitude and shade," as historian Francis Parkman described it, on the Hickman ferry is a great experience. No telling what mood the river will be in the day you're there, perhaps turbulent and angry in the great spring floods, or leaden and sullen under gray winter skies, or serene and soft in the dusk of a long summer's day. Crossing, you'll see and feel the fabled river's grandeur and power, especially out in the middle of the Mississippi where the ferry fights to cut across the current. Here magnificent in its size, sweep and solitude, with nary a building in sight, the river rolls on as it has since time began and as it shall forever. For a few passing minutes—as you leave Missouri and head toward Kentucky, another state, another region—you are part of the great river. The little boat bobs and dips in the current, the Missouri shore grows more distant, the river—rolling, roiling—flows on. Then, before you know it, you touch land: your journey through the great American heartland at an end, you finally leave the Mississippi and bid the Midwest farewell.

Sources and Resources

I   An Introduction to the American Heartland

The Middle West in American History, Dan Elbert Clark (Thomas Y. Crowell Company, New York, 1937)

Midwest at Noon, Graham Hutton (University of Chicago Press, Chicago, 1946)

The Midwest Pioneer: His Ills, Cures, & Doctors, Madge E. Pickard and R. Carlyle Buley (Henry Schuman, New York, 1946)

The Midwest, The Editors of Look, introduction by Louis Bromfield (Houghton Mifflin Company, Boston, 1947)

Midwest Heritage, John Drury (A.A. Wyn, Inc., New York, 1948)

Main Street on the Middle Border, Lewis Atherton (Indiana University Press, Bloomington, 1954)

The North American Midwest: A Regional Geography, John H. Garland, ed (John Wiley & Sons, Inc., New York, 1955)

Missouri Writers, Elijah L. Jacobs and Forrest E. Wolverton (State Publishing Company, St. Louis, 1955)

The Heritage of the Middle West, John J. Murray, ed (University of Oklahoma Press, Norman, 1958)

The Midwest: Myth or Reality, a symposium by Thomas T. McAvoy, et al (University of Notre Dame Press, Notre Dame, Indiana, 1961)

A History of Indiana Literature, Arthur W. Shumaker (Indiana Historical Society, 1962)

The Middle Western Farm Novel in the Twentieth Century, Roy W. Meyer (University of Nebraska Press, Lincoln, 1965)

The Inland Ground: An Evocation of the American Middle West, Richard Rhodes (Atheneum, New York, 1970)

A Literary History of Iowa, Clarence A. Andrews (University of Iowa Press, Iowa City, 1972)

The New Country: A Social History of the American Frontier, 1776–1890, Richard A. Bartless (Oxford University Press, New York, 1974)

Middle West Country, William Carter (Houghton Mifflin Company, Boston, 1975)

The Old Country School: The Story of Rural Education in the Middle West, Wayne E. Fuller (The University of Chicago Press, Chicago, 1982)

II   Indiana

1. Indiana Tourism Development Division, Suite 700, One North Capitol, Indianapolis, Indiana 46204 (1-800-2-WANDER)
   For Indiana state park information: 1-800-622-4931
   For Indiana festival information: 1-800-622-4464
2. Parke County Tourist Information Center, East Ohio Street, Rockville, Indiana 47872 (317-569-5226)
   Turkey Run Inn, Marshall, Indiana 47859 (317-597-2211)
   Ernie Pyle State Memorial, Box 338, Dana, Indiana 47847 (317-665-3633)
   Terre Haute Convention and Visitors Bureau, P.O. Box 500, Terre Haute, Indiana 47808 (812-234-5555)
   Paul Dresser Birthplace, First and Farrington Streets, Fairbanks Park, Terre Haute, Indiana 47802 (812-235-9717). Open May through September, Sundays 1-4 p.m. or by appointment
   Eugene V. Debs Home, 451 N. 8th Street, Terre Haute, Indiana

47807 (812-232-2163). Open 2-5 p.m. daily except Fridays and holidays

3. Vincennes Log Cabin Visitor Center, First and Harrison Streets, Vincennes, Indiana 47591 (812-885-4339)

Historic New Harmony, Inc., New Harmony, Indiana 47631 (812-682-4474)

The New Harmony Inn, New Harmony, Indiana 47631. (812-682-4491)

4. Holiday World, P.O. Box 36, Santa Claus, Indiana 47579 (812-937-4401)

Lincoln Boyhood National Memorial, Lincoln City, Indiana 47552 (812-937-4757)

St. Meinrad Archabbey and Seminary, St. Meinrad, Indiana 47577 (812-357-6611)

Spring Valley Area Chamber of Commerce, P.O. Box 347, French Lick, Indiana 47432 (812-936-2405)

French Lick Springs Golf and Tennis Resort, French Lick, Indiana 47432 (812-936-9981) or (1-800-457-4042) (In Indiana, 1-800-742-4095)

House of Clocks, 225 College Street, French Lick, Indiana 47432 (812-936-4238)

Indiana Railway Museum, Highway 56 and Monon Street, French Lick, Indiana 47432 (812-936-2405). Train trips depart at 10 a.m., 1 p.m. and 4 p.m. April through November on Saturdays, Sundays and holidays

5. Indiana University Visitors Center, State Road 46 Bypass, Bloomington, Indiana 47405 (812-335-6207)

Indiana Memorial Union, University of Indiana, Bloomington, Indiana 47405 (812-335-2536)

Theodore C. Steele State Memorial, Belmont, Indiana 47448 812-988-2785

Brown County Chamber of Commerce, P.O. Box 164, Nashville, Indiana 47448 (812-988-4920)

Brown County Playhouse, Nashville, Indiana 47448 (812-988-2123)

Abe Martin Lodge, Brown County State Park, P.O. Box 25, Nashville, Indiana 47448 (812-988-4418)

Columbus Visitors Center, 506 Fifth Street, Columbus, Indiana 47201 (812-372-1954)

6. Madison Chamber of Commerce, 301 East Main, Madison, Indiana 47250 (812-265-2956)

   Victorian Inn, 801 East Main, Madison, Indiana 47250 (812-265-2471)

   Howard Steamboat Museum, 1101 East Market Street, Jeffersonville, Indiana 47130 (812-283-3728)

   Hillerich and Bradsby Company, 1525 Charlestown-New Albany Road, Jeffersonville, Indiana 47130 (812-288-6611). Tours of the baseball bat operation leave at 10:30 a.m. and 2:30 p.m. Monday through Friday

7. Whitewater Canal State Memorial, Box 88, Metamora, Indiana 47030 (317-647-6512)

   Whitewater Valley Railroad, P.O. Box 406, Connersville, Indiana 47331 (317-825-2054). The train leaves at noon Saturdays, Sundays and holidays from the first Sunday in May to the first Sunday in November; in addition, Christmas trips operate on weekends in December (you can even rent an entire caboose, with a capacity of twenty people, for those holiday trips)

   Levi Coffin House Historic Site, Fountain City, Indiana 47341 (317-847-2885)

   Moore Museum, Earlham College, West National Road, Richmond, Indiana 47374 (317-962-6561, ext. 302)

   Wayne County Historical Museum, 1150 North "A" Street, Richmond, Indiana 47374 (317-962-5756)

   Hill Floral Products, 2117 Peacock Road, Richmond, Indiana 47374 (317-962-2555). The greenhouses are open September through June; for tours, call 317-935-8687.

   Wilbur Wright Historic Site, R.R. 2, Box 258A, Millville, Indiana 47346 (317-332-2513)

8. James Whitcomb Riley Birthplace, 250 West Main Street, Greenfield, Indiana 46140 (317-462-5462)

   Conner Prairie Pioneer Settlement, 13400 Allisonville Road, Noblesville, Indiana 46060 (317-773-3633). The village is open from early April to late November and for special candlelight tours in December.

Zionsville Chamber of Commerce, 135 South Elm Street, Zionsville, Indiana 46077 (317-873-3836)

9. Huntington County Chamber of Commerce, 12 West Market Street, Huntington, Indiana 46750 (219-356-5300)

Wabash Courthouse, 30 South Wabash Street, Wabash, Indiana 46992 (219-563-0661)

Circus City Museum, 154 North Broadway, Peru, Indiana 46970 (317-472-3918)

Elwood Haynes Museum, 1915 South Webster, Kokomo, Indiana 46902 (317-452-3471)

Auburn-Cord-Deusenberg Museum, 1600 South Wayne Street, Auburn, Indiana 46706 (219-925-1444)

Discovery Hall Museum, 120 South St. Joseph Street, South Bend, Indiana 46601 (219-284-9714)

Studebaker National Museum, 520 South Lafayette, South Bend, Indiana 46601 (219-284-9108)

Notre Dame University, Department of Public Relations, South Bend, Indiana 46556 (219-239-7367); The Snite Museum of Art at Notre Dame (219-239-5466)

Miles Laboratories Visitors Center, 701 West Randolph Street, Elkhart, Indiana 46515 (219-262-7966)

Colonel C.G. Conn Home, 723 Strong Avenue, Elkhart, Indiana 46515

Midwest Museum of American Art, 429 South Main Street, Elkhart, Indiana 46515 (219-293-6660)

Amish Acres, 1600 West Market, Nappanee, Indiana 46550 (219-773-4188)

Fulton County Round Barn Festival, P.O. Box 512, Rochester, Indiana 46975 (219-223-5329)

Tippecanoe Battlefield and Museum, Prophet Rock Road, Battle Ground, Indiana 47920 (317-567-2147)

Lew Wallace Study, Wallace at Pike Street, Crawfordsville, Indiana 47933 (317-362-5769)

10. Useful books on Indiana culture and history
The Indiana Gazetter, John Scott (1826)
Twelve Months in New-Harmony, Paul Brown (Cincinnati, 1827)
Readings in Indiana History (Indiana University, 1914)

Indiana Past and Present, George S. Cottman (Max R. Hyman Publisher, Indianapolis, 1915)

The Wabash, William E. Wilson (Farrar & Rinehart, New York, 1940)

Indiana: An Interpretation, John Bartlow Martin (Alfred A. Knopf, New York, 1947)

Readings in Indiana History, compiled by Gayle Thornbrough and Dorothy Riker (Indiana Historical Bureau, Indianapolis, 1956)

My Indiana, Irving Leibowitz (Prentice-Hall, Inc., Englewood Cliffs, N.J. 1964)

Indiana A Self-appraisal, Donald F. Carmony, ed (Indiana University Press, Bloomington, 1966)

Indiana: A History, William E. Wilson (Indiana University Press, Bloomington, 1966)

We Came Rejoicing, Harvey Jacobs (Rand McNally & Co. 1967)

Travel Accounts of Indiana 1679–1961, compiled by Shirley S. McCord (Indiana Historical Bureau, 1970)

Hoosier Caravan A Treasure of Indiana Life and Lore, selected by R.E. Banta (Indiana University Press, Bloomington, 1975)

A Pictorial History of Indiana, Dwight W. Hoover (Indiana University Press, Bloomington, 1980)

The Indiana Years 1903–1941, Walter B. Hendrickson (Indiana Historical Society, 1983)

The Indiana Book of Records, Firsts, and Fascinating Facts, Fred D. Cavinder (Indiana University Press, Bloomington, 1985)

The Indiana Way A State History, James H. Madison (Indiana University Press, Bloomington, 1986)

III   Illinois

1. Illinois operates three tourism offices: 620 East Adams, Springfield 62701, 217-782-7139; Suite 3-400, 100 West Randolph, Chicago 60601, 312-917-4732; 2309 West Main, Marion 62959, 618-997-4371. An Illinois State Tourist Information Center office is at Suite 108, 310 South Michigan Ave.,

Chicago 60604, 312-793-2094. An Illinois traveline gives news of current events in the state: 1-800-252-8987 (in Illinois), 1-800-637-8560 (adjacent states, plus Minnesota, Michigan, Ohio and Tennessee).

2. Holy Family Church, 120 East First, Cahokia, Illinois 62206 (618-337-2880)

   Jarrot House, East First St., Cahokia, Illinois 62206 (618-332-1782)

   Cahokia Court House State Historic Site, First and Elm Street, Cahokia, Illinois 62206 (618-332-1782)

   Cahokia Mounds State Historic Site 7850 Collinsville Road, East St. Louis, Illinois 62201 (618-344-5268)

   Cahokia Mounds Museum Society, P.O. Box 382, Collinsville, Illinois 62234 (618-344-5268). The Society can provide information on the Archeological Field School program through which non-professional archeologists can learn basic excavating and artifact processing techniques on a dig at Cahokia.

   Fort de Chartres State Historic Site, and Peithman Museum, Prairie Du Rocher, Illinois 62277 (618-284-7230)

   Fort Kaskaskia State Historic Site, R.R. 1-Box 63, Ellis Grove, Illinois 62241 (618-859-3741)

   Pierre Menard Home State Historic Site, R.R. 1-Box 58, Ellis Grove, Illinois 62241 (618-859-3031)

   Chester Chamber of Commerce, R.R. 2, P.O. Box 177-A, Chester, Illinois 62233 (618-826-3706)

3. Ma Hales's Boarding House Restaurant, Grand Tower, Illinois 62942 (618-565-8384)

   Crab Orchard & Egyptian Railroad, 514 N. Market Street, Marion, Illinois 62959 (618-993-5769)

   Shawnee National Forest, Forest Supervisor, 901 South Commercial Street, Harrisburg, Illinois 62946 (618-253-7114)

   Kornthal Church, 207 East Whitlock, Jonesboro, Illinois 62952 (618-833-2915)

   Magnolia Manor, 2700 Washington, Cairo, Illinois 62914 (618-734-0201)

   For Superman information: Metropolis, Illinois 62960 (618-524-2141)

Fort Massac State Historic Site, P.O. Box 708, Metropolis, Illinois 62960 (618-524-4712)

Riverview Mansion Hotel, Golconda, Illinois 62938 (618-683-3001)

Cave-In-Rock State Park, Cave In Rock, Illinois 62919 (618-289-4325)

Old Slave House, Route 1, Junction, Illinois 62954 (618-276-4410)

Shawneetown Bank, Shawneetown, Illinois 62984 (618-269-3303)

4. Edwards County Historical Society, Albion, Illinois 62806 (618-445-3612)

Monastery Museum, 110 South Garrett Street, Teutopolis, Illinois 62467 (217-857-6404) Tours available 1 to 4 p.m. the first Sunday of each month between April and November.

Ingram's Log Cabin Village, R.R. 2, Kinmundy, Illinois 62854 (618-547-7123)

William Jennings Bryan Home, 408 South Broadway, Salem, Illinois 62881 (618-548-1236)

Vandalia Statehouse, 315 West Gallatin, Vandalia, Illinois 62471 (618-283-1161)

Richard W. Bock Sculpture Museum, Greenville College, 315 East College Avenue, Greenville, Illinois 62246 (618-664-1840, ext. 321)

Louis Latzer Homestead, R.R. 3, Highland, Illinois 62249 (618-654-7957)

Ratcliff Inn, Main Cross Street, Carmi, Illinois 62821 (618-382-2404)

Robinson-Stewart House Museum, 110 South Main Cross Street, Carmi, Illinois 62821 (618-382-2404)

McCoy Memorial Library, Washington Street, McLeansboro, Illinois 62859 (618-643-2125)

The Peoples National Bank, 108 North Washington Street, McLeansboro, Illinois 62859 (618-643-4303)

Mitchell Art Museum, Richview Road, P.O.Box 923, Mt. Vernon, Illinois 62864 (618-242-1236)

Appellate Court House, 14th and Main, Mt. Vernon, Illinois 62864 (618-242-3120)

Original Mineral Springs Hotel, 506 Hanover, Okawville, Illinois 62271 (618-243-5458)

Schlosser House, Okawville, Illinois 62271 (618-243-6548). The house is open weekends from noon to 4 p.m. or by appointment (618-243-6548).

Emma Kunz 1830 House, 602 Fulton Street, Belleville, Illinois 62221 (618-234-0600)

St. Clair County Historical Society Museum, 701 East Washington, Belleville, Illinois 62220 (618-234-0600)

Mermaid Inn, 114 East St. Louis Street, Lebanon, Illinois 62254 (618-537-4498)

5. Lincoln Heritage Trail Foundation, 702 Bloomington Road, Champaign, Illinois 61820 (217-352-1968)

Springfield Convention and Visitors Bureau, 624 East Adams, Springfield, Illinois 62701 (1-800-545-7300; in Illinois, 1-800-356-7900)

Lincoln Home Visitors Center, 426 South 7th Street, Springfield, Illinois 62701 (217-789-2357)

Phone numbers for other Springfield attractions (all area code 217): Lincoln Home: 492-4150; Great Western Depot: 544-8695; First Presbyterian Church: 528-4311; Old State Capitol: 782-4836; Lincoln-Herndon Law Offices: 782-4836; Marine Bank: 525-9600; State Historical Library: 782-4836; Parks Telephone Museum: 753-8436; Governor's Mansion: 782-2525 (tours 9:30–11 a.m. and 2–3:30 p.m. Tuesdays and Thursdays); Vachel Lindsay Home: 528-9254; Dana-Thomas House: 782-6776; Grand Army of the Republic Memorial Museum: 522-4373; Daughters of Union Veterans of the Civil War National Headquarters and Museum: 544-0616; Illinois State Capitol: 782-2099; Illinois State Museum: 782-7386; Edwards Place: 523-2631; Lincoln Tomb State Historic Site: 782-2717

Lincoln's New Salem State Park R.R. 1 Box 244A Petersburg, Illinois 62675 (217-632-7953). For tickets or information on the stage shows at New Salem: The Great American People Show, P.O. Box 401, Petersburg, Illinois 62675 (217-367-1900); Talisman River Boat: P.O. Box 337, Petersburg, Illinois 62675 (217-632-2219)

Edgar Lee Masters Museum, Eighth and Jackson Streets, Petersburg, Illinois 62675. (217-632-2878)

Clayville Rural Life Center, Route 125, Pleasant Plains, Illinois 62677 (217-626-1132)

Illiopolis Hotel, 608 Mary Street, Illiopolis, Illinois 62539 (217-486-6451)

Lincoln Trail Homestead State Park, Old State Route 36, Decatur, Illinois 62526 (217-864-3121)

Bryant Cottage State Historic Site, 146 East Wilson, Bement, Illinois 61813 (217-678-8184)

Mt. Pulaski Courthouse, Mount Pulaski, Illinois 62458 (217-792-3919)

Postville Courthouse, 914 Fifth Street, Lincoln, Illinois 62656 (217-732-8930)

Lincoln College Museum, 300 Keokuk Street, Lincoln, Illinois 62656 (217-732-3155 ext. 266)

DeWitt County Museum, 219 East Woodlawn, Clinton, Illinois 61727 (217-935-6066)

Clover Lawn, 100 East Monroe Street, Bloomington, Illinois 61701 (309-828-1084)

Stevenson Memorial Room, Illinois State University, Normal, Illinois 61701 (309-438-8800)

Krannert Art Museum, University of Illinois, 500 East Peabody Drive, Champaign, Illinois 61820 (217-333-1860)

World Heritage Museum, 484 Lincoln Hall, 702 South Wright Street, Urbana, Illinois 61801 (217-333-2360)

John Phillip Sousa Museum, Handing Band Building, 1103 South 6th Street, Urbana, Illinois 61801 (217-333-3025)

For information on the Amish country: Arthur Chamber of Commerce, P.O. Box 221, Arthur, Illinois 61911 (217-543-2111)

Arthur's Country Inn, East Route 133, Arthur, Illinois 61911 (217-543-3321)

For a meal in an Amish home, contact Edna C. Miller, R.R. 1, Box 184, Arthur, Illinois 61911. Mail reservations only.

The Little Theater on the Square, 12 East Harrison Street, Sullivan, Illinois 61951 (217-728-7375)

Rockome Gardens, Route 2, Box 87, Arcola, Illinois 61910 (217-268-4216)

Lincoln Log Cabin and the Moore Home State Historic Sites, R.R. 1, Box 175, Lerna, Illinois 62440 (217-345-6489)

Vermilion County Museum, 116 North Gilbert, Danville, Illinois 61832 (217-442-2922)

For information on the stores at Rossville: 217-748-6720

6. Jacksonville Chamber of Commerce, 155 West Morton, Jacksonville, Illinois 62650 (217-245-2174)

For tours of the Capitol Records plant in Jacksonville: 217-245-9631

Lincoln Courthouse, 101 West Third Street, Beardstown, Illinois 62618 (217-323-2774)

Schuyler Jail Museum, Rushville, Illinois 62681 (217-322-6975)

Western Illinois University, Macomb, Illinois 61455 (309-298-1727, Western Museum); (309-298-1594, Business Hall of Fame)

Watson-Riley School Museum, 301 West Calhoun, Macomb, Illinois 61455 (309-837-4855)

Haeger Potteries, 411 West Calhoun, Macomb, Illinois 61455 (309-833-2171)

Dickson Mounds Museum, Lewistown, Illinois 61542 (309-547-3721)

Spoon River Scenic Drive Associates, Box 59, Ellisville, Illinois 61431 (309-293-2143). The first two weekends (Friday, Saturday and Sunday) in October Spoon River valley comes alive with a fall festival featuring entertainment, country cooking, craft shows, flea markets and the autumn foliage.

Monmouth Pioneer Cemetery, East Archer and 6th Street, Monmouth, Illinois 61462 (309-734-3181)

Holt House, 402 East First Avenue, Monmouth, Illinois 61462

Western Stoneware, 521 West 6th, Monmouth, Illinois 61462 (309-734-2161)

Galesburg Railroad Museum, Seminary and Mulberry Streets, Galesburg, Illinois 61401 (309-342-9400)

Carl Sandburg Birthplace, 331 East Third Street, Galesburg, Illinois 61401 (309-342-2361)

Bishop Hill Heritage Association, P.O. Box 1853, Bishop Hill, Illinois 61419 (309-927-3899)

Lorado Taft Museum, Elmwood, Illinois 61529 (309-742-8285)

Peoria Convention and Visitors Bureau, 331 Fulton Plaza, Peoria, Illinois 61602 (309-676-0303)

Flanagan House, 942 North East Glen Oak, Peoria, Illinois 61603 (309-674-1921)

Pettengill-Morron House, 1212 West Moss, Peoria, Illinois 61606 (309-674-4745)

Peoria Mineral Springs, 701 West Seventh, Peoria, Illinois 61605 (309-676-7951)

Caterpillar Tractor Company, 100 North East Adams, Peoria, Illinois 61629 (309-675-4578)

Lakeview Museum, 1125 West Lake, Peoria, Illinois 61614 (309-686-7000)

Dirksen Congressional Center, Broadway and Fourth Street, Pekin, Illinois 61554 (309-347-7113)

Libby, McNeil & Libby pumpkin canning factory, 216 North Morton Avenue, Morton, Illinois 61550 (309-263-2651)

Metamora Courthouse State Memorial, 113 East Patridge, Metamora, Illinois 61548 (309-367-4470)

Melick Library, Eureka College, 300 East College, Eureka, Illinois 61530 (309-467-3721, ext. 219)

7. Putnam County Courthouse, Hennepin, Illinois 61327 (815-925-7129)

United Methodist Church and Meeting House, Court Street, Hennepin, Illinois 61327 (815-925-7094)

Owen Lovejoy Homestead, U.S. Route 6, Princeton, Illinois 61356 (815-875-2207)

Illinois Waterway Visitors Center, Dee Bennett Road at Route 178, Utica, Illinois 61373 (815-667-4054)

Starved Rock State Park Lodge, Box 471, Utica, Illinois 61373 (815-667-4211)

LaSalle County Historical Museum, Mill and Canal Streets, Utica, Illinois 61373 (815-667-4861)

William Reddick Mansion, 100 West Lafayette, Ottawa, Illinois 61350 (815-433-0084)

Time Was Village Museum, Route 251-52, Mendota, Illinois 61342 (815-539-6042)

St. Peter's Church, Washington Street, Sheffield, Illinois 61361 (815-454-2788)

Johnson 1910 Farm, Route 6, Geneseo, Illinois 61254 (309-944-2040)

International Harvester East Moline plant, 1100 Third Street, East Moline, Illinois 61244 (309-762-1978)

Deere and Company headquarters, John Deere Road, Moline, Illinois 61265 (309-752-4207)

Center for Belgian Culture, 712 18th Street, Moline, Illinois 61265 (309-762-0167)

Greater Quad City Railroad Museum, 3105 5th Avenue, Rock Island, Illinois 61201 (309-788-2200)

Blackhawk State Park and Hauberg Indian Museum, Rock Island, Illinois 61201 (309-788-9536)

Rock Island Arsenal Museum (309-782-5021)

Mississippi River Visitors Center, Rock Island, Illinois 61201 (309-788-6361, ext. 338)

Reagan Birthplace, 111 South Main Street, Tampico, Illinois 61283 (815-438-2130)

Reagan Boyhood Home, 816 South Hennepin, Dixon, Illinois 61021 (815-288-3404)

Nachusa Hotel, 215 South Galena, Dixon, Illinois 61021 (815-288-2132)

John Deere Historic Site, R.R. 3, Grand Detour, Illinois 61021 (815-652-4551)

Rockford Area Convention and Visitors Bureau, 515 North Court Street, Rockford, Illinois 61103 (815-987-8105) 1-800-423-5361 (outside Illinois) 1-800-521-0849 (in Illinois)

Rockford museums: Burpee Natural History Museum, 737 North Main 61101 (815-965-3131); Burpee Art Museum, 815 North Main 61103 (815-965-3132); Museum Center/ Midway Village, 6799 Guilford Road 61107 (815-397-9122); Graham-Ginestra House, 1115 South Main 61101 (815-968-6044); Stephen Mack Home, Highway 75, Macktown Forest Preserve (815-624-7600); Erlanger House Museum, 403 South 3d Street 61108 (815-963-5559); Zitelman Scout Museum, 708 Seminary Street 61108 (815-962-3999)

Tinker Swiss Cottage, 411 Kent Street, Rockford, Illinois 61102 (815-964-2424)

Time Museum, 7801 East State Street, Rockford, Illinois 61125 (815-398-6000, ext. 2943). For hotel reservations, the toll-free number (outside Illinois) is 1-800-358-7666

Freeport Art Museum, 121 North Harlem, Freeport, Illinois 61032 (815-235-9755)

Stephenson County Historical Museum, 1440 South Carroll, Freeport, Illinois 61032 (815-232-8419)

Kolb-Lena Cheese Factory, Railroad Street, Lena, Illinois 61048 (815-369-4577)

Mount Carroll Chamber of Commerce, P.O. Box 94, Mount Carroll, Illinois 61053 (815-244-9161)

Campbell Center for Historic Preservation Studies, P.O. Box 66, Mount Carroll, Illinois 61053 (815-244-1173)

AT & T Satellite Earth Station, 7351 West Blackjack Road, Hanover, Illinois 61041 (815-777-2400)

Galena-Jo Daviess County Chamber of Commerce, 101 Bouthillier Street, Galena, Illinois 61036 (815-777-0203) 1-800-892-9299 (in Illinois) 1-800-874-9377 (from nearby states). Except for the Thomas Melville House, at 1009 Third Street, the locations of all the attractions mentioned are included in the tourist brochures available at the Chamber of Commerce. A few of the many Galena bed and breakfast establishments in old houses are: Aldrich Guest House, 900 Third Street 61036 (815-777-3323); Fricke Guest House, 119 South Bench Street 61036 (815-777-1193); The Log Cabin Guest House and Servants House, 11661 West Chetlain Lane 61036 (815-777-2845); The Victorian Mansion, 310 South High Scheet 61036 (815-777-0675).

8. Shiloh House, 1300 Shiloh Road, Zion, Illinois 60099 (312-746-2639). For information on the Zion Passion Play: 312-746-2221

Tempel Farms, Wadsworth, Illinois (312-623-7272)

Waukegan-Lake County Chamber of Commerce, 414 North Sheridan Road, Waukegan, Illinois 60085 (312-249-3800)

Kitchens of Sara Lee, 500 Waukegan Road, Deerfield, Illinois 60015 (312-945-2525)

The Grove, 1421 Milwaukee Avenue, Glenview, Illinois 60025 (312-299-6096)

McDonald's Museum, 400 Lee Street, Des Plains, Illinois 60017 (312-297-5022)

For information on the antique stores in Long Grove: 312-634-3117. For information on those in Richmond: 815-678-4076

Woodstock Opera House, 121 Van Buren Street, Woodstock, Illinois 60098 (815-338-5300)

Union museums: Seven Acres Antique Village, 8512 South Union Road 60180 (815-923-2214); Illinois Railway Museum, 7000 Olsen Road 60180 (815-923-2488); McHenry County Historical Museum, 6422 Main Street 60180 (815-923-2267)

Elwood House Museum, 509 North First Street, De Kalb, Illinois 60115 (815-756-4609)

Fox River Trolley Museum, P.O. Box 315, South Elgin, Illinois 60177 (312-697-4676)

Creative Crafts Center, 840 North State Street, Elgin, Illinois 60120 (312-697-1800)

Kane County Flea Market, Randall Road, St. Charles, Illinois 60174 (312-377-2252)

Garfield Farm Museum, North Garfield Road, Box 403, La Fox, Illinois 60147 (312-584-8485)

Fermilab National Accelerator Laboratory, Batavia Road, P.O. Box 500, Batavia, Illinois 60510 (312-840-3351)

Batavia Depot Museum, 155 Houston Street, Batavia, Illinois 60510 (312-879-1800)

Aurora Historical Museum, Cedar and Oak Streets, Aurora, Illinois 60506 (312-897-9029)

Naper Settlement, Porter and Webster Streets, Aurora, Illinois 60540 (312-420-6010)

The Morton Arboretum, Lisle, Illinois 60532 (312-968-0074)

The Old Graue Mill, York and Spring Roads, Oak Brook, Illinois 60521 (312-655-2090)

Stacy's Tavern Museum, 557 Geneva Road, P.O. Box 283, Glen Ellyn, Illinois 60138 (312-858-8696)

Cantigny, One South 151 Winfield Road, Wheaton, Illinois 60187 (312-668-5161)

Heritage Gallery, 421 Country Farm Road, Wheaton, Illinois 60187 (312-682-7363)

Wheaton College, 501 East Seminary Avenue, Wheaton, Illinois 60187. The Billy Graham Museum, 312-260-5909. Marion E. Wade Collection, 312-260-5908

DuPage County Historical Museum, 102 East Wesley Street, Wheaton, Illinois 60187 (312-682-7343)

Oak Park Tour Center, 951 Chicago Avenue, Oak Park, Illinois 60302 (312-848-1978) and Oak Park Visitors Center, 158 North Forest Avenue, Oak Park, Illinois 60302 (312-848-1976)

Historic Pullman Foundation, 11111 South Forrestville Avenue, Chicago, Illinois 60628 (312-785-8181)

Lemont Cookie Jar Museum, 111 Stephen Street, Lemont, Illinois 60439 (312-257-5012)

Illinois-Michigan Canal Museum and Pioneer Settlement, 803 South State Street, Lockport, Illinois 60441 (815-838-5080)

Rialto Square Theater, 102 North Chicago Street, Joliet, Illinois 60431 (815-726-6600)

Goose Lake Prairie Visitors Center, 5010 North Jugtown, Morris, Illinois 60450 (815-942-2899)

9. Two information centers, each run by a different branch of the Mormon Church, operate at Nauvoo: Nauvoo Restoration Visitors Center, Main and Young (217-453-2237) and Joseph Smith Historic Center, Main and Water (217-453-2246). Information is also available at the Tourist Reception Center on Mulholland Street (217-453-6648).

Hotel Nauvoo, P.O. Box 398, Nauvoo, Illinois 62354 (217-453-2211)

Old Carthage Jail, 307 Walnut, Carthage, Illinois 62321 (217-357-2989)

Quincy museums include: Gardner Museum of Architecture and Design, Fourth and Maine (217-224-6873); Governor John Wood Mansion, 425 South 12th (217-222-1835); All

Wars Museum, 1707 North 12th (217-222-8641); Pharmacy Museum, Fifth and Chestnut (217-224-1000); Lincoln Douglas Valentine Museum, 101 North 4th (217-224-3355).

Wittmond Hotel, Brussels, Illinois 62036 (618-883-2345)

Kampsville Archeology Center, Kampsville, Illinois 62053 (618-653-4316) or (618-653-4395)

Pere Marquette State Park Lodge (618-786-3351)

Bed and breakfast inns in Elsah include: The Corner Nest, (618-374-1892); Maple Leaf Cottage (618-374-1684); and Green Tree Inn (618-374-2821).

Alton Museum of History and Art, 121 East Broadway, Alton, Illinois 62002 (618-462-2763)

10. Useful books on Illinois culture and history

Letters from Illinois, Morris Birkbeck (1818)

A Gazetteer of Illinois, J.M. Peck (Jacksonville, 1834)

Life in Prairie Land, Eliza W. Farnham (Harper & Brothers, New York, 1846)

Historic Illinois The Romance of the Earlier Days, Randall Parrish (A.C. McClurg & Co., Chicago, 1906)

Recollections 1837–1910, Charles W. Marsh (Chicago Farm Implement News Company, Chicago, 1910)

They Broke the Prairie, Earnest Elmo Calkins (Charles Scribner's Sons, New York, 1937)

The Illinois, James Gray (Farrar & Rinehart, New York, 1940)

Old Illinois Houses, John Drury (Illinois State Historical Society, Springfield, 1948)

The Other Illinois, Baker Brownell (Duell, Sloan and Pearce, New York, 1958)

Legends and Lore of Southern Illinois, John W. Allen (Southern Illinois University Press, Carbondale, 1963)

An America That Was, Albert Britt (Barre Publishers, Barre, Massachusetts, 1964)

The Talk of Vandalia, Joseph P. Lyford (Harper & Row Colophon ed, New York, 1965)

It Happened in Southern Illinois, John W. Allen (Southern Illinois University Press, Carbondale, 1968)

Prairie State Impressions of Illinois, 1673–1967, By Travelers and

Other Observers, compiled and edited by Paul M. Angle (The University of Chicago Press, Chicago 1968)

Bishop Hill   A Utopia on the Prairie, Olov Isaksson (LT Publishing House, Stockholm, 1969)

An Illinois Reader, Clyde C. Walton, ed (Northern Illinois University Press, De Kalb, 1970)

Illinois   A History of the Prairie State, Robert P. Howard (William B. Eerdmans Publishing Company, Grand Rapids Michigan, 1972)

The Prairie State   A Documentary History of Illinois   Colonial Years to 1860, Robert P. Sutton, ed (William B. Eerdmans Publishing Company, Grand Rapids, Michigan, 1976)

The Prairie State   Civil War to the Present, Robert P. Sutton, ed, (William B. Eerdmans Publishing Company, Grand Rapids Michigan, 1976)

Illinois   A Bicentennial History, Richard J. Jensen (W. W. Norton & Company, Inc., New York, 1978)

IV   Iowa

1. Visitors and Tourism, Iowa Development Commission, 600 East Court, Des Moines, Iowa 50309 (515-281-3100)
2. For information on the lower Des Moines River valley villages: Van Buren Development Association, P.O. Box 9, Keosauqua, Iowa 52565 (319-293-3207)

   Deliverance Canoe Service, 8th and Texas, Bonaparte, Iowa 52620 (319-592-3607) The Service offers canoe rentals, group trips and shuttle service on a sixty-mile stretch of the lower Des Moines River.

   Bonaparte's Retreat, Bonaparte, Iowa 52620 (319-592-3339)

   Bentonsport National Historic District (319-592-3133)

   Mason House Inn at Bentonsport (319-592-3133)

   Schoolhouse and Wendell Mohr Art Studio, Vernon, Iowa 52565 (319-592-3427)

   Hotel Manning, Keosauqua, Iowa 52565 (319-293-3232)

   John Deere Ottuma Works, Vine and Madison Streets, Ottuma, Iowa 52501 (515-684-4641)

Mount Pleasant Museum of Repertoire Americana. Except during the annual Reunion, the Museum is open only by appointment (319-385-9432)

Midwest Old Threshers, Rural Route 1, Mount Pleasant, Iowa 52641 (319-385-8937)

Harlan House Hotel, 122 N. Jefferson, Mount Pleasant, Iowa 52641 (319-385-3126)

3. Pella Chamber of Commerce, 507 Franklin St., Pella, Iowa 50219 (515-628-4311)

Historical Village and Wyatt Earp Boyhood Home, 507 Franklin St., Pella, Iowa 50219 (515-628-4311) or (515-628-2409)

Scholte House, 728 Washington St., Pella, Iowa 50219 (515-628-3684)

Rolscreen Museum, Main and Oskaloosa Streets, Pella, Iowa 50219

Strawtown Inn, 1111 Washington St., Pella, Iowa 50219. Restaurant (515-628-4043). Lodging (515-628-2681)

Nelson Pioneer Farm and Craft Musuem, Glendale Road, Oskaloosa, Iowa 52577 (515-672-2989) or Oskaloosa Chamber of Commerce (515-672-2591)

Brick Museum, What Cheer, Iowa 50268 (515-634-2778)

Opera House, What Cheer, Iowa 50268 (515-634-2536)

Grinnell Chamber of Commerce, Grinnell, Iowa 50112 (515-236-6555)

Grinnell College, Grinnell, Iowa 50112 (515-236-4508)

Grinnell Historical Museum, 1125 Broad St. Grinnell, Iowa 50122 (515-236-4908)

Jasper County Historical Museum, 1700 S. 15 Avenue W, P.O. Box 834, Newton, Iowa 50208 (515-792-9118)

Maytag Dairy Farms, Box 806, Newton, Iowa 50208 (1-800-258-2437 in Iowa, 1-800-247-2458 from outside Iowa)

Fisher Community Center, 709 S. Center St., Marshalltown, Iowa 50158 (515-753-6645)

Mesquakie Indian Center, Tama, Iowa 52339 (515-484-3620)

4. Amana Society Main Office, Amana, Iowa 52203 (319-622-3051)

Museum of Amana History, Box 81, Amana, Iowa 52203 (319-622-3567), which is also the number for the Amana Heritage Society

The Original Amana Furniture and Clock Shop, Amana, Iowa 52203 (319-622-3291)

Colony Inn: (319-622-3471) Ox Yoke Inn: (319-622-3441) These are not inns that take guests but are popular restaurants in the village of Amana.

Amana Refrigeration, Middle Amana, Iowa 52307 (319-622-5511)

Community Kitchen, Cooper Shop, Hearth Oven Museum, Middle Amana, Iowa 52307 (319-622-3157)

Hahn's Hearth Oven Bakery, Middle Amana, Iowa 52307 (319-622-3439)

Old Fashioned General Store and Gift Shop, High Amana, Iowa 52203 (319-622-3797)

West Amana Store, West Amana, Iowa 52357 (319-622-3104)

Old Broom and Basket Shop, West Amana, Iowa 52357 (319-622-3315)

Ackerman Winery, South Amana, Iowa 52334 (319-622-3379)

Brumwell Flour Mill, South Amana, Iowa 52334 (319-622-3455)

Schanz Furniture Shop, South Amana, Iowa 52334 (319-622-3529)

Barn Museum, South Amana, Iowa 52334 (319-622-3058)

Amana Society Bakery, Upper South Amana, Iowa 52334 (319-622-3059)

Ehrle Brothers Winery, Homestead, Iowa 52236 (319-622-3241)

Amana Home and Blacksmith Shop, Homestead, Iowa 52236 (319-622-3976)

Die Heimat Country Inn, Homestead, Iowa 52236 (319-622-3937)

Holiday Inn of the Amana Colonies, I-80, Exit 225, P.O. Box 187, Amana, Iowa 52203 (319-668-1175)

Best Western Colony Haus Motor Hotel, I-80, Exit 225, R.R.2, Williamsburg, Iowa 52361 (319-668-2097)

Bill Zuber's Restaurant, Homestead, Iowa 52236 (319-622-3911)

For horse-drawn hay rides and (in winter) bob-sled rides at Amana (319-622-3298); for tours of the Colony, contact Village Tours, P.O. Box 121, Amana, Iowa 52203 (319-622-3269)

5. University of Iowa Public Information Office, 5 Old Capitol, Iowa City, Iowa 52240 (319-353-5691)

University of Iowa Museum of Art, North Riverside Drive Iowa City, Iowa 52242 (319-353-3266)

Old Capitol, Clinton St. and Iowa Ave., Iowa City, Iowa 52240 (319-353-7293)

Plum Grove, 1030 Carroll St., Iowa City, Iowa 52240 (319-337-3673)

Herbert Hoover National Historic Site, Box 607, West Branch, Iowa 52358 (319-643-2541). The Hoover Library-Museum (319-643-5301)

Kalona Historical Society, P.O. Box 292, Kalona, Iowa 52247 (319-656-2519)

Kalona Historical Village, Kalona, Iowa 52247 (319-656-2519)

Cedar Rapids Area Convention and Visitors Bureau, 424 First Ave. N.E., Cedar Rapids, Iowa 52401 (319-364-2591)

City Market, Riverside Roundhouse, 1350 A St., S.W., Cedar Rapids, Iowa 52404

Seminole Valley Farm, Seminole Valley Park N.E., Cedar Rapids, Iowa 52401 (319-398-5190)

Usher's Ferry Pioneer Village, Seminole Valley Park N.E., Cedar Rapids, Iowa 52401 (319-398-5190)

Brucemore Mansion and Gardens, 2160 Linden Drive S.E., Cedar Rapids, Iowa 52403 (319-362-7375)

Iowa Masonic Library, 813 First Avenue S.E., Cedar Rapids, Iowa 52402 (319-365-1438)

Czech Museum and Library, 10 16th Ave. S.W., Cedar Rapids, Iowa 52404 (319-362-8500)

Cczech Village Association, 59 16th Ave. S.W., Cedar Rapids, Iowa 52404 (319-364-0017)

Inn at Stone City, Rt. 1, Stone City, Iowa 52205 (319-462-4733)

Turner's East and #5 Turner's Alley, 800 Second Ave. S.E., Cedar Rapids, Iowa 52401. For tours of Grant Wood's studio (319-362-1131)

Cedar Rapids Museum of Art, 324 Third St. S.E., Cedar Rapids, Iowa 52401 (319-366-7503)

The Old Creamery Theater, Garrison, Iowa 52229 (1-800-332-5200)

Herbert Quick Schoolhouse, Grundy Center, Iowa 50638

Waterloo Chamber of Commerce, 229 W. 5th St., Waterloo, Iowa 50704 (319-233-8431)

John Deere Tractor Works, East Donald St., Waterloo, Iowa 50703 (319-292-7801)

6. Bily Clock Museum and Dvorak House, Spillville, Iowa 52168 (314-562-3569)

Vesterheim (Norwegian-American Museum), 520 W. Water, Decorah, Iowa 52101 (319-382-9681)

Fort Atkinson Preserve, Fort Atkinson, Iowa 52144 (319-534-7543)

The Little Brown Church in the Vale. The church is located on the west side of state road 346 a mile east of Nashua, Iowa 50658.

7. Mason City Chamber of Commerce, 17 W. State St., P.O. Box 1128, Mason City, Iowa 50401 (515-423-5724)

Charles H. MacNider Museum, 303 Second St. S.E., Mason City, Iowa 50401 (515-423-9563)

Winnebago Industries, Forest City, Iowa 50436 (515-582-6936)

Britt Chamber of Commerce, P.O. Box 63, Britt, Iowa 50423 (515-843-3867)

8. Humboldt County Historical Museum, Dakota City, Iowa 50529 (515-332-3392)

4-H Historical Museum, Clarion, Iowa 50525

Fort Museum, Fort Dodge, Iowa 50501 (515-573-4231)

Mamie Doud Eisenhower Birthplace, 709 Carroll St., Boone, Iowa 50036 (515-432-1896)

Boone & Scenic Valley Railroad, 10th and Harrison Streets, Box 603, Boone, Iowa 50036 (515-432-4249)

Kate Shelley Railroad Museum, Moingona, Iowa 50036 (515-432-5681)

Iowa State University, Ames, Iowa 50011 (515-294-4777); Farm House (515-294-3342)

Living History Farms, 2600 N.W. 111 St., Urbandale, Iowa 50322 (515-278-5286)

Walden Acres Bed and Breakfast, R.R.1, Adel, Iowa 50003 (515-987-1567)

Winterset Area Chamber of Commerce, Box 55, Winterset, Iowa 50273 (515-462-1185)

John Wayne Birthplace, 224 S. 2d St., Winterset, Iowa 50273 (515-462-1044)

Danish Windmill, Main St., Elk Horn, Iowa 51531 (712-764-7472)

Council Bluffs Chamber of Commerce, 119 S. Main, Council Bluffs, Iowa 51501 (712-325-1000)

Grenville Dodge House, 605 3d St., Council Bluffs, Iowa 51501 (712-322-2406)

Squirrel Cage Jail, 226 Pearl St., Council Bluffs, Iowa 51501 (712-322-9624)

DeSoto National Wildlife Refuge, Route 1, Box 114, Missouri Valley, Iowa 51555 (712-642-4121)

Siouxland Association of Business and Industry (tourist information), 101 Pierce, Sioux City, Iowa 51101 (712-255-7903)

K.D. Stockyards Station, 2001 Leech Ave., Sioux City, Iowa 51107

Chamber of Commerce, 200 Central Ave. S.E., Le Mars, Iowa 51031 (712-546-5306)

Chamber of Commerce, Iowa Great Lakes Area, Highway 71, P.O. Box 9, Arnolds Park, Iowa 51331 (712-332-2107)

Gardner Cabin (712-332-7248)

9. Keokuk Chamber of Commerce, Pierce Building, 401 Main St., Keokuk, Iowa 52632 (515-524-5055)

George M. Verity River Museum, Victory Park, Keokuk, Iowa 52632 (515-524-4765)

Keokuk Hydroelectric Power Plant and Dam, Keokuk, Iowa 52632 (515-524-6363)

Miller House Museum, Keokuk, Iowa 52632

First School House, Galland, Iowa (515-463-7796)

Sheaffer Pen Factory, 301 Avenue H, Fort Madison, Iowa 52627 (319-372-3300)

Burlington Convention and Tourism Bureau, 807 Jefferson St., P.O. Box 6, Burlington, Iowa 52601 (319-752-7004)

Snake Alley Historic District, Burlington, Iowa 52601 (319-752-6365)

Muscatine Art Center, 1314 Mulberry Ave., Muscatine, Iowa 52761 (319-263-8282)

Davenport Convention and Visitor Bureau, 108 East 3d St., 52801 (319-322-1706)

Davenport Art Gallery, 1737 West 12th St., Davenport, Iowa 52804 (319-326-7804)

Putnam Museum, 1717 West 12th St., Davenport, Iowa 52804 (319-324-1933)

Village of East Davenport Association, 2215 East 12th St., Davenport, Iowa 52803 (319-322-1860)

Buffalo Bill Museum, 200 N. River Drive, Le Claire, Iowa 52753 (319-289-5580)

Buffalo Bill Cody Homestead (319-225-2981)

Potter's Mill Restaurant, Bellevue, Iowa 52031 (319-872-4237)

City of Clinton Showboat: contact Gateway Chamber of Commerce, P.O. Box 527, Clinton, Iowa 52732 (319-243-1260)

Dubuque Chamber of Commerce, 770 Town Clock Plaza, Dubuque, Iowa 52001 (319-557-9200)

Old Jail Art Gallery, 720 Central Ave., Dubuque, Iowa 52001 (319-556-1851)

Dubuque Star Brewery, East Fourth St. Extension, Dubuque, Iowa 52001 (319-582-1867)

Silver Dollar Bar, 342 Main St., Dubuque, Iowa 52001 (319-556-9327)

Cable Car Square information (319-556-2750)

Fenelon Place Elevator (319-582-6496)

Redstone Inn, 501 Bluff, Dubuque, Iowa 52001 (319-582-1894)

New Melleray Abbey, Dubuque, Iowa 52001 (319-588-2319)

Guttenberg Chamber of Commerce, 502 S. First St., Guttenberg, Iowa 52052 (319-252-1161)

McGregor Chamber of Commerce, P.O. Box 105, McGregor, Iowa 52157 (319-873-3781)

Effigy Mounds National Monument, Box K, McGregor, Iowa 52157 (319-873-2356)

10. Useful books on Iowa culture and history

Iowa: The Home for Immigrants (Iowa Board of Immigration, 1870)

A Handbook of Iowa (1893)

When the Wildwood Was in Flower, G. Smith Stanton (J.S. Ogilvie Publishing Company, New York, 1910)

Reminiscences of Newcastle, Iowa, Sarah Brewer-Bonebright (Historical Department of Iowa, Des Moines, 1921)

In Cabins and Sod-Houses, Thomas Huston Macbride (The State Historical Society of Iowa, Iowa City, 1928)

Early Algona The Story of Our Pioneers 1854–1874, Florence Call Cowles (The Register and Tribune Company, Des Moines, 1929)

Memories of Fourscore Years, Charles August Ficke (Davenport, 1930)

Ioway to Iowa, Irving Berdine Richman (The State Historical Society of Iowa, Iowa City, 1931)

Robert Gordon Cousins, Jacob A. Swisher (The State Historical Society of Iowa, Iowa City, 1938)

Iowa Through the Years, Cyrenus Cole (The State Historical Society of Iowa, Iowa City, 1940)

Hawkeyes A Biography of the State of Iowa, Phil Strong (Dodd, Mead & Company, New York, 1940)

Iowa, Land of Many Mills, Jacob A. Swisher (The State Historical Society of Iowa, Iowa City, 1940)

Iowa: The Rivers of Her Valleys, William J. Petersen (The State Historical Society of Iowa, Iowa City, 1941)

Iowa in Times of War, Jacob A. Swisher (The State Historical Society of Iowa, Iowa City, 1943)

A Geography of Iowa, H.L. Nelson (University of Nebraska Press, Lincoln, 1967)

Rogues and Heroes from Iowa's Amazing Past, George Mills (The Iowa State University Press, Ames, 1972)

Portrait of Iowa, introduction by Paul Engel, photos by John M. Zielinski (Adama Press, Minneapolis, 1974)

A History of Iowa, Leland L. Sage (The Iowa State University Press, Ames, 1974)

Growing Up in Iowa, Clarence A. Andrews, ed (The Iowa State University Press, Ames, 1978)

Iowa A Bicentennial History, Joseph Frazier Wall (W. W. Norton & Company, Inc., New York, 1978)

Prairie City, Iowa Three Seasons at Home, Douglas Bauer (G. P. Putnam's Sons, New York, 1979)

Iowa, Allan Carpenter (Childrens Press, Chicago, 1979, rev. ed.)

Iowa The American Heartland, (Bankers Trust, Des Moines, 1981)

Gentlemen on the Prairie, Curtis Harnack (The Iowa State University Press, Ames, 1985)

V Missouri

1. Missouri Division of Tourism, Truman State Office Building, P.O. Box 1055, Jefferson City, Missouri 65102 (314-751-4133)

   Missouri Bed and Breakfast Association, P.O. Box 31246, St. Louis, Missouri 63131 (314-965-4328)

2. St. Charles Department of Tourism, P.O. Box 745, St. Charles, Missouri 63302 (314-946-7776)

   St. Charles Vintage House Restaurant and Wine Garden, 1219 South Main Street, St. Charles, Missouri 63301 (314-946-7155)

   Daniel Boone Home, Highway F, Defiance, Missouri 63341 (314-987-2221)

   Wineries in Augusta include: Mount Pleasant Wine Co., (314-228-4419); Montelle Winery and Vineyards, (314-228-4464); Osage Ridge Winery (314-228-4505)

   Augusta Visitor's Association, P.O. Box 31, Augusta, Missouri 63332 (314-228-4410), which is also the number to reserve a room at the Augusta Haus Bed and Breakfast

   Union Electric Callaway Nuclear Plant Visitors Center, P.O. Box 620, Fulton, Missouri 65251 (314-676-8511)

The Winston Churchill Memorial and Library, Westminster College, Fulton, Missouri 65251 (314-642-6648)

Jefferson City Area Chamber of Commerce, 213 Adams, P.O. Box 776, Jefferson City, Missouri 65102 (314-634-3616)

Jefferson Landing State Historic Site, Jefferson City, Missouri 65101 (314-751-3475)

For information on tours of the governor's mansion, held on Tuesdays at 10, 11, 1 and 2 (314-751-4141)

For reservations at the Dauphine Hotel in Bonnots Mill (314-965-4328)

Hermann Visitors Information Center, P.O. Box 88, Hermann, Missouri 65041 (314-486-2017) or (486-2781); toll-free number in Missouri for Hermann information (1-800-437-6266)

Stone Hill Winery, Route 1, Box 26, Hermann, Missouri 65041 (314-486-2221)

Hermannhof Winery 330 East First Street, Hermann, Missouri 65041 (314-486-5959)

Bed and breakfast establishments in Hermann include: Das Brownhaus, 125 East Second Street (314-486-3372); Birk's Goethe Street Gasthaus, 702 Goethe (314-486-2911); Schmidt's Guesthouse, 300 Market Street (314-486-2146); Seven Sisters B & B Cottage, 108 Schiller Strasse (314-486-3717); White House Hotel B & B, 232 Wharf Street (314-486-3200); William Klinger Inn, 108 East Second Street (314-486-5930)

Washington Area Chamber of Commerce, 323 West Main, Washington, Missouri 63090 (314-239-2715)

Missouri Meerschaum Co., 400 West Front Street, Washington, Missouri 63090 (314-239-2109)

Zachariah Foss Guest House, 4 Lafayette Street, Washington, Missouri 63090 (314-239-6499)

Schwegmann House (bed and breakfast), 438 West Front Street, Washington, Missouri 63090 (314-239-5025)

3. The Apple Shed, P.O. Box 251, Clarksville, Missouri 63336 (314-242-3264)

Stark Brothers Garden Center, West Georgia Street, Louisiana, Missouri 63353 (314-754-3113)

Hannibal Visitors Bureau, 320 Broadway, P.O. Box 624, Hannibal, Missouri 63401 (314-221-2477)

Mark Twain Boyhood Home and Museum, 208 Hill Street, Hannibal, Missouri 63401 (314-221-9010)

Schaffer's Smoke House, 308 Broadway, Hannibal, Missouri 63401 (314-221-9547)

Mark Twain Cave, P.O. Box 913, Hannibal, Missouri 63401 (314-221-1656)

Garth Woodside Mansion, R.R. Number 1, Hannibal, Missouri 63401 (314-221-2789)

The Victorian Guest House, 3 Stillwell Place, Hannibal, Missouri 63401 (314-221-3093)

The Bordello, 111 Bird Street, Hannibal, Missouri 63401 (314-221-6111)

The Molly Brown Dinner Theater, 200 North Main, P.O. Box 504, Hannibal, Missouri 63401 (314-221-8940)

Rockcliffe Mansion, 1000 Bird Street, Hannibal, Missouri 63401 (314-221-4140)

Mark Twain Birthplace Museum, Stoutsville, Missouri 65283 (314-565-3449)

Golden Eagle Showboat, 2d and Green Streets, P.O. Box 227, Canton, Missouri 63435 (314-288-5273)

Gregory's Antiques, Route 1, Box 123, Kahoka, Missouri 63445 (816-727-2129)

The Bethel German Colony, P.O. Box 127, Bethel, Missouri 63434 (816-284-6493)

4. General John J. Pershing Boyhood Home, Box 141, Laclede, Missouri 64651 (816-963-2525)

James Cash Penney Memorial Museum, Hamilton, Missouri 64644 (816-583-9997)

Cedarwood Restaurant, Box 177, Jamesport, Missouri 64648 (816-684-6212)

Amish Settlement Tour, P.O. Box 204, Jamesport, Missouri 64648 (816-684-6602)

Fitzgerald Buffalo Ranch, Bethany, Missouri 64424 (816-425-6031)

Benedictine Convent of Perpetual Adoration, Clyde, Missouri 64432 (816-944-2221)

Conception Abbey, Conception, Missouri 64432 (816-944-2211)

Mule Barn Theater, Tarkio, Missouri 64491 (816-736-4185)

Squaw Creek National Wildlife Refuge, P.O. Box 101, Mound City, Missouri 64470 (816-442-3187)

St. Joseph Area Chamber of Commerce, P.O. Box 1394, Seventh and Felix Streets, St. Joseph, Missouri 64502 (816-232-4461)

Pony Express Museum, 914 Penn Street (816-232-8471); Patee House Museum, 12th and Penn Streets (816-232-8206); Jesse James Home, 12th and Penn Streets (816-232-8206); Albrecht Art Museum, 2818 Frederick Avenue (816-233-7003); St. Joseph Museum, 11th and Charles Streets (816-232-8471); Psychiatric Museum, 3400 Frederick Avenue (816-232-8431); Stetson Hat Co., 3615 Leonard Road (816-233-8031); Robidoux Row, 3d and Poulin (816-232-5527)

5. Weston Development Company (tourist information), 521 Main Street, Weston, Missouri 64098 (816-386-2909)

The McCormick Distillery Co., Highway JJ, Weston, Missouri 64098 (816-386-2276)

Weston Historical Museum, 601 Main Street, Weston, Missouri 64098 (816-386-2977)

Pirtle's Winery, 502 Spring, Weston, Missouri 64098 (816-386-5728)

Benner House Bed and Breakfast, 645 Main Street, Weston, Missouri 64098 (816-386-2616)

New Deal Tobacco Warehouse, Highways 45 and P, Weston, Missouri 64098 (816-386-2226)

Jesse James Farm and "The Life and Times of Jesse James" show, Route 2, Box 236, Kearney, Missouri 64060 (816-635-6065)

Claybrook House Historic Site, Route 2, Box 236, Kearney, Missouri 64060 (816-635-6055)

Jesse James Bank Museum, 104 East Franklin, Liberty, Missouri 64068 (816-781-4458)

Clay County Historical Museum, 14 North Main, Liberty, Missouri 64068 (816-781-8062)

Historic Liberty Jail, 216 North Main, Liberty, Missouri 64068 (816-781-3188)

William Jewell College, Kansas Street, Liberty, Missouri 64068 (816-781-3806)

Watkins Woolen Mill State Historic Site, Route 2, Box 270 M, Lawson, Missouri 64062 (816-296-3357)

The Elms, Regent and Elms Boulevard, Excelsior Springs, Missouri 64024 (816-637-2141); toll-free (outside Missouri) 1-800-843-3567

City of Independence Tourism Division, 111 East Maple, Independence, Missouri 64050 (816-836-7111)

Harry S Truman Library and Museum, Independence, Missouri 64050 (816-833-1400)

Truman National Historic Site, 223 North Main, Independence, Missouri 64050 (816-254-7199)

Truman Home: a limited number of free tickets are distributed beginning at 8:30 a.m. at the information center on the corner of Truman Road and Main Street (816-254-7199)

Truman Railroad Station, 600 South Grand, Independence, Missouri 64055 (816-421-4725)

Independence Square Courthouse, 112 West Lexington, Independence, Missouri 64050 (816-881-4467)

1859 Jail Museum and Marshal's Home, 217 North Main, Independence, Missouri 64050 (816-252-1892)

Bingham-Waggoner Home, 313 West Pacific, Independence, Missouri 64050 (816-461-3491)

Vaile Mansion, 1400 North Liberty, Independence, Missouri 64050 (816-833-0040)

Mormon Visitors Center, 937 West Walnut, Independence, Missouri 64051 (816-836-3466)

Fort Osage, Sibley, Missouri 64088 (816-249-5737)

Missouri Town 1855, Lake Jacomo, Missouri 64015 (816-795-8200)

Lone Jack Civil War Museum, Lone Jack, Missouri 64070 (816-566-2272)

Truman Farm Home, 12301 Blue Ridge Boulevard, Grandview, Missouri 64030 (816-761-6505)

Belton City Hall Museum, 512 Main Street, Belton, Missouri 64012

Tourist Information Center, 1211 Main Street, Lexington, Missouri 64067 (816-259-2040)

Battle of Lexington State Historic Site and Anderson House, North 13th and Wood Streets, Lexington, Missouri 64067 (816-259-2112)

Lexington Historical Museum, 112 South 13th Street, Lexington, Missouri 64067 (816-259-6313)

Warrensburg Chamber of Commerce, 118 North Holden, Warrensburg, Missouri 64093 (816-747-3168)

The Country Place, four and a half miles east of Warrensburg, offers bed and breakfast accommodation (816-429-2040)

6. Sedalia Area Chamber of Commerce, 113 East Fourth Street, Sedalia, Missouri 65301 (816-826-2222)

State Fair Community College, (ragtime archive), West 16th Street, Sedalia, Missouri 65301 (816-826-7100)

Missouri State Fair, West 16th and State Fair Boulevard, Sedalia, Missouri 65301 (816-826-0570)

New Lebanon, Route 2, Box 55, Bunceton, Missouri 65237 (816-366-4482)

Pleasant Green Plantation House (816-834-3954)

Ravenswood House (816-427-5562)

Burger's Smokehouse, Highway 87 South, R.F.D. 3, California, Missouri 65018 (314-796-3134)

Boonville Chamber of Commerce, First floor, Courthouse, P.O. Box 8, Boonville, Missouri 64233 (816-882-2721)

Thespian Hall, Main and Vine Streets, Boonville, Missouri 64233 (816-882-7977)

Arrow Rock Lyceum Theatre, Arrow Rock, Missouri 65320 (816-837-3311)

Arrow Rock State Historic Site, Arrow Rock, Missouri 65320 (816-837-3330)

Arrow Rock Tavern, Arrow Rock, Missouri 65320 (816-837-3200)

Arrow Rock bed and breakfast establishments include Cedar Grove (816-837-3441), and DownOver (816-837-3268)

Fayette Area Chamber of Commerce, 116 East Davis, Fayette, Missouri 65248 (816-248-2200)

Stephens Museum, Central Methodist College, Fayette, Missouri 65248 (314-248-3391)

Columbia Convention and Visitors Bureau, 300 South Providence Road, P.O. Box N, Columbia, Missouri 65205 (314-875-1231)

University of Missouri Visitors Center, 103 Heinkel Building, 201 South Seventh, Columbia, Missouri 65205 (314-882-6333)

State Historical Society, Ellis Library, Columbia, Missouri 65205 (314-882-7083)

Shelter Insurance Gardens, 1817 West Broadway, Columbia, Missouri 65205 (314-445-8441)

Maplewood House, 802 South Edgewood, Columbia, Missouri 65203 (314-449-5876)

Moberly Historical Museum, 100 North Sturgeon, Moberly, Missouri 65270 (816-263-7576)

Chance Gardens and Centralia Historical Society Museum, 319 East Sneed, Centralia, Missouri 65240 (314-682-5711)

Ross House and American Saddle Horse Museum, 501 South Muldrow, Mexico, Missouri 65265 (314-581-3910)

7. Onondaga Cave, Route 1, Leasburg, Missouri 65535 (314-245-6200)

Meramec Caverns, Stanton, Missouri 63079 (314-468-3166)

Rosati Winery, Route 1, Box 55, St. James, Missouri 65559 (314-265-8629)

Heinrichshaus Vineyards and Winery, Route 2, Box 227, St. James, Missouri 65559 (314-265-5000)

Ferrigno Vineyards and Winery, Route 2, Box 277, St. James, Missouri 65559 (314-265-7742)

St. James Winery, 540 Sidney Street, St. James, Missouri 65559 (314-265-7912)

For brochures on Missouri's more than thirty wineries: Grape and Wine Program, P.O. Box 630, Jefferson City, Missouri 65102 (314-751-6807); (1-800-392-WINE in-state)

Maramec Spring Park, St. James, Missouri 65559 (314-265-7124)

Memoryville, U.S.A., 1008 West 12th, Rolla, Missouri 65401 (314-364-1810)

Houston House Restaurant, Newburg, Missouri 65550 (314-762-3010); the restaurant is open Thursday to Saturday evenings 5:30 to 8:30 p.m., Sundays noon to 5

Regional Opera Company, Newburg, Missouri 65550 (314-762-2545)

Dillard Mill State Historic Site, Dillard, Missouri 65458 (314-244-3120)

Montauk State Park, Salem, Missouri 65560 (314-548-2525); to reserve cabins at the park (314-548-2434)

Ozark National Scenic Riverways, P.O. Box 490, Van Buren, Missouri 63965 (314-323-4236); the Riverways office can furnish information about outfitters for float trips; Jacks Fork firms include Eminence Canoe Rental, P.O. Box 276, Eminence, Missouri 65466 (314-226-3642) and Jacks Fork Canoe Rental, P.O. Box 188, Eminence, Missouri 65466 (314-226-3434); for the Current River: Akers Ferry Canoe Rental, HCR 81, Box 90, Salem, Missouri 65560 (314-858-3224) and Current River Canoe Rental, HCR 62, Box 375, Salem, Missouri 65560. Summer (314-858-3250); September–May (314-226-5517)

Big Spring Lodge, P.O. Box 602, Van Buren, Missouri 63965 (314-323-4423)

Ozark Trail, Missouri Department of Natural Resources, P.O. Box 176, Jefferson City, Missouri 65102 (314-751-3443)

Mingo National Wildlife Refuge, R.R. 1, Box V, Puxico, Missouri 63960 (314-222-3589)

8. Greater Lake of the Ozarks Convention and Visitors Bureau, P.O. Box 98, Lake Ozark, Missouri 65049 (1-800-392-0882 in Missouri, 1-800-325-0213 outside Missouri)

Bagnell Dam, Union Electric Co., Route 3, Box 234, Eldon, Missouri 65026 (314-365-1002)

Lake of the Ozarks State Park, Kaiser, Missouri 65047 (314-348-2694)

Ha Ha Tonka State Park, Route 1, Box 658, Camdenton, Missouri 65020 (314-346-2986)

Bushwacker Museum, 231 North Main, Nevada, Missouri 64772 (417-667-7609)

Laura Ingalls Wilder Home and Museum, Rocky Ridge Farm, Mansfield, Missouri 65704 (417-924-3626)

Springfield Convention and Visitors Bureau, 320 North Jefferson, Springfield, Missouri 65806 (417-862-5501)

The Landers Theatre, 311 East Walnut, Springfield, Missouri 65806 (417-869-3869)

Outdoor World, 1935 South Campbell, Springfield, Missouri 65807 (417-887-1915)

Wilson's Creek National Battlefield, Postal Drawer C, Republic, Missouri 65738 (417-732-2662)

Branson area information and hotel reservations: 1-800-492-7092 (in Missouri); 1-800-641-4202 (outside Missouri)

Stone Hill Winery, HCR 5, Box 1825, Branson, Missouri 65616 (417-334-1897)

Silver Dollar City, Branson, Missouri 65616 (417-338-2611)

The Shepherd of the Hills Outdoor Theatre, Route 1, Box 770, Branson, Missouri 65616 (417-338-4191)

The School of the Ozarks, Point Lookout, Missouri 65726 (417-334-6411); for the Ralph Foster Museum, extension 407 or 408

A good source of information about the Ozarks is "The Ozarks Mountaineer" magazine, Route 3, Box 868, Branson, Missouri 65616 (417-546-5390); books on the Ozarks are on sale at the magazine's office, Highway 76, nine miles east of Branson and four miles west of Forsyth

George Washington Carver National Monument, Box 38, Diamond, Missouri 64840 (417-325-4151)

National Fish Hatchery, East Park Street, Neosho, Missouri 64850 (417-451-0554)

Ginger Blue Resort, RFD 1, Noel, Missouri 64854 (417-436-2216)

Dorothea B. Hoover Historical Museum, Schifferdecker Park, Joplin, Missouri 64801 (417-623-1180)

9. Old House Restaurant, 2d and Elm, Kimmswick, Missouri 63053 (314-464-0378)

Mastodon State Park, 1551 Seckman Road, Imperial, Missouri 63052 (314-467-5428)

Washington State Park, Route 2, De Soto, Missouri 63020 (314-586-2995)

Missouri Mines State Historic Site, Federal Mill Drive, Box 492, Flat River, Missouri 63601 (314-431-6226)

Bonne Terre Mine, P.O. Box 287, Bonne Terre, Missouri 63628 (314-358-2148)

Arcadia Valley Chamber of Commerce, P.O. Box 3, Courthouse Square, Ironton, Missouri 63650 (314-546-7117)

Ste. Genevieve Tourist Information Center, Main and Market Streets, Ste. Genevieve, Missouri 63670 (314-883-5750)

Hotels in historic buildings at Ste. Genevieve include: Hotel Ste. Genevieve (314-883-2737), and Inn St. Gemme-Beauvais, (314-883-5744)

St. Mary's Seminary, Perryville, Missouri 63775 (314-547-8343)

Altenburg Lutheran Seminary and Church, and Saxon Lutheran Memorial, Frohna, Missouri 63748 (314-824-5404) or (314-824-5906)

Oldtimers Agricultural Museum and Park, Box 96, Altenburg, Missouri 63732 (314-824-5594)

Old McKendree Chapel, McKendree Methodist Church, Jackson, Missouri 63755 (314-243-5396)

Oliver House, 218 East Adams, Jackson, Missouri 63756 (314-243-8131)

St. Louis, Iron Mountain and Southern Railway, P.O. Box 244, Jackson, Missouri 63755 (314-243-1688)

Bollinger Mill State Historic Site, P.O. Box 248, Burfordville, Missouri 63739 (314-243-4591)

Cape Girardeau Tourism Bureau, P.O. Box 98, 601 North Kingshighway, Cape Girardeau, Missouri 63701 (314-335-3312)

Glenn House, 325 South Spanish, Gape Girardeau, Missouri 63701 (314-334-1177)

Cape River Heritage Museum, 538 Independence, Cape Girardeau, Missouri 63701 (314-334-0405)

Southeast Missouri State University Museum, Memorial Hall, Cape Girardeau, Missouri 63701 (314-651-2260)

Hunter-Dawson State Historic Site, New Madrid, Missouri 63869 (314-748-5340)

10. Useful books on Missouri culture and history

Gazeteer of the State of Missouri, Alphonso Wetmore (C. Keemle, St. Louis, 1837)

The Missouri Handbook, Nathan H. Parker (P.M. Pinckard, St. Louis, 1865)

The State of Missouri, Walter Williams, ed (Press of E.W. Stephens, Columbia, 1904)

A History of Missouri, Louis Houck, Three Volumes (R.R. Donnelley & Sons Company, Chicago, 1908)

A History of Missouri, Eugene Morrow Violette (D.C. Heath & Co., Boston, 1918)

Centennial History of Missouri (The Center State), Walter B. Stevens, Five Volumes (The S.J. Clarke Publishing Company, St. Louis-Chicago, 1921)

An Artist in America, Thomas Hart Benton (Robert M. McBride & Company, New York, 1937)

Missouri   Its Resources, People and Institutions, Noel P. Gist, et al, ed (Curators of the University of Missouri, Columbia, 1950)

Stars Upstream   Life Along An Ozark River, Leonard Hall (The University of Chicago Press, Chicago, 1958)

Vanguard of Empire   Missouri's Century of Expansion, Lew Larkin (State Publishing Company, St. Louis, 1961)

Missouri   A History of the Crossroads State, Edwin C. McReynolds (University of Oklahoma Press, Norman, 1962)

Missouri Historic Sites Catalog, Dorothy J. Caldwell, ed (The State Historical Society of Missouri, Columbia, 1963)

Missouri Heritage, Lew Larkin (America Press, Inc., Columbia, 1968)

Missouri Bittersweet, Mackinlay Kantor (Doubleday & Company, Inc., Garden City, New York, 1969)

Missouri   A Bicentennial History, Paul C. Nagel (W.W. Norton & Company, Inc., New York, 1977)

Missouri The Heart of the Nation, William E. Parrish, Charles T. Jones, Jr., Lawrence O. Christensen (Forum Press, St. Louis, 1980)

Missouri A Geography, Milton D. Rafferty (Westview Press, Boulder, Colorado, 1983)

A History of Missouri, William E. Foley, et al, Five Volumes (University of Missouri Press, Columbia, 1971–1986)

Index

Addams, Jane, 106
Amana Colony, 3, 226–234, 395–397; attractions of, 228–229, 230–233; history of, 226–228, 229–230; hotels in, 233, 396; museums of, 227–228, 232, 234; restaurants of, 228–229, 230, 233, 396, 397
"Amana That Was and Amana That Is," 226–227
American Notes, 122
An America That Was, 82–83
An Artist in America, 348–349, 360
An Illinois Reader, 82
Anson, Adrian, 223–224
Apperson, Phoebe, 346
As I Saw the U.S.A., 181
"A Tribute to a Dog," 334–335
Austin, Moses, 367

Bacon, Lydia, 57
Bagnell Dam, 353–354
Baird, Bil, 253–254
Barnum, Caroline, 55–56

Barnum, P. T., 55, 261
Battle of Wilson's Creek, 357
Bauer, Douglas, 8, 200, 255
Beiderbecke, Bix, 274–275
Benton, Thomas Hart, 298, 348–349, 360, 361
Bickerdyke, Mary, 146
Bingham, George Caleb, 331, 340
Birkbeck, Morris, 110–111, 122–123
Bissell, Richard, 276–277
Black Hawk, 10, 165
Blane, William, 4, 121
Bollinger, George, 372–373
Boone, Daniel, 97, 290–292, 294–295, 342, 355
Borah, William E., 112
Brackenridge, Henry, 287–288, 291
Brewer-Bonebright, Sarah, 199
Britt, Albert, 82–83
Brownell, Baker, 83
Browning, Pete, 59, 60
Brown, John, 219–220, 236
Brown, Paul, 37–38

Bryan, William Jennings, 115, 140
Bryant, Francis, 131–132
Bryant, William Cullen, 155–156
Buckingham, J. H., 5–6
Burden, Charles, 334–335
Burger's Smokehouse, 338–339
Butler, Ellis Parker, 262
Byron, George Gordon, 291–292

Calamity Jane, 319
Calkins, Earnest Elmo, 4
Call, Nancy Henderson, 218, 263
Cannon, Joseph, 137
Carmichael, Hoagy, 46
Cartwright, Peter, 184, 185
Carver, George Washington, 359–360
Catherwood, Mary Hartwell, 188
Central Methodist College, 342
Cherry Sisters, 244
Churchill, Winston, 295–297, 338
Civil War, 332, 333–334, 356, 357–358, 368–369
Clark, George Rogers, 34, 94
Clemens, John, 306, 307–308
Clemens, Samuel see Twain, Mark
Cobb, Irvin S., 23
Cody, William, 275–276, 321, 322
Coffin, Levi, 63
Columbia College, 343
Conner Prairie Pioneer Settlement, 66–67, 68
Conner, William, 66
Cousins, Robert Gordon, 222
Croghan, George, 33–34

Davenport, George, 160, 274
DeBra, Sarah Brown, 67
Debs, Eugene V., 31–32, 174–175
Deere, John, 164–165
Dicey, Edward, 102
Dickens, Charles, 102–103, 122, 311–312
Dilliard, Irving, 283
Disney Version, The, 7

Disney, Walt, 7, 314–316
Don Juan, 291–292
Douglas, Stephen A., 81, 116, 131, 132, 133, 144; /Lincoln debates, 101, 136, 146–147, 157, 168, 188, 191
Dreiser, Theodore, 30–31
Duden, Gottfried, 290
Duncan, Elizabeth, 139–140
Duncan, Joseph, 139–140
Dvorak, Antonin, 246–248

Earlham College, 64, 66
Early Algona, The Story of Our Pioneers, 218, 263
Earp, Wyatt, 145, 158, 216, 363
Eggleston, Edward, 57–58
Eisenhower, Dwight, 261, 339
Engle, Paul, 3, 197
Ernst, Ferdinand, 5
Eureka College, 153

Farnham, Eliza W., 9–10, 111–112, 165–166
Ferber, Edna, 99, 209–210
Ferguson, William, 11, 101–102
Ficke, Charles, 211
Field, Eugene, 4–5, 323–324
First of the Hoosiers, The, 57–58
Fischer, William, 4
Fitch, George, 341
Flint, Timothy, 369
Flower, George, 110–111
Floyd, Charles, 266–267

George Washington Carver National Monument, 359–360
Gerhard, Fred, 111
Grace Truman, 330
Grant, Ulysses S., 103, 170–171, 365, 368
Greeley, Horace, 219
Griffin, Walter Burley, 254
Grimes, James, 224–225
Grinnell College, 220
Grinnell, Josiah, 219–220

Hall, Leonard, 350
Handbook of Iowa, A, 199
Harlan, James, 212
Harrison, William Henry, 23, 35–36, 74, 118
Hartt, Rollin Lynde, 198
Hawkeyes: A Biography of the State of Iowa, 205, 213–214
Hay, John, 187
Haynes, Elwood, 70–71
Hearst, James, 7
Hemingway, Ernest, 12, 181, 182
Hendrickson, Walter, 46–47
Herbert Hoover National Historic Site, 236–237
Herbert Hoover Presidential Library-Museum, 238
Hickok, James ("Wild Bill"), 158, 331
Hillerich, J. A., 59
Historic Illinois, 104
Holladay, Ben, 324–325
Holliday, John H., 38
Home Country, 24
Hoosier Schoolmaster, The, 57
Hoosiers, The, 49–50
Hoover, Herbert, 236–239, 263
House of Singing Wings: Life and Works of T. C. Steele, The, 49
Hughes, Robert Earl, 192–193
Hutton, Graham, 3, 10, 11

Illinois, 77–194; Albion, 110–112, 122; Alton, 191–193; Amish country, 134–135; Beardstown, 140–141; Bishop Hill, 148–149; books on, 393–394; Cahokia (French), 85–86; Cahokia (Indian), 86–89; Cairo, 96–97, 99, 101–103; Calhoun County, 188–190; cemeteries, 85, 92, 93, 95, 97, 99–100, 103–104, 129, 130, 135, 143–144, 145, 192, 387; Champaign-Urbana, 133–134; Charleston, 135–136; Chester, 93–94; Chicago, 77, 79, 80–81, 82, 134, 173–174; Danville, 136–137; Decatur, 130–131; Dixon, 162–163; exploration of, 83–85, 86; ferries, 190; forests, 100; forts, 85, 90–91, 92, 103, 105–106; Galena, 170–172; Galesburg, 145–148; health spas, 119–120; historic settlements of, 85, 86, 90–91, 92, 104, 110–112, 122, 130, 148, 182–183, 185; history of, 83–88, 90, 92–95, 97, 103–104, 109, 110–116, 121, 123–129, 142–143, 146, 152, 154–155, 158; Indian settlements in, 86–89, 142–143, 160, 190; inns and hotels of, 89, 107, 119, 121–122, 130, 134, 163, 178, 179, 182, 183, 186, 189, 385, 386, 388, 392, 393; Jacksonville, 139–140; Kaskaskia Island, 92–93, 94–95; libraries, 101, 111, 118, 126, 153, 180; Lincoln, 132; Macystown, 89–90; map of, 78; Metamora, 152–153; Metropolis, 79, 104–105; Monmouth, 144–145; Mormons in, 184–186; Mound City, 104; Mt. Vernon, 119; Nauvoo, 184–186; North Utica, 156; Ohio River country, 104; Old Shawneetown, 108–109; other towns of, 91–92, 93, 99–101, 104, 107–108, 112–115, 117, 118, 119, 132, 134, 135, 137–138, 141–142, 154–155, 158, 163–165, 167–169, 173–184, 190, 191; Ottawa, 157–158; overview of, 77–83; parks of, 92–93, 95, 97, 103, 105, 112, 113–114, 120, 132, 133, 135, 136, 156, 157, 159, 163, 165, 169, 174, 179, 183, 190, 193, 384, 386; Peoria, 150–152; Princeton, 154–156; Quad Cities, 159–160; Quincy, 187–188; railroads, 100; resources, 382–394; restaurants,

98, 135, 191, 383, 386; riverlands, 154–172; Rockford, 166–167; Rock Island, 160–162; schools, 117, 121, 132, 133, 134, 140, 142, 146–147, 153, 163, 169, 180, 183, 184, 191, 387; Spoon River country, 142–144; Springfield, 123–128; Thebes, 98–99; Tower Rock, 97–98; Underground Railroad, 155; Vandalia, 115–117; Waterloo, 89; West Salem, 113; writers on, 79, 82–83, 98, 101–103, 104, 111, 122–123, 134, 189

Illinois, A Bicentennial History, 134
Illinois As It Is, 111
Illinois College, 140
Illinois State University, 133
I'm From Missouri!, 283

Indian, settlements in Illinois, 86–89, 142–143, 160, 190; settlements in Iowa, 224–226

Indiana, 21–75; Auburn, 71; Bloomington, 45, 46–48; books on, 381–382; cemeteries, 33, 60; Crawfordsville, 74–75; Elkhart, 72–73; festivals, 26, 28–29, 381; French Lick, 43–44; Greenfield, 65–66; historic settlements of, 24, 25, 32–40, 62, 66–67, 68; hotels and inns in, 29, 40, 44, 378–379; Jeffersonville, 58–60; Kokomo, 70–71; libraries, 32, 33, 47–48; limestone industry of, 44–45; Madison, 24, 54–56; map of, 22; Metamora, 61–62; Millville, 64; museums, 38, 42, 44, 48, 50, 58, 59, 63, 64, 67, 69, 70, 71, 72, 73, 74, 379–381; Nashville, 49–51; New Harmony, 24, 37–40; North Webster, 73–74; other towns of, 23, 30, 43–45, 48–49, 58, 62–63, 68; overview of, 21 25; Parke County, 26–32; parks, 29, 39, 52,

67–68, 379; Peru, 69–70; resorts in, 43–44; resources on, 378–382; restaurants, 40; Richmond, 63–64; Santa Claus, 41–42; schools of, 32, 46–48, 57–58, 64; South Bend, 72; Terre Haute, 30–32; transportation links, 61–62, 63, 66; Underground Railroad, 63; Vevey, 56–58; Vincennes, 25, 32–37, 75; writers on, 21–25, 42, 49, 50, 54, 57, 65, 67, 68; Zionsville, 67–68

Indiana, A History, 65
Indiana Way, A State History, The, 50, 68
Indiana State University, 32, 46–48
Ingersoll, Robert, 105, 151–152
Iowa, 195–280; Bentonsport, 204–206; Bonaparte, 201–203; books on, 401–402; Britt, 255–259; Cedar Rapids, 241–244; cemeteries of, 210, 217, 238, 243, 244, 247, 249, 258, 267, 275; churches of, 204, 247, 249, 251–252, 268, 278; conventions and festivals, 210, 212–214, 216, 241, 242, 243, 249, 253, 256–259, 260, 264, 275; Council Bluffs, 265–266; covered bridges, 263–264; Des Moines River valley, 201–209; Dubuque, 276–278; forts of, 250, 260–261; historic settlements of, 204, 213–214, 215–216, 224–226, 226–234, 236–238, 239–241, 246–249, 267–268; history of, 198–199, 202–210, 214–216, 228, 229–230, 235, 236–239, 244, 250, 265, 266–267, 271; Indian settlements, 224–226; industry, 221, 222–223, 245; inns and hotels of, 202, 206, 207, 216, 223, 233, 254, 278, 394, 395, 396, 397; Iowa City, 234–236; Kalona, 239–241; Keokuk, 269–271; Keosauqua, 206–209; libraries of, 210, 238,

242, 397; map of, 196; Mason City, 252–254; mills of, 202–203, 205, 206, 228, 231–232, 241, 249, 255, 276; Mount Pleasant, 211–212; Muscatine, 273–274; museums of, 203, 205, 211, 216, 217, 218, 219, 220, 221–222, 223, 227–228, 232, 234, 235, 238, 241, 242, 243, 248, 249, 250, 254, 257, 259–260, 261, 262–263, 370, 374, 275, 276, 277, 395–401; Newton, 221–222; Oskaloosa, 217–218; other towns of, 201, 203–207, 209–211, 218–219, 223, 224, 244–246, 248–250, 254–255, 260–263, 264–265, 267–268, 271–272, 274–276, 278–280; overview of, 195–200; parks, 264, 268, 270, 272, 399; Pella, 215–217; resources on, 394–402; restaurants, 203, 228–229, 230, 233, 396, 397; Salem, 213–214; schools of, 206, 211, 212, 217, 220, 235, 249, 262, 271, 398, 399; Sioux City, 266–267; Spillville, 246–248; State Fair, 210; Underground Railroad, 213; West Branch, 236–239; Winterset, 263–264; writers on, 197–198, 199, 200, 202, 204, 205, 207, 211, 245, 255, 269, 271–272, 273–274
Iowa As It Is in 1854, 269
Iowa in Times of War, 250–251
Iowa, Land of Many Mills, 202
Iowa State University, 262
Iowa the American Heartland, 198
Iowa: The Home for Immigrants, 195, 214
Iowa Wesleyan College, 212

James, Frank, 326–327, 331
James, Jesse, 322, 326–327
James, Thomas, 345
Jefferson, Thomas, 343
Jenson, Richard, 134

Johnson, Samuel, 91
Jones, "Mother," 117–118
Joplin, Scott, 337

Kantor, Mackinlay, 283
Keil, William, 312, 313–314
Kneeland, Abner, 204
Knox College, 146–147

Lane, John, 43–44
Leibowitz, Irving, 24, 54
Lemcke, J. A., 25
Letters from Illinois, 122–123
Lewis and Clark, 193, 194, 265, 266, 288, 325, 332, 341
Lewis, Sinclair, 245
Life in Prairie Land, 9–10, 111–112, 165–166
Lincoln, Abraham, 5–6, 35, 42, 68, 71, 81, 112–113, 116, 118, 121–122, 128–133, 135–136, 137, 138, 140, 144, 147, 153, 161, 162, 163, 187, 212, 266; at Springfield, 123–127; /Douglas debates, 101, 136, 146–147, 157, 168, 188, 191; family, 135–136, 212; houses of, 42–43, 123–124, 129
Lincoln Boyhood National Memorial, 42–43
Lincoln Home National Historic Site, 124–126
Lincoln Log Cabin State Historic Site, 135
Lincoln, Sarah Bush, 135, 136
Lincoln Trail Homestead State Memorial, 113, 130
Lind, Jenny, 55
Lindsay, Vachel, 127
Little Brown Church in the Vale, 251–252
Lorimer, Louis, 372, 373
"Lousiville Slugger," 59–60
Lovejoy, Elijah, 155, 191–192, 289
Lovejoy, Owen, 155, 157, 192
"Lover's Lane, Saint Jo," 323–324

Lyford, Joseph P., 116–117

Madison, James H., 50, 68, 190
Maharishi International University, 211
Main Street, 245
Marquette and Joliet, 83–84, 272, 279
Marquette, Jacques, 83–84, 94, 190, 191
Marquis, Don, 146
Marshall, Thomas R., 23, 312
Marsh, Charles, 157, 158
Martin, Abe, 51–52
Martin Chuzzlewit, 311–312
Mason, Charles, 239
Mason, Sam, 107–108
Masters, Edgar Lee, 143, 144, 146, 152
McKendree College, 121, 184
Meek, William, 201, 202
Memories of Fourscore Years, 211
Menard, Pierre, 93, 95
Mesquakie Indian Settlement, 224–226
Midwest, books on, 3, 4, 8, 10, 377–378; historical overview of, 1–13; map of, 2; perceptions of, 1–13, 181; practical travel advice, 13–20; sources and resources on, 377–378; waterways of, 9–11
Midwest at Noon, 3, 10
Miller, Henry, 87
Missouri, 281–376; Arrow Park, 340–342; Bethel, 312–314; books on, 412–413; caves, 347, 350, 404, 408; cemeteries of, 294–295, 311, 327, 333, 363, 367; churches of, 294, 296–297, 299, 326, 328, 338, 342, 343, 354, 366, 367, 368, 370–371, 373, 411; Columbia, 342–343; covered bridges of, 311, 316, 372–373; dams, 353–354, 355; Femme Osage, 292–293; festivals, 307, 313, 337, 370;

forts, 332; Fulton, 295–297; Hannibal, 304, 305–310; Hermann, 300–301; historic settlements of, 292–294, 299–303, 312–314, 318, 319–320, 369–372; history of, 283–285, 287–289, 290–291, 295–296, 297, 300–301, 311, 315, 320–323, 324–336, 337, 341, 345–347, 348, 355–357, 367–369, 370–376; Independence, 329–332; industries of, 284, 301–303, 325, 337, 345; inns and hotels of, 299, 303, 308, 326, 329, 403, 404, 405, 407, 409, 410; Ironton, 367–369; Jefferson City, 297–298; Joplin, 361–362; lakes, 353, 354, 355, 367; Lexington, 333–334; libraries of, 329, 337, 341, 343, 361, 363, 406; map of, 282; Maramec Spring Park, 345, 347–348; Marceline, 314–316; Mark Twain country of, 304–314; mills of, 288, 328, 349, 372–373; mines, 366–367; museums of, 296, 307, 310, 317, 322, 327, 329, 333–334, 335, 338, 342, 344, 348, 354, 356, 357, 358, 361, 363, 367, 370, 371, 373, 404–412; New Madrid, 374–375; Osage Beach, 353, 354; other towns of, 293–295, 298–300, 304, 310–312, 316–320, 326–329, 339–340, 342–344, 345–348, 351, 352–363, 364–374; overview of, 281–287; Ozarks region, 352–364; parks and preserves of, 290, 309, 316–317, 320, 342, 343, 345, 347–348, 350, 351–352, 354–355, 357–358, 366, 367–368, 371, 373, 408, 409, 411; resorts, 360–361; resources on, 402–413; restaurants of, 289, 301, 303, 312, 319, 326, 340, 348, 404, 407, 409, 410; rivers, 348–350, 353; schools of, 286, 295,

301, 312, 320, 327–328, 330, 337, 342–343, 358, 372, 406, 407, 410; Sedalia, 336–337; spas of, 328–329; springs, 345, 347–348, 350; state symbol, 336; St. Charles, 287–290; St. Genevieve, 369–370; St. Joseph, 321–324; trails, 350–351; Warrensburg, 334–336; Washington, 301–303; Weston, 325–326; wineries, 347, 358, 402–403, 408; writers on, 283, 284, 289, 304, 331
Missouri, A Bicentennial History, 284, 293
Missouri Bittersweet, 283
Missourian Lays and Other Western Ditties, 289
Mormons, 184–186, 271, 318, 332
Morris, James, 181
Mound Builders, The, 88
Music Man, The, 252–253
My Indiana, 24, 54

Nagel, Paul, 284, 293
National Hobo Convention, 256–259
Nature and Destiny of Man, The, 287
Nicholson, Meredith, 49–50
Niebuhr, Reinhold, 286–287
Nixon, Richard, 210
Nordhoff, Charles, 313

Old Drum, 334–335
One Man's Life, 10
"On the Banks of the Wabash—Far Away," 31
Oregon Trail, The, 331
Other Illinois, The, 83
Owen, Robert, 37–38

Paine, Albert Bigelow, 204–205, 307
Parkman, Francis, 331, 375
Parrish, Randall, 104
Parsons, John, 3, 25, 36

Patee, John, 321–322
Peattie, Donald Culross, 80
Peck, J. M., 5
Penney, J. C., 317–318
Pershing, John J., 316
Pigs Is Pigs, 262
Pike, Zebulon, 271, 287
Pinkerton, Alan, 138
Pitts, William, 251–252
"Plaint of the Missouri 'Coon in the Berlin Zoological Gardens," 4–5
Pony Express, 311, 321–322
"Popeye," 94
Porter, Cole, 70
Portrait of Iowa, 197
Powers, Elmer, 200
Prairie City, Iowa, 8, 200, 255
Prince, Harold, 276–277
Pyle, Ernie, 24, 29–30, 32, 48

Quayle, Dan, 23
Quick, Herbert, 10, 244–245

Rapp, George, 37
Reagan, Ronald, 153, 162–163
Recollections, 157
Red Cloud, 225
Reflections of the Last Ten Years in the Valley of the Mississippi, 369
Reminiscences of an Indianian, 25
Reminiscences of New Castle, Iowa, 199
Renault, Phillipe François, 90, 366
Rhodes, Richard, 3
Richman, Irving, 197
Riley, James Whitcomb, 24, 26, 52, 65–66, 68, 75

Saarinen, Eero, 53, 159, 343
Saarinen, Eliel, 53
Sandburg, Carl, 79, 136, 147, 187, 274, 359
Santa Fe Trail, 331, 335, 341
Sappington, John, 340–341
Saucier, François, 86, 90

Saucier, Jean Baptiste, 85–86
Schickel, Richard, 7
School of the Ozarks, 358
Segar, Elzie Crisler, 94
Sevareid, Eric, 248
Shambaugh, Bertha, 226–227
Shelley, Kate, 261–262
Shoop, Homer, 73
Show Boat, 99
Sidey, Hugh, 198
Sioux City Corn Palace, 199, 267
Small Town America, 4
Smith, Hyrum, 185, 186, 187, 327
Smith, Joseph, 184–185, 186, 187, 318, 327, 332
Snyder, Robert, 355
Spoon River Anthology, 143, 144
Stanton, G. Smith, 197–198
Stars Upstream, 350
State Fair, 207
Steele, Selma, 49
Steele, Theodore, 48–49
Steevens, George, 173
Stephens College, 343
Stetson, John, 323
Stout, Elihu, 34–35
Strong, Phil, 205, 207, 209, 210, 213–214, 221
Sullivan, Louis, 220
Sunday, Billy, 224
Superman, 104–105
Sweet Memories of "Old Indianie" in 1870, 67
Swisher, Jacob, 202, 250–251

Taft, Lorado, 149–150, 165, 168, 188
Talk of Vandalia, The, 116
Tarkio College, 320
Tecumseh, 36, 74
Thompson, Maurice, 75
Tinker, Mary Manny, 167–168
Tinker, Robert Hall, 166–167
Tom Sawyer Abroad, 305

Tropic of Capricorn, 87
Truman, Bess, 330
Truman, Harry S., 116, 295, 329–330, 333, 334, 362–363
Truman, John, 362
Turner, Jonathan Baldwin, 8–9
Twain, Mark, 98, 204–205, 270, 271–272, 273–274; in Hannibal, 302, 304, 305–310; writings of, 305, 307, 309–310
Twelve Months in New-Harmony, 37

Umphraville, Angus, 289
Uncle Tom's Cabin, 63
University of Illinois, 134
University of Missouri, 342–343

Van Buren, Martin, 23
Vest, George G., 334–335
Views of Louisiana, 291
Villagers 1840–3, 309–310
Vonnegut, Jr., Kurt, 25

Wabash, The, 10
Wadlow, Robert, 192
Wallace, Lew, 75
Walton, Clyde C., 82
Watkins, Waltus, 328
Webster, Daniel, 102, 140
Western Illinois University, 142
Westminster College, 295
Wheaton College, 180
When the Wildwood Was in Flower, 197–198
Whitman, Walt, 11
Wilder, Laura Ingalls, 356–357
William Jewell College, 327–328
Willson, Meredith, 253–254
Wilson, William E., 10, 65
Wolfe, Thomas, 3
Wood, Grant, 199, 209, 242–243, 275
Wood, John, 188

Woods, John, 109
Wright Brothers, 64
Wright, Frank Lloyd, 181–182, 183

Yates, Richard, 131

Years of Struggle, 200
Young, Brigham, 185, 265, 271, 318

Zuber, Bill, 233